International Education

International Education

Principles and Practice

Edited by Mary Hayden and Jeff Thompson

**KOGAN
PAGE**

First published in 1998
First published in paperback in 2001

Kogan Page Limited
120 Pentonville Road
London N1 9JN
UK

Stylus Publishing Inc.
22883 Quicksilver Drive
Sterling VA 20166-2012
USA

British Library Cataloguing in Publication Data

A CIP record for this book is available from the British Library

ISBN 0 7494 3616 6

Typeset by Kogan Page
Printed and bound in Great Britain by Biddles Ltd, Guildford and King's Lynn

CONTENTS

NOTES ON CONTRIBUTORS

Kevin Bartlett
Kevin Bartlett has held senior management positions in schools in London, Dar es Salaam and Vienna and is currently Director of Windhoek International School, Namibia. Kevin is a former Chairman of the Accreditation Committee of the European Council of International Schools (ECIS). In 1990 he initiated the International Schools' Curriculum Project which, in 1997, became the Primary Years Programme (PYP) of the International Baccalaureate Organization. He is now the chairman of the PYP Curriculum Committee. Kevin has written and taught for the Principals' Training Center for seven years, and has also taught in the international MA programmes of the Universities of Bath and Oxford Brookes. In 1994 ECIS presented Kevin with a special award for extraordinary services to the Council and to international education.

James Cambridge
James Cambridge has been a biology educator in Britain, North Yemen, Lesotho and South Africa in both national and international schools. He is currently a Research Officer at the Centre for the study of Education in an International Context at the University of Bath and his research interests, linked to a doctoral programme, focus on schools in an international context and, in particular, on the organizational and national cultures associated with them.

Barry Drake
Barry Drake is Director of Guidance and Deputy to the Principal at the Li Po Chun United World College of Hong Kong where he also teaches history and Chinese Studies, and has recently been awarded a doctorate for his research at the University of Bath's Centre for the study of Education in an International Context. Barry has extensive experience in international education in various parts of the world including the Middle East, South and South-east Asia, and has also spent time at the United World College of the Atlantic.

Elisabeth Fox
Elisabeth Fox began her teaching career at Santiago College, Chile, where, as Director of the school in the 1960s, she introduced the International Baccalaureate as a pilot project. In 1968 she received the Order of Merit from the Chilean government, then returned to Britain where she was IB Research and Development Officer. Elisabeth was Head of San Silvestre School, Lima, in the 1970s, and

Academic Dean at the United Nations International School, New York in the 1980s, at which time she served on the IBO Curriculum Board and the International Schools Association Curriculum Committee which developed the Middle Years Programme. She returned to Santiago College as Director in 1991 and is currently a member of the IBO Council and consultant to the Chilean Ministry of Education on aspects of educational reform.

Martha Haldimann
Martha Haldimann is American/Swiss and has been involved in international education for 19 years. She is currently an educational and psychological testing consultant in Switzerland for the John F Kennedy International School in Saanen/Gstaad and the International School of Berne, where she is also Learning Support Co-ordinator. Martha consults regularly with schools within the Swiss Group of International Schools (SGIS) and represents SGIS for the Optimal Match: she conducts research projects for SGIS internationally and is a frequent speaker at international conferences.

Mary Hayden
Mary Hayden is a lecturer in the Department of Education at the University of Bath, and has particular responsibilities within the Centre for the study of Education in an International Context and for the direction of the modular Masters level courses offered to over 1000 teachers and educational administrators based in over 60 countries around the world. Her involvement in international education includes a period as IB Subject Officer for Mathematics and Science and, subsequently, IB Research and Development Officer; after leaving the IBO she took up a post at the University of London Examinations and Assessment Council. Mary's MPhil degree focused on issues related to assessment within the IB context: her research interests are based in the field of international education, in which context she is currently carrying out doctoral research and on which she has published extensively.

Colin Jenkins
Colin Jenkins has taught in the Isle of Man, Devon and, since 1971, at the United World College of the Atlantic where he is now Principal. Between 1987 and 1990 he was Deputy Director General and Director of Examinations of the International Baccalaureate Organization (IBO) and is currently a member of the IBO Executive and Vice Chair of the Conference of Heads of International Baccalaureate schools. Colin's academic interests have been in environmental and, particularly, marine education and he is currently leading a movement to broaden the post-16 curriculum in his native Wales by proposing the introduction of a Welsh Baccalaureate.

Mary Langford
Mary Langford was recently awarded an MA in (International) Education through the Centre for the study of Education in an International Context at the University of Bath, where her research was partially funded by an ECIS Fellowship.

After teaching Spanish and ESL, and then working in political and diplomatic circles in Washington DC, Mary moved to Europe and began a career in international school administration. A 'Global Nomad' who attended eight schools in three different languages, she has also served on ECIS accreditation teams and is currently Admissions and Communications Director at Southbank International School, London.

Malcolm McKenzie

Malcolm McKenzie is Principal of Maru a Pula School in Gaborone, Botswana. Prior to moving to Botswana in 1987 he taught at two universities in South Africa. Malcolm has published many articles in the general areas of English Literature and Applied Linguistics. His major academic interest at the moment is to explore ways in which national schools can learn from international schools, and vice versa. Maru a Pula is best described as a Botswana school with an international enrolment: just over half of its students are Batswana and the remainder are drawn from approximately 40 countries.

Edna Murphy

Edna Murphy has spent most of her professional life in international education. She served as deputy head, divisional head or head of international schools in Paris, Brussels and London from 1977 to 1995, when she retired from full-time administration. Having served on the Board of Directors of ECIS for nine years, much of the time spent on accreditation matters, she has continued her work in that area by chairing visiting teams to schools in various parts of the world. In 1981 she founded, and continues to edit, the *International Schools Journal* and has recently agreed to serve as London coordinator of a UNESCO project involving the linking of international with national schools in activities to promote peace through understanding.

Michal Pasternak

Michal Pasternak is Chairperson of the Performing Arts department on the La Châtaigneraie campus of the International School of Geneva, Switzerland; his teaching experience also includes both the English and Canadian state systems. From 1989 to 1991, he was a Research Fellow at the Centre for Global Education, University of York, specializing in the development of interactive teaching approaches using theatre techniques across a range of disciplines. Since 1985 he has been Secretary on the Executive Council of the International Schools Theatre Association (ISTA) and has contributed to wide range of ISTA developments over his period in office. He is a staff member of the European branch of Facing History and Ourselves (FHAO), a non-profit foundation involved in teacher training for anti-prejudice education throughout Europe. Over the past ten years he has served as workshop leader and consultant to major international organizations including UNICEF, WHO and FIET.

Richard Pearce
Richard Pearce has taught at independent schools in Britain and the USA, and at English and American system international schools. After 16 years as Director of Admissions at the International School of London his interest in cultural issues led him to research into the adjustment of mobile children, through the Department of Education at the University of Bath. He is also a consultant to multinational enterprises and families on schooling for internationally mobile children.

Derek Pigrum
Derek Pigrum obtained his MA in Education from the University of Bath, and is currently conducting doctoral research into transitional drawing towards a programme for education and computer-aided design. He is Chief Editor of *Skepsis*, the International Schools Association journal. He has been involved with International Art/Design education for a number of years and is at present the Senior Assessor of the IBMYP Art/Design area. Derek is a painter, graphic artist, designer and writer, as well as a teacher at Vienna International School.

Neil Richards
Neil Richards obtained his first teaching post in Kathmandu, Nepal, and has since worked in the Canary Islands, Egypt, Chile, Lesotho and Japan; for the last 13 years he has held senior administrative posts in international schools. His headship of Machabeng High School in Lesotho led to a particular interest in the composition of staff and staff morale in international schools, and became the basis of a postgraduate research degree completed through the University of Bath. His present appointment is as Headmaster of Yokohama International School in Japan.

Bob Sylvester
Bob Sylvester is Principal of Westwood International School in Gaborone, Botswana. Since 1976 his work in international education in Africa has also included research, teacher training and curriculum development for the United Nations, and responsibility for a K-12 reading programme at the International School of Lusaka in Zambia. His current research activities centre around the nature of international schools and international education, and are being undertaken in relation to a doctoral programme at the University of Bath.

Philip Thomas
Philip Thomas has been involved in the field of international education for over 30 years. As a senior administrator at the International School of Geneva he has been at the forefront of the development of the International Baccalaureate programme, and served for many years as Secretary to the IB Council of Foundation. A long-time advocate of the place of Education for Peace in the curriculum, Phil is now centrally involved in the International Education System Pilot Project, currently serving as its Coordinator.

Jeff Thompson

Jeff Thompson is Director of the Centre for the study of Education in an International Context (CEIC), Professor of Education and currently Head of the Department of Education at the University of Bath. Jeff first became active in international education in the 1960s when at the University of Oxford Department of Educational Studies, and has continued his involvement since that time in a number of different capacities. He was Chair of the IB Examining Board and member of the IB Curriculum Board, Executive Committee and Council of Foundation; he is currently a member of the IB Academic Affairs Board and Chair of the IB Research Committee. His major research interests are linked to the fields of assessment and curriculum, in both national and international contexts.

George Walker

George Walker is Director General of the International School of Geneva and Visiting Professor in the University of Bath, through the Centre for the study of Education in an International Context. George's earlier career was in science education and included a spell as an educational consultant for Imperial Chemical Industries (ICI); he subsequently took a central role in the development of comprehensive education in England. He was deputy head and head in a number of schools in Britain before moving to Geneva, and has participated in a number of ECIS accreditation teams.

David Wilkinson

David Wilkinson is the founding head of the Mahindra United World College of India. David has worked in international education for over 20 years as a teacher and school administrator, in countries including Italy, Lesotho, Thailand and Hong Kong, and has conducted research in international education – particularly within the context of the International Baccalaureate. He has also served on the Council of the IBO.

PREFACE

One of the striking features of the field of international schools and international education is the dearth of written material available within the public domain. The new recruit to a teaching post in an international school who sets out to comb the shelves of a well-stocked academic bookshop or library for background reading could be forgiven for thinking that he or she is about to enter uncharted territory. It is difficult to envisage many other professional contexts where a determined search through databases, whether paper based or electronic, would yield such a low return of relevant sources as is the case when the key words 'international school' are the focus of the search. It was in 1991 that the most recent composite volume dealing with international schools and international education was published as part of the World Yearbook of Education series. The editors of that volume, Patricia Jonietz and Duncan Harris, commented on how rapid had been the change in levels of interest in international education in the years leading up to that publication, in view of the fact that the first international schools were created in the first quarter of the twentieth century. In the short time that has elapsed since the publication of the *1991 World Yearbook* that change has not only continued to take place but has done so at an even greater pace. Changes in the world order, and in the nature of the political systems of many countries throughout the world, have all had consequences for the direction and organization of education in every part of the world. The international schools' network has been affected no less than any other part of the educational sphere, both in terms of the numbers of participating individuals – students and teachers and institutions – and in a development of our understanding of the nature and purpose of international education itself.

This book attempts to update thinking in the area of international education and to propose a rational for future development. It draws on specific contributions from a number of those involved in international education, all of whom are currently participating both in the development of current practice and in guiding the direction which international education may take in the future. A majority of the contributors are involved, through research activities, with the work of the Centre for the study of Education in an International Context (CEIC) at the University of Bath. The Centre itself has established a world-wide reputation for the high quality of its teaching and research activities in the field of international education, and all the contributors have links of one kind or another with the Centre or with individuals who work within it. In fact, the number of teachers and others world-wide who are actively engaged in study through the Centre has grown enormously over recent years and, in preparing material for inclusion in this book, those of us involved directly with the work of the Centre would wish to acknowledge the influence that the work of practitioners throughout the world has had on our thinking and writing. Thus, the perspectives on international education represented in this volume are from a much wider constituency than the list of authors would indicate.

The improvement in practice, represented by much of the work undertaken by those directly involved with international schools, has been widely welcomed. What has not emerged to date, however, is a clear conceptualization of the whole field of international education. This book sets out to engage all of those involved in the search for such a framework, which will form the basis for future development of understanding in an area thus far characterized by diversity, opportunity and expediency.

As general editors we are grateful for the patience exercised by all contributors with the processes of interpretation which we have brought to their own specific fields of expertise. We acknowledge that credit must be given to them for their willingness to share their experiences with the wider community of all those who are working towards a vision of what may, one day, be achieved through a common understanding of the potential international education offers as a contribution to world peace.

Mary Hayden
Jeff Thompson

Introduction to the Paperback Edition
Extending our Understanding of International Education

Mary Hayden and Jeff Thompson

THREE YEARS ON

It is almost three years since the first hardback edition of this book of contributed chapters was published. Such has been the magnitude and nature of the response generated by a great many of those involved in researching, and applying to practice, the principles of international education that the publisher has decided to bring out a further print run of the volume in a paperback edition. As editors we are pleased with that decision, for it will enable even further dissemination of the work to take place, and we are grateful to the publisher, Kogan Page, for such an expression of their confidence. We are also delighted by the reactions to the 1998 volume we have received from those in schools and universities around the world and by the further work and thinking that has clearly followed its publication. One of the most pleasing aspects of the response to *International Education: Principles and practice* has been the interest shown not only by those in the international schools field *per se* but also by teachers, administrators, curriculum developers and others working in national school systems.

DEVELOPING INTERNATIONAL EDUCATION IN PRACTICE

In fact, the positive response to the 1998 book from those interested in the promotion of international education encouraged the generation of a second edited volume, *International Schools and International Education: Improving teaching, management and quality* (Hayden and Thompson, 2000). Our aim in producing this second volume was to invite some of those colleagues most prominently involved in the application of the emerging principles for international education to identify a range of issues that would need to be addressed in translating those principles into practice. In doing so they were asked to place particular emphasis on aspects of the curriculum, human resources and management tasks associated with the organization of the institutions in which they were promoting international education. It is evident that those contributions from the practice dimension are already meeting a need amongst the many other colleagues who are seeking to apply current perceptions of international education to their own practice. They are also addressing aspects of quality provision for international education.

In addition to the collection of contributions to the practice dimension of international education, other individual teachers and researchers have increased our understanding of a range of practically-oriented issues. Florence Kulundu for example, from her school in Lesotho, has undertaken an in-depth study of the CAS (Creativity, Action and Service) component of the International Baccalaureate Diploma programme in order to determine the extent to which CAS, at her school, achieves the aims for that component as a part of a balanced curriculum for the programme overall. A survey approach was adopted amongst the student cadre involved in CAS work at Machabeng International College (Kulundu, 1998; Kulundu and Hayden, 1999). The importance of such work by a teacher researcher is that, in this case, it led to a series of recommendations for strategies leading to a fuller achievement of the aims of the activity. Thus a closer relationship between theory and practice was fostered not only for the teacher concerned but also amongst colleagues within the institution. In a similar way Patricia Wecker has explored some of the factors contributing to choice of an international school by, *inter alia*, parents and students. Building on previous work relating particularly to the place of the formal curriculum, 'third culture kids' and the nature of the teaching staff, it was found that all aspects of the school, including the wider community, should play a part in the generation of a marketing strategy designed to meet client needs (Wecker, 2000). The link between theory and practice was also clearly demonstrated in a study undertaken by Rosalind Stirzaker (Stirzaker, 2000) which investigated a range of issues surrounding staff induction into a bilingual, multicultural school in the Middle East. In building on a review of theory to gather a range of perspectives on such issues, this study was able to arrive at a series of recommendations for improvement in practice which arose from those directly involved in the context under investigation.

ESTABLISHING A MODEL FOR INTERNATIONAL EDUCATION

In the final chapter of this volume Jeff Thompson has proposed a conceptualization of the task facing those who wish to incorporate an approach to international education within the overall educational programme for an institution. Based upon growing evidence from research undertaken at the University of Bath, and elsewhere, it is argued that the appropriate style of learning, leading to the development of individual student characteristics believed to be associated with the generation of international-mindedness, is essentially *experiential* in nature. A consequence of the model put forward is that there rests a responsibility, on the part of those who have been charged with the challenge of organizing the educational programme, to arrange the learning environment for students in such a manner that they will stand the best chance of developing those characteristics as a result of their experience within the programme. The model identifies three institutional dimensions, which, it is held, must be concurrently offered as part of the student experience; they are:

1. an appropriately balanced curriculum;
2. exposure to cultural diversity through human resources; and
3. an institutional administrative regime value-consistent with international education principles.

From feedback received, following the publication of the first edition, it is clear that there are those who have, over the past three years, been involved in testing the validity of the model through their own researches and individual reflections. Such work, attempting to validate and to extend our current understanding of the theoretical principles of international education, complements that of those who have contributed to the development of the practice of international education as outlined above (Hayden and Thompson, 2000). Such enquiry is not yet necessarily recorded in a formally published manner, although some of it will be found in unpublished theses or in papers presented at conferences. It is certainly worthy of note at this point, however, for much of it relates directly to the material contained in this book. With respect to the three institutional dimensions of the proposed model, the following pieces of work, selected from a wide range of investigations known to us, are of current significance.

A balanced curriculum

An important influence on the provision of an appropriately balanced curriculum has been the development, by the International Baccalaureate Organization, of programmes relating to the primary (3 to 12 years), middle (12 to 16 years) and upper secondary (16 to 18 years) phases of education (IBO, 2000). The creation of a curriculum that is effectively a 'K through 12' provision offers appropriate schools, or groups of schools, the opportunity to plan, on an uninterrupted basis, for continuity and progression with respect to some of the central features that are shared by all three programmes. These features include the notion of balance in the selection of materials that promote the acquisition of knowledge, skills, concepts and attitudes, and in the deployment of different approaches to learning. They also include the incorporation of aspects of coherence in each of the programmes, through interdisciplinary study and core elements (for example the Theory of Knowledge in the Diploma programme). The generation of the individual student's personal responsibility for learning is a feature of each of the programmes, and leads directly to the claim that students from IB programmes have 'learned how to learn'. To these features may be added the claim that IB programmes help promote the development of an 'international attitude' in students within those institutions adopting the IB curricula (Hayden and Thompson, 1995). Such claims, and the implications arising from them (many of which are included in the contributions to this volume), are clearly in need of testing through systematic research. In 1999, the establishment of an IBO Research Unit at the University of Bath, UK, as a part of the IBO strategic plan developed by its Director General, George Walker (also a contributor to this book), is intended to meet that need by stimulating and supporting the researches of those in schools and universities around the world (Walker, 1999). The initial priorities for that research have been described elsewhere (Thompson, 1999).

Exposure to cultural diversity through human resources

The importance of the experience of cultural diversity as a contribution to international education is evident from the work of Cynthia Wong, whose research at Bath involved an investigation of the IBO claim that its Diploma programme promotes international understanding. In particular she was interested in the views of former IB students now studying at university concerning the acquisition of international understanding in relation to individual cultural and language identity. A major finding of the research was the perception of students (shared by IB teachers and higher education staff) that multicultural interactions in informal dimensions of the school were more significant in contributing to the formation of an international attitude than was the structure of the formal curriculum (Hayden and Wong, 1997).

Issues relating to the sense of identity felt by primary-aged, globally-mobile children were at the heart of a study by John Nette, (based in Botswana when his research was undertaken but now in Colombia) which focused on children's sense of home and where they belong (Nette, 2000). Such issues would seem to be crucial in the context of the growing numbers of 'global nomads' who follow their parents' professions around the world, and studies such as these are providing a sound basis for the development of our better understanding of the cultural and identity factors which influence such children in their formative years.

Peter MacKenzie has explored, within one school, the utilization of available human resources from the school and its community as a source of cultural diversity for students. MacKenzie, formerly from a school in Switzerland before appointment as head of the secondary section at the International School of Tanganyika in Dar-Es-Salaam, tested the opinions of parents concerning what it meant for students to be 'international' and what they perceived to be the characteristics of an 'international education' (MacKenzie, 2000). In general it was concluded that his sample of parents appeared to go rather further than did either teachers or students in a parallel piece of work carried out earlier (Hayden, 1998) in emphasizing the importance of interaction with people of other cultures in contributing to students being 'international'. The parents did not consider it necessary for students to attend an international school in order to experience an international education. Interestingly, this sample of parents did not value interaction with the local community as a contribution to the development of 'internationalism' so highly as did the teachers or students themselves. They did, however, consider an English language dimension to be an important part of an international education. Admittedly, the conclusions here relate to a specific parental body, and further work is currently being conducted within a wider range of institutional contexts using the same approach to test the wider generality of the findings.

Our understanding of student perceptions of what it means to 'be international' has been extended by the work of Bora Rancic, who analysed questionnaire responses from a large sample of 18-year-olds studying in international schools throughout the world. The findings of this analysis (Rancic, 1998; Hayden, Rancic and Thompson, 2000) suggest that there exists a number of significant characteristics believed by the students to constitute the concept of 'being international'. Pre-eminent among these are open-mindedness, freedom of speech and ethno-relativism. Also important is the firmly held belief that the maintaining of one's own views and culture is not incompatible with being international. A similar piece of work undertaken by Geraint Williams, now based in California, investigated perceptions of the nature of international education by groups of students aiming for differing school-leaving examinations in the USA and UK. An initial exploration of the data obtained indicates different perceptions between such groups (Williams, 2000), a finding which it will be of interest to explore in further depth.

Institutional administration and value systems

The impact of differing styles of organization and administration of schools on the achievement of objectives related to the promotion of international education is a relatively unexplored field of research. Following his own contribution to this volume in 1998, Bob Sylvester has continued to develop his ideas on the ways in which the stated missions of international schools are, or are not, matched to fundamental ethical and operational principles of human unity and human diversity (Sylvester, 2000). His work is additionally interesting because of the consideration he gives to the potential importance of a dimensional and directional model of school missions examined in the light of relevant models from the Bahá'í faith. Sylvester's work involves a systematic documentary analysis of mission statements of over 70 per cent of the school members of the Association of International Schools in Africa (AISA), together with interviews with heads of international schools with experience both on that continent and on others.

An increasing number of teacher researchers are using approaches to enquiry that enable them to explore in systematic ways the relationship between institutional characteristics and the achievement of international education aims. Mark Gray at Jakarta International School, for example, has extended ideas from the school effectiveness and school improvement fields to an investigation of a specific aspect of school ethos: teacher-student interaction and perceptions by teachers and students of the importance of its role in international education (Gray, 1999). Gray has customized ethos indicators from existing literature for use in an international school context, and in this way has paralleled the related work of Paul

Crute from Switzerland, who also developed indicators for effectiveness in an international context (Crute, 1998).

A more holistic institutional approach is being taken by some authors who are employing case study techniques to elucidate the nature of the education offered within their own international institutions, through an exploration of the school's philosophies and ideologies and their relationship to practice. An example of a recently completed study of that kind is the work of Dennis Stanworth at Yokohama International School in which the importance to both process and product aspects of the school's objectives is the stated and shared philosophy (Stanworth, 1998).

THE WAY FORWARD

The above examples of recently completed enquiries, which relate directly to the issues raised in this volume, are cited only as a small sample of the known work of teachers and other researchers who are attempting to extend our understanding of international education, and its application to the teaching, learning and management of schools that are setting out to promote the values of international education. We know, from what many have reported to us, that the contributions in this book have brought to colleagues not only a better knowledge of the challenges involved in implementing international education in schools, but also encouragement and stimulation in making a contribution to that knowledge from their own experiences. We therefore offer this book, in its paperback edition, to an even wider community of those who are interested in the pursuit of a deeper understanding of the nature of international education, and its application to those institutions that seek to bring a high quality international education to all of their students. We would be delighted to receive news of your endeavours.

REFERENCES

Crute, P (1998) Using Ethos Indicators in School Improvement: a case study, Unpublished MA dissertation, University of Bath

Gray, M (1999) Teacher/Student Interaction and School Improvement in an International School, Unpublished MA dissertation, University of Bath

Hayden, M C (1998) *International Education: a study of student and teacher perspectives*, Unpublished PhD dissertation, University of Bath

Hayden, M C and Thompson J J (1995) Perceptions of International Education: A Preliminary Study, *International Review of Education*, **41**, 5, 389-404

Hayden, M C and Thompson, J J (eds) (2000) *International Schools and International Education: improving teaching, management and quality*, Kogan Page, London

Hayden, M C, Rancic, B A and Thompson J J (2000) Being International: Student and Teacher Perceptions From International Schools, *Oxford Review of Education*, **26**, 1, 107–23

Hayden, M C and Wong, C S D (1997) The International Baccalaureate: international education and cultural preservation, *Educational Studies*, **23** (3), 349–52

Kulundu, F K (1998) An enquiry based on a survey research of creativity, action and service (CAS) in Machabeng High School, Unpublished MA dissertation, University of Bath

Kulundu, F K and Hayden, M C (1999) Creativity, Action, Service (CAS) Activities as Part of the International Baccalaureate Programme at a School in Lesotho, Unpublished Paper

MacKenzie, P (2000) Being International and International Education: the perceptions of parents in one European International School, Unpublished MA dissertation, University of Bath

Nette, J (2000) Primary Age Internationally Mobile Children's Sense of Belonging and Identity: a Survey of Standard 5 and 6 Children at Four International Independent Schools in Botswana, Unpublished MA dissertation, University of Bath

Rancic, B A (1998) International Education: student perceptions of what it means to 'be international', Unpublished MA dissertation, University of Bath

Stanworth, D (1998) An International Education at Yokohama International School: from theory to practice, Unpublished MA dissertation, University of Bath

Stirzaker, R (2000) An Investigation into Issues related to the Management of Staff Induction at a Bilingual, Multicultural School in the Middle East, Unpublished MA dissertation, University of Bath

Sylvester, R (2001) A dimensional and directional model of school missions in international schools in Africa in the context of the emerging aims of international education with specific reference to issues of human unity and human diversity examined in the light of relevant models from the Bahá'í faith, Unpublished PhD thesis, University of Bath

Thompson, J J (1999) Student Learning: a focus for research, *IB World*, Vol 21, pp 33-35, International Baccalaureate Organization, Geneva

Walker, G R (1999) *A Strategic Plan for the IBO*, International Baccalaureate Organization, Geneva

Wecker, P (2000) Factors influencing international school choice and the impact of these findings on marketing strategies, Unpublished MA dissertation, University of Bath

Williams, G O (2000) What do students attending international schools perceive as important aspects of an international education; a comparison between groups of students according to the course of study taken, Unpublished MA dissertation, University of Bath

INTERNATIONAL EDUCATION IN PRACTICE

Mary Hayden

The absence of an extensive literature relating to the field of international education and international schools may well lead the new recruit, or the casual observer, to conclude that the concept of an 'international school' is an unimportant phenomenon, playing a minor role in education in perhaps a small number of fairly obscure parts of the world. And yet, to those who have been, or who currently are a part of it, the experiences of the world of international schools and international education are all too real. For many, the international school context raises a whole new set of challenging issues compared with their previous experiences of teaching in a national context: issues related, inter alia, to the multicultural, multilingual nature of the student population, to the transience of the student and teaching populations, to the variety of higher education destinations of the student population, to the nature of the curriculum and to the underpinning management dimension of all these factors. Some of them may be well served by literature generated within different but related contexts: the field of what is known as multicultural education, for instance, is a growing issue in many national contexts. Copious amounts of literature may also be found relating to various dimensions of management and the management of schools, much of which can be interpreted with relevance within the specific context of international schools, as can much of the fairly high profile range of curriculum-focused literature. What appears not to exist, however, is a literature base that focuses on the combination of these issues arising within the context of the international school.

Would it therefore be correct to extrapolate from the dearth of such literature an assumption that little is happening in the field of international schools and international education? Clearly the answer to this (rhetorical) question is an emphatic 'No!' Anyone who has been involved in this field, whether as a teacher, administrator, examiner, a parent of a child attending such a school or as a member of the school board, will know that it is one where much innovation is taking place; a field in which the tiny iceberg tip that is the literature accessible to the uninitiated hides the very large mass beneath the surface that is the large amount of exciting and innovative work being undertaken in many international schools around the world.

In 1991 one of the very few books to have focused on this field was edited by

Patricia Jonietz and Duncan Harris. In collating contributions from a range of individuals with experience of international schools and international education, Jonietz and Harris made a tremendously positive contribution to the field. In the preface Jonietz (1991) highlighted its rapid growth, from a point where the *1964 Yearbook of Education* proposed 'the existence of a new concept – international schools founded with the specific purpose of furthering international education' and, in identifying about 50 international schools and a new organization (the International Schools Association), the same 1964 *Yearbook* concluded that international education was 'not only short on means and not far-reaching enough in its spread, but uncertain of its aims and fundamental premises'. In asking whether this statement was still true in 1991 Jonietz reflected on the period since 1964, in which unimaginable changes had taken place internationally, and in which rapidly increasing numbers of families had adopted a lifestyle bordering on the nomadic, with parents following employment around the world and children increasingly accompanying their parents and requiring an education other than that of the local national system. Contributions to the 1991 edited collection demonstrate just how much had happened in the intervening period so far as this form of international education was concerned: a vast increase in numbers of schools, the growth of the International Schools Association, the development of an international curriculum for the pre-university age range (the International Baccalaureate), a curriculum for the middle years (International Curriculum for the Middle Years of Schooling (ICMYS), formerly the International Schools Association Curriculum (ISAC)), an increase in the number of United World Colleges from one to seven, the development of an international alternative to GCSE (the International GCSE), the subsidizing by government of international schools in some countries (notably The Netherlands), the creation and growth of the European Council of International Schools (ECIS) and the beginnings of an international school system.

In 1998, a mere seven years later, the rate of change is almost frightening in its dimensions. Since Jonietz wrote in 1991 of the creation of new countries, such as Belize and Papua New Guinea, the face of eastern Europe has changed beyond recognition with Yugoslavia being totally transformed and the USSR and Czechoslovakia ceasing to exist. Changes have occurred in South Africa that would have been practically impossible to envisage even as recently as 1991, and previous certainties such as the stability of the 'tiger economies' of the Pacific Rim have been thrown into question. Against this backdrop, the number of international schools has continued to grow, with estimates, including that of Hayden and Thompson (1995a), of approximately 1000 such schools. The International Schools Association, referred to in the *yearbooks* of 1964 and 1991, continues to spearhead developments including the international school system described by Blaney in 1991 and is flourishing in 1998; and the International Baccalaureate and ICMYS/ISAC are now combined in an international curriculum that caters for the entire primary and secondary (K-12) age range, incorporating the original IB, what was the ICMYS/ISAC and is now known as the IB Middle Years Programme, and what developed for primary years as the International Schools Curriculum Project and is now known as the IB Primary Years Programme. The United World College movement now includes ten member institutions, the Cambridge Examinations Syndicate has introduced a pre-university alternative to A level, the Advanced International Certificate of Education, to complement their IGCSE programme, and an international dimension has been introduced to the American Advanced Placement programme. What might be referred to as the 'practice' of international education within this context is clearly, therefore, alive and well.

Perhaps one of the reasons for the relatively low profile of the field of international education is the manner of its growth. As charted by, among others, Jonietz and Harris (1991) and Peterson (1987), as well as by school documentation, this growth could be taken to have started in 1924 when – within four days of one another – two prestigious institutions were founded: the International School of Geneva and Yokohama International School (both of whose current Directors contribute to this volume). From that point, to the point where we are today, the growth has been relatively *ad hoc*, so that 'for the most part the body of international schools is a conglomeration of individual institutions which may or may not share an underlying educational philosophy' (Hayden and Thompson, 1995a). While a number of attempts have been made to categorize or define them (including Leach, 1969; Terwilliger, 1972; Pönisch, 1987; and Matthews, 1988) such schools remain, despite a number of groupings including the United World Colleges, 'Shell Schools', 'IB schools', ECIS-accredited schools and so on, a disparate group.

A related factor contributing to the relatively low profile of international schools is the lack of clarity with respect to a consensus on several issues: what they actually are, the relationship between the schools themselves and the international education many of them profess to offer. Where an assumption often appears to have been made that international education is simply what happens in international schools, recent work (Hayden and Thompson, 1995b) has suggested that the apparent relationship is not quite so straightforward: an international school may offer an education that has no claims to be international, while an international education may be experienced by a student who has not attended a school that claims to be international. If, as this absence of a one-to-one relationship implies, international education may be experienced world-wide in schools other than international schools, the potential field becomes much larger.

Encouragingly, the literature base in the field has been developing rapidly. Although still not of a high profile to the 'outsider', to those who are prepared to persevere the evidence is there to be found. Curriculum-focused publications such as *IB World* have been introduced and are published regularly, a new journal from the International Schools Association, *Skepsis* (edited by one of our contributors, Derek Pigrum), appears regularly, publications such as *The International Educator* and *Newslinks* keep schools informed of news from international schools, and the *International Schools Journal*, founded in 1981 by another of our contributors, Edna Murphy, and now published under the auspices of ECIS, continues to go from strength to strength. In addition it is possible to find not only a small but growing number of articles and papers in such journals, but also masters and doctoral level theses relating to the international school/international education context. Such study is increasingly being undertaken by teachers and administrators whose careers have led them to pursue interests relating to the field at institutions, such as the University of Bath, which offer masters and doctoral level study specializing in the field, and through organizations such as the Principals' Training Center (PTC), which offers workshops and training focused on the development of skills for international school administrators.

Such publications and studies, together with the growing debate about issues which arise particularly in the context of this form of international education, have acted as a stimulus for many of the contributions in this volume, from a range of experienced practitioners within the field who each highlight a particular issue of relevance to this growing context. The contributions are divided into four parts, focusing on four dimensions of international education that appear to encompass between them the issues that are most often the subject of debate in this context: the student, the curriculum (both formal and informal), the school as an organization, and what we have called 'international education for all'.

Part 1, concerned with the student in international education, begins with a reflection based on a lecture delivered at the University of Bath MA programme Summer School in July 1997 by George Walker, currently Director General of the International School of Geneva and Visiting Professor at the University of Bath. Drawing on his wide experience in both national and international education George Walker reflects on the concept of 'home' through a review of a range of classical literature which he relates to the context of the globally mobile international schoolchild. Mary Langford follows this reflection with a consideration of the situation of such children – those who have come to be known as 'global nomads' or 'Third Culture Kids'. Arising from her own research work, as well as from her experience as an administrator in a number of international schools and on ECIS accreditation teams and, importantly, as a one-time 'global nomad' herself, Mary Langford goes on to consider the perceptions of employers, educators and parents with respect to how international schools may best cater for the needs of these young people as they wend their itinerant way through childhood, adolescence and the formal education system. Immediately following this contribution, Richard Pearce considers the wide-ranging and related issue of cultural identity within the environment of the international school. From personal research and from many years of experience working as a teacher in, and consultant to international schools, Richard Pearce's reflections highlight the importance of school culture, particularly within the context of international schools, and the way in which the child develops and maintains cultural identity through school and other influences. Thus a number of important issues are raised at the outset relating to the place of the student in the process of international education. This is important, for the central focus of international schools must universally be the student, whose educational needs they exist to fulfil.

In Part 2 we consider the place of the curriculum within international education. As has already been noted, much has happened both since 1964 and since 1991, in the development of a curriculum appropriate for the international school context, which is other than the adaptation of the curriculum of one national system. Elisabeth Fox, in the first of two contributions, reflects on the emergence and development of the International Baccalaureate from the early 1960s as an appropriate curriculum for international schools. Drawing on a range of sources, including her own seminal article in the *Harvard Educational Review* (1985), and on her extensive experience especially in South America and New York, Elisabeth Fox highlights the observation that an international curriculum may be offered not only in international schools; it may also be found in schools that do not claim to be international but that aspire to offer an international education: this is consistent with findings (Hayden and Thompson, 1995b) which suggest that the concepts of international schools and international education do not necessarily go hand in hand and can exist in isolation from each other. The extent to which the concept of an international curriculum has developed since even 1991, when the most recent *Yearbook of Education* dedicated to international education was published, is emphasized in Kevin Bartlett's contribution, which considers the growing place in schools world-wide for an international curriculum designed for the primary age range. Kevin Bartlett's own role in spearheading this particular curriculum initiative is well known through his experiences while at Vienna International School in Austria and latterly at Windhoek International School in Namibia, and he makes a convincing case for the place of a curriculum designed for the 'international student' at this very formative stage in their development. His continuing leadership of the Primary Years Programme for the International Baccalaureate Organization will provide further opportunity for development of his work to date in this field.

A convincing case is also made by our next contributor, Colin Jenkins, for the place of global issues within any curriculum designed for students growing up in our increasingly interdependent world. A long-time proponent of the crucial place of such issues during his career both at Atlantic College and as Director of Examinations and a member of the Curriculum Board with the International Baccalaureate Organization, Colin Jenkins considers the place of such a dimension within the curriculum as well as some of the associated logistical difficulties. Another arguably vital aspect of the curriculum for the internationally educated student is that of Education for Peace. In charting developments at both local and national levels, Phil Thomas – another long-time advocate, in this case over many years at the International School of Geneva as a major player in the development of Education for Peace for the adult citizens of tomorrow – highlights the importance of this area of the curriculum and the creative work being undertaken through the auspices of the International Schools Association project for which he is the Coordinator. Derek Pigrum's subsequent contribution explores yet another dimension of the curriculum: the realm of semiotics (the study of signs) and creativity. His experiences at Vienna International School, as a teacher of courses including IB Art/Design and as editor of the ISA journal *Skepsis*, as well as personal research, inform this discourse, which includes consideration of the link between creative understanding and the concept of Homo Faber, one of the interactive areas of the IB Middle Years Programme.

Two other vital and related aspects of a curriculum designed for any young person are those of pastoral care and of catering for individual needs, be it in terms of learning disabilities, giftedness, language support in a multilingual context, or any one of a range of other dimensions of what could be termed the non-formal curriculum. Martha Haldimann's consideration of the concept of 'Optimal Match' shows just how important is the place within international schools of an emphasis on catering for the particular needs of each individual student. Martha Haldimann's experience as an educator, researcher and author is drawn on in this account, which highlights just how much is happening through four short case studies from international schools around the world. Barry Drake, in a contribution arising from his own research as well as from his professional experience at Li Po Chun United World College in Hong Kong, goes on to show how the concept of pastoral care has grown to have an important place not only in national contexts but also within the context of an international education environment. The contributions to this section thus highlight the importance of a wide variety of both formal and informal dimensions of the curriculum offered in international schools world-wide.

Part 3 includes contributions relating to various aspects of school and its organization within the context of international education. Neil Richards draws on his experiences in a number of international schools including headships at Machabeng High School, Lesotho and Yokohama International School, Japan, as well as his own personal research, to reflect on the crucial place of staffing within international schools and, in particular, on the recruitment of local-contract teachers in international schools based in the less developed world. Bob Sylvester's research, taken with experiences based in countries including Zambia and Botswana, contributes to his consideration of issues relating to diversity within international schools and the way in which such schools respond in terms of their own mission and philosophy. James Cambridge's discussion of the role of organizational cultures picks up on one dimension of this chapter, in reflecting upon the extent to which studies conducted within the context of a commercial environment can be applied to the international school context. Experience of teaching in international schools in Yemen and Lesotho, and of examining for the IB, clearly informs James Cambridge's work in this area, which is also linked to his research at the University of Bath. Edna Murphy's role within the international school context requires little, if any introduction. Over many years as a teacher and administrator of international schools within Europe, she has also made time to found and edit the *International Schools Journal* and to serve on ECIS accreditation teams in different parts of the world. Edna Murphy's contribution draws on this wealth of experience in highlighting the place of accreditation in the international school, and in reflecting on a number of hypothetical examples of situations in which accreditation might be undertaken with benefit. All of the contributors serve to emphasize the importance of organizational features in the planning and implementation of programmes of education in international schools.

The last section, Part 4, includes a number of contributions focusing on the concept of international education as it applies across a range of contexts, exploring ways in which international education may be made accessible to all. David Wilkinson highlights issues informed by his varied experience as a teacher and administrator in schools based in Thailand and Lesotho and in United World Colleges in Italy, Hong Kong and, most recently, at the newly established Mahindra UWC in India, in reflecting on the extent to which international education is, in practice, an education that can only be offered to the few, and on what steps can be taken to make it an experience available to rich and poor alike. David Wilkinson, like Neil Richards, has been Head of Machabeng High School Lesotho, an experience of international education in the less developed world that has clearly informed current thinking in each case. In the second of her two contributions Elisabeth Fox considers the place of the International Baccalaureate as a curriculum that can be applied in a national as well as an international context by highlighting, as an illustration, developments within Chile, from her own work in a wider world context. Malcolm McKenzie subsequently draws on teaching and administration experience in the UK, South Africa and Botswana, as well as a term spent as a visiting lecturer at the University of Bath, in discussing the meaning of 'international' as applied to education and schools. This contribution is based on talks given to the National Association of Independent Schools in Washington in March 1996, and to the February 1997 Global Connections meeting held in Johannesburg, and is informed by feedback from the audiences at both gatherings. In arguing for consideration of the concept of 'pan-national education' Malcolm McKenzie discusses some of its possible characteristics, as well as the place of partnerships that promote the international dimension of education. Michal Pasternak's discussion, arising from his own research as well as from experience of teaching at the International School of Geneva and in other contexts, reflects on the extent to which 'international education' can actually exist and, in considering possible approaches to international education, reflects on whether such a notion is actually a pipedream to which we aspire but which we may never actually reach.

The last chapter reflects on all these varied and informative dimensions of international education and on what, taken together, they may offer as a model for the future. Jeff Thompson is known to many in the world of international schools and international education through his involvement in the development of curricula and examinations at both national and international levels, and brings together strands from his teaching and research through the University of Bath to formulate a working model for international education that owes a great deal, as he acknowledges, to the themes running through the contributions to this book.

It is clear, then, that much is indeed happening within the world of international schools and international education, and contributions to this volume provide evidence of just a small proportion of the exciting and innovative developments that become clear once an exploration of that world is undertaken. Much had happened between the publication of the *1964* and *1991 Yearbooks of Education*: much more has happened between 1991 and the 1998 publication of this text. The exploration of practice which the book represents also leads to the establishment of a number of principles within international education that have hitherto not been made explicit. We may not know what the future holds, but it would seem to be a safe assumption that developments in the world of international schools and international education will continue apace, and that large numbers of dedicated

professionals will play a crucial role in shaping the path of those exciting and innovative developments that will influence the world of the twenty-first century.

REFERENCES

Fox, E (1985) 'International schools and the International Baccalaureate', *Harvard Educational Review*, **55**, 1, pp 53–68

Hayden, M C and Thompson, J J (1995a) 'International schools and international education: a relationship reviewed', *Oxford Review of Education*, **21**, 3, pp 327–45

Hayden, M C and Thompson, J J (1995b) 'Perceptions of international education: a preliminary study', *International Review of Education*, **41**, 5, pp 389–404

Jonietz, P L (1991) 'Preface', in P L Jonietz and D Harris (eds) (1991), *World Yearbook of Education 1991: International Schools and International Education*, Kogan Page, London

Jonietz, P L and Harris, D (eds) (1991) *World Yearbook of Education 1991: International Schools and International Education*, Kogan Page, London

Leach, R J (1969) *International Schools and Their Role in the Field of International Education*, Pergamon Press, Oxford

Matthews, M (1988) 'The ethos of international schools', MSc thesis, University of Oxford

Peterson, A D C (1987) *Schools Across Frontiers*, Open Court, La Salle, Illinois

Pönisch, A (1987) 'Special needs and the International Baccalaureate: a study of the need for and development of alternative courses to the International Baccalaureate', MSc thesis, University of Oxford

Terwilliger, R I (1972) 'International schools: Cultural crossroads', *The Educational Forum*, **36**, 3, pp 359–63

Part 1

STUDENTS IN INTERNATIONAL EDUCATION

2

HOME SWEET HOME: A STUDY, THROUGH FICTIONAL LITERATURE, OF DISORIENTED CHILDREN AND THE SIGNIFICANCE OF HOME

George Walker

THE CONCEPT OF HOME

> I never fully realized that I was actually leaving my country, which I had
> lived in for all of my seventeen years, until I found myself looking down on
> what had been my house, my school, my town, my whole world, from the
> window of an aeroplane taking me to a country I had never been before, half-
> way across the globe.

That *cri de coeur*, written by a student in Geneva, strikes an immediate chord with
anyone who works in an international school. The disorientation of young people
caused by the temporary, sometimes permanent loss of their 'home' is becoming
the subject of serious academic research. Because of its deep impact on young lives
it has always been the subject of serious literature, and it is through novels that I
want to explore the questions: what is it that defines 'home', how important is it
and is a stable home necessarily an unmixed blessing, and what are the implications for those in international schools?

I start in 1908, deep in the English countryside:

> Once beyond the village, where the cottages ceased abruptly, on either side of
> the road they could smell through the darkness the friendly fields again; and
> they braced themselves for the last long stretch, the home stretch, the stretch
> that we know is bound to end, sometime, in the rattle of the door-latch, the
> sudden firelight, and the sight of familiar things greeting us as long-absent
> travellers from far overseas. They plodded along steadily and silently, each of
> them thinking his own thoughts. The Mole's ran a good deal on supper, as it
> was pitch-dark, and it was all a strange country to him as far as he knew, and
> he was following obediently in the wake of the Rat, leaving the guidance

entirely to him. As for the Rat, he was walking a little way ahead, as his habit was, his shoulders humped, his eyes fixed on the straight grey road in front of him; so he did not notice poor Mole when suddenly the summons reached him, and took him like an electric shock.

We others, who have long lost the more subtle of the physical senses, have not even proper terms to express an animal's intercommunications with his surroundings, living or otherwise, and have only the word 'smell', for instance, to include the whole range of delicate thrills which murmur in the nose of the animal night and day, summoning, warning, inciting, repelling. It was one of these mysterious fairy calls from out the void that suddenly reached Mole in the darkness, making him tingle through and through with its very familiar appeal, even while as yet he could not clearly remember what it was. He stopped dead in his tracks, his nose searching hither and thither in its efforts to recapture the fine filament, the telegraphic current, that had so strongly moved him. A moment, and he had caught it again; and with it this time came recollection in fullest flood.

Home! That was what they meant, those caressing appeals, those soft touches wafted through the air, those invisible little hands pulling and tugging, all one way! Why, it must be quite close by him at that moment, his old home that he had hurriedly forsaken and never sought again, that day when he first found the river! And now it was sending out its scouts and its messengers to capture him and bring him in.

(*The Wind in the Willows*, Kenneth Grahame, 1908)

I hope the immediate impact of that extract will explain why I have chosen to explore the theme of disorientation through the medium of literature. The temporary, or sometimes long-term loss of a stable, identifiable home is a favourite theme in literature and it is no coincidence that many of the examples I have chosen, though classified as fiction, nevertheless have a strong autobiographical basis. Why have I started with a quote far removed from international schools and jet-setting global mobility and rooted instead in the deliberately neutral culture of animals? Quite simply because I believe that the reader's immediate and powerful identification with Mole's emotions confirms that we humans, too, have a deep instinctive need for a home – something or somewhere to which we can belong, with which we can identify, which offers us stability and security.

My mother's home was a village in Northamptonshire, more or less in the centre of England. We have traced her family back over three centuries, and none of her ancestors lived more than about 50 miles from her birthplace. Some of them came from the village of Helpstone and they must have known the poet, John Clare, whose rural surroundings affected him profoundly, indeed psychologically. In 1832 he had to leave Helpstone, a move which he describes in a poem called 'The Flitting'. Here is an extract:

Ive left my own old home of homes

Green fields and every pleasant place

The summer like a stranger comes

I pause and hardly know her face

I miss the hazels happy green

The bluebell's quiet hanging blooms

Where envy's sneer was never seen

Where staring malice never comes

I miss the heath, its yellow furze

Molehills and rabbit tracks that lead

Through beesom, ling and teazel burrs

That spread a wilderness indeed

The woodland oaks and all below

That their white powdered branches shield

The mossy pads– the very crow

Croaked music in my native fields

(from 'The Flitting', John Clare, 1793–1864)
Reproduced with permission of Curtis Brown
Ltd, London, on behalf of Eric Robinson.
Copyright Eric Robinson 1984.

Clare found the move to his new home in Northborough deeply disturbing, and shortly after completing that poem he was admitted to an asylum where he spent the rest of his life. Those two villages – Helpstone and Northborough – are just four miles apart but Clare, like Mole, had become an exile living in an alien land.

In modern, increasingly divided societies, more and more people are forced to live in exile, separated from their homes. Here is part of a poem by the contemporary Ghanaian poet, Ama Ata Aidoo, called 'Homesickness':

This afternoon,

I bolted from

the fishmarket:

my eyes smarting with

shame

at how too willingly and sheepishly
my memory had slipped up
after the loss of my taste buds.

Familiarly in an unfamiliar land,
so strong and so sweetly strong,
the smells of the fish of
my childhood hit hard and soft,
wickedly musky.

All else falls into focus
except the names of the fish.

While from distant places in my head
the Atlantic booms and roars or
calmly creeps swishing foam on the hot sand.

But I could not remember their Fantse names.

They were labelled clearly enough
– in English –

which
tragically
brought no echoes ....

One terrifying truth
unveiled in one short afternoon:

that

exile brings losses like

forgetting to remember

ordinary things.

(from 'Homesickness', by Ama Ata Aidoo)
Reproduced with permission of Dangaroo
Press, Hebden Bridge, West Yorks.

I want those two poems, written 150 years apart, to establish one of the pillars of this chapter, namely that in each of us there is a very strong, almost animal sense of home that forms a part of our psyche. I want to emphasize that point because I shall go on to suggest that most young people seem to adapt rather easily to different physical surroundings; and I shall also be drawing attention to the damaging aspects of too strong an identity with 'home'.

DISORIENTATION AND ADAPTATION

It was in the second half of the nineteenth century that the disorientation of 'homeless' children became a popular theme in literature, reflecting an increasing number of lives thrown into turmoil by the industrial revolution. Tempting though it is, I shall pass by Charles Dickens and I shall also ignore that rich, but eccentrically British, genre of boarding school literature. But we should note in passing that in the best known of them all, *Tom Brown's Schooldays*, written in 1867, it is only on its final pages that we learn that Tom's closest friend has left to join his regiment in India; this is the first hint in the book that there is any existence outside rural Middle England.

Instead, let us move on to 1880 and to the village of Dörfli in Switzerland:

The valley lay far below bathed in the morning sun. In front of her rose a broad snow-field, high against the dark-blue sky, while to the left was a huge pile of rocks on either side of which a bare lofty peak, that seemed to pierce the blue, looked frowningly down upon her. The child sat without moving, her eyes taking in the whole scene, and all around was a great stillness, only broken by soft, light puffs of wind that swayed the light bells of the blue flowers, and the shining gold heads of the cistus, and set them nodding merrily on their slender stems. Peter had fallen asleep after his fatigue and the goats were climbing about among the bushes overhead. Heidi had never felt so happy in her life before.

(*Heidi*, Johanna Spyri, 1880)

After all those television serials, it was rather refreshing to go back to the original text of Heidi which had been read to me as a child some 50 years ago. I had not realized how fast moving children's books seem to the adult reader; events whizz by! And Peter's blind grandmother is a much more cheerful character than I remember her, despite her disability and poverty. I was quite unaware of the cloyingly religious overtones in the second half of the book, which my mother wisely suppressed. To my delight, my most enduring memory of *Heidi* remains intact - the magical description of the snow catching fire as the sun sets in the high mountains. I have now seen that for myself and I can understand why, for Heidi, it became such a powerful symbol of 'home'.

I am sure you are familiar with the story. Heidi is 'dumped' as a five year old on her alienated grandfather. She comes to love both him and the freedom of the mountains where he lives. Some years later she is taken off to Frankfurt to become a companion for Clara, a sickly child. Heidi's acute homesickness in an urban environment makes her physically ill and a wise doctor insists she return to her grandfather. Sometime later (in what was actually a sequel to the original book) Clara visits Heidi in the mountains. The young goatherd, Peter, deliberately destroys Clara's wheelchair so she is forced to walk and she is slowly healed in the invigorating surroundings of her new environment.

The central message is the same as that of John Clare 50 years earlier and our own more than 100 years later: the essential equilibrium between human beings and their physical surroundings. But a number of other criteria for defining 'home', which we shall meet again and again, are apparent in *Heidi*.

1. In the absence of parents (sometimes dead, sometimes away on business) grand-parents play a key role, in this case Heidi's, Peter's and Clara's.
2. Siblings or quasi-siblings like the goatherd, Peter, are a significant part of home.
3. A change of home will often involve an acute clash of cultures, in this case between the naïve simplicity of mountain life and the stuffy, artificial conventions of Frankfurt.
4. There is the importance of education: when it was first published, the book was called *Heidi's Years of Wandering and Learning* and the ability to read, which Heidi is taught and then passes on to Peter, is seen as a vital part of the preparation to move beyond the confines of home.

With the expansion of the British Empire in the second half of the nineteenth century a new genre of literature began to appear. Children's lives were now being disoriented by their parents' 'service' to their nation. Home was suddenly moved to India, or was it with an uncle and aunt in England, or was it really with the nuns of a boarding-school? The best-known author of this period is Frances Hodgson Burnett, and her classic story, endlessly televised and filmed, is *The Secret Garden*. The spoilt child, Mary Lennox, is forced to return to Britain when her parents die of cholera in India. She goes to live with her uncle in a desolate house on the Yorkshire moors. Through the help of a simple local boy, Dickon, she comes to know and love the local flora and fauna. She rediscovers the 'secret garden' that was her aunt's before her tragic death. Mary befriends her cousin, Colin, isolated within the house with a psychosomatic illness, and his participation in the restoration of the secret garden restores his health.

There are obvious parallels here with *Heidi*: the theme of illness and the possibility of cure by achieving a better equilibrium with nature; the importance of the substitute parent – this time Martha, the Yorkshire maid – and of the substitute sibling, Dickon; the many examples of clashes of culture between the exotic Indian background of Mary and the simple, dour Yorkshire people of her new home, as well as the associated problem of communication as Mary struggles to understand the Yorkshire dialect. But we are conscious of a new dimension in this book. *Heidi*, despite all those snow-capped peaks and that heady mountain air, is a claustrophobic novel. The action moves from the tiny village of Dörfli, shut in by its mountains, to Frankfurt, shut in by its buildings, and back to Dörfli again. Despite the beautiful flowers, brilliant sunsets and free-range goats, you feel that Heidi's spirit will never escape out of the valley.

In contrast, read this virtuoso passage from *The Secret Garden*:

> One of the strange things about living in the world is that it is only now and then one is quite sure one is going to live for ever and ever. One knows it sometimes when one gets up at the tender, solemn dawn-time and goes out and stands alone and throws one's head far back and looks up and up and watches the pale sky slowly changing and flushing and marvellous unknown things happening until the East almost makes one cry out and one's heart stands still at the strange unchanging majesty of the rising of the sun – which has been happening every morning for thousands and thousands and thousands of years. One knows it then for a moment or so. And one knows it sometimes when one stands by oneself in a wood at sunset and the mysterious deep gold stillness slanting through and under the branches seems to be saying slowly again and again something one cannot quite hear, however much one tries. Then sometimes the immense quiet of the dark-blue at night with millions of stars waiting and watching makes one sure; and sometimes a sound of far-off music makes it true; and sometimes a look in someone's eyes.
>
> And it was like that with Colin when he first saw and heard and felt the springtime inside the four high walls of the hidden garden.

(*The Secret Garden*, Frances Hodgson Burnett, 1911)

Despite its high walls the secret garden is not a confining metaphor; on the contrary, it inspires a global perspective. Note the deliberate reference to the East and to the sound of far-off music. There are new, unimagined possibilities here and by the end of the book the two cultures – the English flowers, gardens and Yorkshire dialect and the heat and mysticism of India – blend together and bring about Colin's cure. This is a completely new idea, totally absent in Heidi, and in many ways *The Secret Garden* is a truly international book.

HOME AND HUMAN NEEDS

Let us see where we have got to. 'Home' for a young person is a place of physical security with powerfully memorable features, scents and atmospheres. It provides love, affection and human contact from competent adults, who are frequently not the child's parents, and from children of similar ages, who are not necessarily brothers and sisters. In fact it is a place that satisfies the first four of Maslow's hierarchical needs (as discussed for instance, in, Dixon, 1993):

1. of early survival – a source of food, water, warmth
2. of security and safety
3. confirming love and feelings of belonging
4. to learn competencies, win prestige and esteem

although the two higher levels of Maslow's motivation cannot be achieved at home – you have to move out and on:

5. self-fulfilment
6. curiosity and the need to understand

and I shall return to this point.

First, let us put our simple model to the test with a more disturbing form of childhood disorientation that has been a feature of the second half of the twentieth century – the dislocation of home and family caused by war. To illustrate this theme I have chosen the best-known children's novel of this genre, *The Silver Sword*, by Ian Serraillier. It has become a modern classic which has sold over a million copies. Three Polish children, Ruth, Edek and Bronia Balicki (who are aged 18, 16 and eight by the end of the story) escape from Warsaw in 1945 and set off across Europe for Switzerland, where they believe they will find their parents who have been seized by the Nazis (their mother is Swiss). They are joined by Jan, whose own lonely struggle to survive has turned him into a young criminal. In the absence of a home – theirs was blown up by Nazi storm troopers – they are sustained in their seemingly hopeless quest by a vision of a new, secure home in Switzerland and by a symbol for it – the silver sword. In their precarious situation none of the adults can be trusted because they have their own priorities for survival, so Ruth herself becomes the substitute parent, even taking over responsibility for the family's education. Her heroic role and the strong sense of sibling support are the main themes of the book.

It is an exciting adventure set amidst the chaos that existed in post-war central Europe as thousands of refugees wondered in what direction to walk in order to find a 'home'. On the way to safety and security in Switzerland the children establish temporary homes, like this one in Berlin:

There was more food for them at the transit camp, a disused cinema whose floor appeared to contain the entire population of Berlin. After four helpings of soup each, they were given blankets and straw-filled mattresses and ushered into a dark corner of the hall. Here a seedy looking flag and a scribbled notice on the wall indicated that they were in 'Poland'. The electricity was not working, and the only light came from hurricane lamps suspended from the balcony above.

As far as they could see, the whole floor was carpeted with mattresses. They threw down theirs where they stood – in the no-man's land between 'Poland' and 'Yugoslavia'.

This was to be their home while they were in Berlin. It was warm and dry and comfortable, and they were delighted – especially Bronia, who loved to hear Polish voices, as they made it feel like home. Next to her she found a child of her own age, whose mother was as good as Ruth at telling stories and knew many folk-tales that Bronia had never heard.

(*The Silver Sword*, Ian Serraillier, 1956)

The adventure is made even more compelling by its complete lack of sentimentality and by the reader's knowledge that it is based on the true story of a real family. At the end of the book the children do reach Switzerland, where they are reunited with their parents, and the security of their new home is further emphasized by its location in an international Pestalozzi village. But, despite their apparently unlimited capacity to survive, the children have suffered serious damage; it is 18 months before Edek regains his full health and Ruth has a complete breakdown, reverting to childhood after her premature adult responsibilities.

Carrie's War, by Nina Bawden, is again largely autobiographical. Carrie (who is 11) and her younger brother Nick are evacuated from London to a Welsh mountain village in 1939. We are therefore hardly aware of the war and the story is about two different homes. The first is Carrie's new foster home belonging to her substitute parents, the strict Samuel Evans and his bullied sister, Lou. With its 'chapel' atmosphere it is a model of safety, security and predictability, but nearby at Druids Bottom, a prehistoric site of Celtic sacrifice, live the mysterious Hepzibah and the mentally retarded Mister Johnny. This strange, frightening but enticing house, which burns down at the climax of the story, becomes a powerful allegory for Carrie's strange, frightening but enticing new experiences: conflicting adult relationships, witchery, mysticism and death. She is torn between the two homes: the first is predictable, stable but cold, while the second is complex, dark but welcoming.

Here is the description of Carrie and Nick on their first, terrifying, visit to Druid's Bottom:

She ran, and Nick ran behind her, and the creature, whatever it was, the gobbling Thing, followed them. It seemed to be calling to them and Carrie thought of fairy-tales she had read – you looked back at something behind you and were caught in its spell! She gasped, 'Don't look back, Nick, whatever you do.'

The path widened and flattened as it came out of the Grove and she caught Nick's hand to make him run faster. Too fast for his shorter legs and he fell on his knees. He moaned, as she pulled him up, 'I can't, I can't, Carrie...'

She said, through chattering teeth, 'Yes you can. Not much further.'

They saw the house then, its dark, tall-chimneyed bulk looming up, and lights in the windows. One light quite high up and one low down, at the side. They ran, on rubbery legs, through an open gate and across a dirt yard towards the lit window. There was a door but it was shut. They flung themselves against it.

Gobble-Gobble was coming behind them, was crossing the yard.

'Please,' Carrie croaked. 'Please.' Quite sure that it was too late, that the creature would get them.

But the door opened inward, like magic, and they fell through it to light, warmth and safety.

(*Carrie's War*, Nina Bawden, 1973)

[The Gobble-Gobble is simply Mister Johnny trying to talk to them.]

HOME AND PERSONAL DEVELOPMENT

And at this point we turn a corner, because in *Heidi*, in *The Secret Garden* and even in *The Silver Sword*, we are left with the strong impression that 'everyone lived happily ever after', more or less as they were before, despite everything that has happened to them. By contrast, Carrie's disorientation is part of her growing up; the burning down of Druids Bottom is the destruction of her own childhood at the very moment that she is returning to the love of her own home. The external security of familiar surroundings, competent adults and supportive siblings is replaced by an internal struggle between the familiar and the unknown, the reassuring and the alarming, the light and the dark.

Which brings me to a remarkable book that explores these opposites in real depth. Herman Hesse's *Demian*, published in 1919, became a cult novel of the 1960s, the *Gospel of St Demian*. It describes the growth from childhood to manhood of Emile Sinclair. As a schoolboy Sinclair is involved in a foolish incident that threatens to alienate him from his secure home and loving family: he is unable to confess to his parents and this gives him both an acute sense of guilt and a novel sensation of power over them; they no longer own him, he no longer belongs to his home. His dilemma is resolved by a remarkable young man called Demian, who helps Sinclair to tell his parents who, of course, forgive him and welcome him back into the fold. But the relationship is never the same again.

And now with heightened emotions I underwent the ceremony of my readmittance to the fold, the Prodigal Son's home-coming. Mother took me along to Father, the story was repeated, questions and exclamations of praise were showered on me; both parents patted me on the head and breathed great sighs of relief. Everything was marvellous, everything was like the fairy-tales, everything was restored to a wonderful harmony.

... And yet my house was not really in order... I was clinging with all my roots to my former earthly paradise; I had returned home and had been accepted in grace. But it was not Demian's world nor was he suited to it. He too.... was a 'tempter' and moreover my link with the second, evil world with which I never wanted to have anything more to do.

(*Demian*, Herman Hesse, 1919)

We are back in Switzerland where Herman Hesse moved as a protest against German militarism after World War I. This autobiographical novel is built around the work of the great Swiss psychiatrist, Carl Jung, with whose pupil, Josef Lang, Hesse underwent successful psychoanalysis in 1916. Demian, who is killed in Flanders, turns out to be the other half, the outward-seeking half, of Sinclair's personality. They are one and the same person, or more accurately two and the same person.

It is no coincidence that the remaining novels I have chosen to illustrate the disorientation of children are all adult books and no one lives happily ever after. The first derives from the same situation as *The Silver Sword* – but that is the only similarity. Exciting adventure is replaced by grim realism and J G Ballard's autobiographical novel *Empire of the Sun* has been described as one of the most significant novels of World War II. Jim, who is 12, lives a comfortable life with his expatriate parents in Shanghai. When the Japanese take over the city in 1941 he becomes separated from his parents and experiences the appalling conditions of internment camps, labour squads and death marches. Yet, somehow, the boy survives; indeed he not only survives, he thrives and out manoeuvres most of the adults who are portrayed as inept, unreliable and physically weak.

Jim constructs a temporary home in one of the camp huts and reinvents his parents:

Beside the Packard was a small section that Jim had cut from a larger photograph of a crowd outside the gates of Buckingham Palace in 1940. The blurred images of a man and a woman standing arm in arm reminded Jim of his parents. This unknown English couple, perhaps dead in an air raid, had almost become his mother and father. Jim knew that they were complete strangers, but he kept the pretence alive, so that in turn he could keep alive the lost memory of his parents.

(*Empire of the Sun*, J G Ballard, 1985)

Reunion with his parents remains Jim's constant, if distant dream throughout the war, but when it finally takes place it turns out to be an anti-climax:

Jim remembered his return to the house in Amherst Avenue, and his mother and father smiling weakly from their deck-chairs in the garden. Beside the drained swimming-pool the untended grass grew around their shoulders, and reminded him of the bowers of nettles in which the dead Japanese airmen had lain. As Dr Ransome stood formally on the terrace in his American uniform, Jim had wanted to explain to his parents everything that he and the doctor had done together, but his mother and father had been through their own war. For all their affection for him, they seemed older and far away.

The novel is disturbing at every level; Jim has no cultural roots, refuses to display the expected behaviour of a young British schoolboy and does nothing to conceal his admiration for the Japanese and especially their flying skills. Even so, throughout all the horror there remains a compulsive urge to learn.

> 'Now, Jim, I'm sure you've done your prep....' Dr Ransome opened the Latin primer. Although distracted by the prisoners who gathered outside the huts and dormitory blocks, he stared hard at the text. Hundreds of men and their wives, many with their children, were crossing the parade ground. He began to question Jim, who continued to polish his shoes under the table.
> 'They were being loved... ?'
> 'Amabantur.'
> 'I shall be loved... ?'
> 'Amabor.'
> 'You will have been loved... ?'
> 'Amatus eris.'
> 'Right – I'll set you an unseen. Mrs Vincent will help you with the vocabulary. She doesn't mind your asking'

Jim appears to have moved far beyond the need for the security and protection of the home. In Maslow's terms, he has been offered the possibility of self-fulfilment, the satisfaction of curiosity and the need to understand. But at what price? We do not know what happens to Jim in later life (we would need to ask J G Ballard) and the novel ends as, devoid of any love or close human contact, he leaves his former home in Shanghai to attend boarding-school in Britain.

> He stepped on to the gangway, conscious that he was probably leaving Shanghai for the last time, setting out for a small, strange country on the other side of the world which he had never visited, but which was nominally 'home'. Yet only part of his mind would leave Shanghai. The rest would remain there forever, returning on the tide like the coffins launched from the funeral piers at Nantao.

Let us move on a generation to find more familiar ground – the life of the international civil servant – and to the first novel that actually mentions an international school! It is *The Peacock Spring* by Rumer Godden, set in Delhi.

The situation is immediately familiar because Sir Edward Gwithiam is a senior UN diplomat. One day, and for no apparent reason, he sends for his daughters, Una and Hal, to join him in Delhi from their boarding-school in Britain. It turns out to be a cynical device to enable him to retain his mistress, a Eurasian Miss Alix Lamont, as their governess. Una, who is 15, feels betrayed by her father; she starts clandestine meetings in a garden hut with a young, attractive dissident poet, Ravi, who is working as Sir Edward's gardener, and she becomes pregnant. They run away from Delhi and are welcomed into Ravi's Brahmin family, but Sir Edward tracks her down and brings her back home.

'You should at least sit down.' The Inspector-General came to Una and as she did not move, he said, 'It must be painful, after such an adventure, to come home.'

'Home?' Una spoke as if she had never heard of it. What home? she seemed to ask. Then, suddenly, 'There is a little hut at the end of the garden,' she told him, 'where... where...'

No Indian can bear to see a child cry. To Colonel Jaiswal Una was a child and the big policeman went to her and smoothed the tormented hair. 'There, there, *batchi*. It will pass,' but this was not a child and Una disengaged herself 'It will never pass.'

(*The Peacock Spring*, Rumer Godden, 1975)

She loses the baby and is sent back to finish her education in Britain.

This is a truly international novel which contrasts the love and support of the extended Indian family with the deceit and neglect of the rather sad remnants of the British Raj, parading under the flag of the United Nations. The reader is shocked by the pregnancy of such a young girl but the choice of age is deliberate because Una is young enough to begin to change her culture. By the end of the book she is wearing a sari and bathing in the Ganges; it is the adults who display the incompatibility and incomprehension of different cultures and different conventions. Once again, formal education plays an important part. Una is a promising mathematician and Miss Lamont's inability to teach her is what started the liaison with the young intellectual, Ravi. In the end, as Sir Edward is transferred to Bangkok, Una's younger sister is sent to live with her mother in America and Una herself returns to school in Britain, we can all identify with the fragmentation of this unhappy family and wonder if a good education at this or that international school will ever compensate for the damage done when (in Una's words) 'children are posted around like parcels'.

The Peacock Spring conveys a powerful impression of the pressures on the globally mobile family, and of the difficulties the young experience when they try to integrate into an alien culture that is perceived by the adults as little more than a temporary resting place, an extension of the airport waiting lounge.

THE ADULT ROLE

My final choice is different, because for the first time the story is seen through the eyes of the adults; the children play only a minor role. So perhaps this is the moment to glance at the adult characters in the books I have discussed and to note how many of them are portrayed as guilty, neglectful and selfish. We have just seen the miserable example of Sir Edward Gwithiam, but remember also Heidi's aunt, who dumps her five-year-old niece on her grandfather; Mary Lennox's mother, who 'cared only to go to parties and amuse herself', and is punished by a fatal dose of cholera; Carrie's mother, who is clearly having the time of her life driving ambulances in Glasgow. As for the shattered parents in *The Silver Sword* and *Empire of the Sun*, they have their own memories that leave little room for their children.

But the ultimate betrayal comes in *July's People* by the South African novelist Nadine Gordimer. This is an ingenious story of role reversal. Following a black rebellion in South Africa Bam and Maureen Smales and their three children flee from Johannesburg with their black servant, July. After a long and dangerous journey they reach July's village, where he hides them in a hut belonging to his family. They are forced to adjust to the bewildering new style of African village life and, needless to say, after some early bickering, the children integrate without much difficulty. After a few weeks the Smales leave the village for the first time to pay their respects to the local chief. When they return 'home' to their hut the full impact of their situation hits them.

> It was the first time the Smales had had to come home to: the iron bed, the Primus, the pink glass cups and saucers in the enamel basin with its sores of rust, the tin of milk and the general-store packet of sugar covered with a newspaper. Living within the hut they had lost sense of it. But now it was waiting for them. Coming from the stare of the sun into the dim enclosure smelled rather than seen – old smoky grass and earth damp with what spilled from vessels and human bodies instead of dew and rain – they scarcely made each other out. In a tin-bright angle of sunlight drawn by the slide-rule of the doorway, a fowl with a bald neck was sitting on the suitcase of their possessions. Maureen read the labels to herself as if she had never seen them before. Statler-Hilton Buenos Aires Albergo San Lorenzo Mantua Heerengracht Hotel Cape Town. Bam chased the fowl.

> (*July's People*, Nadine Gordimer, 1981)

The adults' sense of disorientation is complete when Bam loses his two symbols of white supremacy, his car and his gun. Finally Maureen can stand it no longer and, when the opportunity presents itself, she deserts her family. Animal survival suppresses the maternal instinct to protect her children; in the end we are all on our own.

> She runs: trusting herself with all the suppressed trust of a lifetime, alert, like a solitary animal at the season when animals neither seek a mate nor take care of young, existing only for their lone survival, the enemy of all that would make claims of responsibility. She can still hear the beat, beyond those trees and those, and she runs towards it. She runs.

The frustration of reading about children in novels is that we do not always know what becomes of them. We know from the sequel that Heidi married Peter and lived happily ever after, but what happened in later life to Mary Lennox, Jim, Una Gwithiam and the Smales' children? Did they survive their disorientation to live happy, fulfilled lives? It seems that everything eventually worked out for the Balicki children; and Carrie, who tells her story as an extended flashback, appears to be a well-balanced adult with a family of her own.

It is only in *Demian* that we follow the child turning into an adult because that is the very theme of the story: Emile Sinclair's lonely search for his own identity.

Only by being conscious of oneself can one find self-knowledge and thereby achieve self-fulfilment. The home must therefore offer more than food and water, more than safety, more even than love and learning; it must offer the means of helping the young person find his or her own identity. 'I am beginning to hear the lessons which whisper in my blood', says Emile Sinclair.

CHILDREN IN INTERNATIONAL SCHOOLS

But what are the lessons for those who care for children in international schools? I believe the most important is the recognition that underneath the much travelled, multilingual, sophisticated exterior presented by many of our students lie some rather vulnerable young people at a crucial stage of their development. Their parents, by definition, are professional people, frequently absent and often too busy to integrate into a temporary new culture. Their grandparents and extended family will probably be inaccessible in terms of distance and sometimes of language.

The school should be aware of the main features of the complex map of each child's cultural identity: where is that physical home, what is the current pattern of language used in the family, who are the key adults, who are the siblings or their substitutes? What have been the defining events thus far in the child's life? Only then is it possible to build a programme of cultural reinforcement of language, literature, drama and music supported by peer group friendships. At the same time the school must be well integrated with its host environment, recognizing that for many students this will determine the stable language and culture of their adult lives. The school's staff and students will often provide the substitutes for the stable adults and the siblings who play such a vital role in family life and which many international families lack. There is plenty of anecdotal evidence to suggest that student–teacher and student–student relationships formed in international schools are unusually strong and enduring. This places a particular responsibility on the school's arrangements for pastoral care, guidance and counselling.

But the most challenging task for the international school is the same as for any school: to support and encourage young people in the search for their own identity, their own self-knowledge and, ultimately, their own self-fulfilment; and that is the fundamental responsibility of every single member of staff.

All children need love, recognition and a sense of belonging, and I will end with a short story called 'Ha'penny' by another South African novelist, Alan Paton, best known for his classic novel *Cry the Beloved Country*. It is based on Paton's experience as warden of a reformatory. Ha'penny, who is 12, has been sent to the reformatory as a punishment for stealing. Every weekend he writes to his mother, two brothers and two sisters in Bloemfontein, but for some reason they neither reply nor come to visit him.

Finally, Paton tricks Ha'penny into admitting that his family and his home do not exist; he has invented them – or rather he has adopted in his mind a family he once met quite by chance. The adult has destroyed even his fantasy home and

Ha'penny falls sick with tuberculosis. The woman, Mrs Maarman, whom Ha'penny has decided should have been his mother, is eventually persuaded to visit him, even though she is from another tribe and hardly knows him.

> She was a decent, homely woman, and seeing that the situation was serious, she, without fuss or embarrassment, adopted Ha'penny for her own. The whole reformatory accepted her as his mother. She sat the whole day with him, and talked to him of Richard and Dickie, Anna and Mina, and how they were all waiting for him to come home. She poured out her affection on him, and had no fear of his sickness, nor did she allow it to prevent her from satisfying his hunger to be owned. She talked to him of what they would do when he came back, and how he would go to the school, and what they would buy for Guy Fawkes night.
>
> He in his turn gave his whole attention to her, and when I visited him he was grateful, but I had passed out of his world. I felt judged in that I had sensed only the existence and not the measure of his desire. I wished I had done something sooner, more wise, more prodigal.
>
> We buried him on the reformatory farm, and Mrs Maarman said to me, 'When you put up the cross, put he was my son.'
>
> 'I'm ashamed,' she said, 'that I wouldn't take him.'
>
> 'The sickness,' I said, 'the sickness would have come.'
>
> 'No,' she said, shaking her head with certainty. 'It wouldn't have come. And if it had come at home, it would have been different.'

('Ha'penny', from *Debbie Go Home*, Alan Paton 1961)

REFERENCES

In each case, for ease of access, a recent edition is quoted.

Aidoo, A A (1992) 'Homesickness', in A A Aidoo (ed) *Angry Letter in January*, Dangaroo Press, Hebden Bridge, West Yorks

Ballard, J G (1994) *Empire of the Sun*, Harper Collins, London

Bawden, N (1993) *Carrie's War*, Penguin, Harmondsworth

Burnett, F H (1995) *The Secret Garden*, Penguin, Harmondsworth

Clare. J (1832) 'The Flitting', in G Summerfield (ed) *John Clare: Selected Poetry*, Penguin, Harmondsworth

Dixon, R (1993) *The Management Task*, Butterworth Heinemann, Oxford

Godden, R (1992) *The Peacock Spring*, Macmillan, London

Gordimer, N (1983) *July's People*, Penguin, Harmondsworth

Grahame, K (1994) *The Wind in the Willows*, Penguin, Harmondsworth

Hesse, H (1995) *Demian*, Macmillan, London

Paton, A (1965) *Debbie Go Home*, Penguin, Harmondsworth

Serraillier, I (1993) *The Silver Sword*, Penguin, Harmondsworth

Spyri, J (1995) *Heidi*, Penguin, Harmondsworth

3

GLOBAL NOMADS, THIRD CULTURE KIDS AND INTERNATIONAL SCHOOLS

Mary Langford

INTRODUCTION

Those seeking to further their understanding of international schools would do well to acquaint themselves with the research on so-called 'Third Culture Kids' and 'Global Nomads'. This recommendation is justified when one considers the number of theorists and practitioners in the field who have referred to the populations of these schools – the kinds of pupils they attract and serve – as part of their overall criteria for describing international schools. This chapter explores current opinion on the profile of these internationally mobile students, and concludes with a discussion about the response of international school educators to the recognition that this growing community of learners have unique academic and pastoral needs that should be understood by those responsible for their education.

With the rapid growth in the number of families moving around the world during recent decades as a consequence of the global expansion of commerce, trade and humanitarian relief, as well as the military and diplomatic infrastructure required to support these activities, educationalists have become increasingly curious about the development of international schools and the 'international education' that many multinational expatriate communities seek for their children. While there is much debate about what exactly constitutes an 'international school' and an 'international education' there is still no clear consensus about the definition of these two terms. Notwithstanding this, a pattern is emerging whereby the criteria for defining international or overseas schools include a description of their populations as a feature. In summary, it appears that there is some agreement that international school populations are characterized by:

1. their multinational composition
2. fairly high levels of student turnover as a consequence of career paths of a professional parent body which in turn may result in childhoods of transiency and international mobility for such students

3. a very strong likelihood that their pupils will not complete their educations or attend university in the country where the international school is located, but rather they will be required to face the challenge of moving on to another foreign location or alternatively of repatriating to their passport countries to continue their educations
4. the strong probability that the cultural development of their pupils will be influenced by the culture of the host country as well as by the various cultures that they collectively represent.

'THIRD CULTURE KIDS' AND 'GLOBAL NOMADS'

While the debate about international schools and international education has been taking place among educationalists, investigation and research of a somewhat different nature has emerged in other arenas which might be broadly categorized as:

1. sociologists, psychologists, teachers, counsellors and other mental health professionals working with children who lived abroad or, alternatively, with adults who as children had lived abroad
2. the corporate, military, foreign service and missionary organizations that were observing common patterns in the experiences of the families they were sending abroad to carry out their various professional duties
3. parents who were raising children internationally as a result of their own careers;
4. educators of internationally mobile pupils
5. adults who spent part or all of their childhoods living abroad and who are now contributing to the discussion based on their personal experiences.

In 1976 Useem published her findings based on research of young adult Americans who had been raised overseas as dependants of professional parents and who had returned to the USA to enter university. Useem, the first to identify the characteristics of these internationally mobile young adults who were experiencing common reactions to their repatriation to their passport country, wrote:

> Although they have grown up in foreign countries, they are not integral parts of those countries. When they come to their country of citizenship (some for the first time), they do not feel at home because they do not know the lingo or expectations of others – especially those of their own age. Where they feel most like themselves is in that interstitial culture, the third culture, which is created, shared and carried by persons who are relating societies, or sections thereof, to each other.

She described these returnees as 'Third Culture Kids', or 'TCKs'.

Although Useem has focused on American TCKs there is literature emerging that indicates that the same characteristics and qualities can be ascribed to young people of other nationalities who share a similar experience of a childhood abroad. McCaig and Schaetti (1993), both (adult) Third Culture Kids who are regarded as authorities in this field, use the term 'Global Nomads', which they define as:

> individuals of any age or nationality who have spent a significant part of their developmental years living in one or more countries outside their passport country because of a parent's occupation. Global Nomads are members of a world-wide community of persons who share a unique cultural heritage. While developing some sense of belonging to both their host culture(s) and passport culture(s), they do not have a sense of total ownership in any. Elements from each culture and from the experience of international mobility are blended, creating a commonality with others of similar experience. Global Nomads of all ages and nationalities typically share similar responses to the benefits and challenges of a childhood abroad. (Schaetti, 1993)

'TCK' and 'Global Nomad' have now become interchangeable terms to describe such internationally mobile children. These common characteristics and similar responses are observed by others writing on the subject, including Pollock, another recognized authority who, in Killham (1990), describes such TCKs as speaking several languages, having cross-cultural skills, and having a 'three-dimensional world view'. In Stuart (1992) he describes their ability to cope in a crisis, their maturity and their sense of independence gained through travel. In Kittredge (1988) Pollock describes their sporadically acquired cultural identity, saying that:

> their crazy-quilt childhoods make them privy to many cultures and owners of none... Knowing a culture is a little like Trivial Pursuit... You collect lots of information – values, bits and pieces of history, the names of athletes, in-jokes, humour, code words – and then store it away. Then, during personal exchanges, you dip back into the data bank and pull them out and make connections with other people.

Pollock in Killham (1990) says that TCKs, because of their broad international perspective, have much to contribute to a future global society 'We have to recognise that part of the role of the third-cultured people of today is to be the culture bridge and culture brokers for the whole generation. The Global Nomad of today is the prototype of the citizen of the 21st century.'

Global Nomads are described by Killham (1990) as a 'silent minority' who possess unique characteristics distinct from those of children who grow up in their native cultures: 'These include superior diplomacy, flexibility, linguistic ability, patience and sophistication'. On the down side, they experience 'insecurity in relationships, unresolved grief stemming from constantly leaving friends through childhood, and rootlessness'.

PERCEPTIONS OF THE MILITARY, FOREIGN SERVICES, MISSIONARIES AND INTERNATIONAL BUSINESS COMMUNITIES

It appears to have been the US foreign service, military and missionaries who initially grappled with the issue of raising children internationally. Perhaps this is because these groups were, in effect, pioneers in the field of moving families overseas by virtue of their extensive experience of relocation long before the business sector launched itself into the international market-place after World War II. (The experience of American expatriate children may well have differed historically from that of the British, whose tradition of boarding-school education enabled them to maintain stronger links with the United Kingdom.) Interest on the part of the corporate sector in the ways in which their employees and their families cope with international moves has led to the publication of articles in many professional journals aimed, in particular, at human resources managers. Quantitative research on the topic is minimal; most of the literature is based on anecdotal evidence and the personal and professional experiences of the authors. Although much of the literature is American originated or appears in American publications, it is evident that the American bias of the TCK and Global Nomad issue is receding as people from many other regions move their families abroad to establish business links in the international arena.

Studies, dating back to the 1950s, of military dependants and the effects of their mobility were reviewed by Hunter (1982), who found that most highlighted the negative, rather than the positive aspects of a military childhood of mobility. She suggested that these children experience a 'unique development process; the military child experiences added stress due to geographical mobility, transcultural experience, transien father absence', among other factors, and found that experts recommended increased contact between military families and local indigenous peoples to facilitate more successful adjustment of military personnel in foreign countries. Packard (1973), writing about military children, quotes a school principal who observed that children of above-average ability tend to adjust to new school situations more easily than those of average or below-average ability. He addresses the age issue, suggesting that three to four and 13–18 year olds are most vulnerable to problems. He cites another school administrator in an affluent New York suburb who believes that problems at school stem from the fact that parents are not easily available because of frequent business and travel commitments. Marchant and Medway (1987) studied military families and found that frequent relocation had a positive effect on social competence, and that the child's response to relocation related to that of the mother. *Brats*, by Truscott (1989), is a collection of vignettes shared by (now adult) military dependants who moved frequently during childhood; stories with which any Global Nomad would easily identify. Wertsch (1991), inspired by her own childhood, has written a book based on anecdotal data that explores all aspects of childhood as experienced by dependants from all the US military branches. Although some of her subjects describe the experience of international mobility as a highlight of their childhood, confusion surrounding the notions of 'home' and 'roots' are an issue for many, as is the constant challenge of adapting and fitting into new social environments associated with every move.

A significant sector of the Global Nomad population is represented by the 'missionary kids' or 'MKs'. Tucker (1989) and Wickstrom (1993) write about the experiences of MKs at boarding-schools (which may differ significantly from international schools) but many of the results of their research about the profile of MKs are consistent with other Global Nomad research.

Werkman (1972, 1975), in his capacity as a psychiatrist under the auspices of the US Department of State (USDOS), contributed to the early study of international mobility in teenagers, although much of his early work focused on the disorders suffered by teens abroad based on case studies of those he saw in his professional capacity. Werkman later extended his research to include investigations of other internationally mobile students whom he compared to a US-based control sample. Endorsing Useem's theory, Werkman (1978) states: 'These internationalists, more knowledgeable about each other than either the countries in which they live or their lands of origin, share attitudes, interests, concern and intrapsychic processes that may well be distinctive and enduring.'

He found the common characteristics included strong nuclear family bonds, fathers who were highly successful professionals with heavy travel commitments, strong emotional ties to servants, a lack of experience of living in the USA, broad cultural experiences that influenced their characteristics, and the ability to form friendships quickly and with intensity. Rodgers (1993), a psychologist, published a quantitative survey on the behaviours of overseas teens as compared to their Stateside peers based on questionnaires distributed to USDOS dependants attending American international schools world-wide.

Lefkow (1994), a foreign service parent, reveals pangs of parental guilt about repatriating his children after a lifetime of international mobility, saying:

> We had committed a cardinal error in bringing our family back to the US for each of our children's senior year of high school. This is possibly the most difficult time for teenagers to adjust to a new school. For them, it was a year marked by loneliness... It can be wrenching to watch one's children return to... find themselves out of place and out of touch.

Wallach and Metcalf (1982) and Eakin (1988) have also offered advice and suggested strategies for childrearing based on their experiences with foreign service children.

Once regarded by the human resources industry as one of the 'soft' issues relating to employee relocation, the priority of managing transition has grown as corporations assess the effectiveness of employees who can be distracted if their spouses and children are not happily settled and adjusted. In an attempt to avoid the alarmingly high expenditures that result from the early repatriation of expatriate employees and their families due to failed assignments, some employers are seeking ways of reducing stress in order to improve the experience for the entire family. Harvey (1985) cites Gaylord who says, 'Research seems to indicate that the wife pays the greatest price for a family's move.' He suggests that children often do not want to move, that the notion of improving father's career is too abstract, and improvement of financial standing is meaningless to many children, saying: 'Their world centres around their friends and their school. Regardless of the reason for a family's move, it holds a built-in sense of loss for them'. He again quotes Gaylord, who finds that children aged between three and five suffer most emotionally, while those aged 14-16 suffer from social frustration – implying that age is a factor in adjustment. Harvey highlights the advantages of overseas schools where more individualized instruction and, in some instances, rich extracurricular activities such as the European schools sports leagues are available to expatriate families. He recommends that families expose their children to the foreign cultures, and emphasizes the strong family ties that develop as a result of life abroad. Brett (1980, 1982), Hubbard (1986), Dunbar and Katcher (1990), Shortland (1990), Benjamin and Eigles (1991), Brewster (1991) and Hausman and Reed (1991) are others who have written for business journals about the effects of company transfers on families and children. Stuart's (1992) views are particularly insightful as she is herself an adult Global Nomad. Speaking from personal experience, she says that 'school is the most pivotal point in helping assimilate a teen and other children into the culture'.

Brewster (1991), a lecturer at Cranfield School of Management, is also concerned about the difficulty of repatriation for families and children.

> Children may have an even harder time, given the reliance of children on approval from their fellows. They don't know or don't dress in the latest styles; they are out of touch with the music that is in vogue; they don't know who the latest (real or cartoon) personalities are; they may be embarrassed by their parents' insistence on spreading ethnic artefacts around their home, or by frequently showing photos of them in a different environment – whilst they are trying hard to fit in to the current one. They may well find it difficult fitting into a 'strange' form of schooling. Smaller children often miss the close personal attention of servants that characterizes many third world environments... Returners frequently describe feelings of discomfort and vague dissatisfaction with their lives, and even those who are overtly well adjusted to their return report long-lasting feelings of restlessness, rootlessness, and being out of place.

PERCEPTIONS OF PARENTS OF INTERNATIONALLY MOBILE CHILDREN

For the benefit of others embarking on international careers, parents are also writing about the reactions and behaviour they can expect from children of all ages, while offering strategies for helping them. They acknowledge the mixed feelings that parents have about the lifestyle their careers necessarily impose on their children. Some of these sources also advise parents on how they can positively interact with the school and what expectations they should have of the school. Gordon and Jones (undated), conducted a study of over 300 women from many nationalities which offers a wealth of anecdotal data on childrearing abroad. Many of the comments from non-American women are similar to perceptions arising from American-oriented sources. Their discussions centre around the importance of flexibility, the linguistic abilities of the children, the heightened importance of the nuclear family in the absence of traditional support systems, and a discussion about the challenge of putting down roots. Gordon and Jones also discuss the problem of parental guilt.

Parental guilt was a major concern in the problems of expatriate wives and until some form of coming to terms with the subject was achieved, more parents, among future generations of expatriates, would be suffering from similar pangs and more children would be burdened by them... We move from country to country because we accept the idea that it is an aspect of today's world and, even more so, of tomorrow's world, but we baulk internally at uprooting our children. We lament the distance that separates them from the rest of their family and fear they will grow up rootless and lost, with no sense of place or belonging... and cause them irreparable harm.

Pascoe (1994), an expatriate wife and mother, published *Culture Shock! A Parent's Guide*, as a resource describing all the aspects of childrearing abroad, from pre-departure through to re-entry strategies. It refers throughout to the Third Culture Kid, and also contains an entire chapter, 'International School Daze', devoted to helping parents understand how overseas schools differ from domestic schools and how to meet the educational needs of their children.

PERCEPTIONS OF EDUCATORS WORKING WITH INTERNATIONALLY MOBILE STUDENTS

The educational community is another sector that has taken an interest in these internationally mobile students, and the literature reflects a growing perception that they have different characteristics and needs. An interview by Yeary (1976) with three teenagers from Teheran American School appeared alongside Useem's TCK article in *Today's Education*. He investigated how they felt about moving internationally on a fairly frequent basis, with emphasis on building relationships, peer pressure, perceived disadvantages and advantages, and asking students how schools and teachers could ease their transition stress. Orientation programmes and buddy systems were recommended. The interview concludes with the question 'Where is home?', to which there were no clear responses. Lykins (1986), a teacher with the US Department of Defense schools overseas, describes TCKs as well travelled, able to speak a second language, tolerant, members of a strong nuclear family, experiencing fewer social problems than 'First Culture Kids', experiencing a constantly changing community, and returning to the third culture after graduation. Downs (1989) writes about the challenges faced by repatriating Japanese students and *Kokusaika* – a process of internationalization that students experience in adapting to life outside Japan. Downs quotes a Japanese student who says 'My bicultural experience allows me to be a flexible person, which in turn allows me to better cope with the chaotic world we live in today.' Simon *et al.* (1990) researched the adjustment process of foreign primary children residing in the USA and found that the degree of culture shock felt by the child was linked to the extent and quality of pre-departure orientation experienced by the mother.

Gerner *et al.* (1992), all experienced international educators, conducted one of the first studies to use proper quantitative research methodology to compare

American expatriate children with expatriate children from other countries. They probed some of the existing myths and assumptions surrounding TCKs which have been based largely on anecdotal evidence. The research sample included students at overseas schools in Egypt and Thailand and at a rural-suburban public high school in the American Midwest, to assess each of these characteristics. Students represented a variety of nationalities. Occupations of the father were representative of the diplomatic, business, missionary and educational communities. The results confirmed the impression that American adolescents who live abroad rate themselves as more culturally accepting, more interested in travel and languages, and more interested in an international lifestyle in the future than their American counterparts. Non-American internationally mobile adolescents also rated themselves as more interested in the above, but they have closer ties with families than the American internationally mobile students. Non-American internationally mobile students also rated higher in their foreign language acceptance than their American internationally mobile peers. Their conclusion was that international living appears to be associated with the formation of a self-perception of cultural acceptance, interest in learning languages, travel and an international future.

Others, including Lykins (1986), Robinson (1984), Willis and Power (1985), Jonietz (1988) and Pearce (1991), Wasaw (1993) have also written offering specific strategies which international schools might implement to better help their internationally mobile students.

THE ADULT GLOBAL NOMAD PERSPECTIVE

Global Nomads themselves are also now contributing to the weight of literature on the topic of childhood international mobility. Smith (1991), drawing on her childhood as an American foreign service dependant in the 1940s and 1950s, describes the many aspects of a childhood abroad on the basis of questionnaires she sent to 300 adult 'absentee Americans' ranging in age from 20 to over 70, who had spent some or all of their formative years abroad because of their parents' work and who had repatriated to the USA. She describes the extent to which families interacted with the local community; the function of the schools, language and cultural exchange; living with danger (brought about at times by political hostilities or kidnappings); and lack of supervision. She analyses the challenge of repatriation and the realization that they will never quite fully reintegrate into their home country. Her research confirms an awareness that life abroad has enhanced the ability of Global Nomads to understand differences in issues and values between people of diverse backgrounds. Multicultural perspectives are seen as an advantage, as typified by the greater sense of tolerance and appreciation of cultural differences. Another trait described by Smith is the 'tendency to focus on the uniqueness of every individual'. The global orientation of the absentee American is another outcome, the result of the difficulty in developing a 'local view' when one relocates with frequency.

Giardini (1993) argues that 'the importance of a fixed geographical location and an image of any one cultural context as homogeneous and bounded do not accurately describe the experience of many childhood expatriates'. Her research was conducted with students who had graduated during a five-year span from the American School of London. She concluded that individual identity among Global Nomads is a dynamic process and that national identity is not restricted to a geographical notion. Although allegiance is normally fixed to family and friends, many feel a kinship with others who have no roots in territory but rather in travel or ideology. Giardini found that all expressed some desire to stop 'having to explain themselves and their reasons for not belonging to any specific pre-established category' and concluded that this should not be in conflict with their status as citizens of the USA, but that 'the ideas presented concerning the ways that the interviewees have come to understand themselves, their national identity and the human experience of community will continue to that progress towards a new nation'.

In a series appearing during 1993 and 1994 in *Newslinks*, Useem and Cottrell report on the findings from years of research conducted by Cottrell, Useem, and Finn-Jordan. In one piece of work their sample included 680 adult TCKs between the ages of 25 and 90 residing in the USA who had lived at least one year abroad as the minor dependant of an American parent. In analysing this survey, a continuation of her earlier work, Useem (1993b) concludes that TCKs are overwhelmingly "committed to continuing their education beyond high school graduation". Typically high achievers, Useem (1993b) found that 90 per cent of her sample had post-secondary education and 40 per cent had completed graduate degrees. However, Cottrell and Useem (1993) state that many of the TCKs do not follow the traditional course of higher education. They drop out, change majors, change colleges, and are often 'out of synch' with their peers. In response to the question of how long it takes to readjust to life in America, the answer is 'never' (Useem, 1993b). Although they adapt, find ways of coping, and find careers that suit them, they never feel totally adjusted. Three-quarters of Useem's (1993b) sample felt 'different' from their peers who had never had an overseas experience. Two-thirds want to have international dimensions in their adult lives. They believe they have more transnational knowledge and skills than they are able to use in a domestic setting (Cottrell, 1993). Eighty per cent use another language regularly (Cottrell and Useem, 1994). Ninety per cent feel 'out of synch' with their peers throughout their lifetime (Cottrell and Useem, 1993).

Adult TCKs are now using their experience to help younger generations of internationally mobile children in their ability to adapt to new environments and to see the advantages that might be gained. In early 1997 a new magazine, *Nomad: The Brat Journal* was launched in the USA. According to Duin (1997), it is 'compiled by four thirty-something editors... who moved 18 times in their Air Force childhood and learned how to smile and bear it, at least in public'. Mansfield Taber (1997), a foreign service dependant, has published a wonderful workbook suited to Global Nomads of any age or nationality to help them develop a better understanding and perspective of their international experiences. Other adult TCKs who have written on the subject include Gordon (1997) and Fail (1995).

THE RESPONSE OF THE INTERNATIONAL SCHOOL COMMUNITY

It was only a matter of time before the two areas of research – that relating to international schools and international education, and that relating to the special qualities of children growing up internationally – overlapped. It might even be said that they are interdependent; international schools are unique because of the preponderance of the Global Nomads and TCKs they serve; these same children develop unique characteristics in part because of the social and academic environment found at international schools. There is some evidence that those involved in international schools – teachers, administrators, governing boards and proprietors, as well as educational consultants– are seeking to improve their understanding of the community they serve, for a number of reasons. International school educators are generally members of the expatriate community they seek to serve and, as individuals, they share similar responses to relocation and changes in language and cultural environment. From a more practical point, international schools are often dependent on the expatriate community for their enrolments (and consequently for their financial base) and, therefore, should be assessing continuously the quality of the programmes they deliver to the expatriate communities that rely on them. Hurn (1993) cites Tung who observes that 'one of the main reasons for... failure among American and European expatriates is the inability of the spouse or family to adjust to living overseas'. It is in the international school community's own interests to understand why families sometimes fail to adjust and how they as educators can help improve the transition process for their pupils. So what is it that educators understand about these Global Nomads and TCKs, and what are international schools doing to accommodate their needs?

Langford (1997) investigated this question by analysing quantitative data derived from a survey of 287 international school teachers and administrators working at 41 international schools world-wide, and qualitative data drawn from interviews with ten highly experienced international school administrators and Schaetti, previously acknowledged as an authority on transition. This research confirmed that international school educators recognize in their pupils many of the unique qualities and characteristics ascribed to Global Nomads and Third Culture Kids, and they agree that these children develop differently from those children who experience domestic stability. They strongly agree that these children, regardless of nationality, experience common traits in their 'approach to relationships', 'linguistic ability', 'flexibility', 'cultural awareness', 'tolerance', and their 'world view'. They also agree that international schools should respond to their internationally mobile pupil populations by providing programmes and strategies to help them adapt to their new cultural environments. The survey data found that educators think their schools are most successfully addressing issues relating to the adjustment of internationally mobile pupils in two areas – 'orientation of new pupils on arrival', and 'acknowledging the educational needs of internationally mobile pupils in the schools' philosophies and objectives'. They also agree that the schools are successful in 'creating or adopting a curriculum that serves internationally mobile pupils'.

The research indicates that there are seven areas that the educators agree should be given greater attention. They are 'pupil counselling', 'provision of in-service training for teachers', 'the development and maintenance of a "profiling" portfolio (containing records, samples of work, test results, teacher comments, assessments, etc) that can accompany the internationally mobile pupil in order to facilitate placement', 'incorporating classroom activities that facilitate the arrival of new pupils', 'parent counselling', 'providing the family with practical local information (eg doctors, housing, community support services)', and 'incorporating classroom activities that facilitate the departure of pupils' (Langford, 1997). These educators seem to appreciate that international schools play an essential part in the lives of their students. This is because, in the words of Gellar, the international school may be 'the one stable place in the child's life'.

Schaetti (1993) states:

The schools have a key role, a pivotal role to play. They can influence the child's arrival, influence the child's departure, they influence the child's arrival in the next location. They have an invaluable role to play in the issue of cultural identity which overrides and encapsulates all of the mobility issues. It is a critical role they play.

The research concludes that international school educators agree that there is more that can and should be done by these schools to serve their Global Nomad populations. These include not only actual strategies such as English as a Second Language and mother tongue programmes that would generally be regarded as good practice, but also an awareness of certain attitudes with which educators should approach the international school community.

It is important to be sensitive to parents' anxieties and to be aware that the successful transition of the pupil is strongly related to the attitude of the parents. Snowball believes 'Schools should do a great deal to make not only the child, but the whole family, as comfortable as possible, as quickly as possible'. Gellar recognizes this, saying that international schools must help the family integrate into the local community. 'You can be the best school in the world, but if you don't have all kinds of activities to involve the parents, you are in trouble. They need to be able to mix and mingle and so on.' Related to this is a willingness on the part of the international school to accept the fact that in some instances it becomes a lifeline for the expatriate community. Gellar describes the burden this places on time and resources, surmising that 'we're not just schools, we're community centres'.

Also important is an awareness of the importance of hiring teachers and administrators who are, as described by Malpass, 'internationally minded', or by Armstrong-Law as having a 'world view', that is people who understand the complexities of working in an environment where so many cultural perspectives and language backgrounds are interacting on a daily basis. Along with this is the importance of empathizing with families and children experiencing culture shock. J Young recommends that this should be explored at interview stage: 'We need to hire the teacher who has a sensitivity and understanding of what we are there for.'

Finally, it is important for educators working in the international school community to be able to recognize and articulate the positive aspects of a childhood of international mobility as experienced by many of their pupils. M Young says, 'International kids are special because they are open minded, and they want to be different. The nomadic life does make them more capable, and more open to the community and to taking a chance'. Armstrong-Law describes international students as 'strong, very successful and from highly motivated families'. Gellar says they are 'more adept at interpersonal relations... They really know a lot about meeting people, about talking to them, about conversation, about being friendly, and about being self-confident'. International educators need to be willing and able to discuss these outcomes with parents, most of whom will have had a different kind of education and therefore come with differing expectations. Murphy explains:

> I sometimes tell parents that they enrol their children at an international school at their peril. The children will be learning different things and in a different way from anything in their parents' experience. The values they learn may not be identical to their [parents'] values. Children may change. They may become independent. They won't just be the same Japanese or Arab children who have learned to speak English. They will become a mix of nationalities. That is what makes it so hard for the parents.

Malpass summarizes the role of the international school, saying:

> The best thing a school can do is to provide a secure, welcoming environment for all its children. It can't protect them totally from these things [adversity and challenges] in life. In the end these things build character and all the changes develop character. As long as the school is warm and welcoming and supportive in all its ways, the children will, for the most part, be okay.

In her 1976 article Useem expressed a concern about what appeared to be a lack of awareness and appreciation on the part of educators, including those working in overseas schools, about the special characteristics and educational needs of Third Culture Kids. Nearly 20 years later Useem (1993a) highly commends educators in overseas schools for their 'contributions to the development of these unusual individuals'. Yet there is more that can and should be done. Gerner *et al.* (1992) estimate that the number of internationally mobile children living outside of their home countries, or having at some point during their childhood lived abroad, exceeds one million, and there is every indication that international mobility and the challenges associated with transition will continue to impact on future generations. The escalating number of new international schools opening their doors in remote parts of the globe is one of the indicators of that growth, and these schools must do their utmost to develop and maintain programmes that serve their pupils. The Global Nomad and the international school are destined to remain interdependent as we enter the new millennium.

REFERENCES

Benjamin, J and Eigles, L (1991) 'Support services to relocated families increase employee job performance', *Journal of Career Development*, **17**, 4, pp 259–64

Brett, J M (1980) 'The effect of job transfer on employees and their families', in C Cooper and R Payne (eds), *Current Concerns in Occupational Stress*, John Wiley & Sons, Chichester

Brett, J M (1982) 'Job transfer and well-being', *Journal of Applied Psychology*, **67**, 4, pp 450–63

Brewster, C (1991) *The Management of Expatriates*, London, Cranfield School of Management in association with Kogan Page

Cottrell, A B (1993) 'TCKs have problems relating to own ethnic groups', *Newslinks*, **XIII**, 2, pp 1, 4

Cottrell, A B and Useem, R H (1993) 'TCKs experience prolonged adolescence', *Newslinks*, **XIII**, 1, pp 1, 26

Cottrell, A B and Useem, R H (1994) 'ATCKs maintain global dimensions through out their lives', *Newslinks*, **XIII**, 4, pp 1, 14

Downs, L D (1989) 'Returning Japanese students often ostracized', *The International Educator*, October, p 14

Duin, J (1997) 'Military brat pack has life, journal of its own', *The Washington Times*, 9 January, p A2

Dunbar, E and Katcher, A (1990) 'Preparing managers for foreign assignment', *Training and Development Journal*, September, pp 45–6

Eakin, K B (1988) *The Foreign Service Teenager At Home in the US: A Few Thoughts for Parents Returning with Teenagers*, The Overseas Briefing Center, Foreign Service Institute, US Department of State Washington, DC

Fail, H (1995) 'Some outcomes of international schooling', MA dissertation, Oxford Brookes University, Oxford

Gerner, M, Perry, F, Moselle, M and Archbold, M (1992) 'Characteristics of interna tionally mobile adolescents', *Journal of School Psychiatry*, **30**, 2, pp 197–214

Giardini, A M (1993) *'The formation of a national identity among US citizens growing up overseas'*, MA thesis, Stanford University, CA

Gordon, C (1997) 'Rootless in Seattle', *The Citizen's Weekly*, 31 August, pp 3–4

Gordon, E and Jones, M (undated) *Portable Roots: Voices of Expatriate Wives*, Presses Interuniversitaires Européennes, Maastricht, The Netherlands

Harvey, M G (1985) 'The executive family: an overlooked variable in international assignments', *Columbia Journal of World Business*, **20**, 1, pp 84–92

Hausman, M and Reed, J (1991) 'Psychological issues in relocation: responses to change', *Journal of Career Development*, **17**, 4, pp 247–58

Hubbard, G (1986) 'How to combat culture shock', *Management Today*, September, pp 62–5

Hunter, E J (1982) *Families Under the Flag: A Review of Military Family Literature*, Praeger, New York

Hurn, B J (1993) 'Pre-departure training', paper presented at conference entitled *The Global Nomad: The Benefits and Challenges of an Internationally Mobile Childhood*, Regents College, London, 23 April

Jonietz, P (1988) 'The effects of relocation on the family system', *International Schools Journal*, 15, pp 35–6

Killham, N (1990) 'World-wise kids', *The Washington Post*, 15 February, p B5

Kittredge, C (1988) 'Growing up global', *The Boston Globe Magazine*, 3 April, pp 13–46

Langford, M E (1997) 'Internationally mobile pupils in transition: the role of the international school', MA dissertation, University of Bath

Lefkow, L L (1994) 'Globally mobile children gain appreciation for Americans and others despite cultural confusion', *New York Times*, 6 March

Lykins, R (1986) 'Children of the third culture', *Kappa Delta Pi Record*, **22**, 2, pp 39–43

Mansfield Taber, S (1997) *Of Many Lands: Journal of a Traveling Childhood*, Foreign Service Youth Foundation, Washington, DC

Marchant, K H and Medway, F J (1987) 'Adjustment and achievement associated with mobility in military families', *Psychology in the Schools*, 24, pp 289–294

Packard, V (1973) 'Nobody knows my name', *Education Today*, 62, pp 22–6

Pascoe, R (1994) *Culture Shock! A Parent's Guide*, Kuperard, London

Pearce, R (1991) 'Understanding national education systems to facilitate transition in international schools, in P L Jonietz and D Harris (eds), *World Yearbook of Education 1991: International Schools and International Education*, Kogan Page, London

Robinson, J (1984) 'Culture shock: information packet for developing stress/culture shock programs for students in overseas schools', workshop presented at NE/SA Teachers' Conference, Colombo, Sri Lanka, 23–26 March

Rodgers, T A (1993) 'Here are findings of a survey on how American teens behave overseas, *State*, October, pp 20–4

Schaetti, B (1993) 'The Global Nomad profile', paper preserved at conference entitled *The Global Nomad: The Benefits and Challenges of an Internationally Mobile Childhood*, Regents College, London, 23 April

Shortland, S (1990) *Relocation*, Institute of Personnel Management, Wimbledon

Simon U, Cook, A S and Fritz, J (1990) 'Factors influencing the adjustment process of foreign school-age children residing in the United States', *International Education*, **19**, 2, pp 5–12

Smith, C (1991) *The Absentee American: Repatriates' Perspectives on America*, Aletheia Publications, Bayside, NY

Stuart, K D (1992) 'Teens play a role in moves overseas, *Personnel Journal*, 71, pp 72–8

Truscott, M R (1989) *Brats*, EP Dutton, New York

Tucker, R A (1989) 'Growing up a world away', *Christianity Today*, **33**, 3, pp 17–21

Useem, R H (1976) 'Third-Culture Kids', *Today's Education*, **65**, 3, pp 103–5

Useem, R H (1993a) 'Third Culture Kids: focus of major study', *Newslinks*, **XII**, 3, pp 1, 29

Useem, R H (1993b) 'TCKs four times more likely to earn bachelor's degree', *Newslinks*, **XII**, 5, pp 1, 27

Wallach, J and Metcalf, G (1982) 'Parenting abroad', *Foreign Service Journal*, June 1982, pp 20–3

Wasow, E (1993) 'Improving the school climate through family collaboration', *International Schools Journal*, **25**, 2, pp 55–9

Werkman, S (1972) 'Hazards of rearing children in foreign countries', *American Journal of Psychiatry*, **128**, 8, pp 106–11

Werkman, S (1975) 'Over here and back there', *Foreign Service Journal*, March, pp 13–16

Werkman, S (1978) 'A heritage of transience: psychological effects of growing up overseas', in E J Anthony and C Chiland (eds), *The Child in His Family: Children and Their Parents in a Changing World*, pp 117–28

Wertsch, M E (1991) *Military Brats: Legacies of Childhood Inside the Fortress*, Harmony Books, New York

Wickstrom, D (1993) 'Boarding school issues and missionary kids', *The Global Nomad Quarterly*, **2**, 1, p 8

Willis, B and Power, P (1985) 'Counselors as a resource for teachers in overseas schools', *Elementary School Guidance and Counseling*, **19**, 4, pp 291–9

Yeary, E (1976) 'Peripatetic pupils: children who globe-trot with parents are a unique breed', *Today's Education*, **65**, 3, pp 99–102

4

DEVELOPING CULTURAL IDENTITY IN AN INTERNATIONAL SCHOOL ENVIRONMENT

Richard Pearce

THE CULTURAL ROLE OF EXPATRIATE SCHOOLS

Anyone associated with international schools is accustomed to being asked in what way the schools are 'international'. The explanation usually starts with a catalogue of nationalities attending, though we know as we speak that this cannot faintly convey the diversity of the community. In the same way an attempt to describe the cultural variety of our classrooms usually begins with a national typology of school systems and cultures. This gives a useful guide to the backgrounds and expectations of the majority of parents, who had a national upbringing, but takes no account of the diversity of cultural experience of their children.

An appropriate definition of culture is given by Berry *et al.* (1992), as 'the shared way of life of a group of people'. This recognizes it as a medium for social communication, and hence both the current outcome and the future means of social conditioning. On the other hand any differences in culture will be barriers to communication and hence to learning. Each of these ways of life has a unitary and coherent nature and is adhered to with a conviction that has affective, personal, and moral dimensions. All this must be recognized as we help the family to adapt to the new reality.

National education systems each have a basis of educational theory derived from a largely national body of research. Even comparative education and multi-cultural education are generally directed towards the solution of locally framed problems. Since mobile students are by their nature exceptions to national typologies, in this chapter students in the international school environment will be treated at an individual level, and because the characteristic of the mobile student is his/her changing social experience I will consider particularly how cultural development is affected by changes of environment. I will propose a model for culture learning and will apply it to common experience in practice.

To work at the individual level one needs to postulate universal properties. The problems of 'universals' in cross-cultural psychology have been outlined by Berry *et al.* (1992) and Lonner (1990). Berry *et al.* propose that the universal validity of a concept or relationship is judged by (a) theoretical grounds for accepting ... invariant across all cultures, (b) empirical evidence to support this claim, and (c) absence of empirical evidence to refute it. These are the criteria which the argument must satisfy.

The importance of school culture

A tiny minority of the schools founded for expatriates belong in Matthews' (1989) category of 'ideology-driven schools'; the great majority are in some measure a market response to the needs of multinational enterprises within a paradigm of compensation for deficiencies in comparison with life at home. The 'home' culture is normally that of the company or community sponsoring the school, and the school follows their national lines. This seems very reasonable given that national typologies define our language, our careers, our mobility, and therefore many elements of our culture. In the workplace teachers adjust their national professional practices to accommodate the variety of cultural and personal needs shown by their pupils, with success which is evident from the academic outcomes.

Why do communities demand familiar schooling, even when on criteria such as literacy rates or gross national product the host country is at least equal to their home? The essential requirement may be linguistic (initially an absolute barrier in the host system), curricular (to ensure provision of home material), institutional (to guarantee home recognition of overseas schooling), or broadly cultural. The appeal of the explicitly national school overseas is shown by their abundance – 933 out of the 1724 schools listed in the *International Education Handbook* (Findlay, 1997).

The family is the unit of demand for schooling because it is the unit of mobility and the unit of childrearing. A deeply felt fundamental human right, recognized in the UN Declaration, is the right of parents 'to choose the kind of education that shall be given to their children'. The parents' stake in the world after their death lies in those who will represent them, and who must therefore learn to share their most valued beliefs and aspirations. Culture, in Berry's definition, is both the medium of communication and itself a communicated message. Consciously or unconsciously this is understood to be a core element of childrearing.

It can be said that the school is an institution developed by a society to make a guaranteed and standardized contribution to the development of members of that society. Yet school systems vary not only in their curricular content but also in what aspects of culture training are felt to be their responsibility. A comparison of national school systems reveals such a range of parameters that it is hard to agree common values, or even a common framework. What is variable in one country is uniform in another; what matters in one country is insignificant elsewhere. Among national educational cultures a universal formula in which the observer simply fills in the blanks is attractive but infeasible. For example, in the USA schools are entrusted with responsibility for giving children of new citizens full access to the cultural opportunities and democratic responsibilities of citizenship; in a multicultural country such as India cultural education is provided in the home, and school is more the source of instrumental education for the working world (Pearce, 1991). Even in a posting where language, curriculum and institutions are mutually recognizable, culture evidently remains incentive enough to justify the founding of national schools.

The culture of international schools

Where they are available national schools accommodate most of the relevant expatriates; it seems likely that the students placed in other countries' expatriate schools are seeking the nearest substitute in the absence of their own. In practice a sample shows that around half the students at international schools are not following their home curriculum. What cultural resource is supplied by the international schools which makes them a valid second choice? Each school has its operating system, commonly following or derived from a well-known national model, and this may be an attractive facility. The great majority of self-defined 'international schools' profess to follow either the US or the English curriculum. Provided they deliver that system the client family is promised a core package of linguistic, curricular, institutional and cultural elements. There is, of course, a price to pay for joining an alien system. Before communication between teacher and student can develop there must be a degree of culture learning which, if it replaces the former culture, amounts to assimilation. This is not the place for an analysis of the discourse through which children learn, least of all with the complicating dimension of inter-cultural communication. For those who wish to read further, Gudykunst and Kim (1992) offer a rich range of insights into this field.

This process of 'fitting in' is a major concern of parents, teachers and counsellors in international schools. In high context societies the teacher–student relationship has a largely affective component; both parties feel a need to win the interest of the other. The alternative, known as low context societies, will need only a formal relationship before learning begins. This modifies the expectations of both parties. Athletic activities are often significantly non-verbal and low context, and are used by schools to open the necessary cultural dialogue despite limits of language.

For some local families who use the school, assimilation may be the purpose of joining. In many less developed countries the local American, British, French, or international school, according to the region's traditional sphere of influence, is a route for the privileged into more developed country economies, or offers an accepted schooling for the socio-economic elite. There are also traditions, in Latin America and Eastern Europe, for example, of bilingual or foreign-language medium schools that prepare students for superior echelons that do business within and outside the country.

But what of the divergences of expatriate schools from the original home model? If host country nationals form a significant group, the result may be an institution whose ethos contrasts with its operating system, to the puzzlement of 'home' country teachers and pupils. Teachers and institutions naturally flex to meet the needs of students who arrive with deficits or dissonance in their school experience. Some schools consciously abjure national identity, and operate a system uniquely adapted to local and current needs, or even to ideologically innovative patterns. Like Esperanto these will be somewhat strange to everyone, but what compensation do they offer? By deliberately modifying their culture these schools show their sensitivity to its importance. Social culture is both a set of markers by which a group of people recognizes their commonality, and in many cases a medium through which the group continues to share elements, present and future. Norms such as clothing or behaviour, values such as love of order or preference for extroversion over introversion, are recognizable markers of national character; language and communicative style are routes by which such characteristics continue to accrue. In developing a unique mix of norms and values the schools practise a relativism that shows respect for more than one formula, and flexibility that could lead to benevolent polyvalence. This situation is widely experienced, whether by design or accident, and has been well described by Willis in 'Columbia Academy', in Japan (1992a, 1992b).

A stranger arriving in the school, whether student, parent, or teacher, will find cross-cultural communication both a marker and a barrier. We may expect adults to be set in their ways and to have difficulty adapting, but childhood is the time for culture learning. In the words of Yasuko Minoura (1992), Professor of Comparative Education at Tokyo University and a leading authority on Japanese bicultural development: 'For young children who have not yet acquired Japanese patterns, there are no differences between Japan and the United States. For young children, almost everything is new and strange.' We need to look at the way in which children 'normally' acquire culture and then see what role the international schools do – and could – play in their lives.

How the child develops cultural identity

The model that follows was devised for a research programme followed through the Department of Education at the University of Bath. The chosen approach is based on two psychological concepts: symbolic interactionism and social constructivism.

Symbolic interactionism derives from the views of Mead (1934) and others that social behaviour is so subject to variations of perception that it is best regarded as relating to the inner symbolic representations of the outer world. You and I do not interact with one another, but with who you think I am and who I think you are. The interior schema of each person is different, and is built up from a lifetime's perceptions which are themselves mediated by the developing self. Social constructivism is an approach pioneered by Kelly (1955), in which the individual is seen as perceiving the world in terms of idiosyncratic scales of norms and evaluations. These scales measure certain 'constructs', some of particularly high salience ('core constructs') and some of lesser importance. The constructs, like the evaluations made on these scales, are acquired through social learning processes, and are very important parameters of the individual's personality. For example, a child reared in a hierarchical society will mentally rank those who are encountered in later life according to a hierarchical scale. The picture these two perceptions give is that children grow up progressively learning a picture of the outside world, and evaluating the world according to constructs which are characteristics of the child's identity.

From a consideration of multicultural societies it is clear that one physical environment can harbour several social groups, each raising children with different cultural norms and values, based on different deep beliefs. Their differentiation is taken to be a learning process, by which evaluative systems are derived. Pioneer work in this field is that of Kohlberg (in Lickona, 1976), who postulated three major stages of moral development, each with sub-stages, in which children acquire a set of moral values. Further work by Bronfenbrenner (Garbarino and Bronfenbrenner in Lickona, 1976) suits the present purpose by putting emphasis on the social experiences through which moral judgement is developed.

The role of adults in children's evaluative development

Haste (1987), commenting on Bourdieu and the French school of social psychologists, postulates that 'there is a *body of cultural and social resources* which frame the individual's understanding of rules, of the parameters of legitimation and appropriate evaluation, and of the local "rules-for-making-rules"' [original italics]. Garbarino and Bronfenbrenner (in Lickona, 1976) are more specific:

> In our view, developmental movement from Level 1 to Level 2 is based on and stimulated by attachment, the primary socialization of the organism to 'belong' to and with social agents. This is the process by which the individual organism becomes an acculturated person. Ordinarily this development of attachment is initially directed toward the parents, but comes to be orientated toward other social agents as a function of the patterns of social interaction that obtain in early and middle childhood.

Vygotsky (in Bruner, 1986) developed the concept of a social framework further, proposing that his 'zone of proximal development' was a field within which the child could develop new concepts given appropriate pedagogical leadership.

Cultural transfer between generations demands a high level of engagement between adult and child. The developmental necessity for a bond between child and adult is clearly met by the social bonding of mother and child, a reasonably presumed universal of child development. Societies show a variety of bonding patterns beyond this point, but it seems appropriate to use a 'western' model of a nuclear family and a local community school for our present purposes. The significant other to whom the child bonds is seen as providing value judgements for the child. This can happen occasionally by precept, but more often by the example of her actions, or by her public evaluations of everyday events that mother and child witness together. To emphasize the importance of the transfer of evaluations I shall refer to this role as that of Validator. Those things that are normally done comprise the norms of that culture, and those that are labelled good and bad establish the scales of values. Beyond norms and values the child also learns what is important and unimportant, and these qualitative scales make up the constructs by which the child measures the perceptible world.

As the social world enlarges so new validators are enrolled. They may be physically significant by their frequent presence, but if they are to become highly salient in the child's world they need parental validation. Validation can also be given to activities and tools such as reading books, which reflects Vygotsky's concept of the 'mediational means' – instruments promoting children's scholastic learning. The process is well summarized by Bruner (1985): 'I agree with Vygotsky that there is a deep parallel in all forms of knowledge acquisition – precisely the existence of a crucial match between a support system in the social environment and an acquisition process in the learner. I think it is this match which makes possible the transmission of the culture...'

The importance of early conditioning

The child's learning environment is now becoming populated with individuals, generalized roles such as 'teacher', and instruments and activities of learning. The child, too, is building up a coherent pattern of things that are good and right. Each new item that extends the cognitive world changes it; naturally the earliest additions are proportionately most significant. The power of conditioning in establishing core constructs that influence the acceptability of later learning is manifest.

Identification with role models is commonly cited as a key process in development, as though the child strove consciously minute by minute to imitate the hero. Weinreich (1983), who has used personal construct psychology (PCP) to study cultural issues, makes an important distinction between empathetic identification, recognition that another person has characteristics one shares, and role model identification, a desire to emulate an admired person. Using the present model one could say that the first case has probably experienced a parallel set of influences in the past, and that the second is an influential validator who is likely to impart constructs in the future.

New data are not merely collected through experience, but fitted into a coherent pattern. A new phenomenon may be a repetition of previous experience or fit within it, but it could also be an extension or a contradiction, which will be cognitively dissonant from the existing pattern. Festinger (1957) considered how we deal with such contradictions, and proposed that as far as possible we make a minimal adjustment to our cognitive world picture. For example, the fox that could not reach the grapes disposed of the problem by simply dismissing them as sour. Such sour grapes continue to be widespread. As Weinreich (1983) postulates: 'When one forms further identifications with newly encountered individuals, one broadens one's value system and establishes a new context for self-definition, thereby initiating a reappraisal of self and others which is dependent on fundamental changes in one's value-system.'

The validation system

Validation is seen as particularly strong where the views of several validators coincide, and relatively weakened where dissonance has marginalized or qualified the judgement. Within a homogeneous society values may seldom be questioned. Expatriation exposes one to particularly sharp contrasts. The validation system can be represented by the social learning system shown in Figure 4.1.

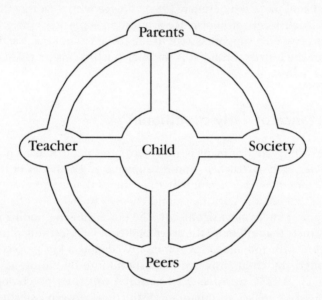

Figure 4.1   The social learning system

In Figure 4.1 the five circles represent parties in the social learning relationship, and the radii the validatory influences, building up in approximately anticlockwise sequence. The circumference shows the links between validators which maintain the consistency of their evaluations in a homogeneous society. The initial bond is between mother and child. A growing awareness of others who behave unlike the mother evokes a sense, first that the mother is a separate unit from the baby, and second that there are several units 'out there'. According to the prevailing social pattern the baby is tended by the father, grandparents, siblings, other adults or elders, and a degree of validatory authority is delegated. As long as there is broad consonance this does not seem to present difficulties. Garbarino and Bronfenbrenner (in Lickona, 1976) even suggest that experiencing a variety of opinions is a prerequisite for developing a sense of objective moral judgements.

If validation is an innate process it must be rewarding for both adult and child. This seems to be the case. We often say that children need firm direction, 'wanting to know where they stand' whether we give praise or reproof. Even as adults we need heroes, though some societies will give them affection and others respect. The pleasures of being important to children are clear to parents, and may account for the otherwise inexplicable popularity of the teaching profession. The power of validated judgements stays with us throughout life, though in a maturing form. Our moral sense becomes necessarily more settled, and is policed at a semiconscious level by a comforting sense of virtue or an unsettling sense of guilt. It may even be possible to trace the validator through barely discernible awareness that so-and-so wouldn't like what we have just done, or a wish that we could tell the long-dead grandparent what we have just achieved. High context societies feel a need for a continuing relationship with validators, and like to make friends before talking business, while low context societies make evaluations using 'internal' judgement based on past validations. The notorious pains of repatriation are sharpened by the rejection of those who have represented, throughout the expatriation, the validators of the 'real' world. They now cannot share or value the returnee's experiences; both have moved on.

Identity

Identity is the individual's sense of his or her own properties; in Weinreich's (1983) words 'the totality of one's self-construal'. This is developed through postnatal experience, and guided by validations. Some such system is necessary for the operation of a moral faculty; without it there can be no moral guidance; without standards for evaluations there can be no decisions, only anomie. It is obvious that the constructs and standards which the child learns to use in viewing the world will also be used in assessing the self. These differ widely between tribes, but will show common features within each unit of the child's experience; the tribe, the family, the school, the nation. Some constructs are shared with others who learned them from the same source; families are aware of a shared identity expressed through shared attitudes. Some may be acquired later in life, as colleagues go through professional experiences together, though it should not be forgotten that shared constructs may draw people into the same career. If constructs are seen as scales on which 'I' is at one point, self-esteem may be viewed as the practice of defining the point occupied by the subject as the optimal value. If the self is not at one extreme, the two extremities are each given pejorative descriptions. As Auden and Isherwood (1935) wrote: 'Beware of yourself; have you not heard your own heart whisper: "I am the nicest person in this room"?'

Adolescence is the onset of reproductive maturity, and with it comes the need to function as an effective adult. The former fluidity and flexibility of values has to solidify. It is clear that the change in status is not always easy, though the phenomenon of the teenage rebellion is only one of a range of possible syndromes. According to Minoura (1993), who looked at national identifications of Japanese children raised in two countries, it is during the period between 9 and 14.5 years that children interiorize a sense of identity that was hitherto flexible, and open to influence from validators. Beyond this stage they 'own' their personal identities, and feel more personally any threat.

The school as a value learning environment

The institution of the school is widely (and in some communities selectively) used to give both simultaneous acculturation and to bond children together. Figure 4.1 shows how a self-recognizing social group around a school can increase consistency and strength of evaluations. The various political frameworks that have arisen reflect a number of forms of community which societies have accepted as channels for such shared activities as direction of their young's development. Although national government is often the unit of school system building, school governance is more often delegated to school districts, local education authorities, or single schools. In The Netherlands, where over 70 per cent of children attend publicly funded, independently run schools, any group with 166 or more children is entitled to public funding to start a school, delivering the national curriculum within their preferred value framework. These cases show a wide perception that schooling is a communal matter, which is even more strongly illustrated in non-western societies (Reagan, 1996).

HOW IDENTITY IS MAINTAINED AND DEFENDED

As a biological aside it is worth mentioning the hypothesis supported by some evidence from palaeontology and physical anthropology (Irwin, 1987) that our species evolved in social groups of about 100–200 individuals (or 400–500, according to Irwin, 1987). Such a group would represent the breeding community, within which a high proportion of genes would be shared. It would be genetically beneficial to those genes to be protected by communal behaviour, altruistic in individual terms but self-interested in terms of the gene pool, and competitive with outside groups. Any behavioural links with a genetic basis would be shared and protected within the tribe, while cultural evolution could superimpose a variety of social patterns which prove beneficial in local situations. The Darwinian advantages of genetic features are clear; by an analogous process beneficial social structures would also tend to survive. To express this in complementary terms, either genetic or social features which did not both protect and isolate the tribe would disappear as it submerged in the overall population.

We may expect, then, to find genetic and social behaviour linking kindred and isolating from others. This is painfully clear in everyday life. With an awareness of 'us' comes an equal and opposite sense of 'them'. The pioneer of social identity theory, Henri Tajfel (1978), proposed that individuals are motivated to achieve a positive social identity, which he defined as 'that part of an individual's self-concept which derives from his knowledge of his membership in a social group (or groups) together with the value and emotional significance attached to that group'. Taylor and Moghaddam (1994) explain that 'this desire will prompt individuals to make social comparisons between the in-group and the out-groups, with the ultimate aim to achieve both a *positive* and *distinct* position for the in-group' [original italics]. Self-esteem is not inevitable. Some societies agree, perhaps as a means of rationalizing the obvious limits of their powers, that their prestige derives from the dominating overlords who hold them in subjection. In general, though, western societies enjoy 'feeling good about oneself'.

Since the markers of a culture are the distinctive evaluations acquired by the child, the distinction between 'us' and 'them' is recorded in terms of the constructs the child uses to evaluate the world. If wealth is one, 'we' have ideal wealth and 'they' are either impoverished or decadent; if directness of speech is a virtue, 'they' are devious and hypocritical. In this way the individual's constructs are used to describe, denigrate or dismiss the outside world. The relationship need not be contemptuous, and may in many ways be respectful, but there is a perception that 'we' alone observe all the proprieties.

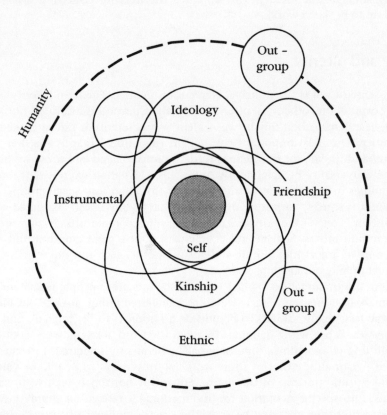

Figure 4.2 Social identities of the self (Vine, 1987)

The identity of an individual may be represented as a Venn diagram, in which the subject belongs to many sets, each one enclosing people of an acceptable level of similarity. Thus I stand in a set of schoolteachers, a set of English speakers, a set of fathers, a set of balding men, and so on. The margins of these sets do not coincide, and in fact they are continuously being renegotiated with fresh social contacts, but they can be summated into a 'fuzzy set' enclosing those I view as my co-culturals at one time or another. Figure 4.2 from Vine (1987) represents the social components of the identity of the individual, without the summated set.

The boundaries of this set can be measured on the evaluative scales formed by my constructs, particularly those known as 'core constructs'. If each of these scales is pictured as running outwards from me to the far extremes, one can draw concentric cultural contours, delimiting those levels of evaluation that are highly or less highly consonant with one's values. Naturally, close relatives who share many similar social experiences with me will be found in the central zones, and those with less in common the outer ones. It is important to remember that identification is dynamic and identifications not total; a teacher may be accepted by a new student as a kindly adult at one moment but devalued the next for criticizing what the child believes to be 'good work'.

Identity and alterity

Individual sense of self is the principal element of identity. The term 'alterity' can be used to express the 'otherness' of people or values beyond the cultural horizon of the self. The demarcation line between identity and alterity is the battlefield of social identity. The most important contour on the cultural map is the division between 'us' and 'them', for this defines those we must defend and those we must attack. The universality of neighbourly antagonism, whether expressed through jokes, calumnies or cannibalism, or the rituals of initiation into social groups, are well known. It is scarcely surprising that religion has so often been associated with warfare, since it is one of the principal means by which communities recognize self and differentiate others. Schism and ecumenism arouse great emotion, but the usual outcome of a doctrinal dispute is flight to another sect, not the rejection of the construct of religious kinship.

The word 'international' as applied to students and other people is sometimes used as a mark of 'otherness'. Since 'we' form a preferred group, anyone outside is in some way less highly valued. To be outside a nation is to be 'foreign', and by implication valued below the national. To avoid the word 'foreign', with its offensive or belittling connotations, 'international' is frequently preferred. In terms of the map of personality either of these words simply refers to people or values beyond the cultural horizon of the group. Since this horizon is relative to each group,there is no specific definition for 'international = foreign'; it simply means 'unlike us', whichever 'us' may be speaking. In the context of 'international schools' the adjective often denotes the dimension of cultural distance rather than any one direction or locus. Much the same could be said of 'globalization', meaning the acceptance of some degree of influence from outside the sponsoring country, rather than any specific institutional structure.

Threats to identity

Any sudden change in the validating system will bring a sharp increase in dissonant experiences. Transfer from primary to secondary school alone is a lifelong memory for many people, though the parents, the home and the surrounding society are unchanged. A move to another country brings a change of every element except the parents. If they have time to spend with the children the cultural discrepancies are splinted, but if the new way of life takes all the parents' attention the children are indeed alone. There are occasional but striking cases of expatriate adolescents who are better students abroad than at home, because in rejecting the schooling their parents support they can embrace the alien system of the international school and perform well in the framework of their teachers and peers.

Since rejection of alterity is a defence of identity, frequently moved children may develop the habit of independence. By declaring themselves indifferent to local friendships and engagements they avoid giving hostages to fortune and suffering when the next move comes. Alternatively, both children and parents have the option, especially on a fixed-term sojourn, of retreating into a tunnel of familiar values and artefacts from which they view the host country. While professionally frustrating for teachers, this strategy has undeniable advantages in cultures where repatriation is known to be difficult.

Each identification with a group has a number of variable properties, making it strong or weak according to the circumstances. For example, as a member of a football team a student may have a core construct of 'being skilled at football'. This was acquired from an earlier validator and has a degree of salience which depends upon its importance at the last location. So, if it was validated by the previous sports coach it will be fairly recent, may be strong, and will be expected to be supported by the new sports coach. In the new school sport may have lower status, skill levels may be higher, or social groups may not be sport based. One's virtuosity could be questioned by either peers or coach, or (in a less expressive culture) the public display of skills may be resented, making the new validators less attractive to the student because of their hostile evaluation. If the previous social bonding within the group of footballers was highly salient to the student a major source of self-esteem has now been taken away and a core construct produces an unfavourable rating.

Group membership varies in its salience and role. Americans are taught that popularity is desirable, but that it is subject to choice and competition. Membership of groups in Japan is obligatory, so individual variations in popularity can only be expressed in anti-social ways, such as bullying or *ijime*. So strong is the national expectation of collectivity that deviant behaviour such as bullying is seen as a national problem, although its frequency is far lower than in the west. Even *ijime* has its social structure, often being carried out by a subordinate who is loyal to the senior bully.

In collectivist societies such as Japan or Thailand there may be no clear verbal categorization of 'me' and 'you' (singular). The Japanese custom of *kawanozi*, in which the first child sleeps between the parents until adolescence, is denoted by a character showing the three as one unit, whose three parallel lines originally showed a river lying between its banks. The fundamental nature of self even in such a collectivist society is illustrated, however, in two remarkable works of literary-psychological analysis by Takeo Doi (1973, 1986). The importance of maintaining outer social behaviour despite inner conflict is accommodated by the institution of *omote* (outer appearance) and *ura* (inner feelings), concepts that are prominent in literature and implicit in daily life. It is as though the self-other horizon were internalized to avoid schisms in the interpersonal world.

The process of culture acquisition

Adjustment of the child to the new international school takes time. Given that the average stay is commonly two to three years, most children can be said to be 'adjusting' most of the time. Clinical symptoms of adjustment are commonly monitored as stress or anxiety, and remediated through counselling. The adjustment necessary for functioning as a student amounts to the culture acquisition that will qualify the child as a member of Tajfel's 'social group', equipping the child first with the common social language to make learning possible, and second the strength of validation to regard the school as important. While many children are helped by being 'buddied' with acculturated co-nationals or with members of the sponsoring culture, some may prefer to avoid the pitfalls of unfamiliar interpersonal manners, and withdraw into a behavioural 'silent phase' while they observe and learn.

It is easy to see that constructs operating within the family and home are less vulnerable than those that depend on elements that are replaced or are altogether absent in the new location. 'I am good in the eyes of my teacher' will take time to develop; 'I am good at Norwegian folk-dancing in the eyes of my friends' can only survive in the memory; 'I always do my homework in the eyes of my mother' can be reinforced daily. A single social group with a core construct that is not widely shared, or a strong validation by someone left behind, will be difficult to replace. The sense of self, the personal identity, will need careful nurturing. Ploys such as wearing school uniform enable a student to fit easily into an unknown field where there is no simple way of knowing local values. A new student often searches for such formulae, but the fit with local norms is more satisfactory if it is achieved by choice than by decree.

THE IMPLICATIONS OF CULTURAL DIVERSITY IN INTERNATIONAL SCHOOLS

If we refer back to Figure 4.1, representing the social learning system of the child, it is clear that several features differ from the static situation. The mobile unit is the two-parents (or step-parent)-and-child sector of the system. The teacher-peers alignment is present in the new school, though always including students at varying stages of assimilation, and the school-society link varies according to the location and the consonance between home and host societies.

Clearly each school has its own ethos. This is as true within a country as between them, and even static families have a scale of values on which the extremes are felt to be worlds apart. On a first expatriation the family need to recalibrate their scale to take into consideration the enormous variety of schools world-wide, but will have some difficulty grasping the reality. This applies equally to teachers. Some of them settle down to a dismissive attitude that simply places all non-home system schools beyond their cultural horizon, which allows them to continue functioning with their original value scale intact. Signs of lack of accommodation include repeated references to markers from the home country as though they were close at hand, or broad, non-discriminating categorizations of local elements as though they were remote. Schools promising their families cultural consistency with home need a degree of value stability, but those intending to teach elements of local experience must have at least some involvement with local values.

Teachers choosing to go overseas have chosen to separate from their compatriots, but usually start out without specific knowledge of the school or its locality. Some information about the institution and location can be sent in advance, but most learning will inevitably happen on site. The typology of international cultural gaps and means of bridging them are dealt with by James Cambridge in Chapter 14. There is general agreement that the most detailed handbook cannot prepare the employee before expatriation, and there is broad general support for any pre-embarkation process of self-examination which promotes an objective attitude to cultures.

The school as an institution needs to ensure consonance between its classroom operations, both academic and social, and the expectations of the parents. The school's part is a matter for internal professional organization; parent liaison is more problematic. International schools have a range of strategies, some of them outstandingly good, for involving families in school life. Among the expatriates they find many competent professionals whose 'trailing spouse' status leaves them with a need to use time and skills. These can act as project leaders, but they will need some balancing influence to ensure that other cultures with different attitudes to school, different languages or communicative styles, and different concepts of duty, are not marginalized in the parent–school organization.

National mix is certainly a matter for careful consideration. It is a common experience within a class that a co-cultural or co-lingual group can form a refuge from the larger group. The model described above makes this obvious: students can maximize the consonance of their environment by staying where views and values are maximally shared. If dissonance is the means of cultural learning this insulation will slow down learning, and schools often react by separating family or national groups. This may be perceived by the parents as effective and desirable, but in the case of collectivist societies it goes against early training. Japanese teenagers, for example, have a social obligation to spend time with their same-sex peers, though their parents are now often aware of the advantages for language learning of being the sole second language speaker.

With substantial groups of students come substantial groups of parents. They too can achieve critical mass at which they can sustain their home culture and create an enclave in which national expectations are unchallenged, remaining remote from local life. In a classic study of Swedish expatriates Torbiorn (1982) found that those who spent most time with compatriots were markedly less content with their posting than those who spent time with local people in the same location. The Parent Teacher Association, or the school, can come under fire from national groups that have a collective tradition or that cling to the validation system – and hence the values – of home. It seems vital for the school to offer its own values and to share these as effectively as possible with their families.

Outcomes of cultural fit and misfit

There is a growing literature covering the pathology of cultural dissonance, and culture shock on expatriation and repatriation. It concentrates on aetiology and remediation, modelled on national practices of diagnosis and treatment. In international relocation the widely shared clinical paradigm often overshadows the prospect of a move, but the Global Nomad literature may help to show mobility in a more positive light. Starting from Useem and Downie's (1976) nationally-based 'Third Culture Kid' model others, including Mary Langford in this volume, are exploring the outcomes in students' lives.

Families patronizing international schools have above-average academic expectations that are frequently met by adopting the selective programmes of the International Baccalaureate (IB). New world school systems tend to offer targets for students of all academic levels, but achieve above-average scores on standardized measures such as Scholastic Aptitude Tests (SATs), Iowa Tests, or PSATs .

Some specific cultural learning difficulties are more easily discernible from classroom performance than overall scores. Students from traditional education systems, say in the Middle East, southern Europe, or post-colonial territories, rely heavily on rote learning. Books are an unquestioned source of knowledge. Practical work has nothing like the value accorded in English schools; the repetition of scientific experiments by children when adult scientists have already done them 'properly' is puzzling. Given that many Islamic communities study the Koran by memorizing it in a foreign language, it is easy to see that the strength of validation for these customs comes from powerful parental and communal sources. Rational knowledge based on experiment or criticism of evidence are altogether alien, and potentially threatening to a conservative society. However, common ground can be found, ironically, in American system schools with their tradition of careful analysis of the rules for winning grades. Where the scoring process is a suitable subject for strategic planning the process is understandable, even if the aim is not. In countries where schooling employs memorizing rather than analysis there is no developmental criterion for promotion. Rapid progress through the school is the mark of a good student.

Second language learning

The new student often has to learn the operating language, most frequently English. This evokes a range of requests. Where English is highly respected, time may be willingly sacrificed. In extreme cases, such as Japanese girls aged 16 or 17, the time taken over second language tuition may cause particular anxiety as it will delay their eligibility for marriage, as well as nullifying or even inverting socially important levels of seniority among fellow students. Where Anglophone education is merely the best substitute for the home system, or where speed of promotion is an absolute virtue, communication problems may be undervalued by the family.

The English as a Second or Foreign Language class often provides a haven for new students. The teachers are particularly experienced in cultural dissonance and frequently spearhead the cultural awareness of the school. Between them, English as a Second Language (ESL) and mother-tongue teachers form a rich reservoir of knowledge and perceptiveness which schools should cultivate. It would be a mistake, though, to see ESL as an emotional casualty ward. There is accumulating evidence (Alston, 1996) that language barriers serve as a protection against stress in newcomers, at least at primary age. It seems likely that the student does not feel fully responsible for situations in which no channels of communication have yet opened, and no validator been recognized. Just as new students slowly enlarge the physical territory in which they feel at home, so their cognitive and cultural world expands progressively with experience. The reverse – immediate recognition of strongly validated responsibilities – may be a major factor in culture shock on repatriation.

The multicultural child

An important area of uncertainty remains. All international schools will be familiar with the 'good international school family'. They arrive with realistic expectations, they are flexible, relaxed, and tolerant of uncertainty, they support the new school in its own terms and not theirs, their children integrate quickly and achieve well, yet on International Day they turn out in national dress and serve national dishes. How do they achieve this ideal cultural flexibility? The western trading nations are predominantly monolingual–monocultural, in the sense that each has an unquestionably dominant culture giving access to national targets. Families – even teachers – raised in such an atmosphere will expect to live in a single system in which each person has one cultural repertoire. Their world is represented by the diagram of culture learning (Figure 4.1) in its simplest form and adjustment means replacing their home culture. From this position any alternative to the national culture may seem a threat. This population has so far dominated the international school-using and -founding community. It seems that the 'good international school family' differs in their acceptance of alterity, their ability to tolerate diversity without feeling a major threat to their own shared cultural identity. This is described by Mary Langford in Chapter 3 dealing with Global Nomads, a grouping of children whose international schooling has given them a distinctive set of characteristics. If we apply the culture learning diagram to them or to the pluricultural societies in which the majority of people in the world live we see that the culture taught and supported within the home is not necessarily practised by their neighbours. A diagram of their social world would show several entities in the 'society' position, and a different pattern of strengths of bonding with the various validators. In such an environment the child will come to accept alterity as normal within the daily social horizon. Such communities may find it relatively easy to accommodate to expatriate life, and not feel threatened if the community outside the front door is different.

This kind of accommodation with alterity may be reached by those who live as members of a stable minority within a dominant or polyvalent community, by those whose parents have two different cultures, as well as by those with overseas experience during childhood. The emergence of a new theatre of international contacts in the Asia-Pacific region will provide us with a diversity of cases which will test this and other current models by which we manage international schools.

REFERENCES

Alston, E (1996) Personal communication

Auden, W H and Isherwood, C (1935) *The Dog Beneath the Skin*, Faber & Faber, London

Berry, J W, Poortinga, Y H, Segall, M H and Dasen, P R (1992) *Cross-cultural Psychology: Research and Applications*, Cambridge University Press, Cambridge

Bruner, J S (1985) 'Vygotsky: an historical and conceptual perspective', in J V Wertsch (ed), *Culture, Communication and Cognition: Vygotskyan Perspectives*, Cambridge University Press, Cambridge

Bruner, J S (1986) *Actual Minds, Possible Worlds*, Harvard University Press, Cambridge, Mass

Doi, T (1973) *The Anatomy of Dependence*, Kodansha International, Tokyo

Doi, T (1986) *The Anatomy of Self: The Individual versus Society*, Kodansha International, Tokyo

Festinger, L (1957) *A Theory of Cognitive Dissonance*, Tavistock, London

Findlay, R (1997) (ed) *International Education Handbook*, Kogan Page, London

Garbarino, J and Bronfenbrenner, U (1976) 'The socialization of moral judgement and behaviour in cross-cultural perspective', in T Lickona (ed), *Moral Development and Behaviour*, Holt, Rinehart & Winston, New York

Gudykunst, W B and Kim, Y Y (1992) *Readings on Communicating with Strangers: An Approach to Intercultural Communication*, McGraw-Hill, New York

Haste, H (1987) 'Growing into rules', in J Bruner and H Haste (eds), *Making Sense of Language: The Child's Construction of the World*, Methuen, London

Irwin, C J (1987) 'A study in the evolution of ethnocentrism', in Y Reynolds, V Falger and I Vine (eds), *The Sociobiology of Ethnocentrism*, Croom Helm, London/Sydney

Kelly, G (1955) *The Psychology of Personal Constructs*, Norton, New York

Kohlberg, L (1976) 'Moral stages and moralization: the cognitive-developmental approach', in T Lickona (ed), *Moral Development and Behaviour*, Holt, Rinehart & Winston, New York

Lonner, W (1990) 'An overview of cross-cultural testing and assessment', in R W Brislin, *Applied Cross-cultural Psychology*, Sage Publications, Newbury Park, CA

Matthews, M (1989) 'The scale of international education', *International Schools Journal*, 17, pp 7–17

Mead, G H (1934) 'Symbolic interactionism', in C W Morris (ed), *Mind, Self, and Society*, University of Chicago Press, Chicago

Minoura, Y (1992) 'A sensitive period for the incorporation of cultural meaning sytems', *Ethos*, **20**, 3, pp 304–39

Minoura, Y (1993) 'Culture and personality reconsidered: theory building from cases of Japanese children returning from the United States', *Quarterly Newsletter of the Laboratory of Human Cognition*, **15**, 2, pp 63–71

Pearce, R (1991) 'Understanding national education systems', in P L Jonietz and D Harris (eds), *World Yearbook of Education*, Kogan Page, London

Reagan, T (1996) *Non-western Educational Traditions: Aternative Approaches to Educational Thought and Practice*, Lawrence Erlbaum Assocs, Mahwah, New Jersey

Tajfel, H (1978) 'Social categorization, social identity, and social comparison', in Tajfel H (ed), *Differentiation between Social Groups*, Academic Press, London/New York

Taylor, D M and Moghaddam, F M (1994) *Theories of Intergroup Relations*, Praeger, London

Torbiorn, I (1982) *Living Abroad: Personal Adjustment and Personnel Policy in the Overseas Setting*, John Wiley, Chichester

Useem, R and Downie, R D (1976) 'Third-Culture Kids', *Today's Education*, September–October, pp 103–5

Vine, I (1987) 'Inclusive fitness and the self-system', in Y Reynolds, V Falger and I Vine (eds), *The Sociobiology of Ethnocentrism*, Croom Helm, London/Sydney

Weinreich, P (1983) 'Emerging from threatened identities', in G Breakwell (ed), *Threatened Identities*, John Wiley, Chichester

Willis, D B (1992a) 'A search for transnational culture: an ethnography of students in an international school in Japan', pt I, *International Schools Journal*, 23, pp 9–25

Willis, D B (1992b) 'A search for transnational culture: an ethnography of students in an international school in Japan, pt II, *International Schools Journal*, 24, pp 29–41

Part 2

INTERNATIONAL EDUCATION THROUGH THE CURRICULUM

5

The Emergence of the International Baccalaureate as an Impetus for Curriculum Reform

Elisabeth Fox

Introduction

The International Baccalaureate (IB) curriculum made its first appearance in the mid-1960s as a series of pamphlets entitled 'the International Schools Examinations Syndicate' (ISES), published under the auspices of the International Schools Association. This Association was created in the aftermath of World War II and the tragedy of Hiroshima at the time of the creation of the United Nations, on the initiative of the International School of Geneva (Ecolint), with the purpose of promoting international understanding and world peace. The ISES project was the outcome of the commitment of a small group of teachers at Ecolint to the concept of international education.

In the light of its subsequent success it is informative to reflect on the way in which the International Baccalaureate, since the days of its inception, has met the demands of the international schools that participated in the original project. The fundamental practical concern of the schools was, in the first instance, to be assured of an education that would facilitate the admission of their students into the universities of their choice in different countries, without having to engage in the lengthy and uncertain process of obtaining equivalence agreements. This meant that those responsible for designing examinations for an internationally acceptable school-leaving credential would need to ensure that the standards of such examinations reflected the 'highest common factor' in all subjects required by the admissions policies of universities in different countries. The demand for upper secondary equivalences came from internationally mobile families whose children were enrolled in international schools, or binational schools in some cases, and who were primarily interested in admissions to British, French, German, and later North American institutions of higher education. The educational leaders responsible for the design of the International Baccalaureate during the exploratory period between 1963 and 1970 were therefore heavily oriented towards European university requirements, and sought out distinguished university professors, initially in France, Germany, Sweden and the United Kingdom, to create syllabuses, outlines of required subject matter, which would synthesize the most demanding features of different national (primarily European) systems. The debate at the time was mainly centred on how to reconcile two fundamentally different approaches: the decentralized system in Britain, which required a high degree of specialization in three or four subjects for university entrance; and the centralized system in France, whose university-controlled secondary curriculum required a broad range of subjects for the *Baccalauréat Français*. A fortunate circumstance was that this debate involved not only policy makers, all of whom were committed to reform within their own countries, and university professors, but also teachers working for a small group of international schools in different locations who were responsible for teaching the syllabuses and conducting pilot programmes in different subjects. The search for 'the highest common factor', the study of different styles of examination questions, and the study of what Alec Peterson called 'the main modes of thinking' (International Baccalaureate Office (IBO) 1985) in different areas of knowledge led to the innovative structure presented by Gerard Renaud to the UNESCO conference hosted by the French government in 1967 (Fox, 1985), a curriculum design whose inherent flexibility and emphasis on quality are at the root of its appeal to a remarkably diverse cross-section of schools world-wide.

Although the development of the IB was examination driven in the first instance it was fundamental curriculum issues – the balance between breadth and specialization, between requirements and choices, as well as the selection of content – which underlay the structure of the programme. An influential contributor to the development of the IB as a curriculum project was Ralph Tyler, Professor of Education at the University of Chicago, whose particular interest was curriculum development and the psychology of learning. Tyler, who worked closely with Professor Benjamin Bloom (well known in education circles for his seminal work on a taxonomy of educational objectives), saw the potential of the International Baccalaureate as a unique enterprise in international curriculum development. Tyler secured the loan from the Ford Foundation that enabled Peterson, as first IBO Director General, to establish a formal research unit at Oxford University. The research was centred on three main studies:

1. a comparative analysis of upper secondary educational programmes in European countries, undertaken in cooperation with the Council of Europe
2. a study of university expectations for upper secondary school students preparing to enter higher education
3. a statistical comparison of IB pilot examination results with those of national school-leaving examinations such as British A levels and US College Board Tests.

The comparative study of different educational programmes provided a foundation for decisions relating to the difficult task of selecting fundamental contents, a common core of knowledge within the various disciplines, that would be acceptable to universities in different countries with a strong tradition of national autonomy regarding the admission of students from their own and other nations. An in-depth review of the several national examination practices paved the way for the scope and variety that has been characteristic of IB assessment during the past 25 years. The second area of research, university expectations, sparked off discussions in IB circles about the aims of contemporary education: the need for specific competences, the ability to apply knowledge and to think critically, the capacity to make independent decisions, the ability to communicate effectively. The international schools participated in this design conversation, contributing their 'experience in the field', a commitment to international understanding, and the importance of experiential learning through the practice of community service. The philosophy of the International Baccalaureate, initially communicated by the research unit and published annually from 1970 in the *General Guide to the International Baccalaureate* as 'General Objectives', gave coherence to the programme and inspired the criteria that govern the construction and execution of the examinations as well as the continuous process of curriculum development. The third aspect of the research unit's work, statistical comparability studies, was conducted in 1970 and 1971 and, although the samples were too small to draw reliable conclusions, the initial indication was that there were positive correlations between IB and national examinations in the limited aspects susceptible to statistical manipulation.

The original 'architects' of the IB project attempted to put aside the constraints of existing systems (in the words of Gerard Renaud: 'the prisoners of old traditions') and to focus on a key question: 'in the context of today's world in "developed" countries, what areas of knowledge and which competences would equip young people equally well for university studies and for a professional career?' The exploration of this question led to the identification of the fundamental educational criteria that link the philosophy of the IB with its basic curricular structure (IBO, 1985):

- priority of personal reflection over mere accumulation of knowledge
- training for independent work, and the practical application of knowledge
- an international perspective in the approach to human problems
- a link between academic and extra-curricular activities – the concept of educating 'the whole person'.

Central to the IB educational philosophy was Edgar Faure's (French Minister of Education during the educational reform of the 1960s) conviction that learning how to learn is the key to meaningful education, and Jean Capelle's (French educational reformer, Dean of the University of Nancy) insistence that students need to use their academic studies to form their own minds in their own way. Capelle's reform of the *Baccalauréat Français* proposed a decrease in the array of subjects required on the grounds that a general education is better acquired by studying half a dozen subjects in depth than by skimming a dozen in order to recall something about each on the day of the examination (Capelle, 1967). The German concept of paradigmatic learning, which required the selection of certain exemplary

67

elements within a discipline to be studied in depth rather than the acquisition of a whole body of knowledge *per se*, brought to the IB by Hellmut Becker (Fox, 1991), was another significant influence on the formation of the IB curriculum. While the French and German reformers were seeking to reduce the number of subjects required for school-leaving examinations, the British were proposing to increase the range of disciplines to provide a less narrowly focused and more complete education for university-bound students. The influence of British thought is reflected in the two-tier ('Higher' and 'Subsidiary' levels) core and option IB curriculum pattern, the combination of general education with specialization proposed by Alec Peterson and the Oxford reformers and consonant with the more flexible high school curriculum in the USA and Canada. The IB reformers sought to embody the concept of *allgemeine Bildung, culture générale*, or general education in the curriculum and examinations, without on the one hand falling into the trap of encyclopaedism which still remains a predominant characteristic of centralized examination-driven educational systems, or on the other engaging in the narrow specialization still typical of upper secondary education in England and Wales.

The IB curriculum framework that was proposed as an experiment at the 1967 UNESCO Conference not only reflected a synthesis of the aims and structures of different national systems, but also presented the concept of the balance between conservation and innovation. The fact that there was direct communication between the authors of this framework, who knew each other personally, and who were leading thinkers in educational renovation within their own countries, undoubtedly helped in the shaping of the elements of flexibility within the IB Diploma Programme which have contributed to its success and rapid expansion. The curriculum framework of the IB, later characterized by Thompson as a hexagon (Hayden *et al.*, in Kellaghan, 1995) (see Figure 5.1) offers a response to the continuing search for balance by including and attempting to resolve such inherent dichotomies as national vs international perspectives; depth vs breadth emphasis; traditional vs modern interpretations; requirements vs choice regulations; theoretical vs practical learning; subject centred vs interdisciplinary approaches.

What distinguishes the overall IB curriculum structure, however, is the inclusion of three special requirements: a common course in the Theory of Knowledge (TOK), an independent Extended Essay, and participation in creative and social service activities. The common course in the TOK leads IB diploma students to investigate 'the main modes of thinking', questioning the nature of different subjects they have studied; to see the relationships between disciplines; to relate what they have learned to personal experience; to understand and apply logic, learning to discriminate between, for example, truth and opinion; in short, to participate in a community of enquiry that leads them to explore the meaning of the universe and to reflect on their place in it. Writing an Extended Essay on a subject and topic of their choice affords students the experience of developing a personal academic interest creatively and autonomously, while at the same time practising the self-discipline, including skills of planning and time management, that independent research of this kind demands. Finally, the requirement for IB students to engage in 'Creativity, Action, Service' (CAS) activities acknowledges that academic excellence alone is insufficient; if the IB claims to promote international understanding then IB schools must give students the means to learn through experience how to take responsible action in the service of others. It also recognizes the importance of physical activity and aesthetic experience in the life of the student, and in the education of 'the whole person'. It is these three fundamental requirements that give the IB Diploma Programme its character as a total, integrated curriculum with varied modes of assessment consistent with the educational values derived from a coherent statement of philosophy.

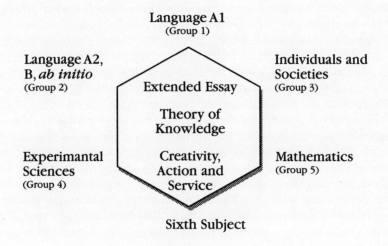

Figure 5.1 The curriculum framework of the International Baccalaureate (Thompson, 1988)

The element of flexibility and choice inherent in the overall IB programme, which enables students from a wide diversity of schools in different locations to select a valid pre-university programme in accordance with their needs and interests, is also apparent within different subjects. In languages schools may choose literary texts from a comprehensive list prescribed by the IBO. Within the field of social sciences ('Individuals and Societies') a choice of units or topics is available in each subject:

in History, for instance, schools decide which region (for example 'the Americas') they will teach, depending on the interest of teachers and students, the location of the school and national requirements. In various subjects 'guided coursework' permits students to explore a theme relevant to their own particular interests. Similarly, the sciences offer a required core with a choice of topics or case studies, and the chance for students to conduct practical experiments in a specific area of interest. Mathematical Studies presents the opportunity for students to apply knowledge to an investigation of their choice, which can be in a different subject. Art/Design requires the completion of an individual diary where students make observations on an artist, period or movement of their choice, as well as requiring the compilation of a portfolio of original artworks from each student which is presented to a local examiner for assessment in conversation with the student.

This degree of choice and flexibility presents an unusual challenge to schools, in terms of making decisions about which subjects to offer and what the range of the total IB programme will be, within the context of their location, the needs of their particular student population and the material and (above all) human resources available to them. Schools entering the programme for the first time often work through a transition period, offering courses in a few specific subjects as an internal pilot scheme, before committing the institution to a curriculum that will lead to the award of the full IB Diploma. A few schools have initially offered a minimal programme, prescribing one subject within each group for the total of six required, virtually eliminating the element of student choice but providing, nevertheless, an education consonant with the IB philosophy. Others, with ample resources and diverse student populations, such as the United Nations International School (UNIS) in New York City, offer an impressive spectrum of courses and array of possible choices.

As one of a small group of original pilot schools UNIS was in fact the first to move away from national examinations and to commit its entire upper secondary curriculum to preparation for the International Baccalaureate. This decision emerged from the particular characteristics and situation of the school. By 1968 UNIS had become the most international of all the participating schools, with an enrolment of 844 pupils from 79 nations taught by 78 teachers of 25 nationalities (Fox, 1985). The great majority of parents were UN employees demanding a common curriculum that would reflect the principles of the UN Charter, and of a standard that would facilitate university admissions world-wide without the necessity of negotiating equivalence agreements. The internationality of the syllabuses was in line with parental aspirations. The decentralized system of the United States gives ample freedom to accredited schools to design their own programmes, and US high school curricula typically offer a range of options from which students may choose. The IB curriculum pattern was compatible with the kind of demanding college preparatory programme expected of schools with a reputation for academic excellence. UNIS was thus in an optimum position to serve as a laboratory for the IB experiment. Another of the pilot schools, Atlantic College in Wales, a sixth form college modelled on the principles of Kurt Hahn and committed to education for peace, made the International Baccalaureate the focus of its programme, gradually replacing the British A level examinations with IB examinations. Atlantic College was the first of what subsequently became a chain of United World Colleges (UWCs) that offer scholarships to students throughout the world to enable them to study together as an international community of scholars devoted to serving their fellow human beings.

As the IB entered the decade of the 1980s there was a growing awareness articulated by schools with large, multicultural student populations, such as UNIS, that what had constituted 'internationality' for those designing the programme in the 1960s, was beginning to be perceived as 'Eurocentred'. In 1980 IBO organized a seminar in Singapore to focus on aspects of Asian culture to examine how Asian thought and education could be incorporated into different IB subject areas. The occasion was a forum for international and national schools in the region to debate with one another and with educational authorities from Hong Kong, India, Japan, Malaysia and Singapore on themes such as the influence of Buddhism and Islam, the Japanese approach to the teaching of mathematics, the meaning of 'east' and 'west' from an anthropological perspective, and multilingual educational reform in Singapore. Proposals for modifications to correct the 'Euro bias' of certain subjects were presented and subsequently endorsed by the 1982 Standing Conference of Heads of IB schools (HSC) in New York. In 1982 a major science conference for IBO was hosted by the Japanese government at Tsukuba University as a token of Japanese interest in the various dimensions of the IB.

In 1984 the Deputy Director General of IBO, Robert Blackburn, who was committed to African education, obtained a grant from NORAD (a Norwegian development agency) to offer an 'African seminar' in Nairobi, the purpose of which was to study ways in which African thought and culture could be integrated into the IB programme of studies. African professors and educators, the majority of them Kenyan, presented a wealth of knowledge and ideas in philosophy, languages, history, anthropology and the sciences. Here the Eurocentrism of the IB was evident, especially in a debate with expatriate teachers and IB examiners during the language working group session where African educators raised two questions.

1. Why should works written in English by distinguished African authors (Soyinka, Achebe, Ngugi) be considered as world literature in translation and not as legitimate English literature alongside works by classical and contemporary British authors?
2. Why should not oral literature be offered for study as a legitimate literary genre alongside the novel, the short story, theatre or poetry?

African teachers made the point that English written by Africans in Africa was as legitimate a native language as English written in the UK, the USA or any other Anglophone country. In claiming that the study of Shakespeare and Dickens was indeed valuable for African students, the teachers also insisted that, if the IB is genuine in its commitment to fostering the understanding of national cultures as a path to learning about other cultures, students should also study the great writers of their own country. They also suggested it would be of value for students in other countries studying English as a native language to include African authors in their selection of texts in English. In making the case for oral literature its proponents stressed that most literature has its roots in this genre, that the enslavement of Africa and the repression of cultural expression had deprived generations of young people from learning about their own heritage. The University of Nairobi had much scholarship to offer in this area, and oral literature, designed from in-depth studies of age-old traditions, was being successfully developed in the teaching of language in schools serving students with different mother-tongue dialects. The languages working group, after a lively discussion, brought forward recommendations supporting the views of the African teachers, and suggesting corresponding modifications of the language syllabus requirements. This incident illustrates the potential of the IB curriculum to be enriched by the constituencies it serves. Dr Tunde Oderinde, a curriculum expert from Nigeria, emphasized the potential of the IB as an international model for African countries in the process of discarding the constraints of the European models inherited from colonial times. In speaking of the need for 'tropicalization' (adapting the programme to the educational priorities of the continent), he lamented that so little was known about the IB, and recommended that IBO launch a communications drive to bring Africa into the picture, and the picture to Africa (IBO, 1984).

Despite the fact that the IB is constantly questioning its own claim to internationality, most recently over the much-debated recognition of the need for more explicit integration of global concerns into the curriculum, new international schools, such as those recently founded in Atlanta, Georgia, continue to appear and flourish with a strong commitment to the IB.

THE IB EXPERIENCE AS A RESPONSE TO THE DEMAND FOR EXCELLENCE IN STATE SCHOOLS

Among the schools that piloted the IB in the late 1960s were three prestigious European state schools; the Lycée Pilote de Sevres and the Lycée Saint-Germain-en-Laye in France, and the Goethe Gymnasium in Germany. Teachers in these schools worked with their colleagues in a handful of international schools to design courses and to bring international education to their classrooms. Two decades later countries in eastern Europe began to see the IB as a possible curriculum model in the quest to 'de-ideologize' schools, and move from uniformity to plurality. During the period of Perestroika the USSR Academy of Pedagogical Science established a research group to undertake a comparative analysis of IB and Soviet programmes. In Bulgaria the IBO became a recognized impulse for change because of its potential for providing a flexible programme with high standards for secondary education. Two schools in Slovenia received authorization to pilot the IB as a national experiment, funded by the state. Furthermore, in 1990 an encouraging endorsement of the success of the IB mission came from the joint conference of the Commission of the European Communities and the Council for Cultural

The IB as an impetus for curriculum reform

Cooperation of the Council of Europe on 'Secondary schools and European/international education in Europe' in Namur, 1990. Fifty-one delegates from 19 European countries attended, and formally recommended that 'the competent educational authorities should consider the extended use of the IB in state schools in Europe as a means to increase the European/international dimension' (Commission of the European Communities, 1990).

Although state schools in France and Germany had participated in the experimental stage of the IB there was little interest at the time from the European public sector. It was in North America, where the national consciousness had been ignited by government publications (such as *A Nation at Risk*) deploring the state of public education, that the IB began to be adopted as a viable programme for state schools in pursuit of excellence. The International Baccalaureate had caught the attention of a number of North American educators during its experimental period. In addition to Tyler and Bloom, Harland P Hanson, Director of the College Board Advanced Placement Program, was an early advocate, cooperating with Peterson and others on the issue of assessment. Lester Pearson, the Prime Minister of Canada, was a supporter because of his commitment to education for peace and the establishment of a United World College in the province of Vancouver. Finally, Blouke Carus, of the Open Court Publishing Company, strongly committed to improving the quality of education, obtained a grant from the Hegeler Foundation to establish a regional office in New York (IB North America: IBNA) to give support to the central office in Geneva. A board of directors was set up to help raise funds and to disseminate IBO policy. One of the directors, Dr Mel Serisky, Principal of the Francis Lewis High School in Queens, New York, saw in the IB a programme for excellence. The entry of Francis Lewis into the programme in 1976 as the first North American public high school to adopt the IB set a historic trend: in 1997 some 215 public high schools in Canada and the US comprised the IBNA schools authorized to participate in the programme. This level of recruitment was initially the result of energetic campaigning by the regional office in the early 1980s, which produced a steady annual growth rate of 20 per cent. IBNA organized well-publicized 'introductory workshops' in different areas of North America, marketing the IB as a programme for the gifted and for academic excellence. A survey of participating schools conducted in 1984 confirmed that the main factors influencing schools' decisions to adopt the IB were academic excellence, the challenge inherent in the syllabuses, the appeal to gifted students, and the opportunity to upgrade and enrich the curriculum school-wide. A subsequent survey, conducted in 1987, confirmed that these were still the primary reasons why North American schools choose to participate in the IB programme. When asked to evaluate the impact of the IB within the schools there was an overwhelming confirmation that the programme had satisfied expectations with regard to rigour, challenge and academic excellence. In addition, the internationality, philosophy and structure of the programme emerged as important factors in its success.

Two significant, associated trends emerged from these surveys:

1. The programme appeared to have a highly motivating effect on both teachers

and students, despite the fact that both groups acknowledged the reality of a heavier workload than they would have assumed under the regular high school programme.
2. The standards required brought about a movement to upgrade the quality of curricula in the last two years of high school within the school system.

In some cases the introduction of the IB affected junior high schools or even elementary schools and, today, all IB public high schools have some kind of pre-IB programme. Although reaction to the IB from feeder schools (junior high schools) has been varied, there is general acceptance that 7th and 8th graders interested in taking the IB in the future must have engaged in serious language study, and have completed 'Algebra 1' by the end of 8th grade. In Florida, a network of IB schools has succeeded in writing pre-IB courses for the state curriculum (Richardson, 1992). By the mid-1980s, public schools in Atlanta, Houston, Winnipeg, Chicago, Milwaukee and Los Angeles, using the IB as a focal or magnet programme with an emphasis on academic standards and excellence, were successful in attracting system-wide enrolments of able students, thus improving their image within the local community and reversing the trend of losing gifted students to the private sector. Ernest Boyer, in his critique of US public education (1983), singled out the IB as a model of quality. Commissioners of Education in California, Florida, Minnesota and Ohio have paid public tribute to the impact of the IB in their states. IBNA reports that today 140 schools act as magnets in one way or another. Some of these have formal entry requirements, as in Florida; others have open boundaries, as in Minnesota; or schools of choice, as in Colorado. In California less formal magnets permit a student to transfer to a school with an IB programme if she or he wants. In some districts the IB has been implemented as a tool for restoring or maintaining racial balance in the school.

One of the interesting features of IB development in the North American public sector is that, despite the incompatibilities between the IB curriculum and the programmes of typical US high schools, the project progressed from strength to strength with ongoing planned support from the regional office. With assistance from experienced IB schools such as UNIS, the Lincoln Park Public High School in Chicago, and Southfields Public High School in Michigan, IBNA pioneered annual in-service staff development courses and discussion sessions for teachers, counsellors and administrators in different geographical locations to facilitate maximum access. The commitment of IBNA schools has given the IB a high profile for excellence which has assisted university recognition and the allocation of public funds for development in the region.

Although one of the first state schools to participate in the IB experiment was Mara College in Malaysia there has been little interest from the public sector in the Asia-Pacific region (IBAP) over the years until recently, with a spurt of growth in Australia and the participation of two new state schools in China. The current President of the Council of the Foundation of the International Baccalaureate, Greg Crafter (formerly Minister of Education for South Australia), believes that educators see the IB as a harbinger for educational change in the context of the economic transition of Australia and its expanding role within the Pacific Rim community of nations. There is an interest in innovative IB courses, such as Economics, and Organization and Management Studies, not normally offered at upper secondary level in Australia, and in the IB experience in Chinese and Japanese as second languages, rather than the customary alternatives of French and German (Goodban, 1992).

The topical relevance of the IB was addressed by Ge Souquing, Director of the Chinese Education Association for International Exchange, at the HSC in Singapore (1980), where he identified the programme as a possible educational model for China (IBO, 1980). It was also foreseen (prior to the Tiananmen Square incident), as a possibility by Ma Li, the Director of Curriculum for the Chinese Higher Council on Education, who believed that in order to meet its goals to modernize society, particularly with regard to economic growth and contemporary human values, Chinese education needed to move away from the traditional, examination-bound mode, and to find ways to achieve up-to-date competences (Fox, 1989). Finally, although the presence of the IB is still minimal in the Middle East and Africa, Machabeng High School in Lesotho, in cooperation with local authorities, has developed a proposal to bring the IB to South Africa as a model for multicultural education.

Clearly the inroads made by the IB, not only into international schools but also into state schools, has been marked, in some regions of the world more than in others. Chapter 17 will consider the particular chase of Chile, where the IB has acted as an agent for educational transformation within the state sector.

REFERENCES

Boyer, E L (1983) *High School: A Report on Secondary Education in America*, Harper & Row, New York

Capelle, J (1967) *Tomorrow's School: The French Experience*, translated and edited with an introduction and notes by W D Halls, Perrgamon, Oxford

Commission of the European Communities/Council for Cultural Cooperation of the Council of Europe (1990) *Secondary Schools and European/International Education in Europe. Mobility, Curricula and Examinations*, Council of Europe, Namur

Fox, E (1985) 'International schools and the International Baccalaureate', *Harvard Educational Review*, 55, pp 53–68

Fox, E (1989) Interview with Ma Li conducted by E Fox in Beijing, February

Fox, E (1991) 'Das Internationale Bakkalaureat', *Bildung und Erziehung*, Aachen, September

Goodban, J (1992) Letter to E Fox from John Goodban, IBAP Regional Director, November

Hayden, M C, Richards, P N and Thompson, J J (1995) 'Validity and reliability issues in International Baccalaureate examinations', in T Kellaghan (ed), *Admission to Higher Education: Issues and Practice*, Educational Research Centre, Dublin

International Baccalaureate Office (1980) *Report on the Standing Conference of Heads of IB Schools, Singapore*, IBO, Geneva

International Baccalaureate Office (1984) *Report on IBO Curriculum Conference, Nairobi 1984*, IBO, Geneva

International Baccalaureate Office (1985) *General Guide to the International Baccalaureate*, 5th ed, IBO, Geneva

Richardson B (1992) Letter to E Fox from Bradford Richardson, IBNA Regional Director, November

6

INTERNATIONAL CURRICULA: MORE OR LESS IMPORTANT AT THE PRIMARY LEVEL?

Kevin Bartlett

INTRODUCTION

The vast majority of students attending international schools are aged between 3 and 12. No one questions the significance of the early years in the patterns of human learning. Indeed, research into the workings of the human brain make a convincing case for these being *the* important years. On the face of it, then, the importance of an international curriculum for the primary years would seem to be self-evident. An international pre-university programme, the International Baccalaureate (IB) has been established for over 25 years and in that period has been recognized as a programme of the highest quality. Yet a common curriculum for younger learners, the Primary Years Programme (PYP) of the IB, has only been established very recently. If an international primary curriculum is of such obvious importance, why has it been so long in coming?

A little history

The answer to that question is to be found to some extent in the history, or per-haps simply the story, of international schools. While international education, and the schools providing it, might have the superficial appearance of a 'movement', this is far from the reality. With the exception of isolated clusters such as the United World Colleges, international schools share no recognized philosophical foundation. There are no deeply held, publicly declared beliefs and values to bind them, to bond them into a coherent global system. They have been created piece-meal, in response to immediate need, in answer to local pressure from globally mobile business enterprises, development aid agencies and diplomats for a (largely) English-medium education of sufficient quality to reduce the potentially negative impact of parental career moves on accompanying children, and to ease re-entry into national systems. Their driving force is pragmatic, not philosophical. Where there has been a compelling practical reason to create an international curriculum, particularly when that reason is rooted in external pressure, then action has been taken. Hence the International Baccalaureate Diploma programme, ensuring university acceptance. Hence the lack of an international primary curriculum.

A little reality

There is a further, practical reason for the absence of an international primary curriculum. Quite simply, until relatively recently, no one has made it a priority. Change requires leadership. This particular change requires global leadership. The chief administrators of international schools represent the most obvious source of this global leadership. They are the individuals who, acting in collaboration, have sufficient authority, power and resources to bring about change at this level, either by pooling the resources of their schools to create a shared curriculum or by joining forces to demand its creation by such bodies as the International Baccalaureate Organization (IBO). These chief administrators are also the key change agents in their own schools. Their support is a necessary condition for change, including the implementation of new curricula. These individuals have been too occupied by the practical demands of their own schools to step back from local and immediate problems and begin to transform them by creating global solutions. Ironically, one of the most compelling reasons for developing an international primary curriculum is the sheer practical benefit of doing so.

AN INTERNATIONAL PRIMARY CURRICULUM: THE PRACTICAL IMPERATIVE

Wheel-reinvention avoidance

For all their geographical diversity, international schools are more similar than different. From New York to Nouakchott, from Vienna to Vanuatu mission statements, school brochures, even teachers, are interchangeable. For all that these schools will often claim to offer unique opportunities they rarely do. Genuine integration of the local culture into the school's programme is rare. Physical climate may change; school climate stays the same. For better or worse there is a recognizable international school culture, most strongly evidenced in the behaviours and preoccupations of the student body. Some may say 'worse' since this culture tends to be heavily western influenced and strong on materialism; a first-time visitor to an international school might wonder if they had wandered by mistake on to an MTV set or a Benetton advertisement.

A further common element in each of these schools is that, at any given time of year, there will be a group of primary teachers engaged in the business of writing curriculum. They will probably be tired, and probably working on the curriculum after a day in the classroom. Few, if any, will have any training in curriculum development. Most of them will be confused, many of them frustrated. The majority will carry the scars of similar earlier efforts in other schools, or even in the same one. They will have a nagging feeling that they are wasting their time, that the fruits of their labours will lie unused on a shelf in a classroom, possibly even their own. Why are they doing this? They are doing it because parents expect schools to follow a written curriculum, because accrediting agencies demand it, because administrators mandate it – even because students deserve it. They may even be doing it because of the myth of ownership; the idea that teachers will be more likely to use a curriculum if they write it themselves. Even if this were true the turnover of staff in international schools makes a mockery of this line of reasoning. In reality they are doing it because they have no choice – because no recognized international primary curriculum has been available. Their more fortunate colleagues, teaching the IB programme to older students, are conspicuously not doing it, for obvious reasons.

In one sense, then, the importance of an international primary curriculum lies in releasing schools from the chore of producing their own. It lies in saving them countless hours of valuable time. It lies in conserving school resources; whether money, energy or time. Especially time – time better spent learning new strategies, becoming more effective at planning, at teaching and at assessing student learning. Time spent doing what teachers are trained to do: implementing curriculum, not writing it. Remaining at the practical level, there are further compelling reasons for developing a common primary curriculum.

RESPONDING TO NATIONAL PRESSURES: THE ISSUE OF QUALITY ASSURANCE

Even assuming that each international school, working in isolation, was able to guarantee the best possible curriculum 'product' from its staff, it would still remain precisely that: a good product produced in isolation. Unfortunately the global workforce served by international schools deserves and, increasingly, demands something very different. They need to know that the educational programmes guiding their children's learning have a wider validity. The clientele of international schools is changing, slowly but surely. British parents now arrive on the doorsteps of international schools well informed as to attainment targets, key stages, and all the other trappings of a national curriculum. While the USA, having less of a centralized political structure, may never move towards a complete national curriculum, national standards have been produced for key curriculum areas. Other national groups come with their own expectations, their own needs and demands. This is not to argue that an international primary curriculum can ever claim to match, objective for objective, a wide range of national curricula with widely differing, even conflicting targets. It is to say that a central organization, with an adequate infrastructure, has ready access to national curricula and can reflect, to the extent desirable, the work of national curriculum bodies. More significantly, a primary curriculum which forms the first stages of a complete, coherent international curriculum for students in the 3–19 age range has a powerful validity of its own. This validity is supported by the fact that the curriculum culminates in a final diploma as widely admired as the IB. It is further strengthened by the spread of the IB into schools in national systems and by the spread of IB-type programmes into national systems. An IB which 'begins at three' is a powerful concept, and one sufficiently reassuring for all but the most sceptical of expatriate parents.

Accreditation based on student learning

It also provides, for the first time, a basis for evaluating the quality of learning in international primary schools. While one could argue that the quality of the IB Diploma programme in a school is demonstrated by its examination results, no such means exist to evaluate the learning of younger students. The commonest way of evaluating the quality of international schools is through the accreditation process, a system which involves schools in producing a thorough self-study and then being subject to an evaluation visit conducted by a carefully selected team of peers drawn from other schools. The process is honest, rigorous and undoubtedly assists schools in the process of structured self-improvement. It is, however, a system that focuses almost exclusively on process. It will inform the accrediting agencies as to whether or not the institution hires and evaluates qualified teachers, whether or not it has a written curriculum and whether or not it utilizes a range of assessment methods. What it will not tell anyone is whether or not the students are learning what they should be learning. It has been likened to a team of biscuit inspectors visiting a factory and leaving without ever tasting the biscuits! The 'inspectors' do so because they have no choice. In the absence of a common curriculum no one has defined what the biscuit should be like. Until recently no one has posed, let alone answered, the question, 'What should primary students be learning in international schools?'

There is a powerful practical case for providing an answer to that question in the form of a clear, coherent curriculum for international primary schools. Such a curriculum enables schools to avoid wasting their resources in reinventing the wheel. It provides an assurance of quality, common benchmarks against which to evaluate learning and common, meaningful assessment data to facilitate student transfer between international schools. However, it is equally important to realize that the significance of an international curriculum transcends the level of practical benefit. It does so because it provides an opportunity to offer students a significantly different learning experience; an opportunity to define international education in ways that set it apart and place it on the leading edge of educational innovation. In assessing the importance of an international primary curriculum it is therefore vital to appreciate the necessity for that curriculum in terms of its unique nature.

AN INTERNATIONAL PRIMARY CURRICULUM: THE PHILOSOPHICAL IMPERATIVE

What do we want our students to learn?

The Primary Years Programme answers this question on several levels. The broadest answer is provided by a set of clearly defined student learning outcomes, set out in Figure 6.1 (IBO, 1997)

These outcomes provide the aims for the curriculum, the driving force for all that follows. They present a broad picture of the type of student that international schools would be proud to send out into the world; a profile of a PYP 'graduate'. They also provide the initial elements in a definition of international education. The line of reasoning can be expressed as follows:

Q. 'What is an international education?'
A: 'One which creates internationally minded people, or "internationalists".'

Q. 'What is an internationalist?'
A. 'A person displaying the following dispositions and attributes.'

When considering these outcomes as the defining terms of internationalism a natural response is to suggest that they would also be desirable in national schools, and are therefore not exclusive to international schools. This is an accurate observation but it misses the point. Internationalism in education is, thankfully, not the sole province of international schools. It is an ideal towards which all schools should strive, but one which carries a greater imperative for international schools, given their access, in their students, parents and staff, to microcosms of wider 'global communities'. The IB Diploma programme is well established in several national systems, for instance in public schools in North America and The Netherlands. The IBO has long recognized the national market for an international curriculum and is inclined to describe the programme as 'not a curriculum for international schools but an international curriculum for schools' (Hagoort, 1994). If this is to be a serious claim rather than merely a marketing slogan then the IBO must commit itself to defining 'an international education' with far greater clarity than at present. To this search for clarity the PYP brings a series of contributions, not least of which is the suggestion that the complete IB programme, from PYP to Diploma, be devoted to the achievement of broad, common targets in the form of a set of student learning outcomes which begin to define the nature of the curriculum.

**WHAT DO WE WANT STUDENTS TO LEARN
Student Learning Outcomes**

Students will be:

Inquirers
Their natural curiosity will have been nurtured, their sense of wonder and love of learning will be sustained throughout their lives and they will have acquired the skills necessary to conduct purposeful, constructive research

Thinkers
They will exercise initiative in applying thinking skills critically and creatively to make sound decisions and solve complex problems

Communicators
They will be able to recieve and express ideas and information confidently in more than one language, including the language of mathematical symbols

Risk takers
They will approach unfamiliar situations without anxiety and have the confidence and adaptability to explore new roles, ideas and strategies. They will be courageous and articulate in defending those things in which they believe

Knowledgeable
They will have spent their time in our schools exploring themes which have global relevance and importance. In so doing they will have acquired a 'critical mass' of significant knowledge

Principled
They will have a sound grasp of the principles of moral and ethical reasoning

Caring
They will show sensitivity towards the needs and feelings of others and have developed a sense of responsibility and personal commitment to action and service

Open minded
They will respect the views, values and traditions of other individuals and cultures and be accustomed to seeking and considering a range of points of view

Healthy
They will understand the importance of physical and mental balance and personal well-being

Reflective
They will be accustomed to examining their own learning and analysing their personal strengths and weaknesses in a thoughtful, constructive mannner

Figure 6.1 Student learning outcomes

From outcomes to action: the essential elements of international curriculum

It is one thing to set targets; it is another to achieve them. How does a child become open minded? In an international context, what does it mean to be knowledgeable? What kind of curriculum makes a person reflective? If these outcomes are to become the daily reality of international schools they will profoundly affect the culture and climate of international schools and, indeed, the intention to bring about systemic change is one of the unwritten goals of the PYP. In order to understand how the PYP may affect the nature of teaching and learning it is necessary to examine rather more closely the structure of the curriculum model. The PYP centres around five 'essential elements' of curriculum; aspects of student learning that put flesh on the bones of the learning outcomes. These elements – concepts, knowledge, skills, attitudes and action – give meaning to the claims of the PYP to offer a truly international curriculum.

Developing conceptual understanding: learning through structured inquiry

The PYP has, from the outset, been concerned primarily with the development of ideas; fundamental concepts that have meaning and significance within and across the traditional disciplines. The programme identifies a set of overarching concepts that have relevance within and across subject disciplines and that are expressed in the form of a set of key questions, shown in Figure 6.2.

Teachers and students use these questions as a springboard for generating ideas. Around these questions they structure thematic units of inquiry. By means of these questions students conduct explorations of significant content. In so doing they not only become more knowledgeable, they also develop certain habits of mind. They become accustomed to seeking a variety of points of view on any given topic, thus beginning to operate in a spirit of open-mindedness. They become used to the idea of personal responsibility. They begin to question the basis of their knowledge, to distinguish between fact and opinion, to seek evidence, to be aware of bias, to consider what it means to 'know' something in the different disciplines. This general commitment to learning through structured inquiry, and these specific questions as the basis for that inquiry, have direct links to the later stages of the IB programme. They represent, most definitely, an 'approach to learning', the phrase used in the IB Middle Years Programme (MYP) to describe its commitment to critical and creative thinking (IBO, 1994). They provide students with the beginnings of the research and communication skills necessary for the extended essay compulsory in the Diploma programme. They echo other appealing aspects of that programme; most obviously the commitment to personal responsibility through social service which is such a feature of the Creativity, Action, Service (CAS) programme and the commitment to epistemological inquiry in the Theory of Knowledge course.

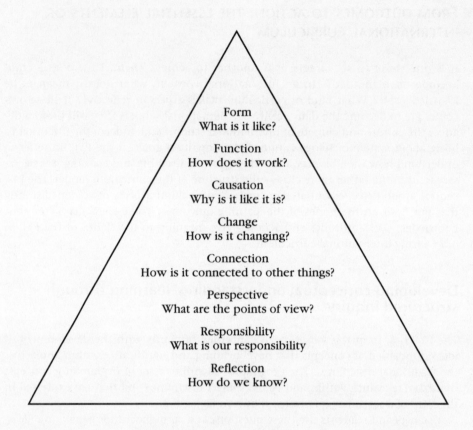

Figure 6.2 Questions for learners

Developing skills, attitudes and a commitment to action: learning through planned activity

Within the context of the PYP teachers plan collaboratively, using a system and format structured around the set of open-ended 'questions for teachers' shown in Figure 6.3.

Integral to this planning is the design of activities that will enable students to acquire a range of cross-curricular skills: from thinking to self-management, from communication to social interaction. Within each unit teachers seek opportunities to foster positive attitudes and to encourage students to engage in constructive action. Students leave the primary school equipped with the necessary skills to succeed in the secondary years, and familiar with the approaches to learning that characterize the MYP (see Figure 6.4).

Stage 1   What is our purpose?

- why are we studying this topic?

Stage 2   What resources will we use?

- which of the available resources best match our purpose?

Stage 3   What do we want to learn?

- open-ended key questions generated by teachers and students that will guide the inquiry by identifying the attitudes, concepts, skills and content to be learned

Stage 4   How best will we learn?

- a range and balance of activities linked directly to the key questions

Stage 5   How will we know what we've learned?

- formative and summative assessment strategies that will be used by teachers and students

Stage 6   To what extent did we achieve our purpose?

- reflections on the degree of success

Figure 6.3   Questions for teachers

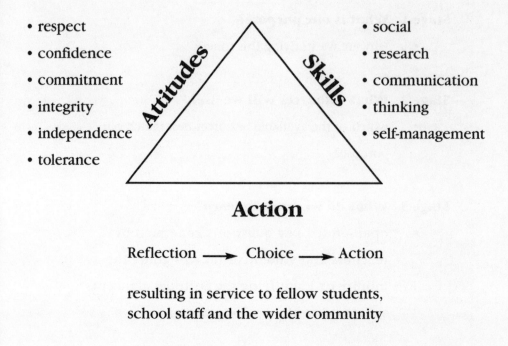

- respect
- confidence
- commitment
- integrity
- independence
- tolerance

Attitudes

Skills

- social
- research
- communication
- thinking
- self-management

Action

Reflection ⟶ Choice ⟶ Action

resulting in service to fellow students, school staff and the wider community

Figure 6.4 Skills, attitudes, action

These skills and approaches have not been developed in isolation but in the context of meaningful subject matter. In deciding on the nature of that subject matter, on a relevant knowledge base, the PYP makes one of its most significant contributions to the debate on the nature of a truly international curriculum.

Developing a shared knowledge base: learning through human commonalities

When developing an international curriculum the question of subject matter or 'knowledge' is perhaps the most difficult to resolve. With students from so many different cultures, in schools so widely dispersed, even if it is possible to decide how they should be learning, is it possible to decide what they should be learning *about*? The question, 'Whose history should be taught?' perhaps sums up the dilemma most succinctly. The response proposed by the PYP builds on the work of the late Ernest Boyer, the distinguished American writer on educational issues. In an article entitled 'An educated person' (1994), Boyer argued that there are certain areas of knowledge which are important for all people. He labelled these 'human common-

commonalities'. His suggested themes included language, art and work. While Boyer may have written primarily for a national audience, the idea of human commonalities has even greater resonance in the context of international education. The PYP takes this idea and develops it into a full programme of inquiry; a way of structuring the subject matter of the curriculum by means of the set of powerful themes shown in Figure 6.5.

Each of these themes is of sufficient depth to be of genuine significance to all cultures, and of sufficient breadth to invite exploration from multiple perspectives. They are prescriptive enough to offer a recognizable structure but open enough to allow schools to reflect the local context. Within the framework provided by these themes teachers and students design individual units of inquiry at each grade level. These units enhance the students' knowledge and understanding of aspects of the theme. Although the programme transcends the barriers of the traditional school subjects it preserves the essence of the disciplines of knowledge. While it may not guarantee that students are exposed to history lessons it will ensure that students are exposed to the lessons of history. This thematic framework provides a vehicle for much of the sequence of conceptual development and skills acquisition integral to the curriculum. Many skills may also be taught through single-subject lessons. The PYP acknowledges the need to focus on the 'tools' of inquiry as well as on the subject matter. There is great potential for combining aspects of units from one theme with units from another. For example, in one PYP-authorized school, the unit 'The miracle of birth' is linked to other Grade 6 units; 'The rights of the child' and 'Move over: The problems of over-population', to form a broader theme to shape a year's work. There is potential, too, for an even more interesting innovation, and one that has major implications when considering the importance of an international curriculum for the primary years. Some PYP-authorized schools are designing a vertical progression of units within each theme, so that the units themselves are sequentially linked. An example is shown in Figure 6.6.

Through this progression students explore some of the major human experiences: birth, exercising independence, forming relationships, living with different generations, coping with bereavement. In examining these from a variety of cultural perspectives they learn how different peoples perceive and address these life-shaping issues. They respond to some of the universal questions of human existence. Through their active engagement in these inquiries they bring their direct and diverse personal experiences into the classroom, to the benefit of themselves, their peers and their teachers.

In designing these sequences within the setting of PYP schools a further point has emerged to reinforce the importance of the primary curriculum and its impact on the years that follow. It has become apparent that the traditional barriers between primary and secondary education present an artificial barrier to the continuous development of important ideas. Figure 6.6 illustrates one of many possibilities for the exploration of significant concepts in a systematic way, providing initial exposure in the primary years and building on this learning throughout the secondary school. The themes suggested in the PYP offer a structure for an international knowledge base that would bring shape and substance to the integration of

Organizing themes for an international programme of inquiry into:

1. who we are
An exploration of the nature of the self; spiritual; of our families, friends, communities and cultures; of our rights and responsibilities; of what it means to be human.

2. where we are... in place and time
An exploration of our orientation in place and time; of our personal 'histories and geographies'; of history and geography from a local and global perspective: of our own homes and journeys – actual and spiritual; of the greater journeys of humankind – the discoveries, explorations and migrations; of human achievement and the contributions of individuals and civilizations; of the descent and ascent of humankind; of the state of the species.

3. how we express ourselves
An exploration of the ways in which we discover and express our nature, our ideas, feelings, beliefs and values through the arts and through our languages, including the language of mathematics.

4. how the world works
An exploration of the physical and material world; of nature and human-made phenomena; of the worlds of applied mathematics, science and technology.

5. how we organize ourselves
An exploration of human systems and communities, of the world of work, its nature and its value, of employment and unemployment and their impact, both personal and global.

6. sharing the planet
An exploration of our rights and responsibilities as we strive to share finite resources... with other people... with other species; of individuals and communities, human and animal, and of the relationships within and among them.

Figure 6.5 Organizing themes for an international programme of inquiry

Who we are

Grade 5: The mystery of life

An introduction to sex education

Grade 6: The miracle of birth

Understanding human birth, birth control and early child care –
how different cultures raise their children

Grade 7: Learning to say no

Making safe and healthy decisions

Grade 8: Making a commitment

Building meaningful relationships – how different cultures
view marriage and divorce

Grade 9: Growing old

Coping with ageing – how different cultures cope with ageing
and care for the elderly

Grade 10: Living with loss

Coping with bereavement – how different cultures deal with
death and dying

Figure 6.6 An example of a sequential progression of thematic units

content areas in the Middle Years programme, and suggest a direction for greater integration of traditional disciplines in the Diploma programme. They offer a central core that would begin to transform the 'sections' of the IB curriculum from three separate, if philosophically similar, curricula into one coherent international curriculum.

AN INTERNATIONAL PRIMARY CURRICULUM... MORE OR LESS IMPORTANT?

How important, then, is the development of a common curriculum for international schools? For those who believe in efficiency it is important for reasons of practicality. The benefits to schools of a shared curriculum are considerable. The pooling of knowledge and experience; the savings in time, energy, money; all point to the sheer common sense of working towards the goal of a common curriculum. The benefits to globally mobile families in terms of security, continuity and quality are equally apparent. For those who believe in the ideals of international education, in the vision of an approach to teaching and learning which can genuinely change schools and the individuals within them, then it is important for reasons of powerful belief. The benefits of a common *international* curriculum, one which sets out to develop internationally minded graduates – individuals who have spent their time in schools engaged in structured inquiry into subject matter of genuine, universal significance – are equally substantial, if less tangible.

Whether one considers the question of an international curriculum from a practical or from a philosophical standpoint one conclusion is inescapable: such a curriculum must begin in the primary school. Skills, habits of mind, attitudes, a common knowledge base – these are not developed in the final two years, or even in the final seven years of a child's life in school. They are developed by many years of contact with important ideas. They are nurtured over many years by methodologies that promote a sense of wonder, that provide the tools necessary to turn wonder into research, that create a climate in which it is safe to take risks and in which the ideas of others are sought out and given value. They are fostered by exposure to a knowledge base that represents the common ground of human experience, and explores that common ground from a multiplicity of cultural perspectives. Crucially, they are developed by starting early. If the IB is truly to become an international curriculum for schools it must become a programme in which the MYP and Diploma programme build on the foundations laid in the primary years. The IB must begin at age three. Without the foundations of the primary years the later years will never yield their full potential. *With* those foundations the IBO will offer a curriculum capable of having a profound effect on the nature of schools and school systems, national and international, world-wide.

How important is the development of a coherent international curriculum? It is profoundly important. How important are the primary years within the international curriculum? They are vital.

REFERENCES

Boyer, E (1994) 'An educated person', in Association for Supervision and Curriculum Development (ASCD), *Yearbook: Towards a Coherent Curriculum,* Alexandria, Virginia

Hagoort, T (1994) 'A message from the president', *IB World*, 6, p 11

International Baccalaureate Organization (1994) *The Middle Years Programme*, IBO, Geneva

International Baccalaureate Organization (1997) *The Primary Years Programme*, IBO, Geneva

7

GLOBAL ISSUES: A NECESSARY COMPONENT OF A BALANCED CURRICULUM FOR THE TWENTY-FIRST CENTURY

Colin Jenkins

A CHALLENGE FOR ALL

The 1990s are the age of globalization. The 1980s were those of the multinational company, and the 1970s and 1960s of a growing awareness of international action to combat tensions of one kind or another. The 1950s and 1940s marked the consequences of the failure to communicate – and before that came the growth of the nation state. Our century marks the evolution of nationalism while other powerful forces point in a contrary direction. We face the new millennium aware more than ever before of our interdependence. The environment, population growth, economic dependence on growth, materialism, and even conscience colour our thoughts and actions. Imperialist thinking, exploitation of natural resources, intolerance of others are all old instincts that prompt self-doubt, guilt and even loss of self-esteem. We all, and especially the young, know that things cannot go on as they are. Power bases throughout the world must now have that niggling doubt about what the future holds.

The 1990s have seen great empires fall – the Soviet Union, South African apartheid, the culture of dictatorship in Latin America, the tests of nuclear missiles and the isolationism of China. New pressures and tensions have increasingly taken their place, which are much harder to control. Population growth, drought, starvation, ozone holes, global warming, crime and social breakdown are not manageable within the nation state. Resolving them requires cooperation, compromise, understanding and respect. Do these qualities emerge by chance or can they be aided by education? Other skills and qualities form the core of educational aims, so why not these? Teaching students about the realities of the future seems to be a responsibility we have no right to shirk if our education is to mean anything. Teaching about these realities without exploring solutions and the action students, as future citizens, can take would seem a barren response to a very real future shock.

Of course there have been responses, and many schools and colleges have been innovative and thoughtful in alerting their students to the world that will be theirs. What seems to be absent is any coherence, system or planning and above all any all inclusiveness and comprehensiveness in tackling the issues. An inspired discussion in class from time to time, in one school or another, seems a long way from facing up to the stark realities which must be the property of everyone.

A CURRICULUM PERSPECTIVE

There is much debate about the place of 'key skills' in national curricula, but little about 'key knowledge' and 'key action'. The step has not yet been taken where an education minister stands up and says 'this is what we have to do – provide key knowledge about the world we face' and 'here is the key action we can undertake to combat the evils that lie ahead'. It is the 'key action' that turns the matter from the defensive and the depressing to the positive and forward looking. Above all a sense of optimism is needed that seemingly intractable problems have solutions. What would or could a minister propose as a suitable curriculum? Do models exist that are predicated on the development of key knowledge and key action? An attempt to respond to such problems has come from the United World Colleges (UWC). The first of ten of these colleges now found in countries around the world was opened in Wales in 1962. Their shared primary aim is stated in the mission statement (revised 1995): 'Through international education, shared experience and community service, United World Colleges enable young people to become responsible citizens, politically and environmentally aware, committed to the ideals of peace, justice, understanding and co-operation and to the implementation of these ideals through action and personal example.'

The students of the colleges are selected on merit and funded by scholarships from some 100 countries. Their role is summed up in the words of the UWC Council President, Nelson Mandela, taken from a speech given to the UWC International Council in Johannesburg in November 1996: 'The virtue and strength of UWC is that it provides small but powerful cells of innovation, catalysts for change, breaking learners of habit and opening broader vistas of experience for both students and educationalists.'

There is little doubt that most of these intentions are met with appropriate strategies in the several colleges, but a telling phrase in President Mandela's comment is 'small but powerful cells of innovation'. The colleges have no reason to apologize for doing what they do and yet the problem of global education seems to require more than 'small cells'. UWCs are but one model in the search for the development of a value system in which interdependence and global well-being is the aim.

Another model is provided by the International Baccalaureate Organization

(IBO). The IB was devised in the late 1960s to provide an internationally acceptable university admissions qualification suitable for the growing mobile population of young people whose parents were part of the world of diplomacy, international and multinational organizations. In its design, though, this utilitarian function was but a part of the curriculum that eventually saw the light of day. What emerged was a liberal yet rigorous and coherent programme that challenged its students to develop a whole range of skills and expertise while at the same time preparing them for specialist advancement in higher education. It is apparent from the mission statement of the IB (IBO, 1996) that more than academic preparation was the aim.

> Through comprehensive and balanced curricula, coupled with challenging assessments, the International Baccalaureate Organization aims to assist schools in their endeavours to develop the individual talents of young people and teach them to relate the experience of the classroom to the realities of the world outside. Beyond intellectual rigour and high academic standards, strong emphasis is placed on the ideals of international understanding and responsible citizenship, to the end that IB students may become critical and compassionate thinkers, lifelong learners and informed participants in local and world affairs, conscious of the shared humanity that binds all people together while respecting the variety of cultures and attitudes that makes for the richness of life.

This mission statement sets lofty targets, but are they achievable and are they being achieved? Certainly the IBO now has programmes in the primary and middle years as well as in the more established and well-known post-16 Diploma programme. It is clear that academic standards need to be high and that something called international understanding is of importance. The 'Baccalaureate' part of the formula is well established and respected, but it is the 'International' we need to explore. IB Diploma students must complete courses in their best language (Language A), a second language, a humanities subject, a science, and mathematics, with the option to select a further programme in any of these areas or studies in art, music or theatre. The syllabuses in each area fulfil international aims. In Language A a component of the course is world literature, studies of literature originally written in another language and from a different cultural tradition. The second language is self-explanatory. Humanities subjects such as history, economics and geography all have programmes in which world or global themes play a significant part, and a compulsory Theory of Knowledge course touches on cultural diversity in the search for knowledge. It is clear that the IB has great strengths, but again the amount of 'internationalism' in a programme depends on which combination of subjects a student may choose. This leads to a feeling that it just misses the target of a truly comprehensive global programme for all.

The IB is itself very international, with examiners and students throughout the world, but this does not impinge on the educational development of any individual student. To its credit the IBO has always attempted to try to provide this deeper internationality – its Blackburn Prize for a social service project, its publications including the work of students from around the world and its frequent meetings, all serve to provide the glue of internationality in its activities. All of this is, however, just a well-constructed net where the mesh is top quality – probably the best available – but there remain all those holes through which students may fall.

Again there have been responses by the IB through, for example, its enlightened system of allowing school-based syllabuses – one of the six courses required of a student may be created at a school or college (and the examination moderated by the IB). This has allowed the development of courses such as Peace Studies, World Religions, the Culture and History of Islam, Marine Science and Environmental Studies. The last three of these have progressed to becoming 'open offer' mainstream subjects. All are contributing to the internationalism of the IB programme, but not to ensuring that all students in the programme follow these courses. They do not block the holes in the net.

A GLOBAL RESPONSE

It was this inadequacy that led to a consideration of some way of making the 'International' in the International Baccalaureate more obvious and more all-embracing – indeed of making it a requirement. It is accepted that the International Baccalaureate programme has a very high standard of rigour, and indeed the huge demands that it makes on students have given rise to complaints from time to time. Adding anything to this heavy programme was therefore seen as being practically difficult and politically impossible, and proponents of the introduction of a compulsory Global Concerns programme ran into great resistance in the councils of the IB. The case was accepted, but the implementation was seen as problematic. The IB does, however, benefit from a number of core requirements, which include a compulsory piece of independent and individual research (the Extended Essay), a course of 100 hours in the 'Theory of Knowledge' and an involvement in creative and physical activities, and community service. Some practitioners felt that it was in these compulsory elements that a Global Concerns programme could be introduced. Recent discussions in IB circles have seen a new mood of determination to include elements that address global issues, although the means by which this may be implemented have not yet been determined.

The question must always be at the front of our minds – are global issues a necessary component of a balanced curriculum for the twenty-first century? It is the case that most of our curriculum in the twentieth century, certainly its latter half, has been unchanging. Syllabuses have changed, of course, as have assessment strategies, but 16+ and 18+ examinations and courses have been merely remodelled to take account of educational research and social needs. No radical thinking has been introduced in which a detailed consideration is made of what young people need in order to face their working lives in the twenty-first century. The context of the years 2010–50 has not really been addressed and it is in these years that today's school pupils will be working and living. We are all subject to the doomsday scenarios of the media and of literature. The Antarctic is melting, it is not safe to sunbathe, tribal and religious conflict and violence are rarely out of the news, the information technology revolution is changing our lives, social structures appear to be breaking down. The mood is of decline and fall and not of optimism – or even of consideration of what the future may bring. Of course, there is the excitement of the year 2000 and the millennium celebration, but on the cold dawn of 1 January 2000 the future will stretch ahead. What will it hold? How are we preparing the coming generations to face it? In education our eyes are firmly on standards, but are they standards for the right things?

Education perhaps should be about standards, but not only so, for it would otherwise result in a sterile and narrow approach. Too often we are concerned about systems, styles of school, programmes and curricula and of the 'needs of society'. These latter are nearly always measured in terms of qualifications and outcomes that relate either to preparation for more education or to suitability for the workplace. Society seems to stop at the office desk or the factory floor in most of our educational strategies and policies. Is it not incumbent upon us to do a little more than that? This depressing scenario might stimulate many countering arguments from dedicated people who have been trying to answer these questions and to introduce broader aims. General Studies courses, model UN debates, exchange visits to foreign countries and much else can be cited as fine examples of the search for more than examination results. How many young people benefit from these? How serious are they? Is there an all-pervading ethos underlying them? Yet again, how many people fall through the holes in the net?

There is, of course, a huge difficulty in trying to establish what does lie before us. Predictions throughout this century have been notoriously unreliable. The Club of Rome report in 1961 predicted all sorts of calamities in the environment and in the exhaustion of resources that are now dismissed as nonsense. The thinkers in that group have been derided as scaremongers. New oil, new gas, new resources are constantly being found – there is no problem! Greenpeace, Friends of the Earth and many other pressure groups have been tarred with the brush of panic merchants and as being 'unrealistic'. While all these people appear to have been proved wrong the television in the background is showing yet another programme on the destruction of the Amazonian rainforest. The case for preparing young people for the future must be at the core of all we do. This preparation must not be about destruction, failure and misery but rather about hope and success, and the actions that will bring these about. That is why we must look at a global issues approach for everyone.

PRACTICALITIES

What would such a course look like and what would it contain? What would it try to achieve? Its texts should not just be Alvin Toffler's *Future Shock* or Rachel Carson's *Silent Spring*, but should be rather more geared to action: to training, not for the workplace, but for an attitude to our common social needs and to producing a healthy, fair planet on which to live sustainably. What do we all want? Health, comfortable homes, happy children with a future. What do we feel unhappy about? Exploitation, injustice, fear of the future. A global concerns education must surely address these concerns and it will be quickly apparent that mere knowledge of the world is not enough. Values, attitudes and the will to act must also find their place. This is dangerous territory as the questions of whose values and whose attitudes begin to surface in the sceptics whose vision does not support this thesis.

There are, however, attitudes and values that are common and that should not cause alarm. Most religions have very specific sets of values clearly and overtly expressed. Billions of people follow these religions, and most of the values can only support ideas of kindness and justice. The secular Bible or Koran is to be found in the declarations of the United Nations. We have all signed up to them through our governments and they are all about attitudes and values. We do not need to be shy or reticent in including them in our education programmes.

At the United World College of the Atlantic we approach our Global Concerns programme with three underpinning guidelines – knowledge, attitudes and values, and action. There is one further element that must also be considered. The last thing such a programme needs is to be seen as yet another course. Students have immediate needs, such as passing examinations, that inevitably crowd out other important needs that seem not essential just now. Nor must it be seen as simply the preparation for another examination. Students need to share in the concept that they are, and certainly will be building the world of the future. They need to be part of the construction and delivery of this educational experience. The sceptics will frown. Are not students supposed to do what they are told? Such cynicism cannot be part of something which is too important for that. Let us not undervalue what young people have to say to us. Perhaps the hedonistic attitudes of western youth have developed because we do not enter into partnership with them. The young will always rebel, but they will also respond to need and to being asked rather than being told. Theirs is the world of the twenty-first century; what do they want it to be? Our job is to use experience and knowledge to support and guide, and to help prevent them from falling into the pits that lie before them – or, in more current mode, the landmines that are scattered unseen on the pathway.

Knowledge

What might they, and we argue should be included in a Global Concerns programme? What do they need to have knowledge of? Many people have tackled such questions. The United Nations has defined four major areas of concern: (i) the environment, (ii) peace and conflict, (iii) food and famine, and (iv) wealth and poverty, and to these we can add or pick out issues of sustainability, north/south inequalities, human rights, technology and change, resources and social issues, including health. The skeleton of a programme emerges from these headings. Where do we find them in our present school curricula?

In international schools there are human resources for the delivery of knowledge in these areas. The students often come from diverse backgrounds or have lived in societies where many of the issues have been far from theoretical. The displaced refugee, the youngster who has walked along the streets of Maputo, the Malaysian who has breathed the polluted smog of 1997, have all experienced the pain of injustice or the signals to what lies in the future. The students of national schools do not, however, just have to think about the problems of Bosnia, Rwanda or Papua New Guinea. They too have the experience of beggars in the street, the insecurities of a crime-ridden society or the pollution from the most recent tanker disaster. The delivery of the 'knowledge' in any Global Concerns programme would seem to gain its strength, not from some didactic expert driving it forward, but from a sense of partnership. We are all in the same boat; should we not all share in rowing it?

This approach would help to avoid the programme falling into that most terrible of all pits – 'if it isn't examined, then I'm not going to waste time on it'. Common sets of values may only become apparent by exchange and shared effort and by showing respect when the ideas may be naive and ill-considered. Critical to the success of such a programme must be the sense of common ownership.

The factual resources available for such a programme are legion. The United Nations and its agencies produce huge quantities of materials. The public media, press, television and factual literature explore these issues in copious quantities. Even fiction writing provides an eloquent eye on the world and on these great issues. The problems in guiding such a course are how to be selective and how to find the time. The first requires experience and knowledge, and as for the time, surely the issue is too important to fall prey to all the excuses that it is not possible. No Global Concerns programme can be introduced in a half-hearted way – it must have the total commitment of the institution and of the people in it. That commitment can only come when people are persuaded of its value and importance. Once persuaded, anything is possible.

Polemic of this kind is, however, not very helpful to the practising educator. What can we do to find room and time for this programme in a crowded curriculum? There are two possible strategies; one is to make it an add-on adjunct to all else the student does, the second is to integrate the themes into the rest of the students' programme. To take the first: it is difficult to see how to find the time and the people to do it. But the people are all of us: we have a responsibility not to sit outside these issues. The question of time is more difficult. Perhaps a two-day workshop in each term could be given over to these issues: worthwhile, but with an air of the 'special occasion' rather than of the all-important core of the educational programme. A successful model that has been tried is to sacrifice one lesson (or more) in each week, but not the same one. Each subject or timetable slot thus loses a lesson only infrequently – in one week it may be mathematics, in the next history and so on. This is hardly going to destroy progress in these subjects and yet the importance of the programme is perceived by all in the institution. The second way is to integrate the themes into the mainstream programme by creating a series of modules which every student would have to cover. Let us say each module accounted for one week of work and there were eight such modules in which the important issues were tabled. What would be lost? Our education should be tackling contemporary issues in any case; a structure for doing so could only enhance the process. Each college or school will find its own best model as suits its own circumstances and there may, of course, be many more to consider.

Attitudes and values

What then are the values and attitudes that will arise from addressing global issues? First and foremost will be that sense of responsibility for others, from the next-door neighbour to the victims of famine or violence in some distant part of the world. A sense of friendship and partnership should also develop. We must do something together for our planet and our society and lose the concept of foreigners, at least in this respect. We are all people – people who live in Ethiopia, people who live in California, people who live in Buenos Aires, people who live next door. We are all people who to varying degrees are suffering the same ills and who will certainly do so in the future. Our education systems do not establish this common interest and give it scant attention in the design of syllabuses and programmes. Could it be that our endangered national and local social structures would be strengthened if the attitudes of friendship and need for cooperation were established as values that we cannot do without if our children and theirs are to have any kind of happy life?

Action

All of this is idealist and 'removed' from reality, but can be made more immediate by bringing in the third element of any Global Concerns programme – action. Schools and colleges are aware of this and many institute and encourage ways in which some support is given to those in need. The United World Colleges have made 'community service' a formal requirement. Students spend significant periods of each working week undertaking responsibilities that cannot be set aside because others depend on it. It is rare to find a student who does not value the experience, even if it was reluctantly or fearfully entered into at first. This is not some 'box ticking' exercise where various tasks must be fulfilled, but rather a total commitment for hour upon hour, week upon week and often year upon year. Many students consider the most important outcome of their studies as not being the diploma or certificate for academic worth, but rather the sense of personal achievement and the feeling of being really useful that comes from service. The International Baccalaureate took this idea from Atlantic College, the first of the United World Colleges, and now includes service as a requirement in its Creativity, Action, Service (CAS) programme. This is a unique and admirable element that neatly turns the International Baccalaureate Organization from being a mere 'examination board' into a system of education.

In the report *The Education of Young People* (1997) the YMCA and five other bodies identify the essential qualities gained by young people from their education as being:

- establishing a sense of values
- coping with change – being flexible and adaptable
- developing a sense of belonging and identity
- developing a sense of usefulness through contributing to the needs of their community
- learning to recognize the value of cooperation and teamwork.

The commitment to community service does all of these things more powerfully than any form of education. In the UK, the late John Smith MP, leader of the Labour Party, and the Prince of Wales have written and spoken eloquently about the ideas of service and of community partnership, but where is the response? It does occur valuably and honourably all over the country, but not comprehensively. The net is there but the holes are big. Well-meaning and experienced people need to put their heads together to find ways of filling the holes. There is no shortage of need, but it is essential that it is the need that becomes the important motivation, not merely hierarchical instruction. Kurt Hahn, co-founder of Atlantic College, expressed it most effectively (1961): 'There are three ways of trying to capture the young. One is to preach at them – this is a hook without a worm. The second is to coerce them to tell them "you must volunteer" – that is of the devil. The third, an appeal which never fails, "you are needed".'

A student of Atlantic College, Julie Payette, now a member of the Canadian astronaut team, said it even more succinctly in 1997: 'Together – we can'.

A GLOBALLY BALANCED CURRICULUM

So much about the balanced curriculum for the twenty-first century seems to need a starting point very different from the traditional. If values, attitudes and a commitment to service to others are the starting point then perhaps the balanced curriculum will look a little different. The skills and knowledge for employment must be there, of course, but they must not, as now, be exclusive of all else.

What hope is there of the introduction of global concerns into our curricula? National developments differ from country to country. If the UK is anything to go by then these issues are far from the centre of thinking. Revisions and proposals for post-16 education fail even to mention the need and are totally preoccupied with a 'don't rock the boat' philosophy. Educators are told to think radically but on condition that nothing must change too much. The starting point is not the twenty-first century or what it will bring: the starting point seems to be what the last 20 years tell us about where we should not go. But the last 20 years are totally irrelevant to what today's young people must face. Of course, there are the radical thinkers. Certainly, in the IB, the Middle Years Programme and the Primary Year Programme adopt an interesting approach that recognizes our interdependence as a species. The IB Diploma is trying, albeit painfully, to resolve ways of doing it – but it is asking the right questions, and sooner or later a solution will emerge. Yet again the IB will be doing things that the orthodox educational world does not regard as possible or even desirable.

An eccentric (in the best sense) effort has been made in Wales to introduce a Welsh Baccalaureate, which includes a global concerns and community partnership element (Jenkins *et al.*, 1997). The eccentricity of the proposal has not deterred the country from demonstrating huge support. Sixty per cent of the schools support it, the university is embarrassingly enthusiastic and major employers, including the Confederation of British Industry, have given it support. Perhaps this is the only measure there is at the moment of the mood of the wider public, those who live outside the doors of a government ministry or the portals of the educational establishment.

UNESCO defines the educational process as being:

- formal: the hierarchically structured, chronologically graded educational system running from primary through to tertiary institutions
- informal: where individuals acquire attitudes, values, skills and knowledge from daily experience, such as from family, friends, peer groups, the media and other influences and factors in the person's environment
- non-formal: ie education organized outside the formal established system that is intended to serve an identifiable learning clientele with identifiable learning objectives.

Jacques Delors, writing in the UNESCO report *Learning: The Treasure Within* by the International Commission on Education for the 21st Century (1996), defines education as being established on four pillars: learning to know, learning to do, learning to live together, learning to be. Ibtissam Al-Bassam, senior programme specialist in the section for humanities, cultural and international education at UNESCO, is promoting cooperation between international schools and national schools on developing education for peace and international understanding.

A recent report *The Education of Young People* published jointly by the YMCA, YWCA, the Scout movement, the Guide and Girl Scout movement, the Red Cross and Red Crescent societies and the International Award Association (1997) subtitles its pamphlets *A Statement at the Dawn of the 21st Century*. These are examples of the sense of disquiet that is beginning to permeate all good thinking people that 'something must be done'. Each of the examples stands high as being well meaning and inspiring, but each falls into the same trap, as have many previous attempts. None is able to guarantee comprehensive cover of students. Each will appeal to a small number who will respond to the ideals expressed. The problem is knowing how to appeal to, draw in and persist with the vast majority who will probably resist. This is too important to be left to well-meaning agencies. The answer lies in one quarter only, and that is in the hands of national governments. UNESCO can work, as it does, to persuade schools, colleges and teachers to respond to its work, but of every 100 documents sent out, how many arrive? How many are read? How many are discarded? How many make anything happen? It is sad to be so cynical about something one supports so wholeheartedly but busy people, with busy lives, do not take kindly to yet more 'junk mail'!

The case is clear, the need is urgent. Who will do anything about it?

References

Hahn, K (1961) Lecture delivered at Bourneville, Birmingham, England

International Baccalaureate Organization (1996) 'Education for life: The mission statement of the IB', *IB World*, 13, p 7

Jenkins, C, David, J, Osmond, J and Pierce, J (1997) *The Welsh Baccalaureate: Educating Wales in the Next Century*, Institute of Welsh Affairs, Cardiff

United World Colleges (1995) *Annual Report*, UWC, London

UNESCO (1996) *Learning: The Treasure Within*, International Commission on Education for the 21st Century, UNESCO, Paris

YMCA (1997) *The Education of Young People: A Statement at the Dawn of the 21st Century*, World Alliance of YMCA, Geneva

8

EDUCATION FOR PEACE:
THE CORNERSTONE OF INTERNATIONAL EDUCATION

Philip Thomas

A CHEQUERED HISTORY IN SCHOOLS

In November 1994 the ministers of education assembled for the 44th session of the International Conference on Education organized by UNESCO in Geneva and adopted a resolution wherein it is stated (UNESCO, 1994) that they will:

2. Strive resolutely
2.1 to base education on principles and methods that contribute to the development of the personality of pupils, students and adults who are respectful of their fellow human beings and determined to promte peace, human rights and democracy;
2.2 to take suitable steps to establish in educational institutions an atmosphere contributing to the sucess of education for international understanding, so that they become ideal places for the exercise of tolerance, respect for human rights, the practice of democracy and learning about the diversity and wealth of cultural identities...

In the same declaration other points seek to eliminate all direct and indirect discrimination against girls and women; to identify the need to improve resources and technologies 'with a view to educating caring and responsible citizens... respectful of human dignity and differences, and able to prevent conflicts or resolve them by non-violent means'; to address the issue of professional development of teachers in the field of what can be described as Education for Peace, and to seek to encourage innovative strategies adapted to the 'new challenges of educating responsible citizens committed to peace, human rights, democracy and sustainable development'.

It comes as a pleasant surprise to learn that such a strident call for placing Education for Peace at the core of education practices in the world's schools has come from education ministers who, in the context of their own national systems, have been traditionally associated with a mission of seeking to produce citizens proud of their national identities and heritage, and willing to give up their lives if proud of their national identities and heritage, and willing to give up their lives if necessary in the service of their country. Educational history over the past 100 years is strewn with the relics of well-intentioned programmes attempting to introduce 'Peace Studies' into schools. It is an issue that has become highly politicized, and few initiatives have successfully outlived the changes of party politics as governments swing from one side of the political spectrum to the other. The 1994 resolution therefore represents a major step forward in recognizing that overcoming prejudice and ideological differences, and addressing the social injustices that are the source of conflict, is primarily an educational process. It also recognizes that this cannot effectively be achieved while education continues to serve purely nationalistic ends. It requires an international education system to seek out and reinforce those values, emphasizing global interdependence.

In a short journal abstract entitled 'Early tendencies of peace education in Sweden', Thelin (1996) offers a brief survey of the situation in his native country and shows how Peace Education became an established concept in the 1980s. However, his researches revealed that it had a much longer history: 'from the second part of the nineteenth century, peace ideas and peace movements grew stronger and stronger in Europe and the United States. Aggressive nationalism, militarism and war heroism were severely criticized. Diplomacy and arbitration were called for instead of violence and weapons to solve international conflicts.' He notes that 400 peace associations existed world-wide by the turn of the century, including the Inter-Parliamentary Union (1889) and the International Peace Bureau (1891). The Hague conferences of 1899 and 1907 were, according to Thelin's researches, 'the first international conferences between governments... convened to discuss how to preserve peace'. However, since neither education nor suffrage had yet reached the masses, 'a rather one-sided emphasis on force and virility, war and war heroes' was more common in the literature used in schools than that portraying a peaceful attitude. Thelin also notes that if any discussion took place it was either in the context of the teaching of history or of religion. He records, with interest, the role of the feminist movement in propagating change, with the Peace Group of Swedish Female Teachers established in 1916.

World War I, Thelin argues, 'functioned as a driving force in convincing public opinion to look upon education as a means for bringing about a changed mentality'. When a new national curriculum was introduced in Sweden in 1919 he notes that history instruction should have had as 'its leading thread(s) peaceful, cultural and societal development'. However the events of the 1930s caused 'disappointment and pessimism' for the peace education movement and kept discussion largely on the macro level (open warfare) rather than the micro level (violence within societies and families). Thelin also shows how peace movements have long been criticized in education for being politically biased, fuelled in post-World War II years by the cold war syndrome. One can conclude that most politicians have sought to keep peace off their educational agendas. Even within such an international organization as the International Baccalaureate Organization (IBO), whose member schools seek to promote international understanding, the Peace and Conflict Studies course developed at Atlantic College has never been adopted by other schools; indeed it came in for a withering attack from the then Minister of Education for the UK, Margaret Thatcher. Neither does peace figure with any prominence as such in the current International Baccalaureate Middle Years or Primary Years Programmes.

Conversely the situation in higher education has been conspicuously more favourable, perhaps reflecting the greater independence enjoyed by universities. Ake Bjerstedt at the Malmo School of Education has been an untiring and prolific writer on the subject. The University of Bradford in the UK, the University of Minnesota in the USA, the School of Peace Education at Carleton in Canada, and the United Nations University in Costa Rica are but a few of the institutions that have built solid reputations for serious research and innovative programmes in aspects of peace education. Strangely, not many of these influences have found their way into practical programmes for use in primary or secondary schools but, since the mid-late 1980s, a major shift has taken place in various aspects of peace education at school level. Much of this can be attributed to the phenomenon of the internationalization of education, although it has been painfully slow in emerging. At last education seems to be facing up to the challenge of the process of globalization.

GLOBALIZATION: PROBLEMS AND OPPORTUNITIES

Osler and Starkey (1996) define globalization as the term:

> used to describe the increasing interdependence of national economies, the integration of financial markets, the increasing power and influence and scale of transnational corporations and media and communications that cover the whole world. A further dimension is provided by the environmental movement. This has raised consciousness of threats to the global commons and the necessity for international co-operation.

Many would wish to argue that this global corporate expansion has its negative as well as positive sides. Many states have to cope with the problem of large-scale unemployment over which they have relatively little control, since the employers are multinational corporations. The increasing international mobility of labour has sometimes led to ethnic tensions and outbreaks of racism and xenophobia. There is an obvious disparity of resource utilization as described by the Bruntland Commission in *Our Common Future* (1987) and there is also the threat of diminishing world resources as observed by the Club of Rome's investigations. Many observers point to the erosion of family values, to the failure to prevent discrimination and to increasing crime rates as insecurity reigns in most societies. Yet despite these very real problems and concerns there have been remarkable changes over the last 50 years which have enabled peace education to be viewed as an essential element in the curriculum of all schools. Some of these changes include:

- profound changes in information technology and communications, which have helped to make the cliché 'the global village' a reality

- an increasing acceptance (arising from the above) of the value of cultural diversity and international understanding
- an increasing acceptance of the value of the interdependence of human beings and the need for greater solidarity
- the gradual acceptance of the principle of sustainable development – of the concept that the environment is a legacy that needs to be protected for future generations rather than being exploited to the maximum by the present.

This major change in accepting the value of internationalism has been due, as much as anything, to the gradual acceptance of universal ethical values that are at the core of international education and of any programme of Education for Peace. A typical proclamation on this point can be found in the report of the Commission on Global Governance (1995) on the occasion of the 50th anniversary of the founding of the United Nations.

> We also believe the world's arrangements for the conduct of its affairs must be underpinned by certain common values. Ultimately, no organization will work and no law be upheld unless they rest on a foundation made strong by shared values.
> We believe that all humanity should uphold the core values of respect for life, liberty, justice and equity, mutual respect, caring and integrity.

It may be worthwhile tracing these developments, mainly associated with human rights, in some detail, as follows.

International conventions, declarations and recommendations at the core of Education for Peace

Students of history and politics are well aware of declarations concerning human rights, such as the Declaration of American Independence (1776) or the French Revolution (1789). As Osler and Starkey remind us, it was the proclamation of the Universal Declaration of Human Rights by the General Assembly of the United Nations that was 'the first occasion on which the organised world community had recognised the existence of human rights and fundamental freedoms transcending the laws of sovereign states' (Evatt, President of the General Assembly, in Osler and Starkey, 1996).

The Charter of the United Nations, signed on 26 June 1945, proclaims:

> We, the Peoples of the United Nations determined
> - to save succeeding generations from the scourge of war, which twice in our lifetime has brought untold sorrow to mankind; and
> - to reaffirm faith in fundamental human rights, in the dignity of men and women and of nations large and small; and
> - to establish conditions under which justice and respect for the obligations arising from treaties and other sources of international law can be maintained, and to promote social progress and better standards of life in larger freedom...

maintained, and to promote social progress and better standards of life in larger freedom...

It took a further three years for these fundamental human rights to be formulated and proclaimed as the Universal Declaration of Human Rights by the General Assembly on 10 December 1948. Following this historic act the Assembly called on all member countries to publicize the text of the Declaration and 'to cause it to be disseminated, displayed, read and expounded principally in schools and other educational institutions, without distinction based on the political status of countries or territories'. I invite readers to reflect on how far this requirement takes place even today. The Universal Declaration is based on the need for human dignity and the rights of all, from which are drawn personal rights (articles 2–11); those of relationships between people (articles 12–17); public freedoms and political rights (articles 18–21); economic, social and cultural rights (articles 22–27); culminating with an international order for the realization of these rights (articles 28–30). The Universal Declaration has subsequently been reconfirmed by a series of regional declarations, and further conventions have been added over the following 50 years.

These charters and conventions thus enable us to distil a set of universal values that are based on what might be called 'international humanism'. The group of practising teachers and administrators undertaking to formulate an Education for Peace curriculum framework for the International Schools Association (ISA)/International Education System Pilot Project have produced the following list as guiding principles:

Dignity
Equality
Liberty
Justice
Responsibility
Security
Solidarity
Democracy.

Some readers may be surprised that the final principle, democracy, is so prominent as a universal value, since it appears so western (based on Greek roots) in its orientation. However, research shows that the issue has been studied widely at a series of international conferences supported or organized by UNESCO.

For educators perhaps the most seminal statement concerning international education is the Recommendation concerning Education for International Understanding, Cooperation and Peace, and Education relating to Human Rights and Fundamental Freedom adopted by the UNESCO General Assembly on 19 November 1974. Here we find almost for the first time a definition of international education intended, in the scope of the recommendations, to apply to all stages and forms of education. In an extract from the 'Significance of Terms' we read the following:

(a) The word 'education' implies the entire process of social life by means of which individuals and social groups learn to develop consciously within, and for the benefit of, the national and international communities, the whole of their personal capacities, attitudes, aptitudes and knowledge. This process is not limited to any specific activities.
(b) The terms 'international understanding', 'co-operation' and 'peace' are to be considered as an indivisible whole based on the principle of friendly relations between peoples and States having different social and political systems and on the respect for human rights and fundamental freedoms. In the text of this recommendation, the different connotations of these terms are sometimes gathered together in a concise expression 'inter national education'.
(c) Human rights and fundamental freedoms are those defined in the United Nations Charter, the Universal Declaration of Human Rights and the International Covenants on Economic, Social and Cultural Rights, and on Civil and Political Rights.

Within the 'Guiding Principles' the following are of importance.

3. Education should be infused with the aims and purposes set forth in the Charter of the United Nations, the Constitution of UNESCO and the Universal Declaration of Human Rights... which states: 'Education shall be directed to the full development of the human personality and to the strengthening of respect for human rights and fundamental freedoms. It shall promote understanding, tolerance and friendship among all nations, racial or religious groups, and shall further the activities of the United Nations for the maintenance of peace.'
4. In order to enable every person to contribute actively to the fulfilment of the aims... and promote international solidarity and co-operation, which are necessary in solving the world problems affecting the individuals' and communities' life and exercise of fundamental rights and freedoms, the following objectives should be regarded as major guiding principles of educational policy.
   (a) an international dimension and a global perspective in education at all levels and in all its forms,
   (b) understanding and respect for all peoples, their cultures, civilisations, values and ways of life, including domestic ethnic cultures and cultures of other nations,
   (c) awareness of the increasing global interdependence between peoples and nations,
   (d) abilities to communicate with others,
   (e) awareness not only of the rights but also of the duties incumbent upon individuals, social groups and nations towards each other,
   (f) understanding of the necessity for international solidarity and co-operation,
   (g) readiness on the part of the individual to participate in solving the problems of his community, his country and the world at large.
5. Combining learning, training, information and action, international education should further the appropriate intellectual and emotional development of the individual. It should develop a sense of social responsibility and of solidarity with less privileged groups and should lead to observance of the principles of equality in everyday conduct. It should also help to develop qualities, aptitudes and abilities which enable the

individual to acquire a critical understanding of problems at the national and the international level, to understand and explain facts, opinions and ideas, to work in a group, to accept and participate in free discussions, to observe the elementary rules of procedure applicable to any discussion, and to base value judgements and decisions on a rational analysis of relevant facts and factors.

6. Education should stress the inadmissibility of recourse to war for purposes of expansion, aggression and domination, or to the use of force and violence for purposes of repression, and should bring every person to understand and assume his or her responsibilities for the maintenance of peace. It should contribute to international understanding and strengthening of world peace and to the activities in the struggle against colonialism and neo-colonialism in all their forms and manifestations, and against all forms and varieties of racialism, fascism, and apartheid as well as other ideologies which breed national and racial hatred and which are contrary to the purpose of this recommendation.

These extracts represent an unequivocal statement that all national systems of education have the duty to promote international understanding and, they justify ISA's decision in 1995 to create a Pilot Project to test the feasibility of an international education system. The fundamental idea underlying the project is that such a system based on shared values, philosophy, mission, curriculum framework and objectives can produce 'active world citizens' intent on creating a better world where peace, social justice and solidarity prevail.

Development of a 'one world consciousness' over the past 50 years and its implication for Education for Peace

It is not easy to bring order to the plethora of activities that have emerged over the past 50 years, which have brought us to the point where some bold initiative can finally place Education for Peace at the heart of the curriculum of the world's varied education systems. The main argument of this chapter is that through their commitment to the concept of the United Nations states have accepted that issues need to be viewed globally, even if solutions have to be found on a local scale.

Thus one layer of activity with great importance for Education for Peace is the strengthening of the UN system which, despite intensive criticism, has had a remarkable impact on the lives of all peoples since its creation. Reference has already been made to the Declarations, Conventions and Recommendations that give substance to a universal system of values. At a more practical level are the myriad contributions of the UN specialized agencies whose publications have provided generations of teachers with ideas and materials to ensure that global issues can be addressed with reference to specific examples or case studies. The work of organizations such as the World Health Organization relating health issues to those of development, or of the World Meteorological Organization in understanding climate issues, have ensured that a global dimension is omnipresent. UNICEF and the UNHCR regularly produce teaching kits related to aspects of Education for Peace. Interestingly, UNESCO itself has not succeeded in producing very many practical materials for schools, although its Associated Schools Project has enabled students and teachers across the world to join in meaningful partnerships in the promotion of international understanding. The work of the International Committee of the Red Cross and Red Crescent can also be recognized in comparable terms. More recently the UN itself produced materials for direct use in schools, aimed at doing something more than just describing how the organization works. To celebrate its 50th anniversary handbooks were produced in English, French and Spanish for primary, middle and secondary schools. Those readers with access to the Internet will no doubt be acquainted with the materials being produced by the UN's CyberSchoolBus team. In keeping with the spirit of the agreements resulting in conventions several regional governmental organizations have produced studies, reports and initiatives emphasizing the need for closer operation. A leader in this area is the Council of Europe, which has played a leading role in facilitating closer cooperation between European states, notably in the area of pedagogy.

The emergence of the UN phenomenon has been supported by the development of separate UN Associations in most states and these have often acted as umbrella organizations for other 'players' to make an impact on raising public awareness of global issues. Thus we find several non-governmental agencies, originally created to address a particular issue mainly through campaigns and fund raising, extending their activities into the field of education and helping to promote the concepts of interdependence and solidarity that are at the core of Education for Peace. Schools world-wide have access to materials produced by such agencies as, for example, Save the Children Fund, Oxfam and the World Wide Fund for Nature.

Other groups of 'players' helping to promote the movement for world peace and security have been the campaign groups or issues-based organizations. To recognize but a few: the work of Amnesty International in the area of human rights has led to chapters being formed at school level all over the world, and the Campaign for Nuclear Disarmament (CND), which kept the issue of nuclear weapons in the forefront of public awareness, enabling those schools who wished to address this issue in terms of global security to do so. Other sources include such organizations as Human Rights Watch, CAFOD and Earth Action, all of which have relevant websites.

Another level of activity has been through those associations specifically targeting the youth range, promoting the spirit of cooperation and international understanding. My first experience of a global dimension came in 1948 at a Ritchie Calder lecture organized by the Council for Education in World Citizenship (CEWC). I was also influenced by 'Dydd Ewyllys Dda' or 'Goodwill Day', which is the message of the children of Wales to the children of the world, broadcast since 1924 by the BBC for the URDD (the Welsh Youth Movement) to commemorate the first peace conference in The Hague on 18 May 1919. The URDD was just one of many fervent patriotic youth movements in Europe in the interwar years, many of which unfortunately adopted intense nationalistic and even Fascist tendencies. The emphasis since 1945 has, thankfully, been on exchange, understanding, and cooperation, as witnessed by pen-pal schemes, school exchanges and encounters such as the International Youth Science Forum held annually in London, or the World

Scholar Athlete games held every four years in the USA. Even multinational corporations, often quoted as another major phenomenon of the second half of the twentieth century, have made significant contributions, although these are sometimes seen as a subtle means of advertising to susceptible future consumers.

The disparate threads of 'peace education'

In keeping with these trends and initiatives several schools of thought have emerged over the past 50 years dealing with issues which could be included in a programme called 'Education for Peace'. Indeed it is the gradual convergence of these separate approaches that allows us now to design a curriculum framework that encompasses them all.

'Peace and Conflict Studies' seems the most obvious place to start. If we take the Atlantic College IB school-based programme as an example, this seeks to analyse the major causes of conflict at an intellectual level and, through case studies, examine the strategies by which conflicts can be resolved peacefully rather than by resorting to violence or war. Some would argue that such analyses should occur within well-planned history programmes at school level. It is far more common to find Peace and Conflict studies programmes at university level, under the influence of leading thinkers in this field. Such 'peace programmes' claim to have a disciplinary base and appear as distinct departments in the institutions in question. In the already overcrowded, subject-specific programmes of our schools, this may be one reason why they do not figure more prominently; another might be their perceived political bias, associated with left-wing movements and thus anathema to any right-wing administrations in office. Associated with such an approach are the numerous projects that advocate non-violence and conflict resolution practices. These, in educational terms, emphasize process and concentrate on the resolution of conflicts at classroom level or the eradication of bullying in schools. As examples of such projects, one can cite the Center for Teaching Peace in Washington, DC, which produces pamphlets for schools explaining the difference between peace studies: 'the literature and history of peacemaking...' and mediation: 'the skill and methods of peacefully settling disputes' (*Peace Times*, 1996).

Concern for promoting international understanding, with schools offering a world perspective to their students, has led to a movement that we can call 'global education'. Several educators have been active in this field, the most prolific possibly being Graham Pike and David Selby operating from the Centre for Global Education of the University of York, UK. In *Global Teacher, Global Learner* (Pike and Selby, 1988), they distinguish what they call the 'four interlocking dimensions of globality' – namely spatial, temporal, the issues and the human potential dimensions. They reject the earlier 'mechanistic paradigms' emanating from advances in scientific thinking in favour of a 'systematic or holistic' paradigm that has been 'influenced and invigorated by the findings of modern atomic physics, but also draws extensively upon the world view of Eastern religions and indigenous peoples and upon recent developments in the biological sciences'. They argue that 'problems cannot be understood within a simple cause(s) and effect(s) framework. They are locked into a dynamic, interwoven and multi-layered web in which interaction and relationship are the principal features.' Their approach suggests that schools should meet five aims in propagating global perspectives – systems consciousness acquiring the 'ability to think in a systems mode... an understanding of the systematic nature of the world... a holistic conception of their capacities and potential'; perspective consciousness recognizing that students may 'have a world view that is not universally shared' and should 'develop receptivity to other perspectives'; have a sense of planet awareness; involvement consciousness and preparedness; and process mindedness, learning being 'continuous journeys with no fixed or final destination' and having 'new ways of seeing the world (that) are revitalising but risky'. Their book is full of examples and practices to allow these themes to be brought into play in the classroom. Their arguments closely match much of the thinking that has gone into the development of the current IB Middle Years and Primary Years programmes, which are also concerned with promoting global vision in schools.

Two other strands have also emerged over the past 30 years. Concern with the deterioration of the world's environment has spawned numerous projects aiming to bring a better understanding of these issues. The current state of thinking is being called either 'education for a sustainable environment' or 'sustainable development'. A vast amount of literature and other media forms have made this topic accessible to most schools and teachers. The approach can best be summarized as the adoption of the viewpoint that the environment is no longer something simply to be exploited, but that we have a legacy that it is our duty to protect for future generations to enjoy. Thus, from being a purely environmental or 'green' issue, it has been widened to incorporate economic and social development. There is therefore considerable overlap with such issues as poverty, unemployment and the obvious disparity between rich and poor societies or nations. It is common also to find another new movement that can be called 'development education'. Here the emphasis is on an active learning process that enables people to understand links between their own lives and those of other peoples. It aims to increase our understanding of the economic, political, social and environmental forces which shape our lives and is intended to examine such issues at all levels – local, national and international. These movements are clearly different facets of what we can call 'Education for Peace'.

Finally, reference needs to be made to the area dealing with 'human rights education' (HRE). Again we see an array of publications promoting a wider acceptance of the need for educators to include the teaching of human rights in schools, especially since the acceptance of the Universal Declaration of Human Rights and the Conventions on the Rights of the Child, for Women and Minority groups. It is probably fair to say that this aspect of peace education is the least developed as far as primary and secondary education is concerned, for a variety of reasons. One of these is the constant extension being made in negotiating conventions on the one hand and delays in ratifying these on the other. Another critical factor is the relative absence of training courses for teachers to make human rights values part of their daily work. Osler and Starkey (1996) highlight such concerns and show that schools have to be seen as communities of citizens, and offer a scale by which the components of citizenship education can be judged on a minimal or maximal scale. They also reproduce the model shown in Figure 8.1 of what they call the human rights curriculum triangle, emphasizing a process in education – thinking, feeling and doing.

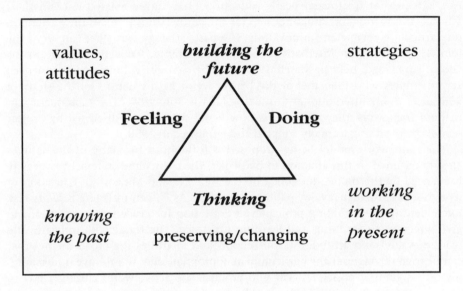

Figure 8.1 Human rights curriculum triangle (Olser and Starkey 1996)

While their conclusion seems to take a radical stance compared with the practitioners of global or developmental education, all of these movements emphasize the need to practise the values now commonly held to be universal in our daily lives. To quote Osler and Starkey:

Many educators have spoken about bringing the world into the school. We are also proposing the reverse. Schools are very special communities. They are communities based on explicit ethical principles. Within the school, the principles of equality and respect for human dignity are particularly valued. For many children, school is the one place where they are secure and where they are valued. Schools at their best are idealised microcosms of society and the world. A significant challenge is to develop this model and see our schools as vehicles for conveying concepts of democracy and human rights to society at large.

The International Education System's Education for Peace curriculum framework

Nearly all of the mission statements of the schools participating in the International Schools Association's (ISA) latest initiative, the International Education System Pilot Project, make reference to peace as a fundamental principle, yet in the various gatherings of the project partners, the teachers and administrators agreed that no formal peace education programme existed K-12 in their schools. It was therefore a natural step for the partnerships to focus their attention on curriculum review and innovation. The basic strategy was agreed upon at the joint ISA/Washington International School Conference, 'Education: Rising to the Global Challenge' held in March 1997. Member schools volunteered experienced staff members who then met at the University of Bath's Centre for the study of Education in an International Context (CEIC) in July 1997. The subsequent curriculum framework they designed is now being studied and discussed by project schools before being formally adopted and published in 1998.

The framework model being proposed is influenced by many of the sources already outlined in this chapter. In particular, the curriculum statement is heavily influenced by the model developed by the New Zealand Ministry of Education in its national curricular review, published in 1993. As is seen in Figure 8.2, the task force identified the guiding principles of Education for Peace which are meant to give direction to teaching and learning for peace. The framework indicates the place of values and attitudes in our schools and identifies the broad themes that can be used throughout the curriculum at appropriate ages to improve understanding of the guiding principles. The end products are active world citizens ready to embrace their responsibilities for building a more harmonious, just and peaceful world.

The purpose of the framework generated by the ISA Project is to provide schools with a blueprint or template to help their staff to plan activities for the promotion of a climate of peace, within the context and needs of their own communities. Education for Peace is a conceptual framework from which schools may devise a programme comprising the recognition and transmission of universal values and enduring attitudes. The initial statement emphasizes the recognition of the following:

1. Each member of the global society is bound by principles relating to human welfare, such as justice, liberty, responsibility, equality, dignity, security, democracy and solidarity.
2. Each member of society is an active participant in a local community and is in turn committed to a global harmony reflective of the diversity of the human population.
3. Each member of the global society must act individually and communally toward guardianship of our world as a whole, guaranteeing the right to a sustainable future.

The implementation of this conceptual framework recognises the practice of peaceful relations at all levels: personal, familial, communal, inter-cultural and global. It entails a process of knowledge acquisition and skill-building which affects the behaviour of individuals and groups and provides a model for the formal and informal curriculum of the school. Education for Peace is a process and condition which permeates all aspects of school life, with implications for learners, teachers, and administrators and it extends beyond the school to society as a whole (ISA, 1998).

The following paragraphs provide a brief overview of the framework.

The 'guiding principles' chosen as the platform for Education for Peace are all drawn from the Universal Declaration of Human Rights and subsequent Conventions. Rather than offer lengthy and complicated definitions of these principles, schools are encouraged to explore and analyse them within their communities so that they are accepted as fundamental norms of human behaviour.

The curriculum framework then outlines the 'core values and attitudes' for enhancing Education for Peace and in this respect the task force recognized the earlier work of the 1994 National Institute for Educational Research Conference on 'Enhancing Humanistic, Ethical, Cultural and International Dimensions of Education in Asia and the Pacific' (NIER, 1994). The values listed are shown in Figure 8.2 and are outlined in greater detail in the framework. They can best be described as emanating from 'international humanism'. It is not expected that these values will be delivered dogmatically. Rather students should be encouraged to examine the context and implications of their own values and those of others to arrive at a set of values that best creates a climate of peace. In so doing, the task force recommends the constructivist approach favoured by the Primary Years programme of the IBO, and in particular the 'Reflect – Choose – Act' cycle which is characteristic of that programme. They also recommend that these attitudes are developed first within the individual and then, through reflection, are examined at group level, in the community, at national level and ultimately on a global scale.

The Education for Peace curriculum framework goes on to analyse the 'skills' necessary to be proactive and effective peacemakers. Broadly categorized into three areas (thinking, communication and personal skills) schools are invited to review whether their pedagogical practices provide sufficient opportunities for a host of essential skills to be developed at appropriate stages of maturity. The framework is based on a heavily process-oriented approach with particular emphasis on skills development. Conflict resolution and conflict avoidance are notably stressed.

The framework is based on a broad definition of the concept of peace as incorporating any issue which is likely to create disharmony in the world. The task force recognized the danger of constructing a new subject that would compete for time and space in already overcrowded school programmes. In contrast, they identified 'major thematic areas' that could be incorporated into existing disciplines, but giving them a different emphasis in keeping with the aim of developing students who 'think globally (and) act locally'. The framework also stresses that these separate elements – human rights, cultural diversity, social justice, population issues, sustainable development, health and housing and the environment – are interrelated

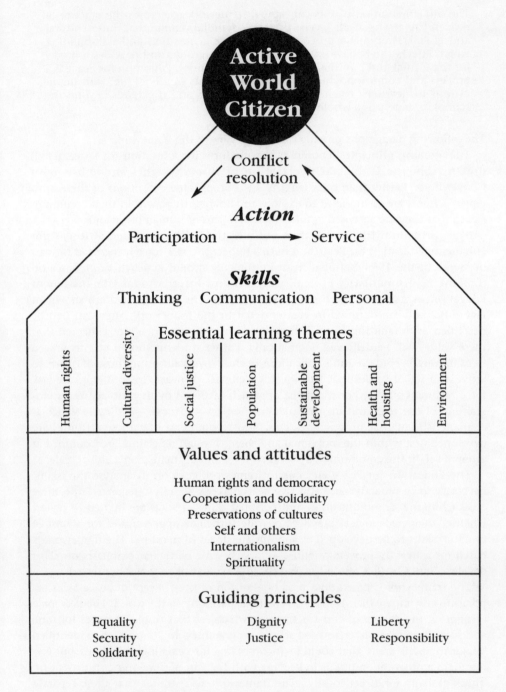

Figure 8.2 Education for peace – curriculum framework

and should not be viewed in isolation from each other. Here the task force see Education for Peace as an 'area of interaction', which is one of the distinctive features of the Middle Years Programme of the IBO. The framework document describes in some detail the issues that should be addressed in each learning area. For example, in the area of human rights, schools are encouraged to examine the rights and responsibilities and the tension that can occur when personal rights impact on those of the family, communities, the nation's rights and those of the global community. They are recommended to examine cases where such rights are violated.

The framework offers suggestions on the 'methodologies' most likely to be successful in promoting the culture and habit of peace. In addition to the formal and informal curriculum, it speaks of the 'hidden' curriculum, of such areas as communications, policies of inclusion and exclusion, of interaction between diverse groups of hierarchical structures and of how the creation of a general climate of tolerance and respect can be enhanced and identified as precepts of peace education. The framework also identifies 'staff development' as a crucial area in establishing a successful Education for Peace programme in a school. Few colleagues will have received formal training in this domain and it may well be necessary for schools to reassess their staff development needs to increase effectiveness in this area. Shared experience is a fundamental feature of the International Education System, which is expected to give considerable attention to this matter over the next few years of its existence.

In its final section the curriculum framework addresses the issue of how to evaluate a school's effectiveness in educating students to be active global citizens. This is seen to be a difficult but crucial task since peace education expresses itself in the domain of affective learning which is not always strictly measurable in a quantitative form. The task group offers schools a list of indicators by which a 'human rights' school can be identified. These are outlined at personal, classroom and school/community levels.

The curriculum framework is supplemented by a series of annexes that will form the bulk of the completed document. These annexes contain extracts of the conventions referred to in this analysis, a bibliography, useful addresses, and details of websites through which colleagues can become more acquainted with the resources available. The larger part of these annexes will consist of classroom practices either designed and used by project schools or those other materials they have found work well on furthering the cause of Education for Peace. The completed publication is expected to be made available during 1998 to all schools through the auspices of ISA, thus making it possible for international, state and parochial schools to bring to life the reforms advocated by UNESCO and its member states.

REFERENCES

Bruntland, G (1987) *Our Common Future: Report of the World Commission on Environment and Development,* Oxford University Press, Oxford

Commission on Global Governance (1995) *Our Global Neighbourhood: The Report of the Commission on Global Governance*, Oxford University Press, New York

International Schools Association (1998) *Education for Peace: Draft Curriculum Framework*, International School of Geneva, Geneva

National Institute for Educational Research (1994) *Enhancing Humanistic, Ethical, Cultural and International Dimensions of Educaton in Asia and the Pacific*, National Institute for Educational Research, Tokyo

New Zealand Ministry of Education (1993) *National Curricular Review*, New Zealand Ministry of Education, Wellington

Osler, A and Starkey, H (1996) *Teacher Education and Human Rights*, David Fulton Publishers, London

Peace Times (1996), Journal of the Center for Teaching Peace, **4**, 1 September–October

Pike, G and Selby, D (1988) *Global Teacher, Global Learner*, Hodder & Stoughton, London

Thelin, B (1996) 'Early tendencies of peace education in Sweden', *Peabody Journal of Education*, **72**, 3, pp 95–110

UNESCO (1994), Forty-fourth Session of the International Conference on Education, Geneva, November

9

SEMIOTICS, CREATIVITY AND INTERNATIONAL EDUCATION

Derek Pigrum

INTRODUCTION

Pushkin's practice of drawing in the margins and among the words of his poetic compositions is a remarkable example of a give and take process between graphic and linguistic signs. I recently acquired Sergei Eisenstein's book, *Über Kunst und Kunstler (Of Art and Artists)* (1977) in which there is an essay on Pushkin. Eager for more clues on Pushkin's creative procedures it was bewildering to find that the first reference to him appeared on the penultimate line of the essay and the second reference on the concluding line, which read *Beginnen wir deshalb mit Pushkin* ('Therefore let us begin with Pushkin'). The reader may have the impression in the next few pages that this author is playing the same puzzling game as Eisenstein when it comes to expectations concerning creativity and international education, but the relevance of 'semiotics' (or the study of signs) to international education will only make sense after a brief overview of the intellectual developments that have produced 'semiotics'. This will be followed by an approach to semiotic 'readings' which contribute to a new perception of cultural diversity encompassed by the concept of 'creative understanding' and a dynamic approach to cultural traditions which combines a concern for both transformation and preservation. This is then related to the concept of a new 'episteme' which the author suggests is imma-nent in some aspects of the International Baccalaureate (IB). The consequences of the new episteme, and its corollary post-modernism, on the concept of creativity is explored in terms of a creative paradigm based on the operation of creative tropes. The link between creative understanding and the new creative paradigm is related to the concept of Homo Faber (man the maker), which is one of the interactive areas of the IB Middle Years Programme (MYP). Finally the prevailing concept of self-expression as the goal of creative activity is juxtaposed to a new paradigm of creativity.

THE SIGNIFIER, THE SIGNIFIED AND THE SIGN

Semiotics has its origins in the 'structural linguistics' of Ferdinand Saussure who, at the turn of the century, saw that language was one of many 'semiotic' or sign systems. The 'sign' is constituted by the signifier and the signified. In the case of linguistics, which was Saussure's field, the signifier is the spoken word, what he referred to as the 'parole', and the signified is the word's conceptual meaning which is the 'langue'. Saussure went on to correct our understanding of language as nothing other than nomenclature (the naming of things) by redefining the linguistic sign as a concept and an acoustic image, both being encoded mental entities which shape the total way of life of humankind. As Lee in Hawkes (1977) says: 'A member of a given society... can actually grasp reality only as it is presented in this code'.

That this encoding may even represent the form which permeates all social behaviour, making social behaviour itself a process of encoding, was the theory of the anthropologist and ethnographer Claude Levi-Strauss, who saw the essential nature of the human mind as a structuring agency, regardless of cultural setting, and gives rise to the theory of 'structuralism'. The 'formalist' branch of structuralism, represented by Propp and Jakobsen, sees in the individual creative act the operation of tacit structural rules. As human beings we invent the world we inhabit by modifying and reconstructing what is given and, as Levi-Strauss says in Elliott (1994): 'there are no natural phenomena in the raw. These do not exist for man except as conceptualisations, seemingly filtered by logical and reflective norms dependent on culture'. Thus there is no innocent eye. As Hodge and Kress (1993) confirm: 'Psychologists of perception have shown conclusively that there is no "pure" act of perception, no seeing without thinking'. In order for perceptions to be communicated they have to be encoded into a 'language'. This primary function of encoding precludes the existence of any pristine range of experiences uncontaminated by encoding.

Roland Barthes, a key figure in the development of semiotics, viewed creativity as a highly conventionalized activity in which 'codes act as agencies – whether we are conscious of them or not – which modify, determine and most importantly generate meaning in a manner far from innocent'. (Barthes in Hawkes, 1977). Barthes (1990) says: 'to signify means that objects carry not only information... ' but also constitute structured systems of signs'. As we will see in the following section, the signifieds of objects depend on the receiver of the message, and the range of readings will depend on knowledge and cultural background. But the object that suggests a meaning is still functional, even at the moment we read it as a sign.

MAN IN A RAINCOAT

In the very last photograph taken of Alberto Giacometti (Giacometti in the Rue d'Alesia 1961, in Stoos *et al.*, 1996) we see a man with his raincoat pulled up over his head crossing a rain-swept street. The raincoat is only one of a parataxis of objects – the road surface, the bleak house fronts, the pervasive ordinariness of the image. In semiotic terms this photograph is a graphic signifier or lexia which mobilizes in the viewer different signifieds or lexicons. The number, identity and depth of these lexicons forms a person's ideolect. The 'language' of the image (the image as text) is composed of ideolects, lexicons and sub-codes. Someone unfamiliar with the figure of Giacometti will produce ideolects of a socio-economic content in response to this image. Someone able to put the name Giacometti to the 'face' in the photograph will have to hand some of the complex lexicons, or signifieds, that this image of the famous artist activates. Apart from whatever knowledge the person has of Giacometti the shabbiness of the artist may well activate the myth, generated by Romanticism, of the artist as living and dying in poverty only to receive posthumous recognition; it might also produce lexia concerned with the supposed eccentricity of artists and their proverbial inability to cope with the practicalities of life. These lexia are not universal, but just a few of the examples of what goes to make up the ideolect of people from occidental cultures in response to the signifier and signified of the sign 'artist'; nor did they exist as part of anyone's ideolect until late into the eighteenth century. As an example of how lexia can provide a creative metaphorical transference we have, in John Berger's book of essays, *Keeping a Rendezvous* (1993), a reading of this image of Giacometti relating the functional sign of the raincoat pulled up over Giacometti's head to a monk's cowl and as a metaphor for Giacometti's ascetic existence, and his almost religious sense of dedication to his art. Readings of this kind, conducted in the classroom context of international education, reveal the different ideolects or sign systems working in different individuals.

One of the best examples of this kind of activity are the studies of Aby Warburg of the interactions, clashes and continuities of certain images within a tradition that took their most arresting form in the last project of his life, the Menosyme (Memory), which consists of a kaleidoscope of permutations, enigmatic and fragmentary, of the life of visual symbols and their 'significance for the psychology of culture' (Gombrich, 1986). To see this project reassembled is to realize that we have still to develop and apply the complex contribution of Warburg and of semiotics to international education. But to what purpose?

NEW PERCEPTIONS

Globalization has cultural dimensions which are producing

> a world-wide culture which is irreversibly displacing, or at least transforming, local cultures everywhere... The power of this culture to erode local differences is so great that it makes one extremely anxious about the possibilities of enhancing or developing those regional specificities that seem a normal and proper human condition (Miller, 1992).

Participation in the performative acts of semiotic readings of graphic and linguistic texts enhances understanding and appreciation of the diversity of individual, culturally determined ideolects, creative projections and imaginings. In a sense this is an ethnographic approach which by creating systems of reference in which the ideolects of persons from different cultures can find a place, constitute a more comprehensive experience.

The structure of such readings could conceivably be based on an adaptation of Panofsky's three levels of meaning (which he applied in an exclusively art historical context) and which consists of a first level of recognition arising from the subjective basis of our everyday experience. The second level is based on the subjective level of our education and culture. The third level is the essential meaning, the subjective origin of which is our world view – 'those beliefs that we ourselves betray, even in the act of interpretation... implicit and unconscious principle, habits, and assumptions which make up our world view' Summers *et al.*, in Lavin (1993). All of these levels constitute what has been described as the individual's ideolect.

There is a principle of ethnography that adds a further dimension to this approach when adapted to education, which is that it is not necessary for a person to have experiential knowledge of all cultures but 'to let himself be taught by another culture' (Merleau Ponty, 1962). Of course, in a very real and beneficial sense this is precisely what happens in international education, the only problem being that the 'other culture' for many students is the 'dominant culture' which is the instrument of the internationalization of culture. How can we avoid the blind alley of an internationalization and commodification of culture and, while enhancing cultural diversity, equally avoid the consolidation of nationalistic thinking?

The 'readings' already outlined are part of the answer, but only if conducted in a way which is based on a concept of 'creative understanding' of other cultures. This notion was first developed by Mikhail Bakhtin, and identifies the most powerful factor in understanding another culture as 'outsidedness'. 'Creative understanding does not renounce itself, its own place in time, its own culture... in order to understand, it is immensely important... to be located outside the object of creative understanding' (Bakhtin in Deveraux and Hillman, 1995). Creative understanding does not mean merging oneself with that culture; 'each retains its own unity and open totality, but they are mutually enriched' (Bakhtin in Deveraux and Hillman, 1995). Understanding another culture, being taught by another culture, involves a 'new perception' of one's own cultural constellation. The most important part of this process is that in creatively understanding and identifying 'difference' we are also required to identify the ways in which we are similar. The perception and understanding of difference can only exist against a background of what is common to cultures, what is shared by diverse cultures. Thus 'in relating to others the choice is not difference *or* similarity; it is difference *and* similarity' (Fay, 1996).

A DYNAMIC VIEW OF TRADITION

This 'new perception' of other cultures and one's own culture has an important sequel for creativity. In the context of international education, Walter Benjamin's letter to Scholem in 1917 (in McCole, 1993), takes on a new importance. Benjamin did not see tradition as something passive, stable, and timeless but rather as a creative field changing through the effects on it of new and creative products. Benjamin saw the process of tradition as including 'the tremendous freedom of overturning' (in McCole, 1993). When we talk of the 'new perception' gained by 'creative understanding' of cultural traditions in the international education context we no longer mean a way of working handed down from one generation to the next, but a development of a consciousness of the past in the present; of the indelible historicity of 'signs'. The production of originality no longer means cutting ourselves off from the past, but rather the capacity to find among other perceptions, of any date or locality, clues for the treatment of one's own specific subject matter. This represents a dynamic and, as we will see, a post-modern view of tradition in which the originality of cultures, including the dominant culture, resides in the way in which each culture groups innovations and discoveries, in a 'composite mixture' that enhances the 'difference' of the culture. Perhaps an anecdotal example will help to clarify this dynamic and indicate the central problem. The author often encourages IB Art and Design students to base their creative thinking on the specificity of their own cultural traditions. In one particular case a student was encouraged to use the highly distinctive traditional form of architecture in his own culture in order to produce a 'new form' inspired by the 'old'. The student experienced work in this direction as producing a dynamic sense of continuity and cultural renewal; his only problem lay in his discovery that almost all of the structures that he had intended to research during his home vacation had been replaced by an international style of architecture with which we are all familiar.

An approach of this kind involves the individual in the active participation of the production and transformation of meaning, making culture something we continually create and recreate by our new perceptions of its meanings and our interpretive and innovative activity.

THE NEW 'EPISTEME'

Foucault is another very important contributor to semiotics. In Elliott (1994), he talks about what he describes as the 'episteme', which he denotes as a fluid system of disparate yet interlocking 'discursive' practices inviting the mind to a new form of thought, a new type of representation and hence to a new world. The International Schools Association Curriculum and its subsequent form as IBMYP, with its central areas of interaction: Environment, Health, Social Education and Homo Faber, in conjunction with the IB constitute just such an invitation to a new form of thought and a new type of representation in the context of international education. In this chapter we can only deal with some aspects of the IB and the IBMYP which have a clear conceptual link to creativity, such as IB and IBMYP Art and Design and the IBMYP interactive area of Homo Faber. (For an investigation of the term Homo Faber see Pigrum, 1996.)

The historicity of the sign is embedded in traditions and artefacts. Creative understanding through semiotic 'readings' produce a new perception and encourage dynamic transformation of artefacts within and across traditions. The concept of Homo Faber can form the vital link between individual and trans-individual creativity, and a dynamic approach to tradition that serves both to transform culture and to preserve diversity. This view of Homo Faber distances itself from a 'discoveries' and 'inventions' view of Homo Faber. As Levi-Strauss (1978) says: 'Too much has been made of all the discoveries; the Phoenicians for writing; the Chinese for paper, gun powder and the compass; the Indians for glass and steel. These elements are less important than the way in which each culture makes... its composite mixture.' What must be avoided is a view of the achievements of other cultures as essentially a static and largely redundant inventory, while emphasizing the most recent technological and artistic achievements of the dominant culture as dynamic and creative. Homo Faber, like the concept world civilization, 'could not be anything on the world scale except the coalition of cultures, each preserving its originality' (Levi-Strauss, 1978).

The author believes one of the main discourses of international education should be the preservation of the diversity and originality of cultures. This cannot be done by viewing Homo Faber and the originality of cultures as closed worlds. It can only be achieved by making the best use of the opportunities in international education for students to test themselves as creators and 'to deepen their understanding of themselves as makers, as Homo Faber' (Porphyrios in Pigrum, 1996). This, in its turn, requires from within the new 'episteme' a discourse geared towards a change in the creative paradigm and in the status of 'tradition' in the post-modernist world.

POST-MODERNISM

The ideas of the writers and thinkers already mentioned, and many others, seeded the growth of the inchoate state we are now in, labelled as post-modern. Post-modernism has arisen out of a phenomenon in the dominant culture called 'modernism' and, like any new concept, has many shades of interpretation, of which I will only mention a few. Modernism was obsessed with starting from 'an impossible zero, a tabula rasa of the mind' (Abbs, 1996). Nietzsche was the first to analyse modernism's preoccupation with breaking with the past in his '*Unzeitgemässe Betrachtungen*' ('untimely meditations') where he showed how modernity looks back anxiously to see whether the past has anticipated its creative achievements. Nietzsche challenges us 'not to be arrogant about the superiority of the present over the past' (Hoy and McCarthy, 1994). In essence, post-modernism is the understanding which we have elucidated earlier in this text that there is no escape from the historicity of the sign. In terms of individual creativity it means we no longer need to follow the injunction to separate ourselves from the past. But it goes deeper than that. 'A core notion in the contemporary debates about post-modernism is the idea that the creative possibilities of modernism are exhausted' (Marcus in Devereaux and Hillman, 1995). This has consequences in terms of creativity, which must be addressed in the context of international education.

BRINGING FORWARD TRANSFERENCES

The new 'episteme' in its post-modern context calls on us to investigate both individual and trans-individual processes in creativity. As Briskman in Dutton and Krausz (1981) says: 'we can only identify and explain creativity by reference to prior products because the creativity of a product resides not in its psychological origins but in its objective relations to other previous products'. Csikszentmihalyi corroborates this in Sternberg (1991), when he writes: 'social agreement is one of the constitutive aspects of creativity; without it the phenomenon would not exist'. This is not to say that the creative process cannot produce readings at a psychoanalytical level, but none of this escapes a structure of meaning. Barthes uses the example of the Rorschach test, which has undergone rigorous scientific analysis and which produces strict topologies of response: 'The deeper we go into the depths of individual reaction the more we identify meanings that are actually simple and codified' (Barthes, 1990). But this does not imply that human beings are little bubbles of culture. Culture shapes us but we also possess our own natures, independent of culture. Culture and society shape our personal and social identities but they do not definitively establish who we are. This is important because structuralism is often seen to have an over-deterministic view of the individual's relationship to culture and society.

However, whether in the sciences or the arts, creative work is organized in so far as it abides by integrating principles. As Chaitin (1996) writes: 'whether it be a substance or a function, the signified of the metaphor is still simply represented by the shape of the signifier'. This is not the same as saying that creative acts proceed from a knowledge of their laws, but neither does it place intuitive and imaginative faculties in opposition to the rational and analytical; rather it presents a view of creativity in all domains as an oscillation between judgemental and intuitive thinking. This is also not to say that creative thinking in art and science is the same, nor does it mean that art is a form of knowledge or a substitute for it. It is rather as Althusser in Elliott (1994) says: 'Art has a certain necessary relationship to knowledge which is more a relationship of difference than identity. Art alludes to reality, enables us to see and perceive and to feel, science enables us to know.' There is a call in the 'new episteme' for a terminology and approach that does not treat imagination and rational thinking as antithetical but as consistent and interdependent in some respects, and at variance in others.

Although we possess and develop creative capacities that are 'sedimented structures' of devices and strategies we are nevertheless unable to explain what elements will trigger them, or the principles that are used in dealing with these elements. Once triggered, however, the producer searches for an apt signifier of the signified. As Hodge and Kress (1993) say, this process 'rests on analogy and is a metaphoric process. Signs are thus always the result of the action of metaphoric process'. (Remember the raincoat and the monk's cowl.) Derrida in his *Of Grammatology* (1977) writes: 'metaphor is the process by which the subjective representation becomes the objective order of designations'. Both these writers echo Nietzsche, who in the Italian writer Fiumara (1992) says: the 'formation of metaphors... by bringing forward new transferences continually manifests an ardent desire to refashion the world'.

One of the keys to a new discourse in creativity is Nietzsche's idea of 'bringing forward new transferences'. This is what Arendt in Benjamin (1970) describes as metaphor 'understood in its original sense of *metapherein* (to transfer)'. This 'bringing forward of transferences' constitutes what the author calls, in his own (unpublished) research, 'transitional' signs that culminate in the finished product. They are in fact intermedial products and are characterized by various kinds of exchanges, displacements, substitutions and recombinations.

In IB Art and Design the importance of these processes is implicit in the requirement that during the two-year course students produce a 'Research Work Book', providing evidence of the growth and development of ideas. In the IBMYP the author, in collaboration with Bob Carignon (Copenhagen International School), introduced the 'Process Workbook'. The idea of this book was based on a kind of Leonardo Da Vinci archive of ideas, observations and creative transferences that could move with the student through all the creative options and indeed through other disciplines, creating links and providing a continuous supply of ideas for the trial and error process of invention.

Briskman in Dutton and Krausz (1981) dismisses any understanding of the creative process without recourse to this kind of intermediary product, representing as it does the 'ineliminable interaction between the creator's psychological states and his own products', and the give and take between the two. The Process Workbook contains the kind of 'sedimented structures' (described by Merleau Ponty in Mallin, 1979) which are further refined and specified, forming a schema of creative thinking procedures. The Process Workbook involves the student in the use of an instrument of creativity that has both historical and contemporary precedents across all domains, keeping before the student the material conditions of creativity and, in terms of Homo Faber, acting as a sobering antidote to mystifications of the creative process. The Process Workbook involves the student in the key operations of creativity.

Metaphor and metonymy

Several general characteristics of creativity, regardless of domain, have been proposed, which include 'analogical thinking, redefinition of problems, recurring themes and recognising patterns and images of wide scope to make the new familiar and the old new' (Sternberg, 1991). These operations of displacement are, as stated earlier, the product of metaphor, but a further displacement is achieved through metonymy; metaphor is the process of displacing one signifier by an associated one and metonymy combines and connects signifier to signifier in a potentially infinite process. Saussure says that human language exists in terms of these two dimensions; the selective, associative and synchronic dimension of metaphor and the combinative, syntagmatic, diachronic dimension of metonymy (in Hawkes, 1977). This is a model of creative processes in which consciousness and the unconscious are both results of the semiotic and symbolic order rather than its cause, and implies both a trans-individual and trans-cultural operation of rhetorical tropes. Through knowledge and application of rhetorical tropes and figures the student can acquire a broad range of creative devices from which to develop individual creative schemas.

This view of creativity is sharply at odds with one which I believe still has a strong following in international education and is based on 'the false and depressing theory of self-expression' (Popper, 1996) coupled to a belief 'that the intuitive and imaginative faculties of the child are repressed by culture, and the primary function of art education should be to restore the earlier pristine state' (Fuller, 1983). As we have seen, there is no pristine state to be restored; there is no source of creative inspiration that is not contaminated by encodings.

Creativity as self-expression or *Das Penelopewerk*

The origins of self-expression as the goal of creative activity were first formulated by Herder at the end of the eighteenth century. His view of expression laid absolute emphasis on the 'voice' of the self rather than on the created object, making the creative act an expression of the whole personality. Herder is 'the true father of the doctrine that it is the artist's mission, above others, to testify in his works to the truth of his own inner experience' (Berlin, 1980). In order to do this the artist must set his face against the past and learn 'not to think in other people's thoughts' (Berlin, 1980). If we avoid all influences and cut ourselves loose from the past then we will have thrown off the shackles that confine creativity and be able to divine the nature of the self in works of true originality. It is this view of creativity which I believe, along with Fuller (1983, 1993) and Abbs (1996), still counts in many people's minds as the essence of creative activity in the arts.

We have already encountered the objection to this position central to structuralism that language creates the greater part of the self, not the self language. But there are other objections. Originality, in Herder's view and in the 'late Romantic condition' we describe as modernism, is only to be achieved by eschewing all influences, past and present. However, some of the most original artists of our time have consistently sought inspiration from the past; Cezanne, Giacometti, Bacon and Corbusier all drew extensively on works of the past. For these artists the relationship between past and present, between influences and originality, merely represents the progressive modification of one mind by the work of another. Valery wrote: 'this derived activity is essential to intellectual production of all types... Originality is when we cannot trace the hidden transformations that others underwent in the mind' (in Said, 1985). Inoculation with the thoughts and images of others lead to those alterations and accentuations that bear a necessary relation to originality of mind. This paradigm, which underpins creativity in the sciences, is distorted by the *Drang* (urge) to self-expression in the arts. As Bakhtin (1990) writes: 'My own axiological relationship to myself is completely unproductive aesthetically; for myself, I am aesthetically unreal. I can be only the bearer of the task of artistic forming and consummating, not its object.' However, it is evident that our singular natures leave their imprint on creative work; this is the style each individual develops, representing the individual bias, essential rhythms, impulses and acquired influences and resources. The role of education is to help the student to take the first formative steps in the development of a style. True originality, however, probably occurs when the individual's style is transcended. This is to view creativity not as a unitary event with a sole participant but as a way of 'determining one's own place in the event of being through others, to place oneself on a par with others' (Bakhtin, 1990).

These new directions do not fall into a ready-made scheme. The author, however, would like to suggest a tentative conceptual framework for a new paradigm of creativity seen as a *Penelopewerk* (the work of Penelope, wife of Odysseus, who delayed her suitors by repeatedly weaving and unweaving a robe), a concept borrowed from the title of an essay by Walter Benjamin on the creative processes of Marcel Proust (Fleckner, 1995). This approach is based on the 'interwovenness' of a number of what I will describe as 'strands'. The underlying strand is composed of rhetorical tropes and figures which have been assimilated at a very deep level and in which 'the I addresses its me' (Mead in Burke, 1962) through inner dialogue and through processes of visualization of the kind we have described in the Process Workbook. Another strand would consist of the operation of influences as an open field of possibilities, where 'acquired ideas are themselves caught up in something like a second life' (Merleau Ponty in Said, 1985). Yet another strand would be technique, the organization of the creative work as a give and take process between material, the body and the mind. Between these and other possible strands there is a constant feedback process through which each acts upon the other in a process of interweaving and unpicking of directions and impulses and of transference into new patterns. The aim of this approach is to help us explore how creative directions arise and become sedimented structures, which possibilities are opened up in this approach and which are closed off, what this approach is good for and bad for and in what ways it entails challenges to received understandings of creativity.

A MESSAGE IN A BOTTLE

Althusser once said that writing was like sending a message in a bottle: 'you can never tell who will come upon your words or what they will make of them' (Althusser in Elliott, 1994). My message is not that semiotics totally domesticates by system the moving forces of creativity; this would be gravely to underestimate the dynamic and unfixed nature, transgressions and restorations involved in the creative process, which I believe are best represented in *Das Penelopewerk* model in which the creator's actions are always being converted into signs that signify ideas; which signs he or she uses in turn to signify other signs and so on in a process of metaphorical association and the combination of metonymy. The complementarity of a dynamic and transformative approach to cultural diversity, and an approach to creativity based on the tropes of rhetoric in a Process Workbook, ensure that Homo Faber incorporates the student's experience of one of the most significant means 'by which humans embark on complex projects to achieve ambitious goals; how they present their plans, how they initiate work on a project,... evaluate tentative drafts... determine when such a project has been completed' (Gardner, 1987). It also means that Homo Faber does not become a licence simply to retell the inventory of humankind's achievements or to construct Homo Faber to the specifications of the dominant culture, thereby accelerating the process of the internationalization of culture.

My message is one that simultaneously calls for the preservation of cultural diversity and the dynamic transformation of culture. This is based on the insight that although our culture does 'make' us in the semiotic sense this is not to be seen as producing mechanical and uniform behaviour, but that a recognition of trans-individual operations of mind, if understood and more consciously manipulated, can enhance the innovative power of our individual natures and our ability creatively to understand other cultures and transform our own.

The IB educational programmes alluded to are part of the meaning structure which nourishes the form of international education. The form is the signifier and is wholly absorbed by the signified; the concept of international education. The form and the concept consists, as Hodge and Kress (1993) say (in terms of linguistics), 'of both behaviours and texts, texts that are traces of semiotic and social action'. The concept is there to be appropriated by the form. Thus the concept is, as Barthes would say, a 'functional tendency', which appears in varying degrees in its form. The 'sign' of international education is a 'turnstile' through which the signifier and the signified, the form and the concept, continually pass, and in which the form attempts to cover the possibilities of representation present in the concept. This chapter is an attempt to narrow the gap not only between the form and the concept, but also between the concept and the emerging episteme of the post-modernist era.

Beginnen wir deshalb mit dem neunen episteme.

REFERENCES

Abbs, P (1996) *The Polemics of Imagination*, Skoob Books, London

Bakhtin, M (1990) *Art and Answerability* (trans Holquist, M), University of Texas Press, Austin

Barthes, R (1990) *The Semiotic Challenge* (trans Howard, R), University of California Press, Berkeley

Benjamin, W (1970) *Illuminations* (trans Zohn, H), Fontana/Collins, London

Berlin, I (1980) *Vico and Herder*, Hogarth Press, London

Burke, K (1962) *A Rhetoric of Motives*, University of California Press, Berkeley, CA

Chaitin, G (1996) *Rhetoric and Culture in Lacan*, Cambridge University Press, Cambridge

Derrida, J (1977) *Of Grammatology* (trans Spivak, G C), Johns Hopkins Press, London

Devereaux, L and Hillman, R (eds) (1995) *Fields of Vision*, University of California Press, Berkeley

Dutton, D and Krausz, M (eds) (1981) *The Concept of Creativity in Science and Art*, Martinus Nyhoff, The Hague

Elliott, G (1994) *Althusser: A Critical Reader*, Blackwell, Oxford

Eisenstein, S (1977) *Über Kunst und Kunstler* (trans Kaempfe, A), Rogner and Bernhard, Munich

Fay, B (1996) *Contemporary Philosophy of Social Science*, Blackwell, Oxford

Fiumara, G C (1992) *The Symbolic Function*, Blackwell, Oxford

Fleckner, U (1995) *Die Schatzkammern der Mnemosyne*, Verlag der Kunst, Berlin

Fuller, P (1983) *The Naked Artist*, Writers & Readers, London

Fuller, P (1993) *Modern Painters*, Methuen Press, London

Gardener, H (1987) *The Mind's New Science*, Basic Books, New York

Gombrich, E H (1986) *Aby Warburg*, Phaidon Press, London

Hawkes, T (1977) *Structuralism and Semiotics*, Methuen, London

Hodge, R and Kress, G (1993) *Language as Ideology*, Routledge & Kegan Paul, London

Hoy, C D and McCarthy, T (1994) *Critical Theory*, Blackwell, Oxford

Lavin I (1993) (cd) *Meaning in the Visual Arts: views from the outside*, Institute of Advanced Study, Princeton NJ

Levi-Strauss, C (1978) *Structural Anthropology:* Vol. 2, Penguin, London

McCole, J (1993) *Walter Benjamin and the Antinomies of Tradition*, Cornell University Press, New York

Mallin, S (1979) *The Philosophy of Merleau Ponty*, Yale University Press, Newhaven, CT

Merleau Ponty (1962) *Phenomenology of Perception* (trans Smith, C), Routledge, London

Miller, H J (1992) *Illustration*, Reakton Books, London

Pigrum, D W (1996) 'The proper study of Homo Faber is process', MA dissertation, University of Bath

Popper, K R (1996) (ed Notturno, M A) *Knowledge and the Body-Mind Problem*, Routledge, London

Said, E W (1985) *Beginnings: Intention and Method*, Colombia University Press, New York

Sternberg, R J (ed) (1991) *The Nature of Creativity*, Cambridge University Press, Cambridge

Stoos T, Elliott, P and Doswald, C (1996) *Alberto Giacometti*, Kunsthalle, Vienna

10

SPECIAL LEARNING NEEDS IN INTERNATIONAL SCHOOLS: THE OPTIMAL MATCH CONCEPT

Martha Haldimann

INTRODUCTION

In international schools, special learning needs students encompass English as a Second Language (ESL) learners, those with learning disabilities and/or students of exceptionally high abilities and talents. In many international schools these special learning needs students, taken as a whole, may represent the majority of students. Thus it is not surprising that the European Council of International Schools (ECIS) has a particular interest in guiding their schools in attempting to meet these students' learning needs.

ECIS, the membership organization for approximately 450 international schools in 90 countries around the world, is the oldest and largest association of international schools world-wide. Every school day about 260,000 students are taught within international schools, representing numerous nationalities and linguistic, cultural, and religious backgrounds (ECIS, 1997–98). The language of instruction is usually English; most schools offer additional language instruction of the host country and may also offer mother-tongue language instruction. Some large international schools, for example, those with over 1500 students, may provide such instruction for 90 or more nationalities. Other schools with smaller student populations of 200, may teach 33 different nationalities. Although many schools in the ECIS *Directory* list learning support programmes in their school descriptions, the concept of such programmes is not defined and may often refer to ESL students receiving English language learning support. Fewer schools refer to special educational needs services for learning disabled students, and very few schools state that, in addition to ESL and special educational needs programmes, they also provide programmes for students of exceptionally high abilities and/or exceptional talents. The *International Schools Journal* has been helpful in publishing articles pertaining to ESL and learning difficulties (including Foreman-Haldimann, 1981a, 1981b,

1983b; Scruggs, and Goldman, 1985; Thomas, 1990; Raynor, 1991; Kusuma-Powel *et al.*, 1992; Sparks and Ganschow 1993; and Hollington 1994). Regarding the special learning needs of those with high academic abilities, one article published in the *International Schools Journal* (Stanley, 1981) described the value of brilliant seventh and eighth grade students taking the Scholastic Aptitude Test (SAT) as an identification instrument through the Center for Talented Youth (CTY) International Talent Search. Foreman-Haldimann, a research writer for the *International Schools Journal*, wrote an overview of the field and cited pertinent research (Foreman-Haldimann, 1982, 1983a). However, only two articles have been published about the needs of 'gifted and talented' students since the Foreman-Haldimann articles (Miller, 1986; Freeman, 1993). In fact Miller found that international schools tend to neglect identifying and providing for the learning needs of this special group of students. Research pertaining to special learning needs populations in international schools is relatively uncommon. Stumpf and Haldimann (1997) found that their research on spatial ability and academic success of students at international schools was the only research project conducted on a wide scale for such institutions.

One source compelling international schools to create programmes for special learning needs students is the ECIS accreditation process (see Chapter 15). Since September 1997 schools have had to meet the guidelines of accreditation for special needs students in the areas of assessment, provision and personnel trained specifically to support students, including those who are ESL speakers, are learning disabled, or have high exceptional abilities and/or talents. The guidelines for special needs education include the following statement:

> There shall be effective procedures for identifying and addressing the special needs of students with learning disabilities. There shall be effective procedures for identifying and addressing the special needs of students of exceptionally high ability and/or exceptional talent. The school shall have an adequate number of trained special needs personnel. If children with learning disabilities or who have remedial needs are admitted, the school shall provide specific curriculum and programmes to meet identified needs (ECIS, 1997).

A self-study guide is provided for schools that are applying for accreditation and, within this guide, special educational needs programmes are examined in a checklist form for areas of assessment and provision for students, including those with learning disabilities, exceptionally high abilities and/or exceptional talents, and ESL (ECIS/New England Association of Schools and Colleges 1997). This is a much valued improvement for special needs education accreditation at international schools and complements a philosophy of education, The Optimal Match Concept, currently being practised in many international schools world-wide.

OPTIMAL MATCH CONCEPT

The Optimal Match Concept is both a philosophy of education and 'the fine-tuning of curricula to match an individual student's demonstrated level and ideal pace of learning' (CTY, 1994). Student learning is based on identifying the zones of appropriate challenge (related closely to Vygotsky's zone of proximal development, Daniels, 1996) and providing instruction for students to work in those zones. Assessment of achievement and abilities, both formal and informal, is considered to be the first step to achieving an appropriate curricular match (US Department of State 1988). The learning needs of students who are ESL speakers, are learning disabled, or have exceptionally high abilities and/or talents are specifically targeted, as are the learning needs of the school's general student population (Advisory Committee on Exceptional Children and Youth, (ACECY), 1993).

The essential elements of the Optimal Match model are:
- a respect for the sense of uniqueness and worth of human individuality, of difference rather than disability;
- a sense of development, of process, of growth, of change in individuals;
- a recognition that all individuals differ and that when these differences are dealt with positively, students will be able to develop their full potential and capitalize upon their own abilities and styles;
- for individuals with special needs, because of a mismatch between what they bring to a situation and what is expected, an active partnership between school, home, community and student is even more critical than it is for other students; and
- the belief that through skilled and sensitive teaching and support, students with differing abilities and talents can find individual paths to success and fulfilment, and can contribute to the fulfilment of other students (ACECY/Institute for the Academic Achievement of Youth, (IAAY), 1997)

The Optimal Match Concept was conceived in 1986 through the Office of Overseas Schools, US Department of State and the Association of American Schools in South America, assisted by an Advisory Committee on Exceptional Children and Youth composed of recognized leaders in the field of education (US Department of State, 1988). 'IAAY is a comprehensive, university-based initiative that promotes the academic ability of children and youth throughout the world.' It lists the Optimal Match as one of four objectives in its mission statement as: 'To hold steadfastly to a vision of education – the Optimal Match Concept – in the face of educational fads, *and* to offer the public criteria for discriminating substantive from superficial education' (IAAY, 1997). The Optimal Match Concept has been described in journal articles (Durden, 1991; Mills and Tangherlini, 1992; Durden and Mackay, 1995), in position papers (Durden and Mills, 1996) and in models (ACECY/IAAY 1997). Schools that decide to embrace the Optimal Match differ in the programmes offered, and it is interesting to note that some, such as the International School of Berne, Switzerland (Burkholder, 1992) and the John F Kennedy International School, Saanen/Gstaad, Switzerland (ECIS, 1993–4) were practising the Optimal Match Concept without realizing that their approaches to student special learning needs were very close to the concept. The concept was introduced at the Swiss Group of International Schools (SGIS) regional conference in Spring 1994 and, although there are many international schools now practising the Optimal Match Concept, the SGIS with a membership of 30, was one of the first regional groups to set a goal of exploring the Optimal Match Concept for its schools (SGIS, 1996). For the purposes of this chapter international schools practising the Optimal Match were requested to submit descriptions of their Optimal Match programmes. The responses from four of the international schools appear below, including concrete practices, theories and concerns by directors of schools or Optimal Match learning centre directors, and acknowledgement of their kindness in permitting their responses to be made here is given with appreciation.

OPTIMAL MATCH PRACTICES AT FOUR INTERNATIONAL SCHOOLS

Escola Graduada (Graded School) de São Paulo, Brazil [Cynthia Silva, Director, Optimal Learning Center]

The Graded School supports the concept of Optimal Match and is incorporating the philosophy into its approach to curriculum at all grade levels; it is included in the school's mission statement. This school was the first to develop an Optimal Learning Center (OLC), in 1987, and has been recommended for the status of model school site for the Association of American Schools in South America (AASSA) by the US Department of State Office of Overseas Schools. We are proud of the confidence invested in us as we strive to enable all students to maximize their talents and capitalize upon their own learning styles in a rigorous and challenging school programme. Candidates who seek admission to the school are carefully reviewed by the Admissions Director, Deans at each school level, Counsellors and, if needed, by the Director of the OLC to be sure that the students who seek admission are indeed an optimal match for the type of programmes offered by this school. It is important to be sure that there is a match between student needs, educational programmes and school resources.

What will this mean for the student? All children learn at different rates, in different styles and at different levels. Within an Optimal Match system, we embrace this dynamic organizationally and attitudinally. In planning a programme of study for the student we consider not only the student's assessed ability and proven performance, but also his or her interest and motivation. We look first to the resources within the school; in the form of staff, materials and training. We want all students to feel supported and challenged. All individuals learn best when appropriately challenged, that is, when they are presented with material which is neither so easy for them as to be redundant, nor so difficult as to be aversive. Some students need individualized work and a variety of teaching approaches. All students need rich learning experiences, both school and community based, which bring meaning to learning. Because of our small class sizes and commitment to the individual child, we give priority to learning about students' unique talents and needs. There is a high level of collaboration among teachers to discuss and provide appropriate support and enrichment to each student where needed. Our professional staff respect the uniqueness and worth of each student and view differences as opportunities, not disabilities. We try to be flexible in our teaching methods and curricula.

The OLC at the Graded School is able to support a range of students with various learning needs. The Center coordinates service programmes for students who have mild learning difficulties (students who have specific difficulties who are within two years of grade level abilities), at the middle and high school levels. The lower school services are more extensive, with alternative programming available to maximize the needs of the developing child. The focus at this level is to be proactive rather than reactive, in order for all children to be able to achieve their optimal levels of performance. The services all begin with full diagnosis, if the child does not already have this information from previous school placement. Referrals to the OLC can come directly from a parent or a classroom teacher who has concerns about specific areas of a child's development. Assessments are performed for students who may be academically talented or gifted, as well as for students who are suspected of having specific learning difficulties. Specific areas that are able to be assessed at the school include Learning Disabilities (LD), Gifted and Talented (G/T), Attention Deficit Hyperactivity Disorder (ADHD), Dyslexia, and English as a Second Language (ESL). Children who may need ESL services are assessed individually and may at times also receive further assessments if a possible learning difficulty and not a language-based difficulty is suspected. A small immersion programme is available for students who have some working English skills but may not be ready for a full English curriculum. ESL classes are offered daily in pull-out small group instruction for students in second through fifth grade and at the high school level.

The OLC also monitors and develops programmes, as needed, for students who are identified as gifted and/or talented. These programmes are created according to the specific needs of each student. Optimal Match for these students can be achieved through cross-grade placements for specific subject or skill areas, independent programmes through grade level or the OLC, classroom differentiation for all students, after-school programmes two to three days a week, pull-out daily accelerated programmes and through mentorships. Students also participate in the Johns Hopkins International Talent Search programme for talented youth. Students who receive support for specific learning difficulties are supported as often as possible within their regular classroom programme. This is done through differentiated instruction, team teaching with an OLC teacher in classrooms, and small group, pull-out remedial programmes. Alternative pull-out programming is used only for students who require alternative instructional methods or curriculum. This type of support is offered on a limited basis, as students who may require this level of support may not be able to maximize their learning potential within the regular programmes at the middle and high school levels. At this time all students who attend the Graded School must be able to meet the expectations of the regular curriculum. Students who require this level of support at the higher levels would not be in an optimal environment for their learning styles. Academic support is offered throughout the middle and high school programmes. This class is restricted to students who have a previously diagnosed learning difficulty and who have specific need for support. Classes meet approximately three times a week in a rotating block schedule format. Students are taught study skills, and have mini lessons in specific areas of academic weakness. Specific lessons could focus on Organization, Note Taking, Summarizing, Paraphrasing, Finding the Main Idea, Learning styles and specific reteaching of regular content from the student's curriculum. Students who take this class earn credit and grades based on their level of motivation and partici-pation, as well as content.

The Director of the Optimal Learning Center is also responsible for staff develop-ment and training as well as preparing ongoing workshops for parents and teachers about current research and teaching strategies. A current library for parents and teachers is available, containing recent publications of texts, journals and activities for use by all to support their children's development. The Optimal Match's best performance indicator is the future performance of the children who have received the benefits of this philosophy of education. 'At the Graded School the question among high school students is not "Are you going to college after high school?" but rather "Which college will you be going to?" In past years almost 99 per cent of the students graduating from the school attended colleges and universities worldwide' (Phyllis Clemsen, College Counsellor).

International School Manila, Philippines [Annette Nyqvist, Optimal Learning Center Coordinator]

The Optimal Learning Center at International School Manila (ISM) was created in August 1992 to coordinate new and existing programmes and services for students with special needs at ISM. The OLC team, led by a coordinator, consists of a school psychologist and a team of teachers with specialized training in learning differences and/or talent development. The OLC model is based on the philosophy that stu-dents vary in their level of ability, achievement, motivation and interest, and that individuals respond best to educational programmes that provide appropriate chal-lenges. When the level and pace of instruction matches the individual's level of achievement and rate of learning, the goal of an optimal match is achievement. In order to provide an optimal match for students with learning differences, who may not be fulfilling their potential in the regular classroom, the OLC develops Individual Educational Plans (IEPs) that are implemented in small group settings. Students with advanced abilities in mathematics and/or language arts may take classes that are designed to remove ceilings and raise conceptual levels, provide opportunities for flexible pacing and individual work, as well as time to interact with intellectual peers. It is recognized that some highly capable students may have a specific learning difference and, in keeping with the optimal match principle, these students may receive services for both special needs. The typical ISM student is a high achiever and often exceeds grade level expectations. ISM does not have the facilities or services to serve students with significant emotional, learning or language problems.

What are the profiles of some of the students who receive services from OLC? An English as a Second Language student with difficulties processing information through an auditory modality who has advanced maths aptitude; a regular education student with exceptional aptitude in mathematics and/or language arts; a regular education student needing learning support in language arts and organization skills with advanced mathematical aptitude; a regular education student with exceptional aptitude in verbal skills, with poor handwriting and spelling skills; a regular education student with spelling difficulties in writing mentorship programme; a regular education student with exceptional aptitude in verbal skills who has difficulty concentrating or sitting still; a regular education student with average abilities in language arts who has difficulties remembering multiplication facts and steps in solving division problems. All of these students have strengths and concerns in other areas, which may include music, art or sports.

Parental communication is considered a vital part of programme development. It is hoped this type of consultative and collaborative effort by all concerned will contribute to a holistic and comprehensive understanding of a student's cognitive learning style. An integrated model of service delivery is advantageous for meeting the needs of students with different educational needs because:

- a variety of specialists are involved in determining the most appropriate instructional intervention for an individual student
- some students have educational needs requiring the services of more than one special programme
- the model provides for a more systematic and comprehensive treatment of a student's learning needs
- assessment services are used to identify a student's cognitive learning style
- it promotes and encourages instructional and institutional flexibility
- it requires collaboration between classroom teachers, guidance counsellors, English as a Second Language teachers, parents, administrators and the admissions office
- the labelling of students based on their cognitive profile is no longer necessary. Instead it promotes an understanding that the bureaucracy of school requires that we label programmes rather than students for the purposes of organizing and managing educational programmes.

American School of Barcelona, Spain [Elsa Lamb, Director]

In 1994 the American School of Barcelona adopted the Optimal Match concept. Its implementation has included the establishment of two student study teams, one in its lower school (grades 1–2) and one in its upper school (grades 7–12); an ongoing staff development effort in the area of special needs; the assigning of interns as tutors to work with highly capable, learning disabled and ESL students; the use of both long-distance learning and independent study programmes in individualizing student instruction; and maximizing the use of local community resources to meet student needs and the better to educate parents about their role in meeting these needs. The American School of Barcelona's Optimal Match referral process and student study team procedures are as follows:

Step One: Teacher and parent meeting is held

a. Student progress is reviewed and problem areas are identified.
b. Teacher explains modifications that have been tried.
c. Teacher interviews parent to obtain developmental history and relevant family information.
d. Teacher and parent agree to what further actions will be taken at school and/or home and put this in writing.
e. If additional actions are agreed on; a date is established to review student progress and programme modifications.
f. If programme modifications prove ineffective, teacher implements step two.

Step Two: Referral is made

a. Teacher completes the referral form, attaches relevant information (anecdotal records, parent interview form, etc) and turns this in to Optimal Match coordinator.
b. The Optimal Match coordinator reviews referral and determines whether more information and/or student observation is needed. If not needed, student is referred directly to student study team.
c. Date for team meeting is set and parents invited to meeting; appropriate participants are notified and copies of relevant information distributed.

Step Three: Student study team meets

a. Referring teacher presents student case by stating problem succinctly, sharing work samples, and sharing relevant background and personal information.
b. Team members participate in problem solving which can include special solutions and interventions (provided by school or outside professionals); establishing alternatives or modifications to regular programme, development of an IEP; and/or referral to outside agencies/professionals.
c. Recommendations are recorded and responsibilities for actions assigned; copies of this are placed in student's file and given to the class teacher/parent.
d. A follow-up date is set for team to meet and evaluate the results of the action taken.

Step Four: Follow-up meetings are held

a. Interventions that have been accomplished are identified.
b. Further modifications, interventions or services, if needed, are recommended.
c. Continued follow-up measures, if indicated, are decided on; responsibilities for these are assigned; and review dates set.

The American School of Barcelona's Optimal Match programme focuses on those special needs present in its student population. Currently this includes physically handicapped, learning disabled, highly capable (ie gifted and talented) and ESL, as well as students with emotional problems who require professional counselling. In order to provide faculty with specific strategies that meet our students' needs an Optimal Match modifications and supports checklist has been developed. The checklist outlines specific strategies in the areas of pacing, environment, presentation of subject matter, materials, assignments, self-management, test adaptations, social interaction supports, and motivation/reinforcement. It is completed at our student study team meeting and copies are distributed to faculty and parents.

International School of Berne, Switzerland [David Gatley, Director]

Getting a curriculum to match the needs of the individual in the classroom is never going to be easy. Understanding and defining the needs of the child is the first major step. This itself will lead to conflict between teachers, between teachers and parents and, in some cases, with the children themselves. Overcoming these difficulties is the job of the school if it is to educate and to develop the children to the best of their ability. Practically this can be attempted in a small school like ours because of small numbers in the classroom. With a maximum class size of 16 children there is a possibility of focusing on individuals within group situations. This would be far more difficult to realize in a larger class situation.

The classroom situation however, as mentioned earlier, is only a part of the issue. How to get all parties focused on the same outcome is much more problematic. It is here that communication becomes the greatest issue to be addressed. What does the school say about matching the curriculum to the child? There can be conflicting statements coming from the school as parents are very aware and very concerned for their own child. A school cannot make sweeping statements that will place great pressures on the school's resources and its teaching staff. If a particular child is perceived to have different needs from the majority of the student body then the implications of this must be looked at and fully understood by all before moves are made to alter the curriculum. Quick fixes are what parents want to see, but in the end they tend to cause more harm than good. A school has to look at the long-term implications and have foresight about what the ramifications of their actions might be. It is better to get it right with considered judgement rather than look for short-term solutions. This is where communication is the crux of the issue. The school that can deliver an optimal match of curriculum to a child is a school where all parties concerned have had an input into the solution. Again a small school has advantages over a large school because of proximity of staff. Even so, procedure, dialogue and documentation must be prescribed so that obvious dangers are avoided.

What seems like a simple issue of delivering to a child's needs is not quite so simple in practice. Education here has always been about balancing the needs of the individual against the needs of the school community and the larger communities outside the school. This is still the case. By delivering what we call an Optimal Match we are trying to redress the balance in favour of the individual.

DISCUSSION

Collaboration, commitment, and communication are common themes reflecting Optimal Match principles at the four international schools quoted. Elsa Lamb wrote of her school's student study team approach and checklist, which emphasizes these themes. Annette Nyqvist described the type of accommodations, extensions and programmes in place at the International School Manila. These practices reflect the school's commitment to meeting their student learning needs. Cynthia Silva at the Graded School, São Paulo, wrote extensively of the comprehensive Optimal Match model practised at that school. 'Graded' has incorporated the Optimal Match model philosophy and approaches at all grade levels, and the Optimal Match approach is included in the school's mission statement. This is an important point. The ACECY conducted a survey of Optimal Match practices at international schools world-wide (Durden, 1996). The most important finding from the survey was the recommendation that international schools should emphasize their commitment to the Optimal Match to the school community by placing Optimal Match approaches in the schools' mission, aims, and objectives statements. Additionally, David Gatley at the International School of Berne clearly states that there must be a school, staff and parent commitment to the Optimal Match process, and cautions against promising more than the school can offer. He emphasizes the importance of communication of all parties involved with the individual student and brings the reader's attention back to redressing the balance of education to the individual student through the Optimal Match philosophy.

The four descriptions of Optimal Match practices at international schools illustrate the diversity of student learning styles and profiles. This calls for adapting the curricula to the student rather than the student being instructed to a fixed curricula. This is central to the Optimal Match Concept, as 'An Optimal Match is the adjustment of an appropriately challenging curriculum to match a student's demonstrated pace and level of learning, contrary to a K-12 curriculum where one size fits all' (CTY, 1994). Maria de la Luz Reyes alludes to an Optimal Match or best fit and challenges the assumption that one style fits all without modifications. She refers to the fallacy of 'the assumption that instruction which is effective for mainstream students will benefit all students, no matter what their backgrounds may be' (Reyes, 1992). Accurate assessment, both formal and informal, is thus an essential component to the Optimal Match. Standardized testing is strongly advocated (Mills and Durden, 1996) at international schools for students with mother-tongue English, ESL students whose level of English permits taking these tests, and students with learning difficulties, allowing test-taking accommodations when necessary. Not only are standardized tests one method for identifying academically talented students, the tests also provide a measure of English language development for

ESL students over time. International students tend to move frequently, and these tests provide an objective measure of basic achievement and abilities where there may be different methods and levels of instruction from school to school. Informal or teacher-made tests may be applicable to one specific school but not to another; therefore, standardized tests may provide the only common basis for measuring student abilities and achievements.

One theme running through all four descriptions of Optimal Match practices is flexibility, which is an integral component of the Optimal Match model. It is well known that, at many international schools, English mother-tongue students are in the minority and teachers are essentially ESL teachers (Bartlett, 1995); flexibility in teaching styles is therefore of the utmost necessity. International school students move in and out of schools frequently, sometimes during the school year, and it is common for a grade to start the year with a set student roster and complete the school year with a 30–40 per cent turnover. This fact leads directors of schools to help teachers develop sensitivity to assessing and matching curricula for their students, especially students with special learning needs, by in-service training, attending workshops, and conferences. In this respect the ECIS Committee for ESL is an important one, aiding the professional development of ESL teachers. Recently the ECIS Committee for the Highly Able and the Special Needs Committee merged into the ECIS Committee for Special Needs/Learning Support. The new committee will be responsible for organizing regional workshops and recommending ECIS conference speakers in the areas of high exceptional abilities and/or talents, learning disabilities, and the emerging field of learning disabilities and high academic abilities and/or talents.

In summary, Durden and Mills (1996) state 'The value of the Optimal Match is most apparent when it is applied to students with obvious special needs – as in the case of highly able children or those with learning disabilities'. But focus on these groups only illuminates the applicability of the concept for all children. Indeed, in thinking about the relevance of the Optimal Match, we might recall the words of seventeenth century physician William Henry: 'Nature is nowhere accustomed more openly to display her secret mysteries than in cases where she shows traces of her workings apart from the beaten path'.

REFERENCES

Advisory Committee on Exceptional Children and Youth (ACECY) (1993) *The Optimal Match Concept: Putting the Pieces together for the Exceptional Student in American-sponsored Overseas Schools*, Office of Overseas Schools, US Department of State, Washington, DC

Advisory Committee on Exceptional Children and Youth (ACECY-IAAY/JHU) (1997) http://www.jhu/-gifted/acecy/acecy.htm. The Johns Hopkins University, Baltimore

Bartlett, K (1995) *Internationalism: Getting Beneath the Surface, Part 2 – The Role of Language*, International Schools Curriculum Project, Vienna International School

Burkholder, J (1992) Letter to the International School of Berne in reference to the Sally Smith Award for Excellence in Special Education awarded to the school, June, Office of Overseas Schools, US Department of State

Center for Talented Youth (1994) *The Optimal Match: A Primer for Change*, Center for Talented Youth, The Johns Hopkins University, Baltimore

Daniels, H (ed) (1996) *An Introduction to Vygotsky*, Routledge, London

Durden, W G (1991) 'The optimal match update', *Earcos Quarterly*, Fall

Durden, W G (1996) *Status Questionnaire*, Advisory Committee on Exceptional Children and Youth, Office of Overseas Schools, US Department of State

Durden, W G and Mackay, L (1995) 'Rediscovering self-reliance in education: The Optimal Match', *Phi Delta Kappan*, **77**, 3, pp 250–51

Durden, W G and Mills, C J (1996) Position paper: *The Optimal Match – The Middle Path toward the Renewal of Education*, IAAY, The Johns Hopkins University, pp 1–5

European Council of International Schools (1997–98) *ECIS International Schools Directory*, ECIS, Petersfield

European Council of International Schools (1997) *School Evaluation and Accreditation: A Professionally Recognized Programme for the Improvement of International Schools World-wide*, ECIS, Petersfield

European Council for International Schools and the New England Association of Schools and Colleges (1997) *School Improvement Through Accreditation: The Instructional Evaluation Guide for American/International Schools*, ECIS, Petersfield

Foreman-Haldimann, M (1981a) 'The effects of bilingualism on cognitive development', *International Schools Journal*, 1, pp 73–81

Foreman-Haldimann, M (1981b) 'The effects of "language shock" and "culture shock" on students in international schools', *International Schools Journal*, 2, pp 74–82

Foreman-Haldimann, M (1982) 'The gifted and talented: Part I – An overview', *International Schools Journal*, 4, pp 55–72

Foreman-Haldimann, M (1983a) 'The gifted and talented: Part II: Research',

International Schools Journal, 5, pp 65–74

Foreman-Haldimann, M (1983b) 'Learning difficulties and the bilingual/multiling-ual international school student', *International Schools Journal*, 6, pp   59–76

Freeman, J (1993) 'The creative cost of high academic achievement', *International Schools Journal*, 26, pp 39–46

Hollington, A (1994) 'A very special international education', *International Schools Journal*, 27, pp 27–30

Institute for the Academic Advancement of Youth (1997) *In-house Bibliography*, The Johns Hopkins University, Public Information Office of IAAY, Baltimore

Kusuma-Powel, O, Kahler, S and Rogers, J (1992) 'Recognizing dysfunctional multi-lingual students in international schools', *International Schools Journal*, 23,   pp 70–4

Miller, B (1986) 'Nurturing gifted children in multicultural international schools', *International Schools Journal*, 11, pp 37–41

Mills, C J and Durden, W G (1996) 'Standardized tests a good option in inter-national school setting', *The International Educator*, 10, pp 1–5

Mills, C J and Tangherlini, A E (1992) 'Finding the optimal match: Another look at ability grouping and cooperative learning', *Equity and Excellence*, 25 (2–4), pp 205–8

Raynor, P (1991) 'Foreign language acquisition and the learning disabled student', *International Schools Journal*, 22, pp 41–6

Reyes, M de la Luz (1992) 'Challenging venerable assumptions: Literacy instruction for linguistically different students', *Harvard Educational Review*, **62**, 4, pp 427–46

Scruggs, P and Goldman, A (1985) 'The case for a special basic skills class in inter-national schools', *International Schools Journal*, 25, pp 67–74

Sparks, R and Ganschow, L (1993) 'Foreign language learning and the learning dis abled at-risk student: a review of recent research', *International Schools Journal*, 25, pp 47–54

Stanley, J C (1981) The predictive value of SAT for brilliant seventh and eighth graders, *International Schools Journal*, 2, pp 39–48

Stumpf, H and Haldimann, M (1997) 'Spatial ability and academic success of sixth grade students at international schools', *School Psychology International*, **18**, 3, pp 245–59

Swiss Group of International Schools (1996) *Minutes from the September 1996 SGIS Committee meeting*, SGIS, Berne

Thomas, M (1990) 'A collaborative consultation approach to special education', *International Schools Journal*, 20, pp 45–54

11

PASTORAL CARE: THE CHALLENGE FOR INTERNATIONAL SCHOOLS

Barry Drake

INTRODUCTION

This chapter seeks to open a discourse on the theme of 'pastoral care' in international schools. It explores just how possible and, indeed, how desirable it is for managers in such schools to take on board the philosophy and mechanisms of pastoral care programmes that are embedded in the specific cultural contexts of particularistic national educational systems. Following an examination of commonalities existing in the provision of pastoral care in national and international schools, the author concludes that innovators in international schools who wish to introduce pastoral care programmes must go beyond national school paradigms to give careful consideration to the differing texture of staffing concerns, to the specific needs of the clientele, to challenges posed by differing value systems, as well as to the varying cultural acceptability of such programmes. The author will argue that the provision of effective pastoral care in an international school will not only contribute to the general development of the individual student but, in terms of 'international education', will afford the opportunity for quality cross-cultural understanding and 'help to negate racist, sexist and negative attitudes [and in[this way the educational and cultural impoverishment consequent upon the exposure only to a mono-cultural, Anglo-centric and parochial environment can be avoided' (Duncan, 1988).

WHAT IS 'PASTORAL CARE'?

The term 'pastoral care' leads to a number of semantic interpretations. What is meant by 'pastoral care' in the UK may be very different from what is understood by the term in the United States or Nigeria. Similarly with the concept of 'guidance'. In England and Wales the term 'guidance' is usually applied to the work done with individual students on specific choices facing them: 'vocational guidance', 'careers guidance' or 'university guidance'. This is similar to the work

146

undertaken by the United States 'college' or 'guidance' counsellor, whereas in Scotland the term is used to refer to the broader aspects of pastoral care. In Canada and Western Australia the term 'guidance' may also refer to specific curriculum programmes, which in England and Wales would normally be labelled personal and social education (PSE). In Canada these courses are usually taught by school counselling staff and have a lot in common with the English PSE and pastoral tutorial programmes (Lang, 1989). In England and Wales the broad programme of support offered to students is designated 'pastoral care' and the timetabled, formal part of the programme described as the 'pastoral curriculum', or PSE. Hong Kong and Singapore, as ex-British colonies, have both adopted the term 'pastoral care' and embarked on a policy of institutionalizing their programmes along English lines (Best and Lang in Lang *et al.*, 1994).

Pastoral care is that part of a school's educational provision which covers 'all aspects of work with pupils other than pure teaching' (Marland, 1974); it is 'concerned with the "health" and functioning of the organisation as well as with individual pupils' (Hamblin, 1981). Pastoral care focuses on the affective domain in its concern for skills and feelings, and in Hamblin's view it ought to aim at building 'responsible autonomy and rational self-regulating principles of moral judgement' (Hamblin, 1986). Pastoral care has been an integral feature of the British educational milieu since the 1970s and has been defined as both a system and a set of ideas (Lang and Young, 1985), though many teachers have found it difficult to differentiate between the two. By the 1980s the British educational inspectorate were of the opinion that all students had to be prepared, while in school, to meet the intellectual and social demands of adult life; to develop an acceptable set of personal values; to be capable of making informed choices and becoming responsible citizens (Her Majesty's Inspectorate, 1980). The Education Reform Act of 1988 actually required schools to provide: 'a balanced and broadly based curriculum that a) promotes the spiritual, moral, cultural, mental and physical development of pupils at the school and of society; and b) prepares such pupils for the opportunities, responsibilities and experiences of adult life' (Lang in Lang *et al.*, 1994). The following year the Department of Education and Science (DES) indicated its broad commitment to pastoral care:

> In detail, pastoral care is concerned with promoting pupils' personal and social development and fostering positive attitudes: through the quality of teaching and learning; through the nature of relationships amongst pupils, teachers and adults other than teachers; through arrangements for monitoring pupils' overall progress, academic, personal and social; through specific pastoral structures and support systems; and through extra-curricular activities and the school ethos. Pastoral care, accordingly, should help a school to articulate its values, involve all teachers and help pupils to achieve success. In such a context it offers support for the learning, behaviour and welfare of all pupils, and addresses the particular difficulties some individual children may be experiencing. It seeks to help to ensure that all pupils, and particularly girls and members of ethnic minorities, are enabled to benefit from the full range of educational opportunities which the school has available. (DES, 1989)

The Department of Education and Science did not attempt to prescribe the methodology by which pastoral care should be provided, and in Britain today there is still little general agreement among educators as to which system provides the most effective format for its delivery or what body of ideas and skills ought to be included in a pastoral care programme. For many teachers a further source of debate has been found in the precise relationship between pastoral care and PSE. In attempting to shed some light on this particular conundrum, Watkins (1993) suggested that it is the 'caring' nature of pastoral care that sets it apart from PSE.

Traditionally pastoral care has been seen by British teachers as a rather reactive process, tending to deal with student problems once they have arisen (Lang and Young, 1985) or, as Hamblin (1993) called it, 'emotional first aid'. While there is a very real need for teachers and/or tutors to deal with the emotional needs of the individual and provide the sort of caring support that will assist the student through times of personal stress and challenge, pastoral care must go further than this. PSE came to be seen as the translation of pastoral care into a more structured curriculum (Best and Lang in Lang *et al.*, 1994) and, as such, was the logical outcome of recommendations by Marland (1974), Hamblin (1989) and others for a proactive pastoral programme that would help students anticipate the various challenges they may face in their lives and deal with them in ways that mitigate against problem formulation. This reflected an awareness that there was a very real need to help empower students to confront, in a proactive way, their emotional crises, anxiety, conflict, values, beliefs; to inform and educate their views and actions on sex, drugs, prejudice, gender equity; to assist them in the pursuit of realistic target setting, self-evaluation and academic progress (Hodkinson, 1994).

Many schools in the UK have, however, continued to separate the delivery of pastoral care and PSE, in the belief that the latter requires more specialist training and, arguably, the creation of a team of PSE teachers. Other educators are of the opinion, however, that 'caring is a function of positive human relationships' which does not necessarily require specific training and expertise (Clemett and Pearce, 1986) and consequently some schools continue to combine the two areas and view PSE as an integral part of the broader provision of pastoral care. For the purposes of this chapter the term 'pastoral care' subsumes both the role of 'carer', in its more inclusive sense, and the institutionalized pastoral curriculum. This is in accord with the view expressed by Clemett and Pearce (1986) that pastoral care covers 'all the non-instructional, generalised aspects of a school's work with pupils and the timetabled curricular interaction between teacher and pupil, whether it is labelled "pastoral" or not'. Differences of opinion over the centrality or marginality of pastoral care in schools have been well highlighted by the conundrum posed by Best (1989): 'Do we teach because we care? Or do we care in order to teach effectively?' For some teachers 'caring' still seems to be seen as lying outside their professional responsibilities. Others see this proposition as an anathema for surely, they would argue, all teachers have a responsibility for 'caring for the pupils in their charge, for putting the ethos of the school into practice, and being aware of the needs of their pupils' (Clemett and Pearce, 1986; Raynor, 1995). Indeed, for some writers pastoral care has become such an automatic expectation of the profession that they claim teachers ought to be able to undertake pastoral tasks without having timetabled PSE lessons (Shaw, 1994).

Moreover, most of the recent literature on pastoral care would seem to subscribe to the view that there should be no artificial separation of the academic and pastoral curriculum which should, instead, be viewed from the Yin and Yang perspective of complementary bipolarity (Marland, 1986; Sceeny, 1987; Hamblin, 1989; McGuinness, 1989; Galloway, 1985; Shaw, 1994). However, as Morphy (1991) has indicated, the reality of practice is often at odds with the theory and the tendency in many British schools, for instance, to appoint one senior manager for the academic programme and one for the pastoral, has possibly reinforced an unwelcome institutionalized split in the two parts of the curriculum. Indeed some writers have seen pastoral care as preparing the way for effective learning and have, thereby, reduced pastoral care to a mere 'underlabourer's' role on behalf of the academic curriculum. This, according to Best (1989), is overly simplistic and unhelpful. Achievement and social development are interlinked and, as Rutter (1991) has argued, it is both artificial and misleading to debate the relative merits of a 'task-oriented, nose-to-the-grindstone' approach, or an 'emotionally supportive' approach designed to make children want to be at school and enjoy their learning; both are vital to optimal learning! Academic growth and learning skills should be of integral concern to any pastoral care programme but such 'care' cannot be limited to the cognitive domain. As Hopson and Scally (1981) suggest, the aim of the life skills section of a pastoral care programme is to empower young people to become more 'confident, assertive and productive in their lives'. In this sense effective pastoral care adds significantly to the 'institutional culture' (Best, 1989) which may, in turn, be further enhanced by the inclusivity of a pastoral care system designed to meet the unique needs of an individual school (Clemett and Pearce, 1986).

PASTORAL CARE IN THE INTERNATIONAL CONTEXT

It has been implied above that the genesis of modern pastoral care in schools lies in the British educational system. Does this necessarily imply that there is an absence of such provision in other educational systems? Is pastoral care, as some of its international critics would have it, an Anglocentric creation embedded in a particular social, historical and cultural milieu?

Until the mid-1970s there seems to have been little in the way of research on the international dimensions of pastoral care, and the earliest literature on the subject would suggest that many other countries had drawn fairly extensively on the UK experience (Dynan, 1980; Lovegrove, 1982). However, what began as a trickle of interest in the 1980s has now become a 'torrent' (Ribbons, 1989). In very recent times pastoral care has become the focus of three international forums, beginning in 1988 with the Singapore Educational Administration Society's conference 'The child's growth: our major concern'. This was followed by pastoral care conferences in Perth (1990) and Queensland (1992), out of which came the important compilation of papers in Lang *et al.*'s, *Caring for Children: International Perspectives on Pastoral Care and PSE* (1994).

Part of the difficulty of comparing the 'caring' approaches of different educational systems lies in semantics. However, despite problems of language, recent literature points to a great deal of common ground. The concepts of pastoral care and PSE, though differently named, are well accepted in many countries. In the USA, despite the alternative route taken towards 'guidance' based on reactive support offered by professional counsellors, there has been a recent move in some states towards 'developmental counselling'. A central feature of the latter has been a greater emphasis on proactive programmes mirroring pastoral care in the UK. Indeed Lang (1989) has demonstrated that a model postulated by Gysbers and Henderson (1988) was strikingly similar, at a conceptual level, to the UK pastoral curriculum. In Hong Kong, not surprisingly, the government is attempting to institutionalize pastoral care along the lines to be found in the UK. Its 1993 and 1995 *Guidelines on Whole School Approach to Guidance,* based on the Education Commission Report No 4, conclude that the responsibility for pastoral care lies with all members of a school's teaching staff: 'In schools with a positive and caring atmosphere, all teachers contribute to helping students develop into whole persons' (Hong Kong Education Department, 1995a). The Education Department went further in September 1995 to issue suggested job descriptions for *Guidance Masters/Mistresses* (Hong Kong Education Department, 1995b).

Singapore began to take a serious interest in the UK model of pastoral care in 1986 when it sent the Minister of Education and 12 secondary school principals on a study tour of the UK. Their findings contributed to the 1987 report: 'Towards Excellence in Schools', which in turn led to pastoral care programmes being introduced into 17 pilot schools. Lang's (1989) study of the Singapore experiment suggests that the decision to implement pastoral care into a system that was extremely selective, examination oriented and very successful in academic terms was 'a fascinating issue in itself', since it clearly represented a view that 'there was a need to produce more well-rounded and fulfilled individuals than can be achieved solely through an emphasis on the cognitive'. Though it is, perhaps, still too soon to draw definitive conclusions from what has happened in Singapore, Lang (in Lang *et al.*, 1994) is convinced that, although there are many cross-cultural issues and questions yet to be resolved, the evidence so far indicates that pastoral care is culturally transferable. Indeed he suggests that the 'problems of pastoral care also appear to be transferable: many of the problems encountered in the schools in Singapore are very similar to those encountered in UK schools'.

Lang and Young's (1985) work in Canada also suggests that there has been some recent convergence with the UK, both in the thinking underpinning 'guidance' and in the actual practice; that there was, in Lang's words, 'an overarching area of concern and practice within the affective domain, which was amenable to analysis, an area best described as "guidance" which informs individual responses (to pastoral care) in particular countries'. It is not just those countries with imperial links to the UK which provide forms of pastoral care. In Denmark the national curriculum prescribes an hour's discussion time once a week for all classes, to be held with their class teacher. In Germany students have long had the opportunity to speak to teachers they can trust (*Vertrauenslehrer*) and have the regular option for political discussion. Portugal is in the process of introducing a form of pastoral care, and Spain may be moving towards pastorally oriented tutorial work (Lang in Lang *et al.*, 1994). Furthermore, a study of recently completed research and research in progress indicates a broadening of interest around the world in the UK approach. These include Chin's (1990) study of pastoral care systems in five English schools that led to recommendations to the Singapore Ministry of Education (1987), and Onyeocha's (1991) research focused on the creation of effective moral education for Nigeria. Firth (1989) and Lam (1991) demonstrated similar interests in relation to the Soviet Union and Hong Kong respectively while, in 1990, Al Tikriti completed a PhD on the development of counselling in Iraqi secondary schools based on the British experience.

The author's own research findings at the Li Po Chun United World College of Hong Kong (LPCUWC) (created in 1992), tentatively confirm the impression of a greater world-wide involvement in some form of pastoral care programme than one might casually have expected. Statistics gathered from the first and second cohorts of LPCUWC students (217 students between 1992 and 1995), drawn from 50 different countries, gave an indication of those who had been provided with various forms of 'life skills' education before they arrived at the college. At the lower end of the scale a mere 14 per cent had been advised on how to deal with severe illness in the family, while only 17 per cent had experienced a 'conflict resolution' programme. Despite the context of our times only 36 per cent had received information on the issue of gender equity and 46 per cent on sexually transmitted diseases. Greater proportions had been exposed to information on sex (53 per cent), drugs (63 per cent), alcohol (58 per cent) and AIDS (59 per cent). As far as study skills were concerned, 50 per cent had received information in class on 'time management' and 50 per cent on note taking, while 60 per cent and 67 per cent had been exposed to revision and examination skills respectively. Within this framework it would appear that cultural provenance did have an impact on the orientation of pastoral care provided to students prior to their arrival at LPCUWC. The statistics suggested that North American and western European educational systems were more likely to offer programmes on sex, drugs, etc than the Hong Kong or Chinese systems. Conversely, the Hong Kong system was more likely to expose students to formal presentations on gender equity and study skills than were the other major cultural groupings. Caution must be exercised in relation both to the limited nature of this evidence and to student memory slippage, but it is interesting to note that the trend demonstrated in a number of such surveys undertaken between 1992 and 1996 was one of increasing involvement (Drake, 1998).

A good deal of this developing international interest in pastoral care has focused on the UK model (if indeed it is possible to talk of a single UK model). There continues to be, however, a wide variety of models for the provision of 'care' in national schools. Despite their differences much common ground exists, even if it is frequently obfuscated by methodology, semantics and systems. Within the international context, as within the UK, differing opinions exist on such issues as whether the delivery ought to be in the hands of specialists, or all teachers, and whether the emphasis ought to be placed on reactive or proactive responses to supporting students. The labels we attach to pastoral care may vary from one part of the world to another, but 'we must not be misled by superficial differences': there is significant commonallty in what educationalists attempt to do beneath the labels (Best in Lang *et al.*, 1994).

PASTORAL CARE IN INTERNATIONAL SCHOOLS

So much for the development of pastoral care in national educational systems around the world: what role does the concept play in international schools and international education? Is it either desirable or possible for international schools to offer pastoral care programmes for their students that may be based on particularistic cultural paradigms? In seeking to answer this question it is essential to keep in mind the broad range of educational institutions that call themselves 'international schools'. There is, of course, considerable divergence of opinion over what makes a school 'international' (Gellar, 1981; Matthews, 1989, Jonietz and Harris, 1991; Hayden and Thompson, 1995a) as, indeed, there is over the relationship between an 'international school' and 'international education' (Belle-Isle, 1986; Hill, 1994; Hayden and Thompson, 1995a). What most of these writers agree on, however, is that it would be dangerous to assume that a school that designates itself 'international' will, by definition, deliver an 'international education'. Nor can it be asserted with any degree of conviction that 'international education' can only be provided, *de facto*, by an 'international school'. Belle-Isle (1986) rejected a broader classification for international schools in favour of the opinion that 'such schools (are not international) which, despite their names and overseas locations, have remained closely related to their national systems through curriculum and programmes'. To Belle-Isle and others a genuine 'international school' must be offering a truly 'international' curriculum. Hill (1994) continued this debate by insisting that it is necessary to distinguish between international and national schools. Hill proposes a classification for national schools along these lines:

> one whose students and staff are predominantly from one country, where the curriculum and examinations of that country only are offered, and where the ethos is national as distinct from international. National schools:
> • serve principally the students of one nationality;
> • are usually located within the one country, where they may be government or fee paying schools with a parent governing body; and
> • may be located overseas to serve their own expatriates such as the numerous American, British and French schools, many of which are funded and staffed by the national government at home and some of which are private.

This pattern, Hill would argue, was substantially different to 'international schools', 'whose students and staff are representative of a number of cultural and ethnic origins, where the IB and/or a number of different national courses are offered and where the ethos is one of internationalism as distinct from national-ism'.

It is this classification that ultimately underpins the arguments that are to fol-low, for it seems that the key to whether a school is 'international' or not is to be found in the answer to the question: what form of broad education does the school provide? For surely an 'international school' must provide an 'international educa-tion'. This, of course, begs the question: what is 'international education'? An 'international education' cannot simply mean an international academic curricu-lum such as the International Baccalaureate (IB) or the International GCSE (IGCSE); in the words of Peterson (1987) it should be a programme in which international understanding is developed. With this is mind, the working definition of a bona fide 'international school' to be used in the rest of this chapter is as follows: an international school is one that has:

1. an international teaching staff
2. an international student body
3. a board of governors that represents different cultural views, especially if it has a substantial impact on policy formulation
4. an international academic curriculum, which goes beyond the simple adoption of 'international' programmes such as the IB or IGCSE, to encourage interna-tional understanding
5. a broad non-academic programme which encourages/facilitates cultural mixing and cross-cultural fertilization (even though, at the time, it might not appear to be happening as extensively as desired: Matthews, 1989).

There will of course be schools that do not completely fit these criteria, but the cor-nerstones of an 'international school' must lie in the existence of (4) and (5) above. Moreover, it is far more likely that an international school will be able to deliver a broad international educational programme successfully if the school can also claim to have (1) and (2) above. Perhaps the least vital of the components listed above is (3), but even here it must be recognized how important a board of gover-nors can be to the formulation of policy that underpins the educational pro-gramme.

The concepts of pastoral care are just as essential for students in such 'interna-tional schools' as they are in national schools. Indeed, 'it is difficult to see what education would mean in any culture if they were not' (Best and Lang in Lang *et al.*, 1994). Personal and social education is presumed by the notion of education itself. 'If education is concerned with changing an individual through promoting growth within a social context, the proposition that education is personal and social is tautological' (Pring, 1988). It is a truism that education is concerned as much with the affective, moral and political domains as it is with the cognitive, whether such education is part of the explicit or the 'hidden' curriculum, and whether it be delivered in a national or an international school. Consequently, the development of a pastoral care programme within an 'international school' (as defined above) is of very real importance. It should certainly receive as much attention as it does in any national system, perhaps more so, since many of the students in an international school are not only facing the normal challenges of adolescence but also have to deal with cultural and other forms of dislocation, often in the absence of extended family and friendship support networks. While there has been limited published work on the sort of challenges facing international school students (Downs, 1990; Powell, *et al.*, 1992; Willis *et al.*, 1994; Akram, 1995) and fairly extensive research on multicultural education (Brislin *et al.*, 1986; Hofstede, 1991; Brislin, 1993; Trompenaars, 1993), there appears to be a conspicuous absence of any relevant literature, published or otherwise, related to the specific issue of pastoral care in 'international schools'. As already stated this chapter is intended to open such a discourse through an examination of two major issues: first, how pastoral care programmes in international schools can fulfil the needs of their students and, second, the challenges facing the development of an appropriate programme in international schools.

THE SPECIFIC NEEDS OF INTERNATIONAL SCHOOL STUDENTS FOR PASTORAL CARE PROVISION

What sort of pastoral care programme should managers offer international students, in terms of both content and methodology? There is no universally accepted answer to this question. In designing an effective programme within the context of the UK Hamblin (1986) suggests innovators need to consider: the formal structure of the school; the neighbouring location; social class and pupil composition; incidence of teacher stress in the school; attitudes within the school towards pastoral care and innovation in general; the availability of training opportunities; and the existing vertical or horizontal pastoral care organization within the school. Every school has its own particular combination of attitudes, potential and available skills which creates a unique corporate spirit and ethos; consequently the pastoral programme must be designed to take this individuality into account. However, Hamblin (1989) offered some valuable thoughts on which life skills ought to be considered for inclusion in a proactive, UK-based, pastoral care programme. He saw it as essential to try: (a) to stimulate the development of personal values and help students clarify them; (b) to provide the skills necessary for achievement, including study skills and the ability to plan ahead; (c) to develop a belief in the need for inner control and the opportunity to exercise it; (d) to promote a wide range of skills necessary for social competence, ranging from standpoint taking to the management of stress; and (e) to help students to learn decision-making skills. These skills are equally important to students studying at an international school, although (a) and (d) might well be extended to include developing an awareness and understanding of differing value systems; and developing those skills required within tomorrow's global community, such as cultural adaptation, which can help individuals transfer from one society to another. Clemett and Pearce (1986) also see the possibility of important common elements in the methodology used in the delivery of pastoral care programmes in the UK:

> Pastoral care is effective in a school when pupils and teachers participate in a coherent programme of skills-based activities enabling a transfer from dependence to independence. Such programmes need clearly defined aims and structured activities and resources designed to specifically meet the developmental needs of the pupils in each school.

Arguably such methodology is equally applicable to international school education but, whatever the methodology chosen to deliver pastoral care, it must be relevant to the needs of both the school and the students. Marland (1974) points out that the real function of a pastoral care system is to help the school attain its objectives, rather than developing a separate sets of goals. Indeed the growing pursuit of effectiveness in education has led administrators to consider much more closely the role played by their pastoral care programme. Galloway (1985) indicated that 'Concepts of school and teacher effectiveness imply the sort of constructive and co-operative pupil-teacher relationships which are one of the characteristics of effective pastoral care'. This line was pursued by Hargreaves (1990), who suggested that 'effective schools are demanding places, where teachers expect and ensure high standards of work and behaviour; at the same time they are responsive to pupils, for the teachers are approachable and, since they value pupils, seek to involve them in the life and work of the schools'. The qualities sought in a progressive school of 'a more child-centred approach, scope for greater self-expression and development of the individual in an atmosphere of warm supportive relationships with adults and a participation of everyone in decision making' (Lambert, 1975) are perhaps best acquired through the school's pastoral care system. Hence, at least in part, the interest shown in this area of the curriculum in recent years. International schools that continue to see the form tutor/home room teacher's role as merely administrative would do well to note the UK experience, where schools in which 'form tutors carry out mainly administrative functions such as taking registers and reading notices, tend to suffer from more disruptive behaviour than schools in which they are actively involved in disciplinary counselling and guidance activities, monitoring academic progress and other pastoral work' (DES, 1989).

However, while increasing cultural heterogeneity is becoming a regular feature of many national systems, the initiators of pastoral care programmes in international schools will generally have to deal with greater variety in educational backgrounds and more extensive cultural diversity. The question may be asked whether in such circumstances it is possible, or even desirable, to create a standardized student support system while being culturally sensitive to all. There is certainly a very real danger that in creating a standardized programme an international school might simply impose a western, and alien model of 'life skills' on other cultures. Moreover, it is important to consider whether the school can, or indeed should expect teachers from different cultures to be willing and able to deliver such a programme in a way that may be best suited to one particular culture. Critics at the 'chalk face' of pastoral care programmes in international schools have maintained that it is impossible to create a programme that meets all needs, and that given free choice neither students nor staff from non-western cultures would welcome such a programme. One must ask, however, whether there is any evidence to support such propositions. (There has been little academic research undertaken on pastoral care programmes in international schools, and even less on the seemingly even more particularistic realm of the upper secondary stage of international schools.) The results of the author's research with international students (grades 12–13) certainly challenges such notions. There have been a number of projects investigating the specific needs of sixth formers in UK schools, which allow some comparisons to be made with the conclusions that follow, which in turn are based on the author's work at LPCUWC. Hamblin's (1989) research indicated that the 16–19 age group would welcome more guidance and counselling in schools 'though it may have to differ from what we have conventionally offered'. Fogelman's work (1972) pointed to the need to prepare students for life beyond the sixth form: particularly what to expect from university-style education. Bailey (1972) suggested the need for more guidance on sixth form subject choices, while King *et al.* (1974), in a study of post-compulsory education in western Europe, found that 50 per cent of British students in the 16–19 age group endorsed the need for 'much more guidance and counselling, whilst 70 per cent of continental students felt the need for this'. A further study by Buckton (1971) of 16–19 year olds in three British educational institutions, a traditional grammar school, a comprehensive school and a college of education, found that 'the large majority indicated that they would welcome guidance and help, so long as it was free from overtones of directiveness and paternalism'.

As part of the author's own research, students at LPCUWC were asked whether they felt the pastoral care programme was helpful or not (Drake, 1997, 1998). In response to the last questionnaire given to the fourth cohort in May 1996, 82 per cent of the respondents stated that the programme offered by the college had been either 'very helpful' or 'helpful'. This was the third year in succession that the students had been so supportive: 87 per cent of the second cohort (1993–5) and 84 per cent of the third cohort (1994–6) had also asserted the programme was either 'very helpful' or 'helpful'. Further confirmation of student support for a pastoral care programme of the sort offered at the college was to be found in the same questionnaire. Students were asked: 'Should the college continue to offer such a programme?'. Eighty-nine per cent of the first, and 86 per cent of the second, cohort replied 'yes'. In subsequent years student support appeared to become even stronger, with 90 per cent of the third cohort and 98 per cent of the respondents from the fourth cohort advocating the retention of the guidance programme. These statistics appear to lend support to the work done in British and European sixth forms, in that the international students at LPCUWC approved of the pastoral programme being offered by the college and felt such a programme was needed by the 16–19 age range. It was of interest to note that this level of student support appeared to be cross-cultural and irrespective of the educational system from which the students emanated.

In terms of the actual content of a pastoral care programme aimed at 16–19 year olds, researchers in the UK have identified a number of key issues: study skills; self- esteem; subject choices; life at university and so on. Data collected in the process of the author's research appears to confirm the interest of international students in these areas (Drake, 1998). At LPCUWC three cohorts of students between 1993 and 1994 were invited to state what subjects they would like to see incorporated into the pastoral programme. It was on the basis of these surveys that the LPCUWC programme was designed. Student responses were indicative of vigorous concern with the pragmatics of university application, examination regulations, life at university, examination skills, career prospects and the 'gap year', and appeared to reflect Fogelman's findings of 1972. Significant interest, however, was also shown by the second and third cohorts in 'stress management' and 'inter-cultural sensitivity'. There was also strong support for discussion to include 'dealing with personal relationships', 'conflict resolution', sex, drugs, AIDS and gender equity. The third and fourth cohorts also demonstrated a concern for 'self-esteem' issues including eating-related disorders and argued, as Hamblin (1989) does, for their inclusion in the programme.

Many international schools of the K-12 or 6–12 structure are in a position to develop a sequential pastoral care programme that meets the ongoing needs of their international clientele as they progress through the school. However, both this type of school and those that deal with a more transitory population have to face the challenge of students who transfer into the international school from diverse ethnic and geographical backgrounds and who, consequently, may have been exposed to a variety of pastoral care programmes in their previous schools, ranging along a continuum of provision from minimal to extensive. It is not enough simply to bolt a national pastoral care programme on to an otherwise international curriculum. The specific needs of both the transitory and the long-term school resident need to be addressed; and what better way of ascertaining those needs than by asking the students themselves (particularly the older ones) what they require from such a programme. The evidence gleaned from the data collected in the author's research project would indicate that international students are likely to support a guidance programme designed to meet the needs of their age range, irrespective of their varying backgrounds, particularly if they feel they have had an input into the programme. Moreover, in terms of what content was held to be desirable, the international students at LPCUWC did not seem to have significantly different needs to those articulated by sixth formers in the UK as identified by researchers such as Fogelman (1972) and Hamblin (1989), although the international nature of the student body and varying educational systems from which students emanate naturally produced some particularity. For instance, when asked for their view on the need for individual units of the programme, student responses were often conditioned by prior provision of pastoral care which, in turn, could well have been linked to a particular educational tradition. It also became clear from a study of 'the perceived needs from a pastoral programme at LPCUWC' (Drake, 1998) that the pastoral team in international schools had to remain sensitive to the fact that some cultures prefer to deal with subjects like sex through dissemination of information rather than discussion. Cognizance must be taken by international schools of cultural heterogeneity, and alternative formats to the delivery of 'pastoral care' units should be offered where it seems appropriate. Flexibility and diversity have to be the keynotes of 'pastoral care' in international schools if the programme is to be effective for the majority of students.

CHALLENGES TO IMPLEMENTING A PASTORAL CARE PROGRAMME IN AN INTERNATIONAL SCHOOL

Staffing the pastoral programme

One of the ongoing debates within the context of British pastoral care education focuses on whose responsibility it is to deliver such a programme. Managers in international schools face the same staffing issues, which may be further complicated by divergent cultural responses to pastoral care, and teachers in international schools articulate exactly the same concerns. They will claim, with much justification, that they have never been trained to provide counselling, to detect and deal with signs of stress and anxiety, and that their own cultural backgrounds would make it difficult for them to deliver certain units of the programme. These concerns certainly reflect the views of educators world-wide. As Soong and Khoo (1994) point out in relation to teachers in Singapore, a lack of ability and experience in delivering such topics as sex education creates a sense of apprehension and a feeling of 'inadequacy, self-consciousness, discomfort, awkwardness and embarrassment'. However, part of what might appear to be a cultural conundrum may in fact be part of a broader pedagogical issue: the lack of training in the delivery of 'pastoral care'.

While the inadequacy of training remains a thorny issue some researchers, of course, continue to suggest that 'caring' is such an integral part of the work of any teacher that it is almost tautological to suggest that teachers need specialized training in order to deliver such guidance programmes (Clemett and Pearce, 1986; Marland, 1989; Raynor, 1995). Few researchers have posited strong arguments in the opposite direction but, in practice, some schools still formally separate pastoral and academic tasks (Morphy, 1991). Teachers in an international school coming from enormously diverse educational traditions may be misled into thinking that their particular educational training has been lacking in comparison to that offered to teachers from another tradition, whereas the reality suggests a commonality: paucity of 'pastoral' training. Even where tutors have received some training in counselling some inevitably feel constrained by the nature of their conflicting roles. Many teachers continue to think that their primary role is to teach and that they cannot be 'all things to all men'. Cross (1995) has indicated a particular conflict between the roles of 'befriender' and 'authority figure'. She argued that older students may well be unwilling to reveal their deeper problems to a tutor, who may also act in some way as an 'assessor'. On the other hand research done by Graham *et al.* (1991) in the UK suggested that teacher resistance to undertaking 'pastoral care' functions stemmed from the fact that 'some felt they were being asked to do "social work", others that it was too demanding of time, and some felt unable to use some of the methods suggested'. All these concerns were expressed by teachers at the author's own international school and were seemingly reflective of general teacher angst rather than culturally specific considerations. Moreover, as Graham *et al.* (1991) suggest, many of these reactions are inevitable when teachers are faced with substantive change to their working patterns. It is important for the pastoral care manager in an international school to be proactive in addressing these problems by stressing flexibility within the programme, involving staff in all stages of the implementation of the programme, and by using the inevitable conflicts as a way of ultimately producing positive growth for the institution. In particular, international schoolteachers have to be persuaded that their particular prior educational training has not seriously disadvantaged them in terms of pastoral care delivery. All tutors will benefit from the provision of common in-service training on the methodology of pastoral care before the programme is fully instituted.

The generality of challenges facing teachers world-wide as they begin to work more extensively with pastoral care programmes should not, however, be used to invalidate the importance of cultural challenges to the delivery of pastoral care. Some international schools will take the carefully considered decision to include *all* teachers, irrespective of culture, in the pastoral team. As with Raynor (1995), the management team of such a school may be of the opinion that:

> pastoral care is not solely the responsibility of designated staff teams within a school, but is the responsibility and obligation of all staff at all times... all staff are responsible for the pupils in their charge, for putting the ethos of the school into practice, and being aware of the needs of their pupils.

As Marland (1989) suggests, the 'tutor is the heart of the school, the specialist whose specialism is bringing everything together, whose subject is the pupil herself, who struggles for the tutee's entitlement, and who enables the pupil to make the best use of the school'. However, to adopt a whole school approach to the delivery of pastoral care is to assume not only that *all* teachers are willing and capable participants, but also that cross-cultural counselling is both appropriate and acceptable.

Cross-cultural counselling

For cross-cultural counselling to work effectively tutors will have to become more aware of the needs of particular ethnic groups. However, it may well be hugely idealistic to expect all tutors to become *au fait* with the particularistic needs of every culture represented in an international school, although if that school wishes to provide more effective cross-cultural counselling it ought, at the very least, to offer regular INSET on the cultural and religious values of the major groups with which tutors have to deal. As an example, high on this list at the author's school would be a greater understanding of Chinese culture, since 50 per cent of LPCUWC students are of this ethnicity. To illustrate the point: non-Chinese tutors would need to note, for instance, that Chinese 'orientation towards children is moralistic rather than psychological' (Ekblad, 1986). Suzuki (1980) also maintains that the Confucian ethic encourages the Chinese to believe that 'individuals have the potential within themselves to achieve fulfilment and happiness. Satisfaction is gained through the person's diligent and sincere efforts to conduct themselves morally and develop their potential.' The emphasis in counselling emanating from a western cultural perspective is currently based on universal human rights, interpersonal tolerance and personal accountability, and this tradition might find itself at odds with a traditional Chinese emphasis on collective allegiance and responsibility, duty, diligence and religious convergence (Everts, 1993).

An international school seeking to develop a pastoral care programme must take these issues into account and seek to allay staff concerns over inexperience and differing cultural attributes. As with the theories related to the management of change in other areas of life, in an international school most teacher concerns can be reduced by the successful provision of INSET prior to the execution of the initiative; by involving staff in all stages of the planning process and by addressing fears related to cultural inhibitions. It would clearly be too idealistic to believe that an international school can completely overcome all cultural impediments to the successful implementation of a pastoral care programme. Some tutors may well continue to find it difficult to conduct 'life skills' sessions in a second language with students of the opposite sex, particularly those taking radically different cultural standpoints. Moreover, some students will still naturally tend to seek out a tutor who speaks the same language for discussions on sensitive personal issues. At the author's school research indicated some tentative support for the view that an important proportion of students (38 per cent) would be more comfortable discussing sensitive issues with tutors of the same culture. Furthermore, it was interesting that a significant proportion of such students were of Chinese ethnicity. To these figures should, of course, be added other students who had expressed the view that for 'some issues' they would prefer to talk to a tutor of the same sex or culture (Drake, 1997, 1998). These statistics were confirmed by more informal interviews with Chinese teachers in the college who indicated the difficulty they faced discussing very sensitive issues in English, and conversely the difficulty faced by Cantonese students articulating their inner emotions in English to a non-Chinese tutor. Problems facing the Chinese students at LPCUWC in their inter-cultural adaptation have been corroborated recently in the data produced by a non-participant observer case study undertaken by Philip Leung of the Chinese University of Hong Kong (1997). Leung undertook a quantitative analysis based on the fourth and fifth cohorts of students at LPCUWC (1995–8). His aim was to investigate how far culture as 'an intrinsic and independent variable... shapes the attitudes and behaviour of students' (Leung, 1997). Leung's results tentatively suggest that Hong Kong students are more collectivist and have 'high power distance attitudes'. As such they need more help to adapt to practices such as cross-cultural counselling. There would appear to be some support in these conclusions for organizing tutor groups more along ethnic lines. However, for pastoral care managers to act upon this evidence, in a way that leads to a realignment of tutor groups on the basis of sex or culture, may not be commensurate with an international school's philosophy of facilitating cross-cultural understanding through ethnically engineered tutor groups.

Values

A pastoral care system will need to be predicated on certain values 'that are appropriate to the school's cultural make-up' (Duncan, 1988). But what sort of value system does an international school subscribe to? That of the founders? That of the society in which the school is located? That of the parents or the staff? In the latter case the challenges are obvious. The value systems of the parents of international school students may well be as diverse as those of the staff, for a true international school will have a wide range of nationalities represented on its teaching faculty. At the author's school, for instance, there have been as many as 13 (1996–7) nationalities out of a staff of 21, with the largest single group being British. What then should be the value system adopted by this school? Should it be that of the majority of students or their parents, or the majority of staff? Should each international school develop a culture of its own with a particularistic value system taking into account the needs of students graduating into a global society? Is it, indeed, possible for an international school to develop a 'programme which includes moral values, without imposing a predominantly western point of view?' (Ellwood, 1996). The difficulty in resolving these questions often leads teachers to take a 'relativist position' to values education (Mattern, 1990; Ellwood, 1996). In the pursuit of objectivity such teachers subscribe to the view that there are no absolutes and that, therefore, the concept of shared values is, at best, a tenuous one. A number of recent researchers have, however, taken issue with the relativist position (Mattern, 1990; Ellwood, 1996; Rodger, 1997). These writers would argue that the international school has a responsibility to provide values education in the sense that 'the student's morality becomes an educated one... [in that this]... entails critical reflection on the "received" moralities of home and other human communities of which the learner is a part, including the school community and the wider society in which it is placed' (Rodger, 1997).

If one accepts that values education should be an essential component of a pastoral programme, the issue still has to be addressed of how to determine what values the international school should promote. A starting point for such a discussion should lie, of course, with the school's philosophy or mission statement (Ellwood, 1996). Within this context the various constituents of the school community (parents, board, students, staff) can be asked for their opinion of the values which ought to underscore modern education. Recent exercises along these lines at the Vienna International School (Ellwood, 1996) and at St Andrew's Scots School in Buenos Aires (Rodger, 1997) suggest a good deal of common ground, and were supportive of Mattern's (1990) assertion that a nucleus of common values does exist to which all people can subscribe; as Rodger (1997) suggests, most of these core values are underpinned by the root value: consideration.

Once a set of values has been identified the school has to move from theory to the practical application of values education. As the research undertaken by both

Ellwood and Rodger indicates, many teachers remain wary of values education, as they do of the broader pastoral programme. Moreover, the diverse cultural backgrounds of those international schoolteachers who are required to deliver values education and cross-cultural counselling as part of a general pastoral programme create the possibility for potential conflict arising from non-convergent cultural perspectives. Duncan's (1988) limited study of the way in which tutors worked in a multi-cultural school in the UK indicated that cross-cultural counselling was of limited value, since many teachers had no knowledge of the backgrounds and needs of students from cultures other than their own and that, therefore, they were not able to cope with 'some of the very interesting but rather delicate issues with which they may have to come face to face'. Pastoral managers in international schools must not ignore these sentiments. Serious efforts must be made to provide relevant ongoing INSET for their pastoral staff to help them adjust to cross-cultural counselling. The school must, at the same time, ensure that they offer students a broad, and flexible range of cross-cultural consultants to whom they may refer.

An international school cannot simply allow a value system to emerge without any considered proactive policy. If values education is left to be delivered in a spontaneous and unplanned fashion it runs the risk of 'being unsystematic; and... [providing] no support for the students' attempts to arrive at a personally reflected and well-informed stance on moral values to live by' (Rodger, 1997). It is not the job of an international school to promote the value system of one component of the school community to the exclusion of all others. The prime function of an international school is to promote international education, which has been defined above as engendering international understanding. What would such understanding be in the absence of an understanding of differing value systems? As Orellana Benado (1995) argued: 'through the appreciation of identities different from one's own, one's own form of life can hope to gain a genuine appreciation of its identity'. The international school needs to articulate a set of values that define the unique identity of that institution while also preparing students to become global citizens. Moreover, as Rodger (1997) suggests, the actual process of defining and articulating these values should engage the school community in an enterprise that fosters a sense of shared purpose and goals. The systematic delivery of pastoral care, of the nature discussed in this chapter, has a particularly important role to play in the development of international understanding, especially in the area of values education. At the author's own school students were asked how far they felt tutor group discussions had helped cross-cultural understanding. Ninety per cent of the respondents to the 1995 survey answered 'occasionally' or a 'great deal'. These opinions converged with views expressed in the 'end of cycle' evaluative surveys given in April/May 1996, where students were questioned as to the value of the tutor group meetings to cross-cultural understanding. Twenty-nine per cent of the first year respondents (fourth cohort) were of the opinion that they helped 'a great deal', while another 56 per cent said they were 'occasionally' helpful (Drake, 1998).

It is also worth noting that a significant number of both Chinese and overseas students seemed to have recognized the impact that western/Chinese culture was having on them in the college. Seventy-four per cent of non-Chinese students felt they had been influenced by Chinese culture while at LPCUWC at the very least 'to some extent', while 66 per cent of Chinese students at the college similarly felt they had been influenced by western culture while at LPCUWC at the very least 'to some extent'.

The author would argue that these responses were as much due to the methodology adopted by the pastoral practitioners at LPCUWC as they were to the actual content of the programme. The focus of most of the 'life skills' units undertaken at the college was to foster an understanding of the varying cultural perspectives and value systems extant within the college community, as well as to explore shared values.

CONCLUSION

The evidence drawn from the author's limited research at LPCUWC tentatively suggests that it is possible for both staff and students in an international school, irrespective of culture, to recognize the need for a pastoral care programme. Although not all students, or tutors, at LPCUWC were totally comfortable with the concept of cross-cultural counselling, the majority saw the need to keep tutor groups ethnically engineered, as it was recognized that what in one sense can be perceived as a 'problem' can, from another perspective, be viewed as an opportunity for more informed communication between students from different parts of the world which, in turn, could enhance the quality of 'international education' offered by the school. A significant aim of 'pastoral care' in an international school is to foster international understanding between the students. Tutor groups, dormitories (in boarding schools) and PSE discussion groups are often constructed so as to afford the opportunity to debate sensitive issues from differing cultural perspectives. The work of Hayden and Thompson (1995b) at the University of Bath has indicated that students in international schools develop more international understanding from what happens outside the classroom than from what is provided inside by the formal academic curriculum. This perception is certainly supported by the author's research at LPCUWC. Here, for instance, the emphasis in 'life skills sessions' for sixth formers was not placed on the routine delivery of items such as basic sex education, as it is assumed that most of our students will have been at least partially exposed to such education in their previous schools. Instead the focus, particularly of discussion sections, was on enhancing international understanding of a range of sensitive issues relating to issues such as differences in the sexual value systems of various cultures represented at the college. One has only to imagine the learning curve arising from a discussion on date rape involving girls from Senegal, the People's Republic of China, Sweden and Indonesia with boys from Nepal, Canada and Pakistan. Or the potential for true understanding of another culture or religion's perspective on pre-marital sex, or homosexuality. Alternatively, consider the impact on a group of international students of two days away from normal lessons debating the arguments for and against the existence of God, or wider issues relating to respective faiths and philosophies. Reflect on the commonalty and differences in international student values such as 'respect', 'consideration', 'work ethic', or political systems such as democracy. There can be no finer way of really getting to understand another culture than through this sort of dynamic interaction. There had been some suggestion that cross-cultural fertilization is rather unidirectional. This view was not supported in the context of LPCUWC, where it was not only Asian students who were influenced by Western culture; quite clearly, influences operated in the other direction as well. Critics of this approach may well posit the dangers of a homogenizing process that could devalue the non-western conventional wisdoms. However, the tentative evidence from LPCUWC suggests that students are more likely to emerge from a pastoral care programme with a stronger conviction in their own religion or culture than they are to find their cultural affinity diminished.

Much of the evidence offered in this chapter has been drawn from research at one particular international school and it has not been the author's intention to suggest that the experience of LPCUWC is directly transferable to other international schools. Each school must, of course, devise a programme that meets the needs of its unique clientele within the parameters set by budgetary and personnel constraints. Introducing an effective pastoral care programme into an international school arguably poses 'change agents' with more challenges than they would face in a domestic school: the heterogeneous nature of an international student body will, for instance, necessitate a rigorous needs analysis, while inevitable disparities in staff experience and skills emanating from varying educational backgrounds will require considerable managerial support. Indeed, the whole process of implementing a pastoral care initiative in an international school requires a great deal of sensitivity, forethought and collaborative planning. It demands commitment by the school authorities to provide the INSET that will allow tutors to become more comfortable with their role as facilitators of cross-cultural discussion and values education, as well as with the demands of counselling. To embark on such a pastoral care programme in the absence of such training (and/or compensatory time allowances) can put an unacceptable strain on human resources; a strain that can be inimical to the aims and objectives of the programme.

Staff concerns over training and their own cultural norms must be placed high on the list of priorities. Within the bounds of corporate responsibility staff must feel they are free to conduct a particular part of the programme as befits their own personal, cultural and religious feelings, but at the same time have to be encouraged to explore new avenues of thought and methodology, as for instance Went (1984) suggests in the context of sex education. This may take time, particularly in a new institution, or in a school where established and intransigent patterns exist. Innovation will almost always bring tension to the institution and it is vital for educational managers to support and protect staff during this process of innovation, especially if a new pastoral programme is but one of many modifications they may be forced to make to their normal pattern of operation. Regular reviews of the programme and receptivity to staff needs are important but time consuming, and can actually contribute to rising levels of friction, fear and confrontation. But it is important to continue inviting staff to offer their input into a programme which they will eventually come to see as their own. With patience and consideration, plus the vital provision of INSET, and an ongoing collaborative style of management, the institution should win over the majority of staff, irrespective of cultural provenance, to the programme.

It is doubtful that all the staff of any school, international or national, will become totally committed to pastoral care, and the variability of tutor interest and involvement will remain one of the biggest challenges for the person charged with coordinating the programme. However, this may be the time for international schools to recognize the importance of pastoral care programmes to the development of the 'whole' individual. The introduction and successful delivery of such a programme will not be without its challenges, but they must not be shirked for the pastoral care programme in an international school offers tremendous potential for substantive cross-cultural understanding. Moreover, the actual process of implementation can bring together the various ethno-linguistic groups on the faculty of an international school in a project that, in turn, can ultimately enhance communication between the cultural subsections of the school and, thereby, help unlock the 'potential across an institution for internationalization' (Hayden and Thompson, 1996).

REFERENCES

Akram, C (1995) 'Change and adaptation: children and curriculum in international schools', *International Schools Journal*, **XV**, 1, pp 39–53

Al Tikriti, K H (1990) 'The development of counselling in secondary schools in Iraq in the light of the British experience', PhD thesis, University of Wales, Cardiff

Bailey, R (1972) 'Factors influencing choice of subjects at advanced level and factors which affect choice of course at university', DSc dissertation, University College, Swansea

Belle-Isle, R (1986) 'Learning for a new humanism', *International Schools Journal*, 11, pp 27–30

Best, R (1989) 'Pastoral care: some reflections and a restatement', *Journal of Pastoral Care in Education*, **7**, 4, pp 7–13

Best, R and Lang, P (1994) 'Care, control and community' in P Lang, R Best and A Lichtenberg, *Caring for Children: International Perspectives on Pastoral Care and PSE*, Cassell, London

Brislin, R (1993) *Understanding Culture's Influence on Behaviour*, Harcourt Brace

Jovanovich, New York

Brislin, R, Cushner, K, Cherrie, C and Yong, M (1986) *Intercultural Interaction: A Practical Guide*, Sage, London

Buckton, A (1971) 'Problems of sixth formers and their implications for a counsellor', DSc dissertation, University College, Swansea

Chin, R M N P (1990) 'A study of the pastoral care systems in five English schools leading to recommendations for a Singapore school', MEd thesis, University of Bath

Clemett, A J and Pearce, J S (1986) *The Evaluation of Pastoral Care*, Blackwell, Oxford

Cross, J (1995) 'Is there a place for personal counselling in secondary schools?', *Journal of Pastoral Care in Education*, **13**, 4, pp 6–10

Department of Education and Science (1989) *Discipline in Schools: Report of the Committee of Enquiry Chaired by Lord Elton*, Department of Education and Science, London

Downs, L D (1990) 'The repatriate Japanese student', *International Schools Journal*, 20, pp 39–44

Drake, B K (1997) 'Pastoral care programmes and their place in international education', *International Schools Journal*, **XVI**, 2, pp 40–53

Drake, B K (1998) 'The development of an effective pastoral care programme in an international school', PhD thesis, University of Bath

Duncan, C (1988) *Pastoral Care: An Anti-racist/Multi-cultural Perspective*, Blackwell, Oxford

Dynan, N (1980) *Do Schools Care?* Education Department of Western Australia, Perth

Ekblad, S (1986) 'Relationships between child-rearing practices and primary school children's functional adjustment in the People's Republic of China', *Scandinavian Journal of Psychology*, 27

Ellwood, C (1996) 'The matter of values', *International Schools Journal*, **XVI**, 1, pp 39–45

Everts, J F (1993) 'Testing the cultural relevance of counselling: a Malaysian case in point', *Asian Journal of Counselling*, **2**, 2

Firth, V E (1989) 'Moral, political, aesthetic/religious education in the Soviet Union and England and Wales', MPhil thesis, University of Lancaster

Fogelman, K (1972) *Leaving the Sixth Form*, National Foundation for Educational Research, Slough

Galloway, D (1985) 'Pastoral care and school effectiveness', in D Reynolds (ed), *Studying School Effectiveness*, Falmer Press, London

Gellar, C A (1981) 'International education: some thoughts on what it is and what it might be', *International Schools Journal*, 1, pp 21–26

Graham, R, Stenhouse, P and Osborne, K (1991) 'Planning a pastoral programme: a new approach', *Journal of Pastoral Care in Education*, June, pp 12–17

Gysbers, N C and Henderson, P (1988) *Developing and Managing your School Guidance Program*, American Association of Developmental Counselling, Virginia

Hamblin, D (1981) *Teaching Study Skills*, Blackwell, Oxford

Hamblin, D (1986) *A Pastoral Programme*, Blackwell, Oxford

Hamblin, D (1989) *The Teacher and Pastoral Care*, Blackwell, Oxford

Hamblin, D (1993) *The Teacher and Counselling*, Simon & Schuster, Hemel Hempstead

Hargreaves, D H (1990) 'Making schools more effective: the challenge to policy, practice and research', *Scottish Educational Review*, **22**, 1, pp 5–14

Hayden, M C and Thompson, J J (1995a) 'International schools and international education: a relationship reviewed', *Oxford Review of Education*, **21**, 3, pp 327–45

Hayden, M C and Thompson, J J (1995b) 'International education: The crossing of frontiers', *International Schools Journal*, **XVI**, pp 13–20

Hayden, M C and Thompson, J J (1996) 'Potential difference: The driving force for international education', *International Schools Journal*, **XVI**, pp 46–57

Her Majesty's Inspectorate (1980) *A View of the Curriculum: HMI Services – Matters for Discussion II*, HMSO, London

Hill, I (1994) 'The International Baccalaureate: policy process in education', PhD thesis, University of Tasmania

Hodkinson, P (1994) 'Empowerment as an entitlement in the post-16 curriculum', *Journal of Curriculum Studies*, 26, pp 491–509

Hofstede, G (1991) *Culture's Consequence*, Sage, London

Hong Kong Education Department (1995a) *Guidelines on Whole School Approach to Guidance (for Secondary Schools) Part 2*, Services Division Education Department

Hong Kong Education Department (1995b) *Administration Circular No 72/95 Appendix B: Suggested Duty List for Guidance Masters/Mistresses and their Teams*, Services Division Education Department

Hopson, B and Scally, M (1981) *Life Skills Teaching*, McGraw-Hill, Maidenhead

Jonietz, P L and Harris, N D (eds) (1991) *World Yearbook of Education 1991: International Schools and International Education*, Kogan Page, London

King E, Moor, C and Mundy, J (1974) *Post-Compulsory Education: A New Analysis of Western Europe*, Sage, London

Lam, C C (1991) 'The implementation of curriculum change in moral education in secondary schools in Hong Kong', PhD thesis, London Institute of Education

Lambert, R (1975) *The Chance of a Lifetime*, Weidenfeld & Nicolson, London

Lang, P (1989) 'What is so special about pastoral care?', *Journal of Pastoral Care in Education*, **7**, 4, pp 21–7

Lang, P and Young, T (1985) 'Pastoral care in English schools: A Canadian Perspective', *Canadian Counsellor*, **19**, 3 and 4, pp 220–30

Lang, P, Best, R and Lichtenberg, A (1994) *Caring for Children: International Perspectives on Pastoral Care and PSE*, Cassell, London

Leung, P (1997) 'Knowing me, knowing you: teaching and learning in a culturally diversified school – a case study of Li Po Chun United World College Hong Kong', term paper, Chinese University of Hong Kong

Lovegrove, E (1982) *Schools within Schools*, Education Department of Southern Australia, Adelaide

McGuinness, J (1989) *A Whole School Approach to Pastoral Care*, Kogan Page, London

Marland, M (1974) *Pastoral Care*, Heinemann, London

Marland, M (1986) *Pastoral Care*, Heinemann, London

Marland, M (1989) *The Tutor and the Tutor Group*, Longman, Harlow

Matthews, M (1989) 'The uniqueness of international education', *International Schools Journal*, 18, pp 24–34

Mattern, G (1990) 'The best of times, the worst of times and what to do about it on a Monday morning', *International Schools Journal*, 19, pp 35–47

Morphy, G D (1991) 'Pastoral care: Stagnation or development? A study of pastoral care in a representative sample of high schools in the county of Hereford and Worcester', MA thesis, University of Warwick

Onyeocha, I M (1991) 'Towards an effective moral education in Nigeria', PhD thesis, London Institute of Education

Orellana Benado, M E (1995) 'Pluralism and the ethics of internationalism', *IB World*, 8, pp 29–30

Peterson, A D C (1987) *Schools Across Frontiers*, Open Court, La Salle Illinois

Powell, O C, Rogers, J and Kahler, S (1992) 'Recognizing dysfunctional multilingual students in international schools', *International Schools Journal*, 23, pp 70–74

Pring, R (1988) in P Lang (ed) '*Thinking about... Personal and Social Education in the Primary School*', Blackwell, Oxford

Raynor, D (1995) 'Perspectives on the pastoral care of the more able', *Journal of Pastoral Care in Education*, **13**, 1, pp 3–7

Ribbons, P (1989) 'Pastoral care: in praise of diversity', *Journal of Pastoral Care in Education*, **7**, 4, pp 28–36

Rodger, A (1997) 'Developing moral community in a pluralist setting', *International Schools Journal*, **XVII**, 1, pp 32–43

Rutter, M (1991) 'Pathways from childhood to adult life: the Role of Schooling', *Journal of Pastoral Care in Education*, **9**, 3, pp 3–10

Sceeny, A (1987) 'Towards the integration of the pastoral and academic?', *Journal of Pastoral Care in Education*, **5**, 1, pp 62–7

Shaw, M (1994) 'Current issues in pastoral management', *Journal of Pastoral Care in Education*, **12**, 4, pp 37–41

Soong, C and Khoo, A (1994) 'Teacher attitudes towards sex education in Singapore', *Journal of Pastoral Care in Education*, **12**, 1, pp 23–26

Singapore Ministry of Education (1987) *Towards Excellence in Schools: A Report to the Ministry of Education*, Ministry of Education, Singapore

Suzuki, B H (1980) 'The Asian-American family', in M D Fantini and R Cardenas (eds), *Parenting in a Multicultural Society*, Longman, New York

Trompenaars, F (1993) *Riding the Waves of Culture*, Nicholas Brealey, London

Watkins, C (1993) *The Value of Pastoral Care and Personal and Social Education*, National Association of Pastoral Care in Education, University of Warwick

Went, D (1984) *Sex Education: Some Guidelines for Teachers*, Bell & Hyman, London

Willis, D B, Enloe, W W and Minoura, Y (1994) 'Transculturals, transnationals: The new diaspora,' *International Schools Journal*, **X1V**, 1, pp 29–42

Part 3

THE SCHOOL AS AN ORGANIZATION FOR INTERNATIONAL EDUCATION

12

THE EMPEROR'S NEW CLOTHES? THE ISSUE OF STAFFING IN INTERNATIONAL SCHOOLS

Neil Richards

An enduring image from the classic cautionary tale *The Emperor's New Clothes* by Hans Christian Andersen is of a large, pink bottom, waddling its way towards its humiliating destiny. Much of the appeal, I suspect, is derived from the ultimate triumph of innocence and honesty, as personified by the young child, who is the only one willing to recognize publicly that the Emperor is stark naked; and the very public, and satisfying, humiliation of the mighty. The bad guys, the swindling tailors, escape, presumably to swindle again, thereby demonstrating that bad guys do sometimes win – rather a dubious outcome for a children's tale, which convinces me that it must be banned somewhere. However, it is very much a tale of vanity and wishful thinking; of peer pressure and conceit; and ultimately, of course, of the triumph of innocence.

THE APPAREL OF INTERNATIONALISM

What has this got to do with international education? Over the last few decades there has been rather a rush to clothe businesses and institutions with the apparel of 'internationalism', and many schools, in particular, have latched on to the assumed marketing potential of this movement, in some cases merely squeezing the word 'international' into their names, or buying into an 'international' examination curriculum. But has this resulted in a radical shift of emphasis, or is it merely a sleight of hand, made possible by the fact that no one really knows what internationalism looks like anyway? And does it really matter?

To a certain extent the use of such terms as 'international school' and 'international education' are misleading, because they imply clearly defined concepts, whereas the reality is that they are loosely applied to a whole range of quite disparate approaches and institutions, with the single most common characteristic seeming to be the existence of, or desire for, a multinational student body. In some

173

cases a clear attempt is made to provide an 'international curriculum', but many schools are firmly committed to curricula that have roots in national systems (most often of US or European origin). This lack of uniformity is highlighted by Hayden and Thompson (1995a):

> Many such international schools have grown up in response to local circumstances on a relatively *ad hoc* basis and, although there are certainly subgroupings controlled by central organisations... for the most part the body of international schools is a conglomeration of individual institutions which may or may not share an underlying educational philosophy.

While there seems to be a distinct danger in attempting generalizations about international schools, any attempt to categorize schools by their characteristics may also prove to be equally problematic. Hayden and Thompson go on to contrast the 'purist' vision of Leach (1969), of a balanced international school having no dominant national influence, with the realistic observations of Peterson (1987): 'one would expect a special influence of the host country and a student body that reflected the local composition of the expatriate community... [as well as] a high proportion of the teachers in international schools to come from English-speaking countries'.

This community influence on international schools is perhaps better understood from Keson's (1991) observations on the early years of their development:

> International schools really began to sprout like mushrooms in the late fifties and early sixties. Following the influx of foreigners who were setting up businesses, developing projects, and liaising between newly interdependent governments, groups of parents got together to provide temporary schools for their children. Cooperative or volunteer arrangements formed the beginnings, but it was not long before the schools moved into permanent quarters, hired proper teachers, and developed an integrated curriculum.

If we accept Keson's observations, which indicate that early international schools, at least, were community driven, it would account for the proliferation of the different types, in many cases closely linked to a national system (such as American, British or French). Their concerns were far more prosaic, and vital, than any philosophy of internationalism; their foci revolved around the academic requirements of the community children, which cannot but still be a central concern of international schools. (The one clear exception to this phenomenon arose out of the idealism of Kurt Hahn, which led to the founding of Atlantic College and the birth of the United World College movement.)

Most international schools are, I believe somewhat belatedly, attempting to articulate their international philosophy but, since so many are 'market driven', a weather eye must be firmly fixed on the needs of the community. It is this alchemy of idealism and pragmatism that determines the individual characteristics of international schools around the world; their clients are not all imbued with a sense of mission, other than to do what is best for their children within the locally imposed limits. This in turn suggests that an analysis of the school community is as important as an examination of the curriculum and philosophy if we are to arrive at a clear understanding of our international schools. Far from exerting a peripheral influence on the continuing development of international schools and any philosophy of internationalism, I would suggest that market forces influence the design, the weave and the very fabric of our international garb and, while this is not necessarily a bad thing, I think we should be a little more honest about what we are looking at, and rather more circumspect in our blanket use of the term 'international' as applied to schools.

IMPLICATIONS FOR STAFFING

My own experiences in international education suggest that the following fourfold community expectations are largely characteristic of international schools.

1. English is the language of instruction (other languages rarely come close, though there are schools which relate directly to national systems, and some schools offer courses through a second language).
2. Standards can be directly related to those of North American or European schools.
3. Qualifications have international currency.
4. The school is founded on a 'western' educational tradition.

Such characteristics are not based on school philosophies but on community expectations. The subtle, and in some cases not so subtle differences in the various curricula are tolerated as long as the essential outcomes are not threatened. Again, this is perfectly reasonable, but it does suggest a chauvinism that belies the use of the term 'international' in its broader, global sense. It also leads to a staffing scenario in many schools that reinforces this chauvinism. In support of an investigation into such murky waters it is worth considering the following passage, taken from the promotional material of a major European international school: 'Over 70 teachers at [the school] share this broad international experience [of the Headteacher], coming from such countries as Australia, Canada, France, Germany, Great Britain, Holland, Ireland, New Zealand, and the United States.'

Can we infer from the above, that no teachers are employed (or employable?) from so-called less developed regions of the world? Or merely that advertising such teachers would not be a positive selling point for the school? Even those schools founded on principles of internationalism and not in response to community forces, the United World Colleges, seem to find themselves in such a staffing cul-de-sac (Sutcliffe, 1991):

> Most teachers on the international circuit are... either British or American. In a small but growing way, this trend is being strengthened by the wish of the IB schools in, for example, Holland and the Scandinavian countries, to recruit British teachers to teach IB courses in the mother-tongue English... Nor do the United World Colleges find it easy to act otherwise, as an examination of

their teaching staffs, and above all the distribution of the responsibilities within their staff rooms, will show.

Sutcliffe's observations, perhaps, underline this central dilemma in many of our international schools: the need to satisfy the demands of the market (community expectations and examinations) whilst remaining true to the idealism of the 'international' philosophies (almost exclusively, it seems at times, articulated and promoted by the professional staffs of the schools themselves).

It may be that where choice exists between good national school systems (able to fulfil community expectations of a 'good education') and international schools, then decisions by parents to choose the latter rest upon a clear philosophy. However, in many countries around the world, international schools are the only institutions that provide a qualification that has international currency, and the only schools where English can be acquired to a high degree of fluency. Also it must be borne in mind that many parents, by virtue of their overseas contractual obligations, have no viable alternatives for their children. The relationship, therefore, between the exponents of 'internationalism' and the many client groups of international schools is certainly ambivalent, and is likely to be based as much on convenience as on any shared commitment to international understanding. It may also account for much of the tension and misunderstanding between philosophy-driven school administrations and community representatives on school governing bodies (and possibly the rapid turnover of headteachers, as highlighted by Hawley, 1994).

Despite this there is a rising swell of optimism, and a firm belief that international education has much to contribute to the security and development of the modern world. Jonietz (1991) confidently claims:

In 1991, internationalism is no longer a dream or an idealistic goal; it is now ... today's young people have futures which do not always depend on national boundaries. Rather, their future universities, their future employers, their future families, and their national interest may be only part of their larger global picture. International schools and international education may teach them to tolerate difference and to seek multinational solutions to problems.

And more recently, from the editors of the *International Schools Journal* (Geller, 1996):

Yet most of the urgent problems facing human beings transcend such [national] boundaries, and can only be solved by cooperative international action. Global thinkers are needed to solve global problems. There is a growing urgency to develop in all young people a real sense of just how small, how fragile, and how interdependent the world has become. For many in international education, this suggests the need to create a new sense of awareness of what it means to be a world citizen, not in the sense of a new political allegiance, but in an abiding awareness of belonging to, and having responsibility for, all humankind.

Heady stuff, but can it be taught, or does it simply ooze out of the formal curriculum?

Much current research is focusing on the concept of an 'international attitude' (Hayden and Thompson, 1995b), and the influence on such an attitude, and it would seem from early findings that, from the students' point of view, the formal curriculum is less of an influence than might be imagined: 'In terms of perceived importance [in respect of an international attitude], formal aspects of school such as subjects taught were placed lower than informal aspects such as mixing with students of other cultures both inside and outside school.'

Interestingly, from the students' viewpoint the attitudes of individual teachers did not emerge as a particularly strong influence in Hayden and Thompson's research findings (although teachers themselves rated this more highly). Is this because teachers are less influential in this respect, or was it merely a reflection of the tendency towards homogeneity in the teaching groups in terms of cultural and educational backgrounds? They also quote one student who, despite attending an international school, felt that her educational experience was not international, but rather: 'a western education, because everything I was taught was delivered in a western point of view, since all the teachers were from the west.'

Surely, if we accept that an 'international attitude' is influenced by aspects other than the content of the formal curriculum, in other words through personal relationships in a variety of situations, then the composition of staff in an international school becomes highly significant. It could be argued that a representative, or zonal spread of nationalities in an international school is the most fitting in terms of the philosophies of internationalism since:

- as attempts are made to broaden the cultural bases of international curricula it makes sense to broaden the spread of cultural representatives on the staff, able to teach or reflect cultural values and not simply allow such values to be interpreted by others.
- if an international attitude is mainly fostered through personal contacts, then the more cultural diversity the better. Since the teachers are an integral, if not vital part of the school community, they too should reflect the racial, ethnic and religious balance in the international community.
- if we do not practise what we preach, in terms of multicultural harmony, respect for other cultures and integration, wherein lies our credibility as international educators? Or is international education becoming a new and subtle form of imperialism?

However, and here is the catch, as long as schools are solely driven by a formal curriculum, even if it culminates in such examinations as the International Baccalaureate Diploma, then staffing policies must be dominated by the need for staff with experience of both the curriculum itself and the educational culture out of which the curriculum was developed. An effective strait-jacket indeed on truly global internationalism.

INTERNATIONAL SCHOOLS AND LESS DEVELOPED COUNTRIES

This dilemma of 'internationalism' versus 'westernism' is probably more marked in international schools in so-called less developed countries, where the nature of many institutions is characterized by such things as differential staff contracts, local student quotas, differential fees and imposed national educational requirements. Good schools will exploit the educational opportunities provided in such an environment, but there is always a danger that the obvious élitism of an international school will become an obstacle to any form of interface with the local educational system or even with the broader community itself. Ironically, this situation may be exacerbated by increasing the numbers of local students within an international school (in my experience usually strongly resisted by the expatriate client groups, and even more strongly resisted by nationals with children already in the school) where all too frequently the fee levels can only be met by the wealthy, which reinforces the general perception of élitism.

One not uncommon feature, but perhaps one of the most contentious issues in international schools in the less developed world, is a salary scale differential between locally employed teachers and teachers recruited from outside the country. This must rest rather uneasily on egalitarian school philosophies, and can hardly be a unifying factor for the school staff. Also, national 'education cultures' can differ quite dramatically – the differing economies and demographic conditions alone will guarantee that – and perceptions and prejudices (held by colleagues, students and parents) are part of the baggage that must be carried by any new teacher who takes up an appointment in an international school. However, when a pedagogical style or methodology is identified with teacher 'types' or, worse, with cultural traits, then there is a very real potential for attitudes to develop into prejudice. Such inclinations are not found solely outside the school gates: teachers and administrators do not come prepacked and sterile; I fear that we are all contaminated to some degree.

This somewhat gloomy view of a multicultural community can be contrasted with the more usual, and propagated image of the international school as a place where cultures meet; where different peoples learn from each other, appreciate the cultural exchange and become emotionally and intellectually equipped for world citizenship. Many international schools, I would suggest, fall somewhere between these two extreme ends of the spectrum, though it is hoped they incline towards the 'harmony' end, but the potential for some schools to reinforce stereotypical images is ever present, as is the opportunity to engender feelings of inferiority or intolerance and even outright racism.

Just as the composition of a school staff is a key element in ensuring that 'appropriate' messages are being transmitted to the community, equally, and inadvertently, it may well be a key element in the transmission of inappropriate messages. Teachers are recruited on the basis of their competency to teach at the required levels. However, as I have suggested, the 'cultural nature' of many international schools is such that their requirements discriminate very effectively against teachers from certain areas of the world, most notably those from less developed countries and non-western cultures. This may not be unreasonable in market-driven

178

institutions as they search for teachers experienced in international curricula, but it does present a 'credibility gap' as far as a school's espousal of cultural equality and values is concerned. The following is a true story, and may serve to illustrate the point.

A member of the teaching staff at an international school in the less developed world was asked if the school employed any national teachers, since there was strong national representation among the student body. The response was: 'Yes, one, but she has lived so long in the United States, and even has an American accent, that she's practically American.' Sadly, it was offered as a justification, and not as a cause for regret.

On the other hand some schools find themselves with a much more balanced staff, more often as a result of financial expediency than any philosophy, but the nature of the curriculum may well discriminate between those who are familiar with a 'western methodological style' and those who are not, resulting in an unhealthy tendency to express this in terms of those who teach 'well', and those who do not – perceptions that have the potential to fan the very flames of intolerance.

STAFF CORPORATE IDENTITY

The findings from a recently conducted case study of local-contract teachers in an international school in Africa (Richards, 1997) suggest that a failure to recognize and respond to the unique problems faced by teachers from less developed and non-western countries is not only an inhibiting factor in the effective development of the school but also threatens the very values espoused by most international schools. The overall picture that emerged from the case study is of a group of teachers with clearly definable characteristics overall, facing classroom, administrative, pastoral and psychological challenges that are quite distinct from those faced by their 'western' colleagues. Taken a step further it highlights some of the problems associated with efforts to create a more zonal spread of teachers on school staffs generally. That problems arise there seems to be little doubt, but the real question that should be asked is: can these problems be overcome, should they be overcome, in the greater cause of internationalism? Or, to return to the opening metaphor, what clothes do we want our Emperor to wear?

Blaney (1991) makes a clear appeal for teacher diversity in our international schools: 'Staff should be carefully recruited so as to represent, without an unreasonable financial burden being placed upon the schools, the major culture areas of the world, and as many nationalities as feasible. This... will also provide the students with a variety of racial, ethnic, and national role models.'

This last point of Blaney's, concerning the provision of role models, is a crucial one. Richards' case study would seem to suggest that the local-contract teachers, for the most part those recruited from less developed country backgrounds, are, at least in some cases, ill prepared to act as effective role models within the context of an international school, but they do have the potential to reinforce the perceived 'superiority' of methodologies and teachers with a western background. Not only did the administrative profile within the school suggest this superiority, but the nature of the rapport between some of the teachers and students suggested that all was not as it should be in the classroom.

> This is the first international environment I have worked in, and I tended to be authoritarian and get too impatient... in national schools here, or even back home, the teacher holds a lot of power.
>
> In the beginning at this school the job was sort of different because I was used to national schools and national curricula.... In national schools, in our African context, people are well behaved and respectful.
>
> Before... I was teaching in a different school altogether – in a national school ...
>
> The students were very different; they were there to learn, everything you told them was true and they wanted to learn more from you. I used mainly lecture methods because that was required.
>
> In an international school the culture is a bit different. You have to earn the respect of pupils much more in an international school. You have to learn to look at international school kids as individuals and treat them individually, that's the difference.
>
> I found an international school a little bit challenging because people come from all sorts of backgrounds and that type of thing... I am not an extrovert as such, I didn't feel that confident.

Far from becoming role models in the school there seemed to be a dangerous tendency, possibly arising out of a lack of complete confidence in an international context, for some local-contract teachers, if not publicly at least privately, to be vilified. When this is coupled with a salary differential it seems to reinforce the belief, and provide concrete evidence that, in the words of one of the case study respondents, 'the school treasures expatriate teachers much more than local ones', with a consequent and understandable effect on morale and commitment. Under such circumstances it is hardly surprising that the case study revealed local-contract teachers themselves perceived that both parents and students preferred expatriate-contract staff. Regrettably, personal experience as an administrator can very largely confirm that this sentiment is an accurate reflection of some parent attitudes. Requests from parents for transfers from one class to another because of lack of confidence in the background or appropriate experience of a teacher are not uncommon. Unfortunately the inevitable refusal does not improve the tolerance of the parents concerned.

Such findings would suggest that further investigation into the composition of staff in international schools and the way in which administrations take cognizance of, and respond to the diversity of educational backgrounds of their teachers is an urgent need, more particularly, perhaps, if teacher recruitment is to have a philosophical base. Clearly, though, any attempt to create a zonal balance of teachers in our international schools is going to run into serious problems. On the one hand, community-driven schools must recognize and respond to the priorities of its client body, which may not be convinced of the wisdom of too great a cultural diversity within the teaching staff. On the other hand, even where great diversity exists, the nature of the 'international' curriculum may be such that it highlights pedagogical (and cultural) difference in a negative rather than a positive way, with a consequent negative effect on any attempt to develop a corporate staff identity. Louis and Smith (1990) suggest that such a corporate identity is of particular concern to the teaching profession, where: 'teachers are... inherently dependent on one another, whether or not they cooperate and collaborate, because the social judgement of their competence will depend upon the performance of their colleagues.'

So how do we, as international educators, extricate ourselves from this staffing dilemma?

In the first place I believe that it is simply not an issue for many schools, and there is no reason why it should be. As continuing attempts are made to create curricula to reflect global issues and to provide the emotional competency to appreciate and value cultural diversity, it seems that many client bodies will be receptive and appreciative (provided we do not tinker too much with the fundamentals of their children's education). The majority of teachers in such schools are likely to be drawn from the cultural traditions of the west, which for many of the client groups is a fundamental requirement. Such schools seem to constitute a clear and very successful group within the international school fraternity (the 'designer label' end of the market, to get back to the original metaphor, selling a specific type of 'international' product). However, there are many others around the world that, either through a staffing philosophy (very few I would suggest), or as a result of financial expediency, have a greater cultural diversity of staff but fail to grasp fully this golden opportunity to demonstrate effective cultural integration and harmony, as opposed to merely teaching it. Do some of our schools, for example, unwittingly demonstrate some sort of cultural pecking order? (For that matter, does international education itself demonstrate this?)

The concept of the 'global village' is frequently invoked in the name of international education, but there seems to be little analysis of the dynamics of this global village: do we, or should we, seek to reflect cultural or ethnic diversity, regional diversity, demographics or just plain old economic clout, within our staff rooms? Perhaps an analysis of the needs of our client groups reveals the answer. Meanwhile, however, we must wrestle with the issue of staff diversity either, as in some schools, in an attempt to rationalize a school philosophy of internationalism, or, as in others, to come to terms with the problems associated with a zonal spread of teachers. Problems that arise out of community perceptions and confidence on the one hand, and out of pedagogical style on the other.

Notwithstanding such difficulties it seems reasonable to suggest that teachers from the less developed world have an important role to play in the development of internationalism and an international attitude within our schools. However, to enable this to happen many schools will have to adopt a more philosophy-driven recruitment policy and, more importantly, provide the professional support to ensure that all teachers are able to adapt to, and give of their best within the educational culture of an international school.

Fortunately the relatively recent development of internationally accessible staff development programmes, delivered *in situ* in many centres around the world, make it possible to provide teachers with a common educational experience, and if a zonal staffing policy is fully integrated with a staff development programme of appropriate calibre then an important step will have been taken towards the provision of a global perspective within those schools that truly desire it and, of course, are able to convince their respective client groups of the benefits. Holly and Southworth (1993) suggest that staff development is one of the foundation stones of the developing school:

> Ranged alongside professional development (ie the long-term process of enhancement of the practitioner's professional – classroom – performance) and career development, staff development (the enhancement of the practitioner's role as a member of staff) has grown in stature and importance the more it has become linked with school development. By and large, staff development is now synonymous with school development, because the staff are the major resource in the Developing School.

This distinction between professional development and staff development is an important one, more so perhaps in the context of an international school than a national school, where 'cultural diversity' and 'unity of purpose' meet head-on. Differences in teaching methodologies, experience, perceptions and contractual status all serve to undermine the unity and consistency that school administrators would hope to achieve. A mismatch between the school system and a teacher could, at the very least, lead to that teacher's morale being adversely affected, but if it occurs with a number of staff members the school, as an effective and efficient organization, will suffer.

Which brings me back to the Emperor's clothes... 'Internationalism', I would suggest, is as much in the eye of the beholder as it is in school philosophies and, although it is very tempting to conjure up an image of rich brocade and fine silks, it must be remembered that such embellishments rest on the rough homespun cloth of the local market (patched up with a few imports, to be sure). The very success of many of our international schools indicates that the Emperor is, on the whole, decently clothed, and at times splendidly and even extravagantly so, but care should be taken to look beyond the tapestry of words, to see what is actually demonstrated by our school systems; to examine their very fabric as it were. And who knows, we might catch a glimpse of raw flesh yet.

REFERENCES

Blaney, J J (1991) 'The international school system', in P L Jonietz and D Harris (eds), *World Yearbook of Education 1991: International Schools and International Education*, Kogan Page, London

Gellar, C (1996) 'Educating for world citzenship', *International Schools Journal*, **XVI**, 1, pp 5–8

Hawley, D B (1994) 'How long do international school heads survive? A research analysis (Part 1), *International Schools Journal*, **XIV**, 1, pp 8–21

Hayden, M C and Thompson, J J (1995a) 'International schools and international education: a relationship reviewed', *Oxford Review of Education*, **21**, 3, pp 327–44

Hayden, M C and Thompson, J J (1995b) 'Perceptions of international education: a preliminary study, *International Review of Education*, **41**, 5, pp 389–404

Holly, P J and Southworth, G (1993) *The Developing School, School Development and Management of Change Series*, Falmer Press, Basingstoke

Jonietz, P L (1991) 'Preface', in P L Jonietz and D Harris (eds), *World Yearbook of Education 1991: International Schools and International Education*, Kogan Page, London

Keson, J (1991) 'Meet Samantha and Sueng-Won, Ilse-Marie and Haaza', in P L Jonietz and D Harris (eds), *World Yearbook of Education 1991: International Schools and International Education*, Kogan Page, London

Leach, R J (1969) *International Schools and Their Role in the field of International Education*, Pergamon Press, Oxford

Louis, K S and Smith, B (1990) 'Teacher working conditions', in P Eyes (ed), *Teachers and Their Workplace: Commitment, Performance and Productivity*, Sage, California

Peterson, A D C (1987) *Schools Across Frontiers*, Open Court, La Salle, Illinois

Richards, N (1997) 'A case study of the implementation of change and its effect upon the job satisfaction and morale of local-contract teaching staff in an international school', MPhil thesis, University of Bath

Sutcliffe, D B (1991) 'The United World Colleges', in P L Jonietz and D Harris (eds), *World Yearbook of Education 1991: International Schools and International Education*, Kogan Page, London

13

THROUGH THE LENS OF DIVERSITY: INCLUSIVE AND ENCAPSULATED SCHOOL MISSIONS

Bob Sylvester

BACKGROUND

The rise and spread of international schools in business and economic centres world-wide has recently attracted the interest of educational researchers. These researchers have questioned the relationship between the traditional model of a liberal, broad-based western education found in many such overseas schools and the concurrent development of progressive and world-minded attitudes in students. Over the past 20 years, especially since the fall of the eastern bloc powers and the rise of the Pacific Rim economies, increasing numbers of international schools of many types, sizes and outlooks have emerged to serve expanding multilateral business, professional and diplomatic constituencies. Since the 1960s, when international schools were first established in significant numbers (Leach, 1969), the total membership of the United Nations has risen from 75 in 1969 to its present level of 185 nations. In the same time frame the number of non-governmental organizations has risen from a modest few hundred in the 1960s to a present estimate of about 30,000 (Commission on Global Governance, 1995).

It is increasingly evident in the advertising industry that a global perspective is being exploited directly by multinational corporations whose world markets are being shaped, articulated and cultivated with images and symbols of 'one planet', 'one world', 'one market-place' and 'a small planet'. At the same time universities in the western world have become visibly more diverse as they have attracted the best and the brightest students from virtually every subcontinent. Many of these university undergraduates are products of an international school education. Increased access to knowledge centres and research pools, especially in education, is creating strong reasons to explore the core meaning and direction of the type of education provided by international schools and its relation to students' views of the world. One could argue that, despite the rush to gain from the benefits of a western education, the emerging world view of students in international schools may well be increasingly non-western in outlook and is most certainly deeply diverse in its perspective.

International schools themselves are useful sites for such research into an emerging world view in that they often present, in a dynamic setting, transplanted educational communities, sometimes foundering in overseas regions. These schools are often faced with conditions that pose unavoidable dilemmas related to diversity of student, parent, governance or management constituencies.

This chapter will attempt to highlight and expand recent work at the Centre for the study of Education in an International Context (CEIC) at the University of Bath, which has explored the relationship between international schools and the loosely defined field of international education. The direction of that education will be questioned here and a model of universals of education proposed recently (Hayden and Thompson, 1996) will be examined in some detail. The literature surveyed will include both the extensive research in multicultural education (Banks, 1986; Gay, 1994) as well as the chronologically older work in global education (Becker, 1973). Reference to multinational business studies (Trompenaars, 1995) will also be made.

While studies of prejudice (Allport, 1979) and peace issues (Pike and Selby, 1988) can be traced to a time before World War II, and while multicultural education has a literature base stretching over two generations (Banks, 1994), the study of world-minded attitudes in international schools has only recently been questioned, let alone pursued in any depth. In a series of published articles over the past three years two researchers have sought to identify the dimensions of international education as expressed (or not) in international schools (Hayden and Thompson, 1995a, 1995b, 1995c, 1996). In a small-scale study of perceptions of international undergraduates they (1995a) examined the role of the non-formal curricular culture. This study hinted that the formation of world-minded attitudes may not primarily be a direct function of the formal curricular structure, at least as perceived by the students themselves. It is more likely in this view a more direct outcome of the movement of students between and among their several ethnic, linguistic and cultural worlds in their informal contacts outside the classroom.

Becker (1973) addressed the issue of students' world view in describing the many levels of cultural attachment that operate simultaneously in the world of the student:

> As Paul Bohanan, an anthropologist, has pointed out, students and teachers, like everyone else, live in a two-storey culture. There is large-scale culture, which is shared to a greater or lesser extent by much of the world and has many versions and varieties, all of which interlock into an international worldwide, large-scale culture... At the same time we are part of a small-scale world of family and community, characterized by common interests, sympathy, and face to face relationships.

Hayden and Thompson (1995c) contrasted the apparent distinction between international schools and the sometimes distinct pursuit of international education.

While their review of the literature on international education cited the notions of 'global citizenship', 'global mobility' and 'third culture kids,' they also highlighted some grounds for considering a significant segment of international schools as transplanted national schools. These schools were, for political and economic reasons, established in an overseas location. The descriptor 'international' in these cases often serves to confuse and deflect one from the central mission of these schools, which is to provide an authentic national experience outside the boundaries of a home country. While their survey also cited a model that distinguished market-driven international schools from ideology-driven ones, the authors questioned the utility of providing any more of a detailed structural model to describe schools all over the world that may not, in any event, even share a common philosophic view of the world.

In a further exploration of the boundaries of curriculum Hayden and Thompson (1995b) scrutinized the notion of the completeness of identity between the products of international schools and those intended aims and products of international education. As they pointed out, it is not the worldly distance travelled that is important to the intellectual transformation of the student and teacher towards a broader world view, but rather the degree to which the individual steps out of a culture-bound process of thinking, learning and viewing of the world.

More recently Hayden and Thompson (1996) have proposed several 'universals of international education' which may or may not be present in international schools world-wide. This chapter will seek to expand and explore those proposed universals with specific reference to the questions of diversity expressed in each of the constituent elements of international schools – parents, students, management and governance. The chapter will also attempt to describe a road in which there are two divergent directions that schools may travel when faced with diverse populations. At least one direction chosen could give rise to the potential of a truly world-minded and truly liberal educational experience. Another path is described that is bounded by limits of culture, ethnicity and national purpose. It is assumed in this chapter that diversity is the fuel that propels these schools down either road.

While seeking to identify those factors that either facilitate or offer resistance to 'unlocking the potential within the international school' (Hayden and Thompson, 1996) the authors have proposed that the characteristics shown below, described as the 'universals' characterizing international education in any institution, may constitute an essential list of properties that allow international schools to move in the direction of what is considered here as an 'inclusive' school mission:

- diversity in student cultures
- teachers as exemplars of international mindedness
- exposure to others of different cultures outside the institution
- a balanced formal curriculum
- a management regime value consistent with institutional philosophy.

These universals are to be found at the institutional level, as Hayden and Thompson (1995c) have pointed out in previous reviews of the literature on international schools, which set out defining characteristics for international education:

> Terwilliger... perceived there to be four main requisites for a school to be classified as international; the enrolment of a significant number of students not citizens of the country in which the school is located... A board of directors made up of 'foreigners and nationals in roughly the same proportions as the student body being served', a teaching body made up of teachers who have themselves 'experienced a period of cultural adaptation', and a curriculum which is a distillation of the best content and the most effective instructional practices of each of the national systems.

While Hayden and Thompson (1996) have subsequently sought to identify 'universals' of international education, their effort naturally gives rise to a need to explore and to articulate those dimensions that are consistent with the universals in what this chapter calls 'inclusive school missions'. In addition, it would be of value to identify a divergent direction on this road and articulate those dimensions that stand in distinction to the universals of international education which, for the purposes of this chapter, will be called 'encapsulated school missions'. What follows is a perspective on both directions. First we will explore the inclusive school missions.

INCLUSIVE SCHOOL MISSIONS

Deep and utilized diversity of student and parent cultures

It is assumed for the purposes of this descriptive assessment that a threshold of 30–40 student nationalities is probably required for diversity to have a significant and positive impact on the mission of international schools. At this threshold these inclusive schools are open to all constituencies and strive to eliminate or at least diminish any sense of a dominant student subculture while seeking continually to attract wider and wider aspects of diversity. The student subculture is therefore explicitly open to newcomers. Becker (1973) presents the notion of 'multiple loyalties and multiple roles' when addressing the needed emphasis in approaching global education. Inclusive international schools expect diversity and accept student diversity as an enriching act and not one requiring a ritual of acceptance into the dominant subgroup. Banks (1995) cited an opposing tendency towards assimilation rather than acculturation as being a key feature, historically, of western schooling. As Gay (1994) has pointed out in regard to the school's responsibilities towards its diverse constituencies: 'The incompatibilities or discontinuities between the culture of the school and those of different ethnic groups need to be major issues of analysis in making decisions about educational programs and practices that reflect and promote cultural diversity.'

Students in these inclusive schools recognize their attitudes as distinct from their parents'. Schools' programmes with deep diversity tend to encourage students to investigate multiple perspectives without evangelizing one cultural orientation.

With parents representative of several cultures or civilizations students in any one class cannot help but be challenged into a wider world view. As one political analyst (Huntington, 1996) has recently proposed: 'Instead of promoting the supposedly universal features of one civilization, the requisites of cultural coexistence demand a search for what is common to most civilizations. In a multicivilizational world the constructive course is to renounce universalism [of one civilization above the others], accept diversity and seek commonalities'.

Students therefore learn to move between the borders of cultural perspectives with a much higher level of comfort and understanding than would be possible in a school with a narrow nationally based mission. This sophisticated worldview, while generated originally from the fact of travelling widely in the world at a school-going age, is enhanced through increasingly non-formal, intimate contacts (Hayden and Thompson, 1995a) with 'foreign' students at a very personal level.

Teachers as exemplars of world-minded views

Schools with an open-ended plan of recruiting the best teachers world-wide will fall easily into the mould of multilateral international schools (Leach, 1969) and there-fore of an inclusive school mission. Diversity in recruiting has only limited value if the orientation of those teachers does not include their view of themselves as world citizens. Teachers from such inclusive schools view the development of world-minded attitudes in students as central to their task as teachers.

The concept of educating for world citizenship is embedded in the Charter of the United Nations (United Nations, 1983), the Universal Declaration of Human Rights (United Nations, 1983) as well as The Convention on the Rights of the Child (United Nations, 1989). These documents have been adopted universally. One recent document presented to the United Nations Conference on Sustainable Development set out a model for the attributes of training for world citizenship (Baha'i International Community, 1994):

> World citizenship begins with an acceptance of the oneness of the human family and the interconnectedness of the nations of 'the earth, our home' [quoted from Rio Declaration]. While it encourages a sane and legitimate patriotism, it also insists on a wider loyalty, a love of humanity as a whole. It does not, however, imply abandonment of legitimate loyalties, the suppression of cultural diversity, the abolition of national autonomy, nor the imposition of uniformity. Its hallmark is 'unity in diversity'.

Teachers in such a setting exhibit and contribute to multiple models of teacher training and instructional approaches. They consciously seek and learn from diverse training models outside of their own original training. As Laszlo (1989) has pointed out: 'Respect for the differing views of others, and a readiness to learn from them are among the most difficult human virtues. They are, however, among the most needed.'

Points of contact rather than distinctions characterize their search. Their conduct in the classroom is characterized by an approach to questions of diversity in a principled manner. These world-minded teachers seek out the underlying principles of an issue and try to instil in their students a principled approach to decision making. These teachers would themselves demonstrate in the classroom an overt appreciation for all the cultural groups in the school. As Mattern (1991) has passionately proposed:

> We must become a truly discrete branch of the profession, committed to the identification of those elements which are basic to the concept and practice of global citizenship, and skilled in the art and science of transmitting them to those for whose education we are responsible... I could hope there might be some schools and teachers bold enough to ask their students to explore one further element in a system of values which, if not totally universal, certainly has very good credentials... In which the common condition and mutual responsibility for one's fellow members of the race are taken as essentials of the social fabric.

School gives students opportunities to explore diversity

The mission of such an inclusive school evokes the consciousness of the unity of the human family in a direct and explicit manner. The basic values expressed challenge the community towards an acceptance of the several notions of the unity of humankind, human solidarity and the brotherhood of man. As Connell (in Skilbeck, 1988) has highlighted: 'Central to education for international life is a recognition of the unity of mankind in a commonly shared world.'

The school therefore exhibits an engagement in the contiguous cultures (conventionally known as 'local cultures') which would not themselves be seen as being distinct from the school environment. Inclusive schools such as these tend to see their role as servants to the surrounding cultures and not 'above' or apart from them. This is evidenced in multiple connections rather than occasional 'window dressings' or school outings geared towards cultural enrichment. As Leach (1969) has outlined:

> The truly multilateral international school must be devoted to the principle that the highest common denominator between and among the various contributing national elements is essential. Rather naturally, the whole world becomes the local parish for the multilateral international school. Each major tradition can be analysed for its strengths and usefulness. Once this course has been decided upon and the essential unity of mankind therefore underscored, the possibility of achieving a result which will enrich each national heritage is made possible.

A world-minded approach is evident throughout the curriculum and at all levels. At the upper levels students would be trained in a high level of dialogue that would require compassion, suspension of judgement and a rigorous assessment of the facts of any position. 'Unity in diversity' is inevitably an underlying theme within these multiple perspectives and opportunities to explore diversity. All student minorities are to be acknowledged and their position protected within the bounds of a consultative ethos and practice.

A balanced formal curriculum

These schools do not view curriculum development as a culture-bound process. The development of curriculum would not have as its aim the protection of one specific cultural orientation but would seek to have as broad a focus as possible. This process would be informed by a continuous search for the best curriculum tools and models world-wide. The adoption of texts from only one source, however effective, would in itself be a culture-bound activity. While textual choices would often be prepackaged, adapting these texts would precede the adopting of such materials. The curriculum would be explicitly designed to prepare students to re-enter a variety of school environments and cultural orientations. The sources of knowledge in this exercise would be global and the view of humanity universal. As pointed out by Banks (1995) quoting Horsman, this universal view of the human condition is not a recent notion: 'Prior to the development of colonisation and before the mid-19th century, a theory of unity of humans had been developed in Europe and was highly influential... This Enlightenment view held that "mankind was of one species, and that mankind in general was capable of indefinite improvement".'

The inclusive school may be open to external review by peers world-wide: not just for the purpose of simple accreditation but also for collegial exchange, student partnerships and expanding understanding of the need for a global approach to learning and teaching. The school therefore uses the curriculum to move students between and through frontiers of thought and perspective. History, geography, literature and the sciences are all viewed from the widest angle with contributions from all the world's civilizations. As pointed out, world citizenship and a sane patriotism are both held up as the fundamentals of civic-minded education. As Sowell (1994) articulates: 'Just as national labels may implicitly overstate the social cohesion of the groups under those labels, so may these national labels obscure the international ties among some groups whose cohesion extends across national borders.'

Good citizenship training is still at the heart of the social sciences, especially in a multilateral international school. The new science of civics calls for wider loyalties and multiple loyalties (Becker, 1973). As outlined by Banks (1986): 'It is essential that schools in western democracies acculturate students rather than foster tight ethnic boundaries, because all students, including ethnic minority students, must develop the knowledge, attitudes and skills needed to become successful citizens of their cultural communities, their nation states and the global community.'

As Dubos (quoted in Becker, 1973) concluded regarding the inevitability of multiple loyalties: 'As we enter the global phase of human evolution, it becomes obvious that each man has two countries, his own and the planet earth.'

Management regime consistent with institutional philosophy

In such inclusive school programmes part of the mission would inevitably be to prepare all students in the broadest sense for entry into their respective school systems. This may at least be presented as a goal of preparing students to enter multiple school systems. The hidden ideology of such schools would also be diminished, as the school's ideology would have to be explicit for the minority perspectives to be protected. The more explicit a school ideology is the less fragile the school culture and climate will tend to be. A culture of consultation would tend to replace purely democratic practices in a multilateral and inclusive school culture. This is a natural outcome when no one constituency dominates the decision-making process. The management of the school would exhibit a preference for such consultative mechanisms, with stakeholders being defined in the broadest sense and decisions being 'built up' over time through a process of consensus. As Trompenaars (1995) has noted in his large-scale study of multicultural business practices:

> The individualist society, with its respect for individual opinions, will frequently ask for a vote to get all those noses pointed in the same direction. The drawback to this is that within a short time they are likely to have reverted to their original orientation. The collectivist society [not a political description] will intuitively refrain from voting because this will not show respect to the individuals who are against the majority decision. It prefers to deliberate until consensus is reached. The final result takes longer to achieve, but it will be more stable.

Management would also display an affection for a problem-solving approach in which agreement on facts and determination of operating principles becomes commonplace. Even with a mature problem-solving approach schools with deep diversity will be presented with multiple dilemmas, which cannot be resolved in quick fashion. Consensus building is a key skill in this regard.

In keeping with all of the 'universals' proposed by Hayden and Thompson (1996) it may be useful at this point to reflect on the stated aims of international education as put forward by Leach (1969) in his major study of the contemporary state of international schools. He proposed that the philosophy of what he called 'integral international education' would be, first:

> to incorporate not only the highest common denominator between and among known national and ethnic education techniques, but to exclude nothing that is common to man. Second, it would seem reasonable to stress those elements which affirm the solidarity of mankind as an entity in such a way that the one-time international school students will find themselves 'at home' in all cultures and human situations. But more important, they should feel their lives incomplete in less than universal situations.

ENCAPSULATED SCHOOL MISSIONS

Schools with an encapsulated mission can be contrasted with 'inclusive' school missions using the same analogy of 'universals'. This, in some cases, results in attributes that would stand as divergent and in other cases present qualities that fall short of the universals. But in all cases they would present a very different direction in their mission and aims. The notion of an encapsulated school mission could be said to be resonant with the literature of multicultural education in which Banks (1986) presented a model that included several stages of ethnic and cultural development. The first stage is described as 'cultural captivity' and the last as 'globalism and global competency'.

Stage two – 'cultural encapsulation' is characterized by ethnocentrism and cultural separatism. While the encapsulated school mission may not suffer from total captivity because it is at least aware of its surrounding pluralism, it does not have a clear framework of the whole world and its peoples as its educational field of focus.

A summary of the encapsulated qualities is proposed below and is point for point related, in contrast, to the universals proposed by Hayden and Thompson (1996):

- limited diversity of parent/student cultures
- teaching limited to culture-specific pedagogy
- school tends to manage the multicultural experience
- curriculum is narrowly targeted
- value system a product of an imported school culture.

Limited diversity of parent/student cultures

While diversity may be a distinguishing feature of this type of international school the depth of the diversity presented does not tend to move the school away from its focus on whatever national programme it has chosen to pursue. One or more clearly identifiable groups dominate these schools, and all other groups in the school stand outside the central sphere of influence. In the same way, one student subculture dominates the life of the school. It may have over 20 nationalities but there are abundant examples of exclusive international schools with student populations from 15–30 nations which attract such diversity without having to question or abandon their nationally based curriculum.

Teaching (teachers) limited to culture-specific pedagogy

The most sensitive question to be asked in addressing schools with a culture-specific pedagogy would be: 'Where, predominantly, are your teachers recruited from?' In schools where one group of teachers forms the dominant group an entire world of teacher training assumptions is naturally implanted into the school culture.

This, of course, would also hold true for the administrators, who are very often recruited from one dominant source. Despite a rather deep level of diversity of student culture schools with teachers from one recruiting source would find it difficult to engender truly world-minded views of teaching and learning.

School tends to manage the multicultural experience

Because one or two student cultures dominate these encapsulated school cultures the view of the world held by many of the students is largely 'foreign' or 'distant'. Great efforts are then made by the dominant group to help their students 'feel at home'. This is done very often by ensuring that the materials, rites, holidays and traditions are carefully representative of the dominant home culture. Students would also be expected to embrace their parents' worldview. The transmission of the culture of the dominant group along with the parents' worldview (highlighted by Allport, 1979) would in fact be the underlying aim of the school mission: 'Most children never enlarge their sense of belonging beyond the ties of family, city, nation. The reason seems to be that those with whom the child lives, and whose judgement he mirrors, do not do so.'

Diversity is seen as desirable but not at the core of the school's mission and therefore is subordinated to the need to pass on the central cultural values of the school. Diversity is managed by a series of predetermined policies which ensure the continuation of this dominant, nationally based school culture. Unfortunately, as Trompenaars (1995) has cited, it is the corporation with 'the best integrated diversity' that excels. Management of diversity and the use of diversity as a human resource and educational tool are two very divergent paths on the road of international education.

Curriculum is narrowly targeted

The central mission of encapsulated international schools is to prepare students for entry/re-entry into one specific nationally based school system. In a few cases it may prepare students to enter more than one national system but even this extended effort would be to the exclusion of preparing students for the wider context. The dominant group is thereby protected explicitly in the school's mission. Under these conditions the curriculum can justifiably be said to be bound by national borders and interests. It is at this point that the description 'overseas schools' comes into play and that these schools perceive themselves as detached from their home base and culture.

As a matter of policy the curriculum is developed from prescribed sources of knowledge consistent with national goals. These goals are then reinforced with recruiting and textual decisions being made on the basis of 'country of origin' rather than (necessarily) merit. Any accreditation process would be designed to ensure parents that the industry standards of a specific country are being met or exceeded.

The level of protection afforded a national group by the focus of a curriculum may well be a litmus test of the direction of a school's mission. The overall degree of protection afforded a dominant subculture could therefore be viewed as a signal of the direction of a school's mission within this directional model addressed in this chapter. By contrast, the newly articulated mission of the International Baccalaureate Organization (IBO, 1996) includes the notion of preparing students to be 'conscious of the shared humanity that binds all people together while respecting the variety of cultures and attitudes that makes for the richness of life'. As Blaney (1991) has proposed in his ideal for international schools: 'Educational systems, rooted mainly in national concerns and constrained by national ideologies, cannot educate young people to live meaningfully (happily and effectively) in a world society which is global, whose interests, concerns and needs – along with its major problems – transcend national boundaries.'

Value system a product of an imported school culture

While the contiguous cultures (local cultural reference points) are recognized and in some cases celebrated in these schools they do not feature as sources of knowledge, nor are they attributed with the capacity and tools to prepare students meaningfully with life skills. The value system of the school is largely implicit because it reflects the dominant student culture. As Banks (1986) highlighted in his review of multicultural education in western societies:

> The school is a microculture where the cultures of students and teachers meet. The school should be a cultural environment where acculturation takes place: both teachers and students should assimilate some of the views, perceptions and ethos of each other as they interact. Both teachers and students will be enriched by this process and the academic achievement of students from diverse cultures will be enhanced because their cosmos and ethos will be reflected and legitimized in the school.

The encapsulated school mission is self-defining. It is limited by its own vision and its underlying fear of what lies 'outside' the boundaries of a known national tradition. It learns from its diversity but only at arm's length and without a conviction, passionately held, that there is a wisdom and knowledge in the full range of human diversity. The proposed universals of international education may provide us with a new way of looking at schools and learning, but to prosper in the education of human beings we must change our overall view of the world. While educating children to be productive citizens of their land of birth and loyalists of their ethnic perspective we also have a moral opportunity to present to them, as well, a view of the world in all its completeness. As Ward (quoted in Commission on Global Governance, 1995) so clearly challenged:

> The most important change that people can make is to change their way of looking at the world. We can change studies, jobs, neighbourhoods, even

countries and continents, and still remain much as we always were. But change our fundamental angle of vision and everything changes – our priorities, our values, our judgements, our pursuits. Again and again, in the history of religion, this total upheaval in the imagination has marked the beginning of a new life... A turning of the heart, a 'metanoia', by which men see with new minds and turn their energies to new ways of living.

The greatest challenge, under these circumstances, facing multilateral international schools today is one of worldview. This challenge addresses itself to each of the stakeholders – teacher, student, parent, administrator and trustee. The response to this challenge will in itself define a future for these schools.

REFERENCES

Allport, G W (1979) *The Nature of Prejudice (Unabridged)*, Addison-Wesley, Reading, MA

Baha'i International Community (1994) *World Citizenship: A Global Ethic for Sustainable Development*, Baha'i International Community, New York

Banks, J A (1994) *An Introduction to Multicultural Education*, Allyn & Bacon, Boston, Mass

Banks, J A (1995) 'The historical reconstruction of knowledge about race: implications for transformative teaching', *Educational Researcher*, **24**, 5, pp 15–25

Banks, J A (1986) *Multicultural Education in Western Societies*, Praeger, New York

Becker, J (1973) *Education for a Global Society*, Phi Delta Kappa Educational Foundation, Bloomington, Indiana

Blaney, J J (1991) 'The international school system', in P L Jonietz and D Harris (eds), *World Yearbook of Education 1991: International Schools and International Education*, Kogan Page, London

Commission on Global Governance (1995) *Our Global Neighbourhood: The Report of the Commission on Global Governance*, Oxford University Press, New York

Gay, G (1994) *A Synthesis of Scholarship in Multicultural Education*, http://www.ncrel.org/catalog/multicult.htm, 22 July 1997, Seattle

Hayden, M C and Thompson, J J (1995a) 'Perceptions of international education: a preliminary study', *International Review of Education*, **41**, 5, pp 389–404

Hayden, M C and Thompson, J J (1995b) 'International education: the crossing of frontiers', *International Schools Journal*, **15**, 1, pp 13–20

Hayden, M C and Thompson, J J (1995c) 'International schools and international education: a relationship reviewed', *Oxford Review of Education*, **21**, 3, pp 327–45

Hayden, M C and Thompson, J J (1996) 'Potential difference: the driving force for international education', *International Schools Journal*, **16**, 1, pp 46–57

Huntington, S P (1996) *The Clash of Civilizations and the Remaking of World Order*, Simon & Schuster, New York

International Baccalaureate Organization (1996) 'Education for life: the mission of the IB', *IB World*, 13, p 7

Laszlo, E (1989) *The Inner Limits of Mankind: Heretical Reflections on Today's Values, Culture and Politics*, Oneworld Publications, Oxford

Leach, R J (1969) *International Schools and their Role in the Field of International Education*, Pergamon Press, Oxford

Mattern, W G (1991) 'Random ruminations on the curriculum of the international school', in P L Jonietz and D Harris (eds), *World Yearbook of Education 1991: International Schools and International Education*, Kogan Page, London

Pike, G and Selby, D (1988) *Global Teacher, Global Learner*, Hodder & Stoughton, London

Skilbeck, M (ed) (1988) *Readings in School-based Curriculum Development*, Paul Chapman, London

Sowell, T (1994) *Race and Culture: A World View*, Basic Books, New York

Trompenaars, F (1995) *Riding the Waves of Culture: Understanding Cultural Diversity in Business*, Nicholas Brealey, London

United Nations (1983) *Basic Facts about the United Nations*, United Nations, New York

United Nations (1989) *United Nations Convention on the Rights of the Child*, http://childhouse.uio.no/childrens_rights/dci_crc.html, 3 July 1997, New York

14

Investigating National and Organizational Cultures in the Context of the International School

James Cambridge

Introduction

There are numerous definitions of culture in the contexts of organizations and national societies. They range from the concrete to the abstract, but at their core they all tend to refer to shared meanings and values. The layers of an onion are often presented as an analogy for culture; some aspects of culture lie on the surface while others are deeper. Some attributes of culture, such as tangible products and artefacts, are explicit – they are easy to observe but may be difficult to interpret. Other attributes of culture are less tangible, comprising norms and values, and basic assumptions; these implicit attributes of culture cannot be observed directly, that is without the construction of data collection instruments. Interpretation of research data can be difficult and confusing because different authors define culture in different ways. The discussion that follows will consider the contrasting views of cross-cultural differences proposed by Geert Hofstede, and Fons Trompenaars and Charles Hampden-Turner. A framework for analysis of cross-cultural congruence, and its possible application to the international school, will also be considered.

The range of cross-cultural interactions in the international school

International schools often have a highly diverse teaching staff and student body. Teachers are recruited from many different countries, including the host country in which the school is located, and they bring with them a variety of professional experience. They also have a variety of educational values which influence their actions and expectations. The student body may be even more diverse. The following description of a hypothetical international school has been generated from informal interviews conducted by the author with teachers in a variety of locations. A composite picture is presented; no resemblance to any specific institution is intended or should be inferred!

Interaction within the staff

Teachers are contracted to work at the international school on a variety of different terms which, it is argued, reflect their potential commitment to their jobs. There is considerable turnover among some sections of staff, particularly among those expatriate workers who are engaged on local terms. Such expatriates living locally are often – but not exclusively – female, and the reason they are in the country is because they are accompanying their spouses who work for multinational corporations and development aid agencies. It is likely that if their spouse leaves they will leave too, possibly at short notice. Other expatriates are employed on more lucrative terms which, it is intended, reflect their longer-term commitment to the school; they are expensive to recruit from abroad but they comprise experienced teachers, often in particularly critical subjects, and many of them occupy key positions in the school such as head of department. They are paid an overseas allowance as an inducement to work at the school, which is located in a poor, undeveloped and not particularly fashionable country. They also receive other emoluments, such as generous flight and baggage allowances, subsidized housing and free tuition for their children in a country where there is no free education. In view of the expense of recruiting expatriate teachers it is desirable to engage them as working couples; it may even be possible to attract them with the inducement of only one overseas allowance between them.

Teachers within the national system are relatively poorly paid but, while the terms of employment and salary scales at the school are better than in the state education sector, the presence of the expatriates is a source of some resentment among the staff recruited from the host country. This is because of the wide pay differential between themselves and the expatriates and the apparent 'glass ceiling' to promotion of host country teachers. Only one member of the senior administration team and the teacher responsible for coordinating teaching of the local language are host country nationals with positions of responsibility. The host country teachers themselves feel that they are being treated unfairly but, in meetings of the board of governors, there is pressure to recruit and retain as many expatriates as possible. This sentiment is not only expressed by expatriate parents of school students but also those members of the board who are themselves host country nationals. It is not difficult to understand their point of view; they see the school, and the international examinations for which students are prepared, as a way of obtaining college places in the USA, Canada, Australia and the UK. They would prefer that the teachers at the school were experienced in these examinations and fluent native speakers of English.

Interaction within the community

The school governors have worked on a mission statement that articulates the educational values of the organization, but it is doubtful whether this has the wholehearted support of all the staff. Different educational values are expressed by various members of the school community. These differences include contrasting beliefs and attitudes about the purposes of education, the nature of teaching and learning, the nature of the subjects being taught, the purposes of educational assessment, and relations between adults and young people. There are also contrasting outlooks about the relationship between the individual and society, gender roles, and the nature of authority.

For example, some members of the community see the school as an agent of social change; they are inspired by the spirit of internationalism in the school, which brings together so many teachers and students of different nationalities, and they feel that this contributes to peace and understanding between nations. Others are more pragmatic; there are not sufficient numbers of expatriate children in the country to make a school that serves a particular national community an economically viable entity, but there is a demand in the local educational market to supply a service that satisfies the widest range of consumers. The spirits of pragmatism and an internationalist aspiration are not mutually exclusive, however, and the development of an international outlook is both an outcome of this type of organization and an important ingredient contributing to the culture of the school.

Some sectional interests in the school community are disturbed by the international outlook of the school and the ways in which it influences their children, who come home speaking an international slang vocabulary, with a taste for different styles of food and dress, and who have acquired different values from those of their parents. This happens to adolescents in cultures the world over, of course, but many parents wish to defend and propagate the traditional values of their home cultures and are prepared to support the school despite, not because of, its internationalism. For them the school is a means to an end of obtaining good educational qualifications that are recognized internationally, but they are worried by the 'lowest common denominator' approach to cultures. Many of the students may be described as 'third culture' children, with the language and culture of their homes being different from the language and culture of both the international school and the host community. Internationalism and national chauvinism can be identified side by side in the same institution. Indeed, some teachers and parents take the view that the traditional values of their own national cultures are being overwhelmed by the 'international style' of western liberal humanism that embodies the so-called internationalism of the school. Their attitude is that tolerance of all points of view, or cultural relativism, is not the hallmark of having strong values but, rather, the outcome of a lack of values.

Teacher–student interactions

Contrasting models of teaching and learning can be identified among individuals from different national cultures. What should be the relationship between the teacher and the student? Is it based on a view of the participants as equals, or is there inequality in the relationship? Should the student address the teacher by title, or should they be on first-name terms? In what direction should the communication be between them? Is the teacher expected to initiate and dominate the relationship, or should the student ask questions of the teacher? In some cultures it is considered impolite for children to question their elders, in which case a deficit view of teaching and learning is likely to prevail, with the task of the teacher being to fill the learner with knowledge. By contrast a developmental view of teaching and learning requires dialogue and feedback between the participants. Active learners, it is argued, must be able to control their own education (Bentley and Watts, 1989). The 'international' curriculum of many schools assumes that the students are active learners, but there may be situations in which students or their teachers are more comfortable working in a more passive learning style. Under such circumstances differences in educational values can come to be interpreted as discipline problems. Students who are used to working in one way may become agitated when confronted with another approach. Teachers may feel threatened because they are no longer in control when they are questioned by students. They may feel that they will lose face in front of their students if they admit that they cannot answer a question; there may be a premium placed on appearing to know everything. For them, education may be seen as an accomplished body of factual knowledge rather than a process for gaining access to that knowledge.

In certain societies it is considered undesirable to stand out as an individual from the group. A teacher with individualist values who asks a student from a more collectivist or communitarian culture to speak up in front of the class may be answered by a resentful silence. Other strategies, such as small group work and discussion, may need to be adopted to encourage student talk and avoid mutual frustration.

One view of educational assessment, particularly of the formative type, is that 'there is no failure, only feedback'. To what extent is this perspective shared by teachers and students? What is considered more important; the knowledge and skills acquired by learning or the certificates gained as a result? How far would a teacher or student be prepared to cheat in order to gain such a certificate? Anecdotal evidence indicates that there is a wide range of attitudes to the security of assessment materials before or during an external examination. There are stories of students being given the answers to examination questions and of questions circulating before the examination is sat. In justification it may be argued that such activities indicate that the teacher is demonstrating solidarity with the student against a common opponent, the examiner. In an assessment system that operates on high stakes examinations the future career of the student will be damaged by failure and, furthermore, the teacher can lose face. Teacher and student may live in a society whose cultural outlook places a higher premium on guile and craftiness than it does on the notions of honesty that prevail elsewhere. Values that appeal to particularism, in the form of the personal needs of the student, may be judged to be more important than appeals to universalist concepts such as impersonally upholding arbitrary rules.

The international school is an arena for a variety of cross-cultural interactions that include interactions within the teaching staff, between the school and the host community, and between members of teaching staff and the student body. Schools may be driven by aspirations towards internationalism or have more pragmatic, economic reasons for their diversity. Cultural diversity may be welcomed by the parents or students to varying extents. It can be a source of some tension as misunderstandings between individuals take place. This is particularly true in the classroom where different expectations of students and teachers about the nature of teaching and learning can be interpreted as discipline problems.

THE SCHOOL AS A CULTURE

How can cultural differences with respect to educational values be described and analysed? Two general approaches to theory are to be found in cross-cultural psychology and international organizational management. There is an extensive literature addressing the school as an organization. The publications of Charles Handy comprise a useful and accessible introduction to the study of organizations; his accounts of the contrasting cultures of organizations using the metaphors of the club, hierarchy, network and individual (and their corresponding 'gods of management') are both entertaining and illuminating (Handy, 1993). Other metaphors for organizations are the family, Eiffel Tower, guided missile and incubator (Hampden-Turner and Trompenaars, 1993; Trompenaars and Hampden-Turner, 1997). Other authors, particularly Morgan (1997), develop further and extend the repertoire of metaphors that may be applied to organizations. The 'culture' metaphor is important, but it is also useful to bear in mind others such as 'the organization as a living organism' and 'the organization as a political system'.

THE SCHOOL AS AN OPEN SYSTEM

Contingency theories of organizations view them as open systems that carry out exchange with their environment. This is Morgan's view of 'the organization as a living organism'. The organization takes in raw materials and processes them to form products as an output; the barrier between the organization and the surrounding environment (which may be expressed in technological, cultural, economic and political terms) is permeable and there is exchange in both directions. Positive and negative feedback loops keep the organization on track, and enable it to respond to changes in the environment.

International schools are organizations located within communities of stakeholders and others with diverse interests that may be in competition. The students and their parents, and the teaching staff, may come from a number of different countries and, depending on the school and its location, there may be either intimate or distant relations with the host country community. In some schools, for example, there may be a large proportion of students and/or teachers from the host country, but in other schools there may be none. There may be legal, economic, educational, linguistic or religious reasons that account for the degree of participation of host country nationals in the international school but, whatever the degree of participation, the school will be profoundly influenced – either positively or negatively – by the host environment within which it operates. As such, international schools may be described as open systems because 'they are dependent on their external environment in order to survive and are, therefore, open to influences and transactions with the outside world as long as they exist' (Hanna in Harris *et al.*, 1997).

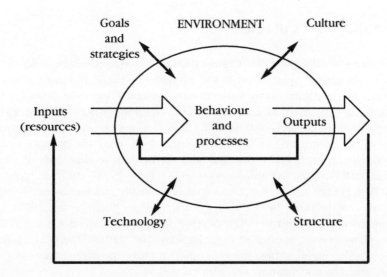

Figure 14.1 An organization as an open system (after Harrison, 1994)

Numerous models of organizations as open systems are to be found in the literature. The example given in Figure 14.1 is a modified version of the model described by Harrison (1994), which is particularly attractive because of its explicit reference to culture as part of the environment of the organization. All such models have particular features in common, which include: a boundary between the organization and the environment, which may or may not be permeable to exchanges between them; inputs into the system, which comprise the various physical and human resources that enter the school such as books, equipment, students, teachers and support staff, as well as 'software' resources such as technologies of education; transformation of inputs by the behaviour and processes of the organization into outputs, which will comprise intended outcomes (such as learning by the students, in the case of an international school) but which may also include unintended or negative outcomes. The activities of the organization are kept on track by monitoring which comprises positive and negative feedback.

Hanna points out that: 'by definition, everything outside the system's boundary is the environment... [It] provides the inputs and must accept the outputs, must support the purpose, and provides feedback to the system. Thus its influence on the life of the system is critical' (in Harris *et al.*, 1997). The international school may interact with its environment in different ways; it may attempt to ignore the environment, by adopting a closed system approach, or by seeking to control its environment. Neither of these approaches would appear to be sustainable in the long term, but a third approach is to seek to achieve a balance between the needs of the organization and the demands of the environment. The international school may attempt to influence changes in parts of the environment while changing itself in some respects. Bate (1994) proposes that organizations are constantly undergoing change, either to develop ('change of position') or to stay the same in the face of a changing environment ('homeostasis'). Thus, the political nature of the international school is underlined, in that its continued existence requires continuing renegotiation and reconciliation between conflicting interests.

Lachman *et al.* (1994) argue that the influence of the environment on the organization, for practical purposes, may be reduced to two key factors: the availability of resources (inputs) and cultural values. While this is admittedly a gross over-simplification it is a useful approach in that it establishes a framework that enables us to generate certain hypotheses about the structure and functions of the international school and that points a way forward. I shall return to this point later.

THE SCHOOL AS A POLITICAL SYSTEM

Contrasting attitudes to national cultures contribute to the development of the institutional politics of the international school. Interest groups at different distances from the centre of institutional power and influence will see things in different ways. Hawley (1995) writes that:

> power struggles [emerge] from different cultural philosophies and economic backgrounds of the board of directors... The challenge of managing a multinational school board (and multinational school) should be recognized by school heads and board members alike... it would be helpful to acknowledge that some effort must be made to understand how different philosophies and cultures could lead to misinterpretations and disagreements.

An organization in perpetual conflict can be ineffective, but to what extent is an organization more effective in the absence of conflict, particularly if this is at the price of cross-cultural conflict having been driven underground? Unitarism is the condition where one culture predominates in an organization; this is in contrast with pluralism, where more than one culture is given expression. Unitarism is frequently equated with 'strong culture' that, in turn, can be equated with organizational effectiveness. It is often said that those in power have the least idea of what is going on in an organization since it is hidden from them. Thus, in practice, strong organizational cultures can turn out to be the least effective. Members of an organization whose cultures are not recognized or valued by the dominant organizational culture can become radicalized within the context of organizational politics or alienated. It is therefore in the interests of organizational effectiveness to understand the ways in which cross-cultural differences can be managed.

Acculturation is the process by which cultural differences are resolved and cultural change and adaptation between different groups takes place. Following a cross-cultural psychological framework Cox (1993) recognizes four possible outcomes of acculturation: assimilation, a one-way adaptive process in which an organization's culture becomes the standard of behaviour for all joining it; separation, in which members of different cultures are unwilling or unable to adapt to an organization's culture and seek some autonomy from it; deculturation, when neither the culture of entering members nor that of the organization is influential or highly valued in framing the behaviour of incoming members; and pluralism, a two-way process of learning and adaptation in which both the organization and members entering it from various cultural backgrounds change to reflect the cultural norms and values of others.

The international school can be viewed as an open system that is influenced by the environment of its host country, whether it embraces or isolates itself from it. Resource availability and cultural values have been identified as two key factors that influence the environment. Unitarism and pluralism are identified as two contrasting approaches to the management of organizational culture. The rivalry between different cultural values can lead to political struggles for power and influence in the organization.

There has been an expanding literature about cultural diversity in organizations over the past couple of decades and an influential voice in this field has been that of Geert Hofstede, who reported a massive study conducted by questionnaire among employees of the various national branches of the multinational IBM corporation (Hofstede, 1980, 1991). Factor analysis of attitude data at the level of countries yielded four discrete factors around which Hofstede constructed four dimensions: power distance, individualism, masculinity and uncertainty avoidance. Construction of scaled indices in each dimension enabled Hofstede to resolve different national cultures and describe them. This approach has not been without its critics but, as Hickson (1996) comments, Hofstede had 'frail data, but robust concepts'. The extent to which his concepts have been used as a paradigm for further research is reviewed by Søndergaard (1994), and there can be little doubt that Hofstede's ideas have been very influential on the work of many researchers.

HOFSTEDE'S DIMENSIONS APPLIED TO INTERNATIONAL SCHOOLS

The prospects for the application of Hofstede's dimensions to the study of teachers and learners in organizations such as international schools are limited. Hofstede emphasizes that the dimensions cannot and should not be used to stereotype the attributes of individuals because they refer to the central statistical tendencies of populations at the level of countries. As a result, it would not be valid to apply these dimensions to the analysis of data at the level of individuals. Inevitably data from teachers in international schools would consist of responses from small numbers of individuals in numerous geographically dispersed units. Hofstede's dimensions were derived from several thousand cases in matched sets, but matched data of this magnitude are unlikely to be generated from teachers in international schools. However, even if they cannot be applied to the study of teachers and learners, the dimensions may be applied to the analysis of cross-cultural issues.

In a paper which discusses cross-cultural teaching and learning Hofstede (1986) identifies four situations in which problems may arise: differences in societal positions of teachers and students in the two societies; differences in the relevance of the curriculum for the two societies; differences in profiles of cognitive abilities between the populations from which the teacher and student are drawn; and differences in expected patterns of teacher–student and student–student interaction. In his discussion of differences in societal positions of teachers and students Hofstede draws attention to: the families from which teachers and students are recruited; whether the educational system is élitist or anti-élitist; the role of employers in education; the role of the church or the state in education; whether there is a private education system next to a public sector one and their respective statuses; whether the government prescribes the curriculum or whether the teacher or school are free to define their own; who pays for education; how well teachers are paid; and the societal status of teachers. These considerations are of particular relevance to the study of the international school. Parents frequently choose an international school education for their children in preference to the other educational arrangements that are available in a country. Their choice may be determined by the nature of the curriculum or the language of instruction. International schools are, in many countries, seen as élitist institutions that not only serve the educational needs of the international business and diplomatic communities but also the host country economic élite. As such they may be private islands of plenty in contrast to an impoverished local public education system. Certain international schools have been founded by government or religious institutions but they are frequently independent of, or at 'arm's length' from the direct influence of government. Funding for international schools may come from a wide variety of sources, including school fees paid by parents or their employers, and subventions from the host government or a foreign government. In an otherwise impoverished educational system teachers may be relatively well paid. Indeed, the school may find it necessary to recruit and retain teachers in an international market; the payment of inducements to certain members of staff may generate a two-tier salary scale among the teaching staff, with highly paid international expatriates and a more poorly paid locally recruited cohort. The social status of international school teachers may vary from country to country; in some societies they will be respected as 'intellectuals', whereas in others they will be treated as servants.

Considering the differences in relevance of the curriculum, Hofstede draws attention to the usefulness of the curriculum content. How does the content of the curriculum address the needs of the learner? Hofstede's paper refers specifically to educational exchanges between economically developed and less developed countries in the context of business management education, but its comments can be applied to a wider range of examples. There is likely to be a lack of relevance for many students if they are exposed to the curriculum of a particular national grouping; this has been a driving force in the development of an international curriculum such as the International Baccalaureate. However, it may be argued that the concept of the 'international' curriculum is limited to the development of one that propagates the values of western liberal humanism. In practice this may be what the varied interest groups in the international school require: an internationally recognized matriculation examination. In other words, the relevance of the curriculum is frequently determined in terms of its usefulness outside the country where the school is located.

Discussing differences in profiles of cognitive abilities between the populations from which the teacher and student are drawn, Hofstede draws attention to problems arising from ethnocentrism. This is emphatically not an argument for a racialist interpretation of intelligence, but is in favour of recognition that particular cultural phenomena, such as ways of writing idiographic scripts, impose demands for certain kinds of learning such as pattern recognition and rote learning. What is presented as an 'international' curriculum, however, may be limited to preparation of students for culturally specific examinations that will assist in entry to universities in developed countries.

Hofstede draws attention to how differences of values influence cross-cultural interactions when discussing the differences in expected patterns of teacher–student and student–student interaction. Reference is made to the four-dimension model of cultural differences, and contrasts are made between cultures in approaches to teaching and learning. For example, in small power distance societies there is a stress on impersonal 'truth' that can in principle be obtained from any competent person, students are allowed to contradict the teacher and education is learner centred, with a premium placed on initiative. By contrast, in large power distance societies the stress is on personal 'wisdom', which is transferred in the relationship with a particular teacher, the teacher cannot be contradicted and education is teacher centred, with a premium placed on order. In strong uncertainty avoidance cultures teachers interpret intellectual disagreement as disloyalty, whereas in weak uncertainty avoidance cultures intellectual disagreement is interpreted as a stimulating exercise. In what are known as 'masculine' societies students compete with each other, whereas in 'feminine' societies they practice mutual solidarity. In 'collectivist' societies teachers are expected to give preferential treatment to some students (based, for instance, on ethnic affiliation or on recommendation by an influential person), but in 'individualist' societies teachers are expected to be strictly impartial.

Discussion with practising international schoolteachers about these differences leads to the conclusion that many of them could be placed simultaneously in two or more of Hofstede's dimensions. This does not make the differences (which have been drawn together by Hofstede from the literature), or indeed the dimensions invalid, but it does suggest that a different approach is necessary in order to create a context for differences in values. Hofstede expresses the differences as paired statements; they articulate the alternatives that embody dilemmas that must be reconciled by teachers and learners; thus it may be more useful to the study of international schools if they are reinterpreted in terms of the 'valuing processes' of Hampden-Turner and Trompenaars (1993).

A FRAMEWORK FOR ANALYSIS OF CROSS-CULTURAL INTERACTIONS

Lachman *et al.* (1994) propose a framework for analysis of factors contributing to effective adaptation of organizations and management practices transferred across cultural boundaries that appears to be applicable to the international school. Close inspection of this framework reveals that it is the product of a contingency view of the organization, in that the environment within which the organization is situated influences its structure and function. However, it is a model of the organization as an open system in which the influence of the environment is stripped down to two key factors, namely 'values' and 'resources availability'.

By 'values' Lachman *et al.* specify 'cultural values', using a definition of culture as 'a system of patterned meanings or the collective mental programming of a social group' (Hofstede, 1980). They make a distinction between 'core' and 'periphery' values, arguing that particular value dimensions are not held equally strongly in all societies at all times. There is a hierarchy of values in each society. The periphery values are most subject to modification in the short term but the core values are more resistant to change. Which values are at the core and which are at the periphery are likely to vary from society to society. In other words different things are important to different people, but there is a pattern to the ways in which values are important according to the national cultures from which the people come.

With notable exceptions, it may be argued that educational institutions are organizations that operate in an environment of scarcity, leading to difficulties in resources availability. These may be manifested in terms of shortages of economic or human resources; for example, budgetary expenditure may not match school fee income, or recruitment and retention of teaching staff appropriate to the needs of the school may be difficult. Economic and human resource scarcity, which are inputs into the organization, will have a profound influence on its structure and function.

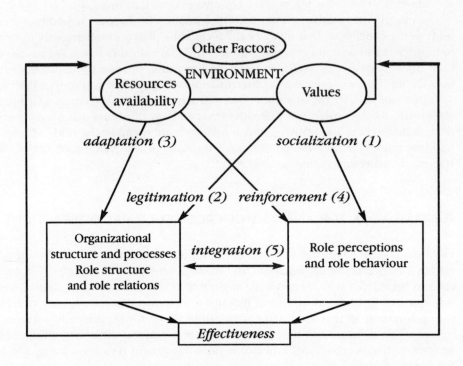

Figure 14.2 A theoretical framework for cross-cultural analysis
(Lachman et al., 1994)

The framework shown in Figure 14.2 identifies five linking processes at work in the interactions between values and environmental factors such as resources availability.

1. *Socialization* describes how the behaviour of individuals in the organization is determined by the values they bring with them; the values of individuals are not necessarily congruent with those of the organization. Teachers and students bring their own attitudes about the teaching–learning process into school; these vary between national or societal cultures. These will comprise beliefs about what school is for (educational ideology), attitudes about the way in which adults and children address each other, how questions may be asked, and in what contexts questioning of teachers by students is permissible. Body language, eye contact between individuals and dress codes are determined by, and convey the values of individuals. As has been observed above, differences in cultural values can be translated into discipline problems at school, for example when the

expectations of behaviour by teachers and students are incongruent.
2. *Legitimation* occurs when cultural values permeate organizations by defining organizational processes, role structures and role relations as culturally acceptable, relatively neutral, or in conflict with culturally prescribed norms and, therefore, unacceptable. Organizational metaphors, such as the 'family' and the 'guided missile', (Hampden-Turner and Trompenaars, 1997) or the 'club' and the 'network' (Handy, 1993) not only reflect the power relations in organizations but are also an outcome of cultural values.
3. *Adaptation* describes the process by which economic or other contextual constraints are absorbed into organizational structures and practices. Taking the example of an international school in a developing country, the existence of differential pay scales for expatriate and locally recruited workers is a commonly observed phenomenon. One salary scale is adapted to the local economy while the other is adapted to competition in the world employment market. There is a lack of congruence between the host country economy and other national economies from which the expatriates are recruited at a higher rate of remuneration.
4. *Reinforcement* describes how the scarcity of economic resources influences individuals' adherence to certain values, by reinforcing specific choices within the legitimized range. Again taking the example of an international school in a developing country, economic inequality as a result of adaptation, as described above, is translated into social inequality. This may then create a climate in which attitudes about the inferiority of local educational culture are reinforced, leading to divisions among the work-force. Morgan (1997) discusses how the organization may be seen as a political system; sections of staff become politicized as a result of reinforcement. Radical sections of the staff want change, whereas conservative sections argue that managers must be allowed to manage, a defence of the status quo. A dilemma arises when management attempts to maintain a unitarist outlook in the face of rising pluralism.
5. *Integration* describes the interface between role expectations and behaviour, on the one hand, and prescribed structures and processes on the other. To what extent are values and expectations of an organization congruent with and reflected by the values and expectations of the participants?

There are also *feedback loops* so that, while culture influences the organization, the organization itself can have an influence on the surrounding environment, its culture and available resources. An international school can be seen as a centre of excellence within a country, encouraging other institutions to change and develop by fostering good relations with the host community, or it can be the focus of local resentment if it is seen as an élitist institution identified exclusively with serving expatriates and rich host country nationals.

Although it remains speculative at the time of writing, it is proposed that this framework will be applied to the analysis of qualitative data about cross-cultural interactions in international schools, framed in terms of the dimensions constructed by Hofstede, and Trompenaars and Hampden-Turner.

Summary

Culture is one of the metaphors that can be applied to the description and analysis of organizations. In the context of the organization as an open system culture can be viewed either as an input (independent variable), output (dependent variable or product) or a process. Many definitions of culture can therefore be proposed, including 'software for the mind', 'shared meaning', 'artefacts and products, norms and values, basic assumptions' and 'the process for reconciling dilemmas'. Culture can be described as an input variable in four dimensions (Hofstede, 1991), and as seven valuing processes (Trompenaars and Hampden-Turner, 1997). The interactions between two key factors, values and resource availability, can be applied to the analysis of organizational culture (Lachman *et al.*, 1994) and application within the context of international schools is planned in the near future.

References

Bate, P (1994) *Strategies for Cultural Change*, Butterworth–Heinemann, Oxford

Bentley, D and Watts, M (1989) *Learning and Teaching in School Science: Practical Alternatives*, Open University Press, Buckingham

Cox, T (1993) *Cultural Diversity in Organizations*, Berrett-Koehler, San Francisco

Hampden-Turner, C and Trompenaars, F (1993) *The Seven Cultures of Capitalism*, Piatkus, London

Hampden-Turner, C and Trompenaars, F (1997) 'Response to Geert Hofstede', *International Journal of Intercultural Relations*, **21**, 1, pp 149–59

Handy, C (1993) *Understanding Organizations*, Penguin, London

Harris A, Bennett, N and Preedy, M (1997) *Organisational Effectiveness and Improvement in Education*, Open University Press, Buckingham

Harrison, M (1994) *Diagnosing Organizations: Methods, Models and Processes*, 2nd ed, Sage, London

Hawley, D (1995) 'How long do international school heads survive? A research analysis (part II)', *International Schools Journal*, **14**, 2, pp 23–36

Hickson, D (1996) 'The ASQ years then and now through the eyes of a Euro-Brit', *Administrative Science Quarterly*, **41**, 2, pp 217–28

Hofstede, G (1980) *Culture's Consequences: International Differences in Work-related Values*, Sage, Beverly Hills, CA

Hofstede, G (1986) 'Cultural differences in learning and teaching', *International Journal of Intercultural Relations*, **10**, 3, pp 301–20

Hofstede, G (1991) *Cultures and Organizations*, HarperCollins, London.

Lachman, R, Nedd, A and Hinings, B (1994) 'Analysing cross-national management and organisations: a theoretical framework', *Management Science*, **40**, 1, pp 40–55

Morgan, G (1997) *Images of Organization*, Sage, London

Søndergaard, M (1994) 'Research note: Hofstede's consequences – A study of reviews, citations and replications', *Organization Studies*, **15**, 3, pp 447–56

Trompenaars, F and Hampden-Turner, C (1997) *Riding the Waves of Culture: Understanding Cultural Diversity in Business*, 2nd ed, Nicholas Brealey, London

15

INTERNATIONAL SCHOOL ACCREDITATION: WHO NEEDS IT?

Edna Murphy

BACKGROUND

When the first barbarian tribe successfully invaded its neighbour the chances were that an international education of a kind ensued, assuming the lives of the vanquished were spared. When a missionary finding himself on a foreign shore first tried to teach the natives his language and religion he, too, was involving himself in an exercise in international education, assuming his life wasn't lost in the process. International education of one sort or another has been going on for a very long time and has evolved, fortunately, into a rather less risky undertaking. Today the term usually refers to the movement that has gained momentum in the latter half of this century – a movement that saw the creation of hundreds of 'overseas' schools throughout the world and that was fuelled by the same mix of convenience and idealism.

There are as many reasons for offering education in a foreign or international context as there are kinds of international schools. Those working in diplomacy, business, law, medicine, education, the performing arts, religion, health, the environment and similar professional fields are frequently expected to spend time abroad. Some simply prefer to live abroad, or do so for the tax advantages it offers. Some are sent by companies to build dams, tunnels or bridges in countries that lack the technology or trained personnel to do the job themselves. In any event, if there are children in the family sent abroad, they will need to be educated. Schools have, in the past, been set up abroad by – to name but a few – the French, Swedish and Japanese governments, the US Department of Defense, oil companies, the Michelin Tyre Company, and by private groups with an interest, such as parents, teachers and entrepreneurs. Schools that were set up for one national group, such as the Americans or the British, have tended eventually to take in children of other nationalities who wanted that style of education, or just an education through the medium of English. These schools now call themselves (and are called by others) 'international schools'. It is not unknown for an international school to be the only school of its kind in a foreign city or country, with no opportunity to exchange ideas and share solutions with colleagues in the same field, and no ready access to books and materials in English – these are just two of the features that contribute to the feeling of isolation prevalent among educators in international schools. It was not long, therefore, before schools in Europe banded together to form a professional organization to arrange events that would bring administrators and teachers together at set times during the year. The organization, the European Council of International Schools (ECIS), was conceived in Beirut in 1962 and born in Geneva in 1965. Five years later – in Lausanne – ECIS put together a framework for school improvement that became today's programme of evaluation and accreditation.

It is a commonplace that schools – and the community from which they draw their students – benefit from some outside evaluation by fellow professionals: every country has its system of inspection. In England and Wales the Office for Standards in Education (OFSTED) is now responsible for this task; in the United States it is shared by six agencies according to geographical region. These organizations draw their strength from the fact that they are dealing with schools whose philosophy and curriculum are thoroughly familiar. The many truly international schools, those that did not fit easily into a national system, whose curriculum might be considerably different from that of the host country and might be delivered in a language other than the local language, felt that, especially in the sensitive area of assessment, they required a different approach. The first ECIS accreditation instrument was very much based on existing American accreditation practice, adapted to take into account the varying and different circumstances of schools abroad. Some American schools abroad were, and still are part of an accreditation programme with the US-based Middle States Association of Colleges and Schools, the Western Association of Schools and Colleges, the Southern Association of Colleges and Schools, and the New England Association of Schools and Colleges, all of which began to accredit overseas schools in the 1970s and 1980s. Now many, mostly US-style international schools have a joint accreditation with ECIS and one of the above-named accrediting programmes. At first the ECIS accreditation procedure was rather informal, leaving much leeway for the professionalism and ingenuity of the visiting team members to find expression but, as the programme grew, procedures were gradually standardized and codified. In The *ECIS Guide* (ECIS, 1997) standards were spelled out in every area of the school's operation, checklists of best practices were drawn up against which the school would have to measure itself and, finally, an assessment component was added.

THE ECIS ACCREDITATION PROGRAMME TODAY

The main aim of the ECIS accreditation programme 'is to provide an opportunity to improve the quality of the education offered at the school through a process of self-examination followed by an objective external appraisal, and to attest to the quality of the evaluated school' (ECIS, 1997). Each school is evaluated against how well it matches up to two basic benchmarks; first, the school's own philosophy and objectives and, second, the ECIS standards for accreditation. These standards were first developed by the ECIS Board's Accreditation Committee and then widely reviewed by colleagues in the international school community. The whole accreditation procedure, including the standards and the literature connected with it, are regularly reviewed by the accreditation committee with input welcomed from the wider community of member schools.

The accreditation process, as refined and improved over the years, is a continuous one and consists of several steps before the cycle is completed and the process starts all over again. These steps are: the Preliminary Visit and Report; the Self-study; the Team Visit and Report; the Decision on Accreditation; the One-year Report (and, sometimes, Visit); the Five-year Visit and Report. The next step is the Preparatory Visit, which is the Preliminary Visit to a school already in accreditation and takes place approximately ten years after the first Preliminary Visit, marking the first step of the second accreditation cycle. These steps are examined in more detail below.

Step 1: The preliminary/preparatory visit and report

The school itself must make the first important decision, that is, to begin the process, and must then communicate this decision to ECIS. A Preliminary Visitor is then sent to the school where he or she spends a couple of days studying and observing every aspect of school life and assessing its readiness to enter the process. This is a very important step, designed to prevent an institution from starting the process before it is ready. The Preliminary Visitor's task is twofold: first, to clarify for the whole school community the evaluation process and its procedures, with emphasis on the Self-study upon which the school will shortly embark, and, second, to produce a Report noting broad areas of strength and weakness. This gives the school a general idea before the Self-study begins of the areas on which it needs to start work. The Preliminary Visitor also works out with the Head of school the timeline for the Self-study and the Team Visit which will follow.

Step 2: The self-study

The Self-study that follows an affirmative decision of the Preliminary/Preparatory Visitor is the most important part of the accreditation process, both in the commitment of time and effort involved and in the benefits to be derived by the school. It requires a school to examine its philosophy and objectives, and its fundamental beliefs about education. The Self-study is organized by a Steering Committee and involves the whole community: the board of directors, administrators, teachers, ancillary staff, students and parents. The school is guided in its work on the Self-study by the *ECIS Guide to School Evaluation and Accreditation*, which is a complete, step-by-step guide to the whole process. The final Self-study will be divided into as many of the following sections as are applicable to the school:

A. Philosophy and Objectives
B. Organization and Administration
C. School Staff
D. Early Childhood Programme
E. Elementary Curriculum Programme
F. Middle School Curriculum Programme
G. Secondary School Curriculum Programme
H. Special Education Services
I. Guidance Services
J. Health Services and Safety
K. Student Services
L. Student Life
M. Library/Media Centre
N. School Facilities
O. Finances and Financial Management
P. Assessment of Student Learning and Achievement

For each section listed above the school committee in charge assembles and analyses appropriate data, views its current practice in the light of its own philosophy and the standards for accreditation, considers a set of accepted effective practices and writes a statement of conclusions. This statement includes a plan for improvement, and most schools start to implement as much of this plan as is both approved and feasible before the Visiting Team arrives. Every staff member should have meaningful assignments, preferably including one related to his or her own area of duties or expertise, and one involving a whole-school operation. Board members, parents, older students and ancillary staff normally serve on committees alongside teachers and administrators, where their input would be appropriate. The Self-study should present an honest, broad view of the school and should not reflect the views of any minority group within the school. When the Self-study is completed a copy is sent to ECIS and to the Team Chair. If it is accepted by ECIS as a properly conducted and complete Self-study the school is then ready for the Visiting Team.

Step 3: The team visit and report

Teams are assembled by ECIS from administrators and teachers in international schools who have been selected for their outstanding professionalism and expertise, and who normally have some experience in the work to be done – either by having participated in one of the frequently offered ECIS workshops for prospective team members and Chairs, or by serving on previous teams, or both. Many have undergone accreditation at their own schools. The Chair will have had much experience as an ordinary team member and usually as a co-chair as well. Teams range in size from seven to over 25 members, depending upon the size of the school and the complexity of its programmes and facilities. The Team visits the school, for at least four working days, to see it in action. Team members visit classrooms, talk to students, parents, members of the staff and board, and examine all aspects of the school in light of the Self-study, the school's own philosophy and objectives and the ECIS standards for accreditation. These standards do not presuppose any specific model of excellence, nor do they seek to impose the methods of one school upon another; they are designed simply to ensure that a school is offering a broad general education of a high quality. It should be mentioned here that, while all teachers are observed once or twice during the Team Visit and many are consulted, no assessment is made of individual teacher performance; nor is critical reference ever made to any teacher in the Report. The Team puts together a detailed report which addresses each of the sections in the Self-study. For each section there is a brief factual description of the part of the school under study, after which the Team summarizes its perceptions of that section. This is followed by a list of commendations and recommendations. The Report also contains the Team's judgement as to whether the school met, did not meet or exceeded the ECIS standards for each section. The Visiting Team then considers the complete Report and reaches a consensus on its recommendation as to whether or not accreditation should be awarded. The Report, and the Team's recommendation with respect to accreditation, are sent directly to the ECIS Accreditation Committee by the Team Chair, and a copy of the Report, if accepted, is sent to the school.

Step 4: Decision on accreditation

The ECIS Accreditation Committee carefully reviews the Visiting Team Report and considers the Team's recommendations concerning accreditation. The Committee then makes its own recommendation, upon which the ECIS Board of Directors acts. The decision may be:

- to award accreditation or re-accreditation
- to award accreditation or re-accreditation with specific qualifications (eg addressing a safety or health issue, or meeting a standard immediately before the award is granted)
- to postpone accreditation or re-accreditation for some specified reason(s)
- not to award accreditation or re-accreditation.

Any adverse accreditation decision may be subject to appeal by the school. Adverse accreditation decisions are defined as either postponement, denial or termination of accreditation or re-accreditation.

Subsequent procedures

The monitoring procedures include a One-year Report and a Five-year Report, as follows.

- The One-year Report, prepared by the school during the year following the award of Accreditation, responds to the recommendations contained in the Visiting Team Report. In each instance the school must indicate if it has completed the recommended course of action, if it is in progress, if it is planned for the future (and if so when), or if it has been rejected. In the last instance the school must give a valid reason why it thinks the recommendation was not well founded. When there are several quite serious recommendations to be responded to, a Visiting Team may recommend that another visit, usually by one person, be made to the school to coincide with the completion of the One-year report.
- The Five-year Report (not a full Self-study) is prepared by the school, again referring back to the recommendations of the Visiting Team, and describing any new features of programme, facilities, and so on, that may have emerged since the last report. At this time a two-person, on-site visit is required. Obviously this is not the thorough review that a full Visiting Team carries out; the five-year visitor works from the previous Visiting Team Report and the school's One-year Report. His or her job is to see how the plans for improvement are progressing. Changes are noted that are sometimes far-reaching: a new head, perhaps, or a new building, or both. Sometimes a new course of study has been introduced, such as the International Baccalaureate. Sometimes it is a combination of such developments. The Five-year Visitors may then take on some of the aspects of a Visiting Team as their Report must address all these factors. Again, recommendations are made at this juncture, and the path to improvement is indicated.

SOME FICTIONAL 'CASE STUDIES'

Perhaps the best way to convey what a school evaluation can do is to posit three fictional schools and to suggest ways in which they might be improved by the accreditation process.

School A

School A is a small school located in an African country which was once part of the British empire. English was then the official language, but since independence it has been heard less and less frequently. The once-thriving English school, established primarily for expatriates, was threatened with closure when those who had remained after independence left during a recession. The decision was consequently made that, in order to continue in operation, it must take in local children. To do this it felt it had to reduce the tuition fees, since local families were probably less able to afford the sum that companies were willing to pay: the Board did not object to this because they were fee-paying parents themselves. The staff was also much reduced, although a few of the 'old guard' remained for continuity. New teachers were found largely among 'trailing spouses': women whose husbands were working temporarily in the area. The school song and shield seemed a bit out of place, and the curriculum and materials varied from classroom to classroom, depending on what had been left behind by the previous occupant of the room. Another change from the past was that many of the local children now started at the school with little or no English. The last long-serving head had gone back to England ten years earlier when the majority of his countrymen left, and since that time there had been a succession of heads, none of whom stayed long enough to effect any changes. The one-storey buildings on the modest campus had begun to fall apart. The finances were shaky, but a new head had just arrived and everyone was hoping for the best.

School A is typical of many small schools that started out with an educational offering geared to an expatriate clientele, but whose community and circumstances so changed that a new programme became necessary. The Preliminary Visitor's report would be the first feedback that School A would have as to its status as an educational institution. One of the main recommendations in this report would surely be that the school rethink its philosophy to suit its new circumstances, and that its staff agree upon and commit to writing a school curriculum and an English as a Second Language (ESL) programme suitable to the needs of the children it now enrols. The school would probably be asked to reconsider its hiring practices, which had resulted in a high turnover when the teachers' spouses were transferred, as often as not in the middle of the school year. The school would then have to embark upon its Self-study which, with a bit of leadership and luck, would bring together the old and the new guard on the staff and draw in the teachers of the host country language and other specialist teachers who, up to this point, had been rather isolated. Together they would work through the necessary steps outlined in the *ECIS Guide to School Evaluation and Accreditation* for the completion of the Self-study. They would have to reach an agreement about a philosophy for the school, about whether its admissions criteria were clear, and even, perhaps, whether the school's logo and song were still appropriate. Not all problems would be solved during the course of the Self-study, but the process would tend to weld the disparate elements of the community into a functional whole, and to provide the school with a framework that would make possible its continuous, not just immediate improvement. Next the Visiting Team would, in its comprehensive report, provide a blueprint – an action plan – for the school for the foreseeable future. It might find much to commend, beginning with the school's new philosophy; it would probably find that all the ingredients or potential for an excellent school were there, just needing to be pulled together. One of its recommendations might be that the Board re-examine its tuition fee level, with an eye to determining whether or not it supported the kind of education they would like their children to have. It might also recommend that the school explore whether the hiring of spouses, who might not match the vacancies exactly and who, in any case, might have to leave in mid-year, is a false economy. If School A has gone through the process carefully and in a professional manner it should be vastly improved over the course of the first accreditation and will have the machinery in place for continual self-improvement in the future.

School B

School B is a different story. Established just after World War II in one of the most popular of European capitals, this large nursery through grade 12 (ages 3–18) school is sited in an elegant manor house with numerous outbuildings on a large and leafy campus on the edge of town. Enrolment has never been a problem. Originally the school had been founded by and for the American community in this city but, with the American presence declining steadily for many years, the school has long since turned to the 'international' community to take up the slack. It has changed its name, its philosophy and its curriculum to match the new student body, and has established a good reputation for academic standards both locally and throughout Europe. The Board of Directors, composed largely of multinational corporation executives guided by the commercial imperative, wanted the school to increase its 'market share'. They were concerned about competition from two new international schools that had recently opened in the area, and decided to embark on an expensive and extensive building and refurbishment programme to attract a higher percentage of prospective students than previously. Not wishing to raise the level of tuition fees sufficiently to cover the full cost of these works, the Board increased class sizes and executed a restructuring operation that meant the reduction of staff 'extras' such as a counsellor, two school secretaries, the school nurse, the psychologist and some of the foreign language and special needs teachers. The head was against most of these measures, but he was a voice in the wilderness: there was almost no interaction between the Board and the divisional principals. By himself he was not able to stop the measures being implemented.

School B, let us assume, has been in accreditation for two decades, and it is now time for a Preparatory Visit. The Preparatory Visitor will have picked up on the lack of support staff, and perhaps some disaffection among the staff about class size. Teacher complaints would have been obvious to the administration but, to this customer-orientated Board, what really counts is parent opinion. Parents would surely have complained in the Community Survey, which constitutes Part One of the Self-study, about increased class sizes and the time it takes for the telephone to be answered at the school office. Those parents whose children were directly affected by the change would be particularly concerned. In its Self-study the professional staff would have identified as a problem the difficulty of carrying on the individualized or differentiated programme – which had been in effect for the past ten years – with so many children in the class. References to differentiation and specialist help, they thought, would also have to be omitted from the school's literature. The Self-study committee on Philosophy and Objectives would have noted that the school's literature needed to be changed to reflect the school's changed circumstances: for example, as they no longer had Special Needs support, they should not take in children who needed such support, and as the upper limit of class sizes had been raised to 26 they could no longer claim to give pupils individual attention. In the Sections on Guidance and Special Needs they would have to give themselves a rather poor grade. Since members of the Board would have been on several of the committees responsible for writing the Self-study they would have had the opportunity to hear from the professional staff the educational argument for keeping those 'extras'. This might have brought them to the conclusion that they had made the wrong decision. Coupled with the fact that they had underestimated the negative impact of their decisions on parents, this process might have enabled them to see things from a different perspective. If not, at least it had the virtue of clarifying a confused situation.

The Visiting Team would find a great deal in this school to commend. It had certainly moved with the times and had been a leader in the field of international education. Several of its teachers had reputations for research and curriculum development that went well beyond the confines of the school campus. The school had a well-endowed library and the laboratories were first-rate. There was an excellent and long-serving staff and a supportive and active parent and alumni group. All this and more would be commended by the Visiting Team. They would also want to establish, however, whether or not what the Board had set as policy was reflected in both the school's literature and in the practice found in the classrooms. They would make a judgement as to whether or not the children in the school were being fully served by the new policies. If they felt they were not they would say so, and it would then be incumbent on the school to respond to that recommendation. Through the Self-study, and later through the Visiting Team's Report, the Board might come to realize that what had seemed to them to be policies of a purely financial nature had serious educational consequences, and respond to balance the situation.

School C

School C was founded after World War I by a visionary who believed that world peace could only be achieved by education. Before the school opened he had drawn up the philosophy and objectives of the school, set its curriculum (which included peace studies and several foreign languages), and opened it to children from all over the world. Students were selected by an entrance examination, and those who proved to be unable to keep up were asked to leave. Because the school had sprung 'fully armed' from the head of the founder and had not, like Topsy and like most international schools, 'just growed', and because the school had a certain degree of renown and was financially secure, successive heads over the years felt little need to make any significant changes, resting squarely and comfortably on their laurels. The staff consisted of a very high proportion of long-serving teachers: pay and work conditions were very good so they were loath to leave. Teachers were given the curriculum to teach and did not complain that there was not much money spent on staff development. Textbooks were geared to the examinations that the students were expected to take, the pass rate for which was exceptionally high. There was one parent–teacher conference per year and one report sent home annually at the end of the school year. There was no other involvement of parents in the school, which always had a waiting list.

This school did not feel the need for an outside evaluation; its waiting list spoke for itself. It was financially sound and had a good teaching staff. What changed the minds of the trustees and the administration was the fact that several international schools in the area had already successfully achieved accreditation; the trustees consequently thought it best, for marketing reasons, to do the same. The school was surprised to see the findings of the Community Surveys. They learned that parents had serious complaints about the school. They appreciated the high standards and rigorous curriculum, including an emphasis on foreign languages, but deeply regretted that they were not well informed about their children's progress. The parent–teacher evening was poorly organized: queues were very long and parents were able to see only two teachers in the course of the evening. Furthermore the conference took place in the hall where everyone could overhear the conversations. Nor were teachers very well equipped to answer specific questions, having no material on hand to serve as evidence of a student's progress or lack of it. Parents whose English was not very good (and there were many in the context of this international school) were left in the dark about school events because they were unable to read school notices. In the sections of the Self-study dealing with curriculum teachers noted that the school had not kept up with the times. Textbooks contained out-of-date maps, incorrect political and scientific information, and were suffering from severe 'wear and tear'; there was no information technology to speak of, beyond the odd computer brought in by a teacher. The staff did not rate itself very highly in any of these curriculum-related areas.

When the Visiting Team arrived they found that much change had already taken place since the Preliminary Visit and the Self-study. The school was commended for encouraging parents to form a Parents' Association, one of whose jobs would be to welcome newcomers to the school and to make sure that they received notices in a language they could read. They had reviewed and reorganized the parent conference arrangements, and were planning to have them twice a year. They had also increased the budget allocation for textbooks and for staff development to keep teachers up to date in the field of international education. The school was also commended for the high achievement of its students in the senior examinations, and for its successful foreign language programme. The Visiting Team noted, however, that the school was deficient in its support for students with special needs, and offered inadequate instruction in information technology. It was further recommended that the school take a look at its financial management: the school had a large reserve and no real financial problems, but there was evidence of carelessness in the accounts department: among other things, the accounts had not been externally audited in two years. Furthermore several safety standards had not been met. The host country fire inspector had recommended in his last report that several urgent actions be taken, including the improvement of the fire alarm system: it was only when a member of the Visiting Team asked for a full-scale fire drill that the head realized that the work had not been carried out. The Report came as something of a surprise to this school which, given its reputation, its student achievements and its dedication to the lofty goals of internationalism, was understandably accustomed to thinking that there was little need for improvement. To their credit, however, the trustees and administration realized that they had become lax over the years and that there was much to be said for a process that encouraged such ongoing self-examination. In their first-year report they were happy to say that they had put everything to rights, and that they were planning to keep active the committees that had been involved in the Self-study to monitor those areas on a continuing basis. The head also commented that they displayed their accreditation plaque with pride.

Summary

There are many benefits to the school from the accreditation process. The overarching good that comes from it is that the school becomes part of a programme of self-examination and improvement that is ongoing and cyclical. Once begun, the process that ends in accreditation or re-accreditation becomes part of the ethos and organization of the school, and exists so long as the school wishes it to, or unless it falls seriously below the required standard. The process itself is, in each phase, designed to get a school to a certain standard and to keep it there. First there is the external and objective evaluation as to whether or not the school is accreditation worthy. Then, if it is judged to be so, the school embarks on a Self-study, which is probably the single most important part of the process, as it forces the school to examine all aspects of school life against its own philosophy and objectives as well as against the ECIS standards. This study has the added benefit of bringing all constituencies of the school together, many for the first time, with cross-fertilization and better communication the outcome. If there is a strong Steering Committee, and the jobs are conscientiously done, there is nothing that comes close to the Self-study for welding the disparate elements of the school into a team. For each teacher, furthermore, the Self-study offers the opportunity of seeing the school from different perspectives, at least one of them being school-wide; an opportunity not normally available to teachers in the course of their work.

The Team Visit and Report are bound to improve morale, as the Team's commendations give the *imprimatur* to much of what the staff is doing. The Team's Report, irrespective of the accreditation decision is, effectively, a blueprint – an action plan – for the school in the short as well as the long term. Many schools decide that the structure mounted to produce the Self-study is worth keeping on a permanent basis. The 'identity confusion' seen in many schools in transition is given a name and a focus. The necessity to write one-year and five-year reports keeps the momentum going. New administrators and teachers at schools in accreditation have an analysis and action plan to guide them through their first years at the school. Ultimately, if the outcome is the awarding of accredited status, the morale of the staff is given a well-deserved boost, and momentum for school reform is pretty well ensured. It is a source of satisfaction to schools to know that they have undergone a rigorous process of evaluation by experienced colleagues and have been found worthy of accreditation. This places the school alongside over 120 international schools world-wide. In addition, more and more peripatetic parents are becoming familiar with the process of accreditation and are beginning to feel that placing their children in an unexamined school is a risk they do not wish to take.

In conclusion I would like to remind readers of Immanuel Kant's observation that 'Out of the crooked timbers of humanity no straight thing was ever built'. Schools are human institutions and, as such, will always remain imperfect things in need of improvement. Where human beings are concerned, there is always a need to fight the forces of inertia. Who needs accreditation? Every school does.

REFERENCES

European Council of International Schools (1997) *ECIS Guide to School Evaluation and Accreditation*, 6th ed, ECIS, Petersfield

Part 4

INTERNATIONAL EDUCATION FOR ALL

16

INTERNATIONAL EDUCATION: A QUESTION OF ACCESS

David Wilkinson

INTERNATIONAL SCHOOLS AND INTERNATIONAL EDUCATION

The urge to include a world-wide view in the education of the young is not new. In 1580 Montaigne wrote: 'This great world... is the mirror into which we must look if we are to behold ourselves from the proper standpoint.' In a growing number of schools around the world, both within and outside state systems of education, children from many different cultures are being educated together in the same classrooms. Among these many schools are those which consciously call themselves 'international'. Such schools have increased dramatically in number and diversity in the past 40 years. They now form a recognizable, if loose network, served in the main by the International Baccalaureate Organization (IBO) whose Diploma, Middle Years and Primary Years Programmes often form the basis of their educational programmes. Although some such schools provide scholarships and bursaries for students in financial need, the overwhelming majority charge fees. As such they have often been described as élitist and hence of little relevance in the widest global terms.

This rapid growth in the number of schools that call themselves 'international' has given rise to numerous attempts to provide a working definition of international education. A recent review by Hayden and Thompson (1995) shows how foresighted Montaigne seems to have been. Hayden and Thompson describe how recent definitions have moved towards the experience of the students themselves. The key elements are exposure in the school to a curriculum that is consciously international in content and approach (to which the teaching staff are committed) by students with a wide diversity of cultural backgrounds. Hayden and Thompson's article raises a further issue that seems not to be included by others who have sought to provide a definition. If international education is to lead to a set of beliefs and attitudes towards other cultures, it cannot be fully realized unless students are educated by teachers who represent a wide variety of cultures and provide the means by which students can cross such frontiers. In 1987 Alec Peterson wrote, in the context of the development of the International Baccalaureate (IB): 'we sought not to produce a generation of rootless "world citizens", but one of Americans, English, French, Germans, Mexicans, Russians and others who understood each other better, sought to co-operate with each other and had friends across frontiers'. No matter how well intentioned, a monocultural staff cannot effectively provide the mirror of this great world.

There is growing acceptance of international education as a sound and important alternative to a national education by colleges and universities around the world. The recognition of the Diploma in universities in over 100 countries, supported by a growing number of comparative studies, indicates that an international curriculum can provide at least as solid a base for university study as does any national curriculum. There appears to be some evidence to suggest that children who have lived in several countries other than their own and who, formally and informally, have received an education that crosses cultural boundaries, are higher achievers and are better adjusted than their socio-economic compatriots who have remained in the home country. Willis *et al.* (1994) suggest that such children, to whom they refer as transculturals or transnationals, 'represent a privileged élite for whom international education plays a pivotal role in personal development'. They go further and propose that such people will be at the forefront of advances in the next century. A key component of the experience of such individuals has been the adoption of 'a multiple cultural identity'. In its broadest sense their experience of international education takes them beyond the limitations of their own cultural identity. The benefit of this is not only of practical value in a world of increasing internationalization; it is evidently of positive value to the growth of the individual. It may be useful therefore to examine how different types of international schools have focused on the experience of their students as the key to providing an international education. In doing so it will be possible to identify the key features of the experience, not only to describe but also to enquire as to its potential value. What factors appear to limit this? Can any educational experience be described as international if it is limited in access by financial or cultural constraints? In what follows the author's recent experience has been drawn on in exploring such issues.

THE NATIONAL CONTEXT FOR INTERNATIONAL EDUCATION

Machabeng High School in Lesotho was founded in Maseru, the capital of Lesotho, by a group of parents in 1976. The aim was to enable their own children to continue the non-racial education they had experienced while at the Maseru English Medium Primary School. As this was essentially a British-style primary school overseas it was natural that Machabeng should open with a British curriculum, a British headmaster, and a staff of whom the majority were British educated. From its very beginning, however, the student population, although in the main comprised of Lesotho nationals, had a strong international mix. By 1985 the school had over 200 students in grades 7–10, a teaching staff of 17 and over 40 nationalities represented across all staff and students. The curriculum remained strongly British in character and all students in grade 10 entered for the Cambridge Board GCE O-Level examination. In the nine years since its founding, however, significant changes had taken place in the national mixture of its student body. Lesotho had become a major recipient of aid from the European Community; the United States also had a large aid programme in the country. Pressure from parents had mounted on the school to provide a curriculum more appropriate to the needs of all students and at the same time to extend the education provided to grades 11 and 12. The school had, from its foundation, regarded itself as international: the Sesotho word *Machabeng* means 'international'. It is interesting, therefore, to examine the manner in which this international school reflected on its own curriculum, found that this did not guarantee its students the experience of international education, and set about ensuring that it would make this available.

In early 1985 members of the school's governing board met with the then Minister of Education, Dr Ebenezer Malie, and discussed the school's unique role within the country. Dr Malie had agreed that the school must provide an education appropriate to the needs not only of Lesotho nationals enrolled within it, but also to the children of the wide range of other nationals working in and for the country. He set out to investigate the International Baccalaureate programme and, in doing so, sent his Permanent Secretary to visit the United World College of the Atlantic. This visit resulted in the decision to appoint a head of school who had IB experience and who would take responsibility for implementing the IB programme. The first response to the desire for international education on the part of parents was the introduction of a curriculum that was recognized as international in character. At this stage the prime movers for further change became the headmaster and teaching staff, working together with parent representatives. Introduction of the IB programme had a significant impact on the style of teaching and on the scope of the curriculum in the junior years of the school. In the absence of a ready-made curriculum for the middle years much was done to internationalize the extra-curricular provision while retaining the O-level programme. The change with the most significant impact on the school, however, was the decision to diversify nationalities of the teaching staff through recruitment of teachers to replace those leaving. This met with some resistance from a number of parents, representing several nationalities, who felt that the British O-level programme was best taught by British or British-trained teachers. Opposing this were those who argued that only through teachers representing their own cultures was it possible to provide an international ethos in the school. Indeed, several African members of staff doubted that even this would enable the school to escape from the domination of its first world, predominantly western view. In practice, however, all agreed that the only hope of making the day-to-day experience one that would help students cut through the narrow assumptions of any national educational system was through a staff that not only represented different nationalities but was also trained in different educational systems.

Hand in hand with these changes went the search for scholarship funding to open up the school to a much broader cross-section of Basotho society. There was strong support for this move from all constituents of the school community. Underlying their support was the feeling that if the education provided was to be relevant to a wider range of students, that wider range must relate not only to nationality but also to social background. Moreover, as many of the expatriates whose children were students at the school were in Lesotho in order to work for the benefit of the nation as a whole, it seemed ironic that the school attended by their children should benefit only the wealthiest sector of the local society. In a limited way, the aim of diversifying the student body was achieved with the support of the European Community Commission, which donated a line of scholarship accounting for one-third of the entry to the IB programme each year. These scholarships were awarded on merit to Basotho students who had completed the equivalent of Ordinary Level in their national system. Machabeng was therefore a school that set itself the goal of becoming more relevant to the needs of a wider spectrum of its students. Without consciously attempting to do so it changed its interpretation of itself as an international school. In 1985 it had a student body representing over 40 nationalities. By 1990 it had, in addition, an international curriculum and a teaching staff actively committed to catering for the diverse needs of as many as possible of its nationalities. Without ever making this an explicit issue, its community had decided that attending an international school did not guarantee an international education.

THE UNITED WORLD COLLEGE CONTEXT

The founding of a new United World College (UWC) raised quite different issues. Here was the opportunity to build a school around a definition of international education. The opening of Li Po Chun College in Hong Kong and of the Mahindra College in India are clear examples of how the founders interpreted 'international' in an educational context. At the outset, the opening of the United World Colleges (which, in those days, catered for boys only) to those from all social classes was regarded as a top priority. Lord Hankey wrote of the scholarship scheme for Atlantic College: 'This is not only an international affair, but it is intended to operate right across social distinctions of class, income and origin' (Hankey, 1966). The UWC movement itself imposes certain requirements. The proportion of the student body representing the host country should ideally be in the order of 25 per cent. The remaining 75 per cent of students should be chosen in such a way as to represent each continent, each major religion, and to have as wide as possible a spread of ethnic groups, languages and cultures in the college. It is evident that, in this ideal situation, the wide mix of nationalities is seen as a vital component of an international education. The curriculum followed by the UWCs is not prescribed, although each of the ten existing colleges bases its educational programme on the International Baccalaureate. The enormous importance attached to the cross-cultural component of an international education can be seen in the co-curricular programmes. Events such as international evenings, in which students representing a particular area of the world put on for the others a display of the cuisine, music and dance of their region, are of major importance. Such events, together with programmes addressing world affairs and global concerns, are conscious efforts to take the students' experience across national boundaries.

At both the Li Po Chun and Mahindra Colleges the need for a strong international mix in the founding teaching staff was a major consideration. Staff were selected to ensure that about half would represent the host country, while the other half would be from as wide a spread of nationalities as possible. In this way the founding staff of the Mahindra College, for example, only 15 in total, represent six nationalities from four continents. A further element is present in these two UWCs. The international nature of an education does not have meaning unless it has a clear, real relationship to what is national. The structure of the IB recognizes this through its inclusion of students' mother tongues as one of the six components of the curriculum. Moreover, the service component of IB's Creativity, Action, Service (CAS) programme offers and encourages a link with the wider community in which any IB school is located. The recruitment of a very significant proportion of citizens of the host country, at both Li Po Chun and Mahindra Colleges, recognizes the importance of the rooting of each college in the host country. This is not a token gesture; it is fundamental to the concept of crossing frontiers and is the only answer to those who see international education as equivalent to the education of a multinational and first world-dominated élite. International education must break away from the Anglo-Saxon mould currently imposed on it if it is to become truly global, rather than the prerogative of the wealthy from the wealthy nations. At the IB Heads' Conference in Jakarta in March 1996, a paper was delivered by Mrs A S Desai, the Chairperson of the University Grants Commission in India. Speaking on the topic 'Little room for sympathy, plenty for sensitivity', she noted that: 'Inequalities between countries are the basic cause of diversity; they also perpetuate an exploitative environment' (Desai, 1996). She went on to observe that students at IB schools very largely represent a multinational élite and that 'they need to develop a knowledge base which gives them the potential to influence decisions to create a more equitable world'.

This call acknowledges the potential value of an international education. It supports the view that those educated in this manner will, as adults, have a major influence in the next century. It goes further, however, by saying that those educated in this manner will be leaders in the next century. Desai also laid out what those individuals ought to do when in a position of leadership. Such an approach had from the very beginning been fundamental to the United World College movement. Kurt Hahn, whose thinking has inspired the UWCs from their earliest days, conceived the idea of an education that could transform 'the love of liberty, and the love of country' into a common love of all mankind. Built into the very existence of the colleges is the strong belief that one cannot separate international education from a set of values. Foremost among these is that those thus educated must be inculcated with the strength of purpose to act on the basis of their privileged experience. The crossing of frontiers is not sufficient. Having crossed the frontier, the manner in which one acts is crucial.

WIDENING THE CONTEXT

If such a philosophy is accepted then the definition of international education should be widened further. Not only is this an education that exposes students from a wide variety of cultural backgrounds to a curriculum that is consciously international in content and approach, delivered by a committed and multicultural staff; it must be based on a clear set of values. Comfortable acceptance of the global status quo is not among these values. International education must be a force for change. A school that purports to provide an international education must address the issues that divide deeply the rich and poor of our world. It is not sufficient to provide programmes of global issues, or for privileged students to commit themselves to service. Such dimensions of a student's education are important in themselves, yet by themselves they do not change attitudes. How then may the international school network go beyond its present situation and become not only a source of future leaders, but also of leaders committed to equity and justice for all of the world's citizens? At the root of the issue, perhaps, is the question of access to international education. In the present situation, who delivers this type of education and to whom is it delivered? The international schools are overwhelmingly English medium, staffed largely by native English speakers and attended mostly by the children of members of a narrow social band. Do these three factors inhibit the aim of multiculturalism? Are they interrelated? To what extent are international schools actually taking steps to widen the social base of their student body and the cultural base of their teaching staff? Do they believe that they should?

Writing in the sixteenth century the Czech philosopher Comenius said: 'let all people in all lands learn all things'. This is surely the clarion call of international education. Yet our present network of international schools merely scratches the surface. There are, of course, major constraints associated with extending the reaches of international education, at the forefront of which is the high cost per student of this form of education. There are many factors that contribute to this high cost. Yet, if international education is to have a significant impact on the world, it must reach out beyond its present narrow confines. One particular problem is that the cost, although high, is not unrealistic in the countries of the developed world, yet is out of reach of all but a tiny minority in the remainder of the world. In countries of the developing world, the cost of an examination entry for the International Baccalaureate often exceeds the cost of a year's education at even privileged schools within the country. The cost of employing teachers from the developed world further ensures that the cost per student is excessive. These factors place enormous obstacles in the way of a school, however anxious it may be to open access to a wider social cross-section of the society it serves. Yet, if international education is to have significant relevance, can the schools afford not to become more accessible? Moreover, access to the schools means access to the IB programme. Hence the claims of the IB to relevance are linked strongly to the participating schools' beliefs in accessibility.

The issue of accessibility has, since the very beginning, been at the core of the United World College movement. The very existence of the colleges depends on the maintenance of scholarship fund-raising programmes to ensure that entry is based on merit alone, rather than on the financial circumstances of the student's family. This principle has proved to be very far sighted. Built into it was the tacit belief that an educational experience cannot be international unless it is shared across cultures and across the social spectrum of each culture represented in a college. This is at the heart of the issue. The internationally mobile families, whose children form the core of many international schools and who make up the majority of IB examination entries, increasingly share a set of values and attitudes quite different from those of their own or their host countries. In themselves these values, including openness, self-sufficiency and tolerance of difference, are important. They are, however, only one subset of the values of a wider and much less privileged world. They can only be honed and shared through wider contact, through which they will form the mature beliefs of a new generation that is committed to changing the world, and changing it for the better.

A greater commitment to scholarship fund-raising within the network of schools providing international education would ensure wider accessibility. Even so, in practical terms this would have little global impact. The most hopeful practical approach would be to turn to the role of the teacher: as an agent for the promotion of international understanding, the teacher is crucial. As role models and representatives of their own cultures, teachers may well be more influential than a student's peers, certainly in the lower age ranges. Already organizations like the European Council of International Schools (ECIS) are making it possible for teachers to map out for themselves a career as international educators. Certain university education departments have established centres dedicated to the study of international education and provide courses for teachers wishing to develop a deeper professional understanding. The concept of a recognizable 'international teacher' is beginning to take shape, imbued with the values inherent in this form of education. These are important contributions. More than these, however, would be a concerted effort to formalize and, through this, to increase greatly teacher exchange schemes between national and international schools. The aim of such schemes would be to build a greater body of professional, international educators who can move freely between their own national systems and the network of international schools. Such teachers, if representative of the widest possible spectrum of nationalities, could profoundly change the nature of international education. Teacher exchange schemes already exist within the international school network. They are, however, small scale and notoriously difficult to implement. Differences in pay scales and terms and conditions between countries and between schools place severe obstacles in their path. Add to this the problems of moving teachers with families, and the difficulties seem almost insurmountable. A closer link between the international school network and national authorities may provide the best pathway towards success in this respect. There is already considerable interest in international education on the part of several national educational authorities. Such interest could be formalized and developed to provide more opportunity for teacher exchange. The recognition of the value of international experience for teachers in schools of national systems will provide a driving force.

As it comes of age international education has taken on a recognizable quality. It has proved that it can provide a highly appropriate foundation for students whose working lives will be in the world of the twenty-first century. The small band of educators in the International Schools Association (ISA) and in the United World Colleges could hardly have dreamed of the outcome of their pioneering work less than 40 years ago. The very success of international education, however, has brought with it new responsibilities. It has been carried forward very much as the privilege of the rich – it should not remain so. The task ahead is to broaden its social and cultural base by making this form of education more widely available to students and to teachers throughout the world. At its best education has always been about change. It has been driven forward by those who had a vision of a better world. This is not a time for those in international education to sit back and feel well satisfied. It is a time to reach out and become more relevant to all the citizens of the global village we inhabit. Peterson put it very succinctly in closing his book, *Schools Across Frontiers* (1987): 'Unless the next generation of the young are brought up in such a way as to stimulate, liberate and educate their natural propensity to make friends across frontiers'... we the educators are failing in our responsibility to our children.'

REFERENCES

De Montaigne, M (1958) *Essays* (trans J M Cohen), Penguin, Harmondsworth

Desai, A S (1996) 'Little room for sympathy, plenty for sensitivity', paper delivered at the Conference for Heads of IB Schools, Jakarta, March, and reproduced in part in *IB World*, 12, pp 19–22

Hankey, R, Lord (1966) letter quoted in A D C Peterson (1987) *Schools Across Frontiers*, Open Court, La Salle, Illinois

Hayden, M C and Thompson, J J (1995) 'International education: the crossing of frontiers', *International Schools Journal*, **15**, 1, pp 13–20

Peterson, A D C (1987) *Schools Across Frontiers*, Open Court, La Salle, Illinois

Willis, D B, Enloe, W and Minoura, Y (1994) 'Transculturals, transnationals: the new diaspora', *International Schools Journal*, **14**, 1, pp 39–41

17

THE ROLE OF THE INTERNATIONAL BACCALAUREATE IN EDUCATIONAL TRANSFORMATION: CHILE AS A CASE STUDY

Elisabeth Fox

The current trend toward democratic styles of government in Latin America, accompanied by a thrust towards market-oriented economies, has brought about a widespread and overt demand for 'educational transformation'. An interesting example is the case of Chile, where President Aylwin, in 1992 shortly after his election, recognized that to sustain the country's growth would require a massive effort to modernize education nation-wide, particularly in the public sector which had suffered a marked decline in quality in the previous two decades. Accordingly the Chilean government established and institutionalized a national project: *Mejoramiento de Equidad y Calidad de la Educación* MECE (improvement of equality and quality in education) under the authority of the Ministry of Education (MINE-DUC), with substantial initial assistance from the World Bank. The preliminary needs analysis conducted by the MECE leaders was confirmed in 1995 by a national survey that demonstrated the interest of the government in encouraging maximum participation at all levels in the purposes and design of educational reform. In 1996 President Eduardo Frei Ruiz-Tagle reaffirmed the key importance of education as first priority on the occasion of the official opening of the National Congress (Frei, 1996):

> There exists a consensus with respect to the central role that education plays in sustainable development and the political will to recognise it as a national priority, and thus to generate conditions for its effective modernisation... the nation has expressed, in many different ways and circumstances, the conviction that the maintenance of our economic growth, the overcoming of poverty, the amplification and consolidation of our democratic livelihood and the improvement of our quality of life, depend fundamentally on the capabilities of our people. It is therefore incumbent upon the educational system to procure an education of quality for all.

As a first step to addressing the questions engendered by this considerable task, of how to identify and manage the profound changes implied by its extensive aims for reform, the Ministry of Education invited proposals for a number of specific research projects. One of these, awarded to a team of researchers from the Centre for Educational Research and Development (CIDE) in Santiago, centred on a comparative analysis of the educational systems of nine selected countries that had undertaken and enacted educational reforms, with a focus on elements relevant to the Chilean situation. Included in the overall project was a separate study of the International Baccalaureate (IB) which had attracted the interest of the MINEDUC planners because of its reputation as a quality programme reflecting the approaches and practices of several countries, and which might therefore serve as a useful model for the redesign of upper secondary education in Chile.

The development of the IB from its early days in the 1960s has been described in Chapter 5. News of its development arrived in Santiago in 1965, at a propitious moment in the history of Chilean education under the leadership of Eduardo Frei Montalva (the current president's father), when the national curriculum commission was seeking new models and structures that would better serve the needs of the country's children. One of the schools that participated actively in educational reform at the secondary level, in consultation with the National Centre for Training, Experimentation and Pedagogical Research, was Santiago College, a bicultural English Language independent school which, initially together with the Instituto Nacional, a leading state secondary school, began to explore the model of the comprehensive high school, a possibility that was being discussed at the time by a group of Chilean experts working with the World Bank. Santiago College was looking for a curriculum of a high enough standard to warrant recognition by universities overseas, that would also enable an increasing number of internationally mobile students to study together with their Chilean peers instead of in totally separate academic tracks. A teachers' committee representing each subject within the school worked for two years to integrate the ideas and pilot courses being developed by International Schools Examination Syndicate (ISES) (which during this period was legally incorporated in Geneva as the International Baccalaureate Office) with the objectives and requirements of the national reform. As spelled out in 1964 by the Integral Planning Commission for Education in Chile (Ministerio de Educación Pública, 1964):

General education aspires to attain the optimal development of
- reflective thinking, a critical spirit, creative capacity, and the will to act, the discernment of individual and social values and the disposition to participte responsibly in economic and social life,
- he capacity to adapt constructively to the changes that operate in individuals and societies;
- a concept of the world and of life, inspired by the highest values of our culture, which integrate thought and conduct.

These learning outcomes for students were based on the general objectives identified by the planning commission as a follow up to the Conference on Education and Socio-economic Development in Latin America, held in Santiago in 1962. The general objectives guiding the development of the IB curriculum structure reflect a similar philosophy. An essential consideration in designing a curriculum that would move a philosophical position from a statement on paper to concrete action was to ensure that each subject would offer a foundation of substantial knowledge, and would develop the capacity for critical thinking through stimulating questions that would motivate students to apply their knowledge creatively. Another crucial element was to provide a curriculum structure that would enable students to make sensible choices according to their interests and abilities. In 1967 Santiago College presented to the Chilean National Council for Education a proposal that synthesized the requirements of the new national curriculum with the demands of the International Baccalaureate pilot programme. The proposal was approved (Decree No 53) by the Chilean National Council for Education on 25 May 1968 as an experimental plan for secondary education.

In Latin America the two independent bilingual schools that joined the IB pilot project in the 1960s, the British School in Montevideo, Uruguay, and Santiago College in Chile, were precursors of the majority of IB schools in Latin America that have adopted the IB as an educational programme that can integrate two different cultures (Anglo/Hispanic) and curricular approaches. Nevertheless there was minimal growth in the Latin American region until the 1980s brought a period of rapid acceleration; in 1989–90 IB Latin America (IBLA) had the highest growth rate of any region, with participating schools in Argentina, Brazil, Chile, Colombia, Costa Rica, Ecuador, Peru, Mexico and Venezuela. At the end of the 1985–6 school year 27 IBLA schools were enrolled; in 1991 there were 68, an increase of over 150 per cent; in 1997 there were 119 participating schools, including a small but increasing number of national state and private Catholic institutions. Two important decisions undoubtedly contributed to this spurt of interest: the introduction of a second examination session in November (as an alternative to May), a date that respects the school calendars of the southern hemisphere, and the authorization of Spanish as the third 'official' IB language (in addition to English and French) enabling students in Hispanic America to write all examinations in their mother tongue. Another significant contribution is the appeal of the educational mission of the IB as summarized by Director General Roger Peel in his formal visit to Argentina in 1987:

> It is important to us that our students *learn how to learn* rather than that they learn how to memorise. We wish to give them an opportunity to analyse, to interpret, to decide, to draw their own personal conclusions. Thus, a History examination is not reduced to seeing whether the student knows what happened. What matters is the student's *interpretation* (Fox, 1992).

In an address to the IB Council in 1990 (Stoyle, 1990), the IBLA regional director, Peter Stoyle, cited the principal reason of the success of the IB as being that it offers a modern, more ample programme, in contexts where education has lagged behind due to the power of tradition and a way of teaching that is incompatible with the needs of today's world. Latin American educators are facing dilemmas similar to those confronted by the 'architects' of the IB curriculum in the 1960s. One of the reformers, a former Argentine Minister of Education, claims that in this IB plan, 'I have been able to observe the balance between the rigour of scientific learning and the valuing of individual creative effort'. Another, the President of the Organisation of the Catholic Universities of Latin America, sees in the IB 'a discovery of creativity within a secondary education which today lacks study skills and reflects insufficient training in basic intellectual aptitudes' (Fox, 1992).

Responses to a recent survey of IBLA schools show that, while they share the respect of fellow schools in Australia and North America for the rigour of the IB curriculum, the main appeal of the programme is its internationality and capacity to open students' minds in the contemporary world. The philosophical values and motivating influence of the IB on both teachers and students come across as a major benefit for participating schools, which claim that teaching methods and study habits have undergone fundamental changes for the better. The introduction of the IB appears not only to have raised academic standards; schools also perceive that the IB in action fulfils its objective of educating 'the whole person': particular mention was made of the role of Creativity, Action, Service (CAS) and Theory of Knowledge in this regard. In general, students are seen to be acquiring intellectual and social skills with which to face a world of change. The IB seems to be more compatible with Latin American than with North American curricula, although a number of schools have restructured their administrative organization to be able to meet IB standards. Chilean schools have been hampered by the incompatibility of the type of learning, acquisition of knowledge and intellectual approach required by IB examinations with the primarily memorization skills demanded by the tests required for admission to Chilean universities.

With Chile entertaining active trade relations with China and Japan, nearing full membership of NAFTA (North American Free Trade Agreements), and poised to formalize its de facto business partnerships with neighbouring countries by entering the MERCOSUR (South American Common Market), global awareness has become an important issue for Chilean educational reform. During 1996 the MECE authorities invited a group of IB teachers from different schools within the country (14 schools in Chile currently offer the IB) to participate in working parties responsible for the redesign of the National Secondary School Curriculum. Of particular interest to the reformers were the philosophical integration of the IB programme, the concept of a common course in the Theory of Knowledge, the flexibility allowing for varied subject choices by students, and the rigorous standards required. This illustrates the direct interest of the Chilean government in the IB as a relevant source from which to draw ideas which pertain to the globalization of national education.

What, then, does the IB have to offer in the context of educational priorities identified by Latin American educators? IBO Director General Roger Peel has frequently emphasized the mission of the IB to be available to education world-wide as a complement to national systems, not as a competitor. However, part of that mission is the conviction of IBO that its courses should be available to young people from every level of society; the inclusion of state schools is therefore an important priority for IBLA expansion. This position was strongly endorsed by IB school heads at their regional conference in Montevideo in 1982. An important seminar in Cocoyoc, Mexico, resulted in the enrolment of the first IB state school in Latin America, La Escuela Preparatoria Federal Lazaro Cardenas, in Tijuana on the border with California. The IB state schools in southern California have, in fact, played a leadership role on the west coast of the United States in developing IB programmes within the context of serving the needs of (among others) a large Hispanic student population. The growth of the IB in California received strong support from Education Commissioner Bill Honig, and IB North America (IBNA) encouraged joint seminars and activities between Tijuana and the southern California schools. Tijuana is an interesting case of cooperation between two regions, IBLA and IBNA. The second state school to join the IB in Latin America, in 1984, was El Colegio Nacional y Comercial de Vicente Lopez in Buenos Aires, a city that now has 25 IB schools – the largest number of any city in the world (Fox, 1992). In a report to the IBO Governing Council the regional director attributes this to the Argentine context, where the impetus for economic growth coupled with hyperinflation and social problems has led to a search for innovative educational solutions.

In Ecuador a group of IB schools is cooperating on a project they designed, together with the Department of Curriculum of the National Planning Centre, which incorporates the International Baccalaureate into a curriculum reform of the National Science Baccalaureate to rationalize the number of required subjects, based on the criterion that the quality of knowledge is more important than the quantity. The project contemplates a restructuring of the curriculum, and therefore of the administrative organization of the participating schools. An analysis of the existing curriculum identified two major flaws, an inconsistent epistemological foundation and a lack of integration, which have brought about major problems: insufficient grounding for students to make career choices (irrelevance); an excessive number of subjects and examinations; fragmentation of knowledge; superficial study; thematic encyclopaedism. The IB is offered as an alternative which will provide curricular integration, through direct experience and the study of specialized subjects in depth, and the globalization of knowledge (Fox, 1992).

The first school in the Chilean public sector to join the International Baccalaureate is the Liceo Luisa Saavedra de González (Nº 7) for girls, a prestigious state institution drawing students from a broad socio-economic spectrum and diverse locations in and around Santiago. In 1994 the headmistress, Sylvia Artigas, saw in the IB a concrete possibility for engendering the fundamental changes required by the MECE reform. The school community responded to the enthusiasm of the leadership, and with the approval and support of the Municipality of Providencia and the Ministry of Education, together with INSET assistance from IBLA and the Chilean Association of International Baccalaureate Schools (ACHBI), the Liceo was able to initiate an IB programme in 1995 with an enrolment of 51 students. Despite the lack of financial resources (the parents undertook a fund-raising campaign to help meet the costs) and absence of formal recognition from the traditional universities, the Liceo Nº 7 has become a leading advocate for the IB in Chile.

An important feature of the Chilean educational reform is the allocation of resources (which include World Bank funding) to schools in the most impoverished areas of the country. This has been reflected in the reforms that were enacted for the first cycle of 'basic education' (ages 6–9) in 1996, and are now being institutionalized for the second cycle (ages 10–13) in 1997 after a period of consultation and participation of teachers in the process of programme development. Intense discussion and research is presently under way for secondary education (ages 14–18), with the purpose of launching the new national curriculum for this level in 1998. In the drive to emphasize quality the government identified 51 secondary schools with 'at risk' (impoverished) populations, and invited them to submit proposals that would meet criteria for excellence, guaranteeing state funding for five years to the best projects. This group of schools has been named 'Montegrande' in honour of Gabriela Mistral, Chilean teacher-philosopher, who was awarded the Nobel Prize for Poetry in 1945. Chilean reformers liken the journey Mistral made from her humble village in Montegrande to far-away Stockholm to the challenge Chilean teachers must assume today in managing change as they enter a global society. The MECE authorities, informed by the experience of the Liceo Nº 7, see the International Baccalaureate as a possible project for the Montegrande schools in the drive to offer quality education to a broader sector of the population and, to that end, on 6 October 1997 sponsored a nation-wide seminar in cooperation with the Chilean Association of International Baccalaureate Schools. The purpose of the occasion was to familiarize interested schools with the IB educational philosophy, curriculum structure, and course objectives and requirements in different subject areas. In his address inaugurating the seminar, IBO Director General Roger Peel stressed the significance of the occasion as an example of the growing relationship between the IBO and national systems.

Over the years, as an independent organization, IBO has had the freedom to explore and pilot a variety of curriculum and assessment initiatives, drawing from varied ideas and practices world-wide. This has been an enriching process, enabling the IB to serve as a complement to national systems, and as a model for innovation in a variety of different contexts. In his closing remarks Jose Pablo Arellano, Minister of Education, formally invited schools to consider introducing the IB as a pilot example within the proposed national secondary curriculum framework.

In the 1960s, during the IB'S early pilot days, Chile was the first country to recognize the fledgeling project by legally authorizing it as a national experiment. Thirty years later, at a time of renewed cooperation, the aspirations of the IB founders ring through Director General Roger Peel's expectations for the IB students of today and tomorrow (IBO, 1997):

Is the IB just another variant of the proliferation of national systems around the world, or do we in fact provide a service that transcends such boundaries in ways that are unique? The answers to such questions depend to a large degree on our interpretation of 'international' and how we choose to infuse it into our curriculum. From my own perspective, the honesty of the IB stems from the fact that we require all students to relate first to their own national identity – their own language, literature, history and cultural heritage, no matter where in the world this may be. Beyond that, we ask that they identify with the corresponding traditions of others. It is not expected that they adopt alien points of view, merely that they are exposed to them and encouraged to respond intelligently. The end result, we hope, is a more compassionate population, a welcome manifestation of national diversity within an international framework of tolerant respect. Ideally, at the end of the IB experience, students should know themselves better than when they started, while acknowledging that others can be right in being different.

In the context of Chile the influence of such sentiments is proving to be widespread, in private and public sector alike.

REFERENCES

Fox, E (1992) 'Un caso de estudio para Chile: El Bachillerato Internacional', Proyecto Mece/Media, Santiago (research document)

Frei, S E Presidente Eduardo (1996) *En el inicio de la legislatura ordinaria del Congreso Nacional*, Santiago, 21 May

International Baccalaureate Organization (1997) *Brochure*, IBO, Geneva

Ministerio de Educación Pública (1964) *Algunos Antecedentes para el Planeamiento Integral de la Educación Chilena*, Ministerio de Educación Pública, Santiago

Stoyle, P (1990) *Report to the Council of Foundation of the International Baccalaureate*, IBO, Geneva

18

GOING, GOING, GONE... GLOBAL!

Malcolm McKenzie

INTRODUCTION

The first part of this chapter is an investigation of the meaning of the word 'international' in its application to both education and schools. I contend that, through lack of rigorous definition, the precise meaning of the word has been and still is cloudy and confused in the phrases 'international education' and 'international school'. This contention is by no means novel. My illustration, however, might be. I take the statement of aims of the International Baccalaureate Organization (IBO), essentially five brief points, and show that the word 'international' is used with five different meanings: non-national, pan-national, ex-national (as in expatriate), multinational and transnational.

The second section of the chapter expands on the pan-national in schools. I claim that this meaning of the word 'international' is the most obviously ideological and the most clearly significant when considering global initiatives, interconnections and influences in education. I suggest some values that are or could and perhaps should be characteristic of any pan-national thrust in education. I raise, in passing, the important question of whether international education is the prerogative of international schools. A brief consideration of some basic, comparative characteristics of national and international schools brings me to the conclusion that 'the international' in education, at least in the pan-national sense, can occur in any school. Its locus, however, will differ in different types of school and school context.

The third and final part of the chapter introduces the concept of 'partnership' as a tool for introducing or enhancing the effective delivery of certain aspects of an international education. I look at a specific school, Maru a Pula, in relation to this idea of partnership. I argue that partnerships, in addition to perhaps more obvious areas such as the curriculum, can be extremely useful in making any school programme more international. I explore, and illustrate four kinds of partnership: within the 'stable' school community; with the 'temporary' school community; between the school community and its immediate 'outside'; and between the school community and a new school-related community abroad.

FIVE MEANINGS OF INTERNATIONAL

The various curricula and examinations designed and promoted by the IBO are used by many international schools as a major aspect of their delivery of an international education. In its statements of aims the IBO uses the word 'international' a number of times. This is to be expected of the organization that has pioneered so successfully an approach to the education of school students that sets out deliberately to be international in its perspective and range. In the admirably distilled expression of the IBO, these aims are threefold (IBO, 1994). They are:

- to improve and extend international education and so promote international understanding
- to facilitate student mobility and provide an educational service to the internationally mobile community
- to work in collaboration with national education systems in developing a rigorous, balanced and international curriculum.

The means to reaching these aims is through the manufacture of two complementary educational products, described in the same document:

- an internationally recognized pre-university curriculum
- a university entrance examination, the IB Diploma, which gives access to higher education world-wide.

Even a cursory glance at these three aims and the two attendant ways of achieving them reveals how much is at stake and how extensive the IBO project is. The organization sets out to link its curriculum to the promotion of understanding between countries, and to use national systems of education where appropriate to develop a curriculum that is international in the sense that it is global in range. These two aims ride in tandem. Ancillary to these, it wishes to serve our late twentieth-century nomads, the internationally mobile community, by providing in countries across the globe an education that is consistent and that will give access to the best universities anywhere.

Now permit me to digress briefly into the realm of animals. We all know that dogs have four legs and a tail and we find it easy to distinguish between these parts. That canny American, Abraham Lincoln, is reputed to have said that you can call a tail a leg but that does not mean that a dog has five legs. It will, however, still retain five, long, thin extensions to its body. The international aspect to education seems to share the same number of possibilities. These are neatly encapsulated in the statements quoted above, which I gloss in the following way. The extension of 'international education' refers to a system that is non-national, and therefore not subject to the requirements, standards, demands and orientation of a particular, national system. 'International understanding', through the juxtaposition of its two words, seems broader than this. Here we have something more than the merely non-national; this type of sympathetic mutuality is pan-national, an enterprise that seeks to build bridges between countries. An internationally mobile community seems clear; the members of this community are those expatriates who can safely be said, for the most part, to be ex-national. When we come to the 'international curriculum' that is worked out through collaboration with national education systems we seem to be dealing with a phenomenon that is multi-national in much the same sense of the word that a comparative educationist might mean. Finally, an 'internationally recognized' secondary school qualification for university entrance suggests a concern with a transnational certificate, which will legitimately promote the educational aspirations of the children of the ex-national community by allowing them to cross educational borders with the same ease that a valid passport permits movement from one country to another.

I contend that much of the discourse of international education uses the qualifier 'international' with these five different meanings and seldom attempts to define them or to say which is being used when. We do not seem to know which is the tail nor when it wags the body of the dog, propelling the other parts: those four legs. This makes it difficult to conduct any rigorous discussion of international education or international schools. The IBO statement of aims does not, of course, set out to demonstrate my five meanings of 'international'. That it does so unintentionally but with wonderful clarity is, however, a useful illustration of my contention. There is, let me add, nothing inherently negative about this fluctuating quintuplet of meanings. Even a cursory glance through any directory of international schools will reveal a rich range of different types, each of which offers an international education that cannot be encapsulated easily. It is, however, useful to know what our various meanings are as well as when and how we employ them. If we do not, we are like children playing the party game whereby a tail is pinned on a picture of a donkey. We try to pin this tail to the body and have much fun doing so; but when we take off the blindfold we are confounded by the haphazard nature of our sense of direction!

THE VALUE AND VALUES OF PAN-NATIONAL EDUCATION

I need now to declare a personal interest. The meaning of 'international' that interests me most is pan-national. The pan-national works consciously to reduce tensions and misunderstandings across nations by promoting global initiatives, knowledge and empathy through education. It is the most obviously ideological of my five meanings in that it seeks to produce students who are not only citizens of the world but participants in trying to produce a future world fit for all its citizens. It is not sufficient for pan-national education to be satisfied with a curriculum that draws on various national systems and an examination certificate that entitles students to university openings around the world. These are important, yes, but they must be underpinned in pan-national education by a set of values congruent with the drive for international understanding. In this sense, pan-national education is truly global in its perspective. What then might such values be?

Going, going, gone... global!

All educational systems have their underpinning values. Sometimes these are spelt out, sometimes they are hidden; usually there is a combination. I am aware that many attempts have been made to elucidate the values that could, or should, contribute to the definition of the pan-national thrust in education that is growing as our century draws to its close. I am also aware of the problems in venturing into any discussion of values. It interests me that some of the more interesting of these attempts have been made by teachers working in international schools, such as the *Principles for an International Education* put together by the faculty of the International School of Geneva (1994). They are:

- encouraging important international values
- supporting the student's language development
- ensuring an international dimension to the curriculum
- recognizing the importance of global issues
- providing a breadth and balance of education experience
- adopting an innovative approach to learning and teaching
- providing appropriate student services
- showing respect for, and integration with the host country.

These principles are general and, in some cases, not specific to a pan-national emphasis. This last point is significant as it is all too easy for those working in international education to assume, complacently, that their schools are inherently capable of doing things that national schools are not. Taken together as a set of eight, however, they have the unmistakable flavour of arising out of the context of an international school and of being assembled by people working with the daily and routine aspects of such a situation.

In 1996 I was on leave from my school, Maru a Pula, as a visiting Lecturer at the Centre for the study of Education in an International Context (CEIC) at the University of Bath. I participated for a term in a Masters module on international education and international schools with a group of teachers from schools, national and international, around the world. During that term we spent some considerable time defining and refining our set of values for the international education that sets out to be pan-national. Those who have undertaken any process like this know only too well that it entails haggling over the choice and meaning of words which inevitably become invested with significance particular to the people in the process. I have no doubt that this is true of the IBO statement of aims analysed earlier. Viewed objectively and evaluated from the outside such formulations will be assessed differently, just as I did in looking closely at the word 'international'. Readers of the following set of eight values that we developed are likely to engage in a similar type of analysis, and I welcome this in advance.

Our eight values characteristic of pan-national education were:

1. worldmindedness
2. open mindedness
3. the promotion of a sense of global interdependence

4. the promotion, conjointly, of a sense of individual and cultural self-esteem
5. the promotion of a commitment to world peace and development
6. a relish for the withering of prejudice
7. a passion for learning as process and product
8. respect for, and tolerance of other cultures and cultural diversity, leading possibly to 'interculturality'.

These values require some teasing out and illustration. 'Worldmindedness' (Sampson and Smith, 1957) is a sociological concept which refers to an attitude that sees the world as an oyster. There is nothing especially novel about that. After all, the global village is a concept that has become domesticated and now inhabits the backyard of many people's minds. Even the neologism 'worldmindedness' is over 40 years old. However, an attitude that sees the world as an oyster might be concerned only with the ruthless exploitation of pearls. It is imperative, therefore, that worldmindedness be accompanied by open mindedness, an attitude that is essentially generous, open and non-grasping.

In expatiating on my first two values I have deliberately used the word 'attitude' a number of times. As Hayden and Thompson (1995a) have highlighted recently, the inculcation of 'an "international attitude" outside the formal curriculum' is, from the perspective of students, a defining factor in their experience of an international education. The combination of worldmindedness and open mindedness describes in very general terms just such an attitude. The former promotes a global consciousness; the latter ensures a conscience appropriate to this. These are the twin towers between which the pan-national bridge is hung.

The remaining six values are more focused and specific and follow on easily from the combination of the first two. A sense of global interdependence is easy to understand and accept, I hope, on the conceptual level. It is no more nor less than John Donne's famous plea against insularity, which still echoes with resonance down the centuries. Although easy to comprehend, and to teach through the academic curriculum, it is often difficult to give practical substance to this value in schools. Community service, emphasized so much in different systems of international education and made a formal part of the IB curriculum, comes into its own here. Think global, act local is a recent commonplace. Through community service, however, this phrase acquires gravity and punch. If students and teachers learn interdependence through community service in their local contexts a genuine feeling for global interdependence is just a short step away. A very different matter, that of the insistence by some schools that their students and, in certain cases teachers, become conversant in at least two languages, can be an important promoter of this value.

The word 'conjointly' is a critical aspect of the expression of the next value, relating to the promotion of self-esteem. Self-esteem is a feature of much modern thinking on education and underlies, for instance, the thrust towards programmes of Personal and Social Education. The insight that individual self-esteem enhances effective academic learning is now widely accepted. Cross-cultural encounters, in education and elsewhere, have led to the equally firmly accepted notion of cultural self-esteem. It is in international schools, however, that these two come together inevitably. Hence the importance of the conjoint: in schools where there are many nations and cultural groups represented individual and cultural self-esteem are promoted by piggybacking each other. In schools that are more homogeneous individual self-esteem remains just as important and attainable a target: it is to be hoped that the development of cultural self-esteem in such schools will become more expansive and global in outlook and will not be at the cost of 'alien' cultures. This is a real challenge for many national education systems.

The next two values could be collapsed into one and many might wish to do this. In our discussions, however, it was felt that an active delight in countering prejudice was absolutely vital if real substance were to be given to any professed interest in promoting world peace and development. That little 'and' has a causal value: world peace is linked to appropriate development. This value, where it exists, will probably find expression in the formal academic curriculum. A proactive attitude against prejudice, on the other hand, is more likely to be diffused within and throughout a school. This should be easy to develop naturally in schools which are multinational or multicultural.

A balance between the processes and the products of learning should be a feature of well-constructed educational programmes, whether national or international. An increasing number of educationists would agree with this seventh value and many would go on to say, in addition, that this is much more than merely a matter of assessment. It is no accident that the IB programme lays store by this, discretely in the Theory of Knowledge core course and integrally in its emphasis on the acquisition of transverse skills within a framework that is individually constructed. In the Middle Years Programme of the IB this is even more clearly delineated in the Areas of Interaction that underpin that course.

The eighth and final value is complicated and problematic. Respect for and tolerance of cultural diversity seems an obvious component of the pan-national enterprise. Does this then lead to cultural relativism? Or is it possible to make informed judgements on and about the various aspects of different cultures and perspectives? The notion of intertextuality is well developed in literary theory. In a nutshell, this allows a reader to assess in a principled way the merit of a piece of writing through comparison, often historically, to other texts of a similar nature. When it comes to culture, a question that has to be faced squarely by pan-nationalism is how to assess the relative demands and expectations of the different groups that make up a diverse community, such as a multicultural school. Interculturality might provide an answer. In Botswana, for instance, corporal punishment is a traditional and quite acceptable way for adults to discipline children and it is used in many schools. In my school many of our parents expect their children to be beaten if they misbehave. The fact that they are not, and that corporal punishment is not practised at Maru a Pula, is difficult to justify without appearing to slight the culture of our community and context. Interculturality, which allows for reasoned comparison and contrast, suggests a philosophical way through this problem.

By its very nature this list of eight values must be tentative. It makes no claim, either, to be comprehensive. But each point is general and the total wide ranging.

I presented this list of values to the 1996 National Association of Independent Schools (NAIS) Conference in Washington. After discussion there was general acceptance of these values and agreement that a global range was covered by them and that little of significance had been left out. One of the presenters sharing that particular platform with me, Eton Churchill, teaches on the Course of International and Cultural Studies at the Kyoto Nishi High School in Japan. He wrote me a letter six months later, in September 1996, in which he recounted his experience of presenting these eight values to a group of Japanese educators in August that year. Before offering them my list he asked them to generate their own, after having explained carefully the goal of the task. Eton commented :

> I found that these 'values' coincided pretty well with those you put forward in Washington with the exception of two omissions. The Japanese educators did not bring up the need to have a 'relish for the withering of prejudice' and the sense of individual self-esteem was not mentioned in any of their discussion. After their list was made, I pointed out these two additional 'values' and asked how important they were. The feedback indicated that they felt that individual self-esteem was important, but there was very little mention of an aggressive approach to the elimination of injustice.

It would be fascinating to take such comparative research further into the pan-national aspect of international education. I suspect that such research would show that areas of difference and divergence would be far fewer than those of agreement and convergence.

If this is indeed the case, that the pan-national aspect of international education is underpinned by a set of values and attitudes that are not too difficult to agree upon, then it would seem to follow that any school is capable of delivering this type of education. Hayden and Thompson (1995b) have argued just this in their exciting claim that international education is characterized at its most fundamental level by a 'movement across frontiers by ideas'. Although it is not easy to define the differences between national and international schools, as such attempts tend to become overly schematic and ignore areas of overlap, these differences are usually located in the composition of the student and staff bodies, the curriculum, and ownership and accountability (Hill, 1994). A national school, even if multicultural, will tend to have a relatively homogeneous staff and student group. Any pan-national direction adopted by such a school will have to be deliberate and will most likely be located in the curriculum. In an international school, on the other hand, the promotion of the values I have adumbrated, or those like them, might well take place in a more subtle fashion, through the ethos generated by the intermingling of students and staff drawn from many nations. It is important to remember, however, that such heterogeneity is not a sufficient condition for this to happen.

'PARTNERSHIPS' THAT PROMOTE THE INTERNATIONAL

I deliberately revert here to the term international, which I use interchangeably in this section with the catch-all 'global', as the different partnerships that I shall describe can and do promote some or all of the five meanings of international. In addition to obvious ways in which the international dimension to education might be promoted, such as from within the academic curriculum and, also, through the diversity that some schools enjoy, many types of partnership can contribute to this endeavour. A useful starting point here is to see the school as a set of possible communities between which partnership links can be built that will augment the school's global connections and consciousness. In this brief conclusion, I hope to hint at some of these possibilities, many of which are not novel but the range of which is seldom exploited.

Partnerships within the 'stable' school community

The stable school community consists of those people, most obviously students and staff, who work at the school. This community will, however, include alumni, parents, governors and, perhaps, others. Many self-styled international schools, of widely differing types, enjoy a diversity within the student enrolment that promotes internationalism almost automatically. At Maru a Pula, for example, although it has always been policy to draw just over half our students from Botswana, the remainder come from about 40 different countries. We feel that the Batswana learn hugely from this global exposure and that the students from other countries gain through becoming, in a small way, a part of their host country.

Clearly, teachers also form part of the stable school community. How many schools, international in certain respects, have a teacher composition and profile that is basically homogeneous? In my experience, many. The same, generally speaking, seems true of school governing bodies. Terwilliger (1972) pointed out that the composition of the board of directors of an international school should 'ideally, be made up of foreigners and nationals in roughly the same proportions as the student body being served'. Terwilliger admits that this is an ideal, and ideals are seldom reached: yet they remain worth striving for. Within the stable school community of teachers and governors it should be possible to promote greater partnership between nationals and non-nationals than we have in many schools that claim an interest in the international.

Partnerships with the 'temporary' school community

Temporary additions to the stable school community from another country or continent can create exciting possibilities. When I consider the temporary school community I include student groups that visit from other schools and countries, individual student exchanges, scholarship possibilities for students in developing countries to go to schools in developed countries, young people becoming teacher assistants during a gap year, and teacher exchanges and teacher visits. At Maru a Pula we encourage all of these and our global consciousness as a school benefits considerably as a result. We have well-established links with certain schools in the United States, for example, which offer grade 12 scholarships to our O-level graduates. In return we take students from these schools to spend our winter term, their summer vacation, with us. This is a programme with obvious mutual advantages in the area I am considering.

Adding to the stable school community with temporary recruits has further possibilities that are not often explored. Teacher exchanges are notoriously difficult to arrange, as it is usually hard to find an exact or even feasible fit when swapping. Short visits, however, are much easier to organize. More and more schools, quite rightly, set store by staff development and inservice training. How many realize that useful, and not too expensive inservice training can be had by spending a few days or a week at a time in schools in other countries? When teachers at Maru a Pula take a term of study leave and spend part of that time in three or four schools with which we have some form of school-to-school link, they often come back feeling that this experience is the most valuable part of their leave. Turning again to governing boards, which in many schools with a consciously international impetus (and, of course, others) can be crucial decision-making bodies: how often do we encourage the stable community of governors to enrich their perspective by taking on temporary visitors? I am trying to develop with a group of schools around the world a relationship that would allow governors, if they happen to be visiting a country where there is an associate school, to visit that school and even to attend a governors' or trustees' meeting if one happens to coincide with the visit. The advantages of being able to tap such a reservoir should be enormous.

Partnerships between the school and the 'outside' community

I use the word 'outside' deliberately, to refer to the community surrounding the school, its local context. I do so because so few schools, in my experience, have any genuine or sustained contact with their ambient society. It may well be the case, despite protestations to the contrary, that many international schools are especially at fault here. On the other hand, a recent and growing emphasis on community service within some national education systems is ensuring some redress of this 'problem'.

Community service learning is an obvious way in which to promote and nurture the interdependence that I stressed in the previous section. It matters not that there is no geographical crossing of frontiers; there certainly is a crossing of frontiers by ideas in projects where advantaged students engage in active service with disadvantaged outsiders. In some cases, such as through an organization like the Round Square and the international service projects that it organizes for its member schools, community service can take on an international aspect: usually, however, although charity begins at home and might, geographically speaking, stay there, the consciousness that it promotes can certainly cross many borders. At Maru a Pula we started the first chapter of Amnesty International in Botswana: the activities of this group clearly take students in imaginative and empathetic ways beyond our borders. Other services, however, such as working with disabled or abused or orphaned children, or teaching English in deprived inner city areas or nearby villages, do develop a sense of that mutual interdependence that I suggested earlier is a crucial value of pan-nationalism.

An important adjunct to the community service partnerships that take students and teachers outside the school are community inreach partnerships, which make facilities of the school available to the community nearby. At Maru a Pula many groups, sporting, educational and cultural, use our facilities after hours and over weekends. I was showing a British visitor around the school one evening a few years ago and he was amazed to see an adult football team practising on our soccer field. He was even more surprised when I told him that the Mochudi Chiefs practised at Maru a Pula most evenings and that it was an easy symbiosis that had existed for many years. Our flagship in this area is a theatre named Maitisong, the Setswana word for a traditional story-telling gathering around a campfire. Maitisong is effectively the national theatre of Botswana and we are unusually privileged as a school to boast a theatre with such status. It is run as a community partnership project and used by the school for only a small percentage of its time. There are shows there most weekends by visiting and local artists and large audiences are drawn from our city, Gaborone, and elsewhere.

Partnerships between the school community and a new school-related community abroad

There are some similarities between this type of partnership and my second type. Here, however, I am thinking of partnerships that are less directly mutual than exchanges and that might often entail relationships between developing and developed countries. Let me give some examples. First, we have established at Maru a Pula two private fund-raising charities, one in the UK and the other in the USA. The President of the American Friends of Maru a Pula is, by right, a member of the Governing Council of the school. Second, a school in Boston holds an annual dress-down day for Maru a Pula and channels the funds raised, usually about $1500, to our bursary fund. Finally, the University of Bath has for the past three years been running Masters level education courses at Maru a Pula, which are attended by teachers from Maru a Pula, elsewhere in Botswana and from other countries in our region. In all cases we see a school community creating a new school community abroad in ways that are novel, that promote global awareness and that, in the last two cases, beg the interesting question: which is the school community and which the new school-related community abroad?

Writers on internationalism or globalism in education often feel forced to adopt a position that is either ideological or pragmatic. In my section on values I was overtly ideological. I hope that this section on partnerships has given some very pragmatic hints on how an international dimension to the education offered by schools of all types might be promoted and developed by taking the school community and making it go global.

REFERENCES

Churchill, E (1996) Personal communication, September

Hayden, M C and Thompson, J J (1995a) 'An investigation of perceptions of international education in an undergraduate population: a preliminary study', *International Review of Education*, **41**, 5, pp 389–404

Hayden, M C and Thompson, J J (1995b) 'International education: the crossing of frontiers', *International Schools Journal*, **XV**, 1, pp 13–20

Hill, I (1994) 'The International Baccalaureate: policy process in education', PhD thesis, University of Tasmania

International Baccalaureate Organization (1994) *The International Baccalaureate: An International Curriculum and University Entrance Examination*, IBO, Geneva

International School of Geneva (1994) *Principles for an International Education*, International School of Geneva, Geneva

Sampson, D and Smith, H (1957) 'A scale to measure world-minded attitudes', *Journal of Social Psychology*, 45, pp 99–106

Terwilliger, R I (1972) 'International schools: Cultural crossroads', *The Educational Forum*, **36**, 3, pp 359–63

19

Is International Education a Pipe Dream? A Question of Values

Michal Pasternak

Experiencing internationalism

In 1971 Marshall McLuhan pre-empted the discussion on the viability of international education with the observation that:

> years before he reaches the classroom, the small child of our time is engaged in data-processing on a large scale. Our schools are still arranged on the assumption that serious information is not available until the student reaches the classroom. For the child who lives in an environment constituted by information such educational assumptions are unrealistic (McLuhan, 1971).

The child of the 1990s may begin her day with a news report on a war somewhere in the world, graphically illustrated with explicit scenes provided by a CNN international camera. As she munches her international breakfast of products from far-off places she may switch to *EuroNews* for an update on the latest decisions taken at the European Parliament. But not for long: a quick flick of the wrist and a Japanese cartoon, dubbed into English, will hold her attention for a fleeting ten minutes. As she sits on her German-built school bus some fruity chewing gum, straight from friends in the USA, is passed around. The school day begins with assembly and finishes with the final bell. Between these two daily markers the extended outside world has been reduced to a single geography lesson. Back home, in the evening, 15 minutes' French homework is quickly completed to leave time for a computer game, set in 'darkest' Africa, while a Johnny Clegg and Savuka compact disc blares rhythmically in the background. The evening meal pizza (Mum's been to the supermarket again) provides family focal time for a discussion on the forthcoming holiday in the Caribbean. A final 30 minutes' TV, an adventure film in Urdu, and another international day comes to an end.

For such children their everyday links with international foodstuffs, multicultural entertainment and global information broaden their horizons to encompass nearly the whole world into their range of experiences. Occasionally the contact is immediate and concrete, like the feel of less expensive clothes from eastern Europe or the Far East, where the source of the product is only vaguely perceived. At other times the contact is 'second-hand', such as a picture on a TV screen or the printed word. Sometimes the language will be obscure and difficult to follow, in need of aggravating subtitles. Whereas on other occasions international icons, such as those found on a washing label, facilitate comprehension. These routine international experiences and daily exposures to the different cultural influences of the global network are intrinsic forms of international education. Certainly the young people are, as the *Collins Concise English Dictionary* specifies, in the 'process of acquiring knowledge' 'concerning... two or more nations or nationalities'.

The question of whether international education exists, or not, is a conundrum to be considered by a party of pedagogical professors puffing their pipes in an opium parlour. International education is a reality. However, there are several important uncertainties within this situation that need to be explored. First, education by its very nature instils a set of values in the recipient, so the questions must be, what are these international values and who decides them? The second issue of dubiety concerns where the formal education system fits in relation to this prototype of international education.

Before any discussion on values can begin I would like to clarify a perception of the nature of international communities. Within the 'global village' (Berry, 1977) several different degrees of international communities can be identified. First there is the community which is nationally based influenced by trade, economic and media values of internationalism on one side and the formal education beliefs of national interest on the other. This body could be termed a *domestic international community* ('domestic' because values are mainly determined by the tension between home, school and lifestyle factors). The second group have migrated to another cultural setting and strive to find a balance between the carried values of their origins, the formal beliefs of the host country and the internationalism of a modern lifestyle. This group could be designated an *osmotic international community* ('osmotic' because different school and lifestyle values filter through to come into contact with powerful home values). Finally there is that group of individuals described as 'global nomads': 'people of any age or nationality who have lived one or more pre-adult years outside of their passport country because of a parent's occupation' (Schaetti, 1994). These individuals could be called a *globally nomadic international community*.

VALUE SYSTEMS

Members of each of these communities experience varying degrees of tension between the different value systems influencing their development. Figure 19.1 shows, in diagrammatic form, a relationship between these three examples of communities. As one moves from left to right along the spectrum so, every day in that community, possible contacts with a variety of intercultural, multi-ethnic and global values increase. In other words the degree of opportunity for international education in some form intensifies. However, it must be stressed that each community experiences some degree of international education.

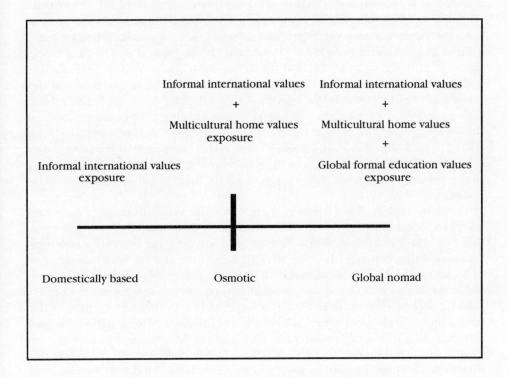

Figure 19.1 A spectrum of international communities

As can be seen from Figure 19.1 at least three different value systems act on an individual. These can be either supportive in nature or conflicting. They are described as follows:

1. The informal international value system
   As previously intimated, this process tends to function effectively and implicitly within the everyday structure of the society.
2. The home value system
   This code of behaviour stems from the values held by the parent(s) and has its roots in family socialization.
3. The formal education value system
   This system of values are those inculcated through attendance at an institute of formal education organized within the structure of the society.

Clearly the three systems are interdependent and each individual creates his or her own broad framework of values from the equilibrium that results within the dynamic of the systems. Before we engage in a more detailed examination of the forces behind these value systems, however, it would perhaps be worthwhile to clarify the word 'values'. 'Values are guidelines for individual behaviour' (Thompson, 1993) that help us compare our actions and outlooks. As can be seen from the example above, values are 'like culture,... not genetically inherited but... learned and inculcated from birth' (Thompson, 1993). Beare *et al.* (1992) draw on the work of Hodgkinson (1978) and the values model he created in 1978. In this paradigm Hodgkinson outlines three levels; the *transrational,* the *rational* and the *subrational.* The first level he perceives as being idealistic, based on belief, ethical code or, indeed, an act of faith. This level he sees as being unique and personal to the values holder. The second tier of values Hodgkinson distinguishes are those related to social interaction and reason. These values he discerns as humanistic and utilitarian. The final set of values in the model are those grounded in emotion and strong personal preference. Hodgkinson identifies these as behaviouristic, 'asocial and amoral'.

In life we tend to move between these strata, our values fluctuating from one level to another as decisions are taken which sometimes lead to action. The complexity of choice of values with which we are constantly faced is like 'a tightrope that man walks, between his desire to fulfil his wishes, and his acknowledgement of social responsibility' (Bronowski, 1976). It is, therefore, no wonder that the added complication of an informal international perspective compounds the values-forming process of education. Here is a factor that is outside the control of the home, since it is socially impervious; beyond the influence of most national school systems, since it is only loosely addressed; and yet has dynamic impact on the other two values-forming institutes. A special case in this situation is the international school. These institutions form a loosely associated world-wide network and attempt to approach formal international education from both a philosophical and practical standpoint.

To return to the informal sector, it has been established that a type of informal international education contributes to the value systems of all countries. But, back to the question – who decides the nature of these values? Very few nations do not have a McDonald's restaurant or peak TV viewing figures when a popular soap opera is being broadcast. This perspective was reinforced while watching a recent news programme on the topic of the World Cup. A group of Indians from the Altiplano region of Brazil were being interviewed on the progress of their national team. The cameras followed the interviewer into a modest lean-to tent. As the camera adjusted to the light a group of people could be seen huddled round a small TV set. To the consternation of the interviewer, the programme they were intensely watching was not the World Cup final between Brazil and Italy but a Portuguese translation of the Australian soap opera *Neighbours*.

The media is clearly a powerful force in the values-forming 'game'. But who controls the media? In response to this question we find ourselves moving into the area of national vested interest, money and power.

Perhaps the discussion can now be extended to include the second social values-forming institution: that of formal education. A similar question to that posed on the origins of the values inherent within informal education – ie who decides the nature of these values? – must be considered. Figure 19.2 presents a rather cynical response to this query by proposing a power-base structure in formal education. The initial question, 'Why education?' evokes the reply formulated by Lawton (1978) in relation to the curriculum being 'a selection of the culture of a society'. This, in turn, prompts two questions. One on the homogeneous nature of a society, and another on who makes 'the selection' proposed by Lawton. The response to the first question is seen in the daily rising figures of political, economic, and humanitarian immigrations that constantly change ethnic and cultural compositions within nations. So, if societies are not homogeneous we once again return to the question – who makes 'the selection'? The responses proposed are different types of power manipulating forces within society, eg political power, economic power, technological power (eg computers, military weapons), media power (eg BBC, CNN) or/and religious power (eg fundamentalist Muslim states).

The outcome statement of this chart suggests that power is a dominant factor in the choice of values perpetuated in a school and proposes the definition that 'education is an open system in a society created by those elements in power positions in order to perpetuate their values'. The extension of this principle into international education results in a similar definition that 'international education is an open system in the "global village" created by those elements in power positions in their societies in order to perpetuate their values'. In my experience, this definition would seem appropriate if used to describe many of the so-called international schools. The concept of an open system suggests some interaction with local communities but the knowledge, skills and attitudes models delivered are nearly always western European or North American in origin.

This power analysis of education would also seem to be true in the informal sector where the fulfilment of personal wishes, mostly in the form of economic profit, promotes national values into an international setting. Of course one of the implicit roles of formal education is, as Bronowski (1976) stresses, to balance the human desire to fulfil personal wishes and yet acknowledge social responsibility. Informal international education does not have these restraints so a greater responsibility must lie on the complementary formal international education system.

However, this flow chart really only presents a single ideological perspective of formal education. Deal and Nolan (1978) would identify this as an example of one of their four models, 'school as a filling station', where students are empty vessels waiting to absorb the rules, values and mores of the past. This view would correspond to the Carl Rogers' 'jug and mug' theory of education (Rogers, 1983). The 'school as a greenhouse' ideology ('Ideologies reflect the intellectual patterns of any culture of movement. An ideology conditions what individuals believe and value and how they view the world': Deal and Nolan 1978), however, views the school as a free learning environment where the young person's innate qualities can organically develop. The more revolutionary ideology of 'the school as a tool' regards students as change agents constantly challenging the social order. The final Deal and

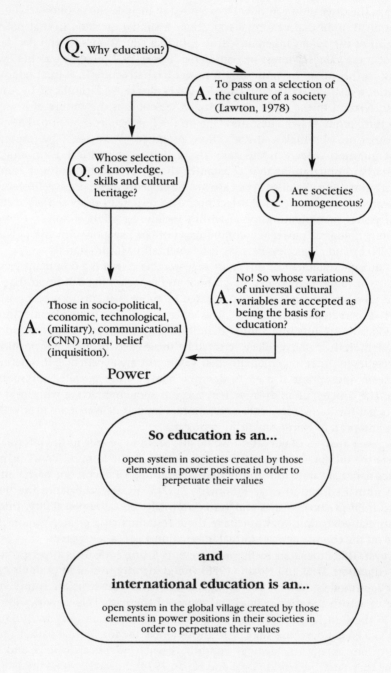

Figure 19.2 A power-based model of international education

Nolan ideology considers 'the school as a marketplace' where constant social inter-action, negotiation and bargaining among students themselves and between the learners and outside social forces will result in educational growth.

My instinct is that no school is a clear-cut example of any one of these ideolo-gies. Most schools are varying combinations of these philosophies depending on the political forces that influence it. Perhaps here we come to the crux of interna-tional education in the formal sector. As intimated before the 'personal desires' power of informal international education needs the balancing perspective of social acknowledgement in the formal education sector. But, just as the ideological bal-ance of a school varies with the political forces acting upon it, so the ideological elements within international education must vary depending on external environ-mental factors (eg local culture, language, pluralism of local society); political cli-mate (eg power base of school – national, UN, European, independent, etc) and internal policies (eg traditional, progressive, open) of the institution. But what are these elements that contribute to an international education?

GLOBAL EDUCATION

In September 1992 a foundation-wide curriculum development group from the International School of Geneva, Switzerland, began work on a 'curriculum charter'. The introductory section of the charter describes it as 'a start, not a finish', thus stressing the vital nature of international education, and goes on to present the doc-ument as 'a framework that provides a shape for the curriculum'. This 'framework', the draft continues, 'needs completing [and] is therefore a first chapter which we hope will stimulate discussion and change'. The first two important elements of international education, as perceived by this establishment, now begin to become clear: First, an atmosphere where healthy discussion is fostered and, second, the ability of the institution to respond to the nature of its whole environment.

Another important aspect of the document was a section entitled 'Encouraging the values of international education'. The opening paragraph of this section, shown below, perhaps gives a clue to those elements of international education referred to previously.

> Section C... We believe that the ethos and the educational programmes of the International School of Geneva should develop values that will help students, teachers and parents of different nationalities, abilities and interests to work together in harmony. This we believe is the fundamental task of 'international education' and one of growing importance in a world that is shrinking, yet increasingly divided.

From this statement one can begin to see elements that point the way to the 'spirit' of international education. The 'work[ing] together in harmony' suggests a search for commonalties and shared components between different peoples to bring about change. And the 'development of values that will help [people] of different nationalities' infers a respect and celebration of diversity and uniqueness between individuals and groups. But there is a certain familiarity about these elements. For example, the first element, of unifying to bring about change, seems fundamentally similar to Deal and Nolan's 'school as a tool' ideology and the concept of *global education*. The second element, of acknowledging and affirming differences between people, implies the 'school as a marketplace' ideology proposed by Deal and Nolan and the concept of *multicultural education*. The introduction of these two existent educational philosophies now begins to concretize the 'pipedream' of international education, as shown in Figure 19.3.

Figure 19.3 The pipe reality of international education

Generally, these two philosophies of learning are poorly understood and ill defined. Global education is often thought of as being an aspect of world geography and viewed with suspicion. The claim that global education creates a 'watering down' of cultural differences and reduces the individuality of ethnic groups is another frequently levelled criticism. Multicultural education also comes under assault from many areas. The problem that lies within multiculturalism is finding a balance between observing the common elements of cultural identity and recognizing the characteristics that make each culture unique. 'To neglect part of this problem results in, on one hand, a relativism which denies the very possibility of intercultural understanding, or, on the other hand, a superficiality which emphasizes folklore and the bizarre' (Walkling, 1990). Multiculturalism is clearly the pedagogical battleground between the so-called 'saris, samosas and steel bands' approach and the narrow dogmas of ethnocentricity.

However, as many international schools are beginning to discover, these two disciplines can exist in a complementary fashion. Global education, by stressing the interdependent nature of dimensions such as time, space and issues, manages to defuse the potential conflict zone of cultural relativism by urging five aims, discussed in depth in Hanvey (1976):

A question of values

1. Systems consciousness

   Through which students acquire:

   - 'the ability to think in a systems mode;
   - an understanding of the systemic nature of the world; and
   - an holistic conception of their capacities and potential'.

2. Perspective consciousness

   Through which students:

   - 'recognize that they have a worldview that is not universally shared;
   - develop receptivity to other perspectives'.

3. Health of planet awareness

   Through which students:

   - 'acquire an awareness and understanding of the global conditions and of global developments and trends;
   - develop an informed understanding of the concepts of justice, human rights and responsibilities and are able to apply that understanding to the global conditions and to global developments and trends;
   - develop a future orientation in their reflection upon the health of the planet'.

4. Involvement consciousness and preparedness

   Through which students:

   - 'become aware that the choices they make and the actions they take individually and collectively have repercussions for the global present and the global future;
   - develop the social and political action skills for becoming effective participants in democratic decision making at a variety of levels, grassroots to global'.

5. Process-mindedness

   Through which students:

   - 'learn that learning and personal development are continuous journeys with no fixed or final destination;
   - learn that new ways of seeing the world are revitalizing but risky'. (Pike and Selby, 1988)

Global educators attempt to fulfil these aims across the recognized curriculum regardless of how the knowledge content has been organized. An example of this approach applied to western recognized knowledge disciplines can be seen in Figure 19.4 with the student at the centre of a global system (taken from Bartlett, 1993).

The global village
Social, political and economic systems

The world as a physical system

Studies in human management: anthropology economics; politics; science; etc

Studies in physical sciences; maths; physics; geology; technology, etc

The human species

Studies in characteristics of humans; history; literature; religion, etc

Individual Learner

Studies in biology; zoology; biochemistry; ecology, etc

The world as a biological system

Studies in ways and means of human communication and expression: language, arts, etc

Studies in the bases of choice and decision making; philosophy; logic religion, etc

Communicative and expressive systems

Evaluative and belief systems

Figure 19.4 The world's systems and the curriculum

To the eye of a western educator, all the subject content areas described in Figure 19.4 would immediately be recognizable. However, the organization of knowledge into systems models reinforces the interdependence between these disciplines. A striking similarity can also be perceived if Figures 19.4 and 19.5, showing the sciences of Islam, are compared.

With this cultural association we have moved to the second element in the 'spirit' of formal international education, the perspective called multiculturalism.

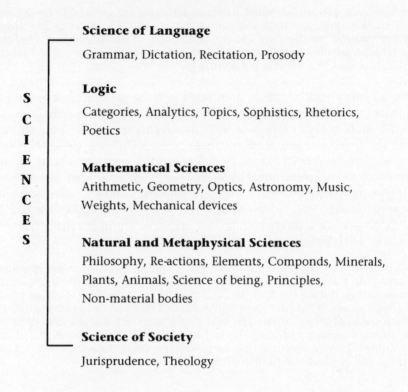

Science of Language

Grammar, Dictation, Recitation, Prosody

Logic

Categories, Analytics, Topics, Sophistics, Rhetorics, Poetics

Mathematical Sciences

Arithmetic, Geometry, Optics, Astronomy, Music, Weights, Mechanical devices

Natural and Metaphysical Sciences

Philosophy, Re-actions, Elements, Componds, Minerals, Plants, Animals, Science of being, Principles, Non-material bodies

Science of Society

Jurisprudence, Theology

Figure 19.5 The sciences of Islam (source unknown)

MULTICULTURAL EDUCATION

Many countries have struggled with this concept. Some, such as Canada, have committed themselves with an intent of purpose, stating that multiculturalism is 'a mandatory social skill that is just as essential as literacy. In education, it is no longer an option, but an integrated part of any well-developed program' (Cech, 1990). In Britain, the 1985 Swann Report, entitled *Education for All*, echoed this view in its recommendation that 'Multi-cultural understanding has also to permeate all aspects of a school's work. It is not a separate topic that can be welded on to existing practices' (Massey, 1991). But what does multicultural education mean in a practical sense? Perhaps this rhetorical question is best answered with a section from the introduction of a resource book to the Canadian project Globalchild, which is committed to fostering multicultural opportunities in early childhood education (Cech, 1990):

> The Globalchild approach sees culture as ever changing rather than static and fixed. As people change, so does culture, and no one activity or adjective can

263

epitomize a nation. So-called national activities are inevitably linked with activities originating half-way round the world... Throughout the project many cultural parallels are drawn; others wait to be discovered. One field tester who labelled an activity as Italian was reminded of this by a Pakistani child who said 'No, it isn't. We do that too.'

Effective multicultural education must begin with the personal, link to the cultural and then back to the personal. Ervin Staub is an American psychologist whose book *The Roots of Evil* (1992) deals with 'the conditions and processes which gave rise to the Holocaust and other instances of mass violence' (Deutsch, 1992). In many ways these instances could be considered the opposite extreme to international education, where national ideologies due to 'monolithic societies' subtended by 'high national self-esteem, a sense of entitlement and an underlying sense of insecurity' (Staub, 1992) led to international destruction. Towards the end of the book Staub presents factors which he feels are important in 'changing cultures and the relations between societies'.

Schools can teach about diversity and commonality. George Orwell, in Homage to Catalonia, described his profound change in attitude toward the enemy when during the Spanish Civil War he saw from his trench an enemy soldier pull down his pants and relieve himself. Schools (and universities) can teach students about differences, in customs, ways of life and values of people in different groups and their shared humanity and shared needs and shared yearnings. To accomplish this, it helps to move beyond abstractions and concretise and particularise human beings.

He continues that:

[by] helping students enter the framework of other cultures, schools can let them see how cultures and subcultures evolved differently because of different circumstances and different choices. By coming to see culture as a mode of adaptation and to appreciate the functions of different customs, especially if this is combined with a range of personal experience, students may come to accept quite varied ways of life (Staub, 1992).

The rider that Staub adds, 'a range of personal experience', points the way to two more important elements in formal international education. For identification of these factors, we must return to the other two ideologies of Deal and Nolan (1978) described earlier. The 'school as a filling station' approach underlines the importance of external information and experiences. This 'journey outward' through life and the ensuing knowledge and skills that are acquired form our socialization 'backpack'. The nature of the information we receive, our ability to communicate and our skills in detecting bias determine how we will view other individuals and groups. Any school should provide the opportunity for developing these qualities as part of the education process. However, with the impact of informal international education, the formal sector must place greater emphasis on the variety of different culture experiences through the 'journey outward' in terms of the knowledge (curricula) and skills, for these will contribute heavily to the acquisition of international attitudes and values.

A question of values

Yet, if the 'journey outward' is critical in formal international education so also is the complementary voyage suggested by Theodore Roszak in his book *Person/Planet* (1978), the 'journey inward'. Once again the concept, the 'journey inward', is reflected in one of the four ideologies outlined by Deal and Nolan. The 'school as a greenhouse' doctrine of education seeks to draw from the student that which is within. This ideology promotes the creation of an environment in which the 'innate' qualities and learning styles of each individual, which have been stifled by socio-political forces, are encouraged to blossom. Houston (1982) attempts to diagnose some of these forces and identify those 'innate' qualities which, she maintains, have atrophied in most individuals to result in an 'extremely limited consciousness'. Her observations include:

- The divorce of mind from body

  The divorce of mind from body..., it is claimed, leads to a progressive deterioration of human capacities such as perception, conceptualization and creativity – in short, our ability to learn and to understand our environment.

- The blunting of the senses

  Through the television screen we receive distorted and disjointed images of the world, employing only the senses of sight and hearing; in the supermarket, the pervasive odour of refrigeration plant, card-board packaging and chemical cleaning agents robs our senses of the pleasures attaining in fresh, unprocessed food... And yet we can also employ this technology to transport us, complete with our limited sensory awareness, to distant lands where our senses are indulged in unfamiliar sights, sounds and tastes. Is it any wonder that we fail to understand, in a profound way, the beliefs and practices of people, who are foreign to us?

- Outmoded physiological responses

  [Our] brain mechanisms... have changed very little, though the environment in which we live has. The result is a residue of inappropriate and ritualistic behaviour, as witnessed daily in the reports of violence and destruction.

- The failure to empower each other

  Through [the] process of neglect we not only miss the opportunity for empowerment for ourselves, but also fail to recognize and value richness, and diversity of experience in others... we all too readily judge other peoples and cultures from our own limited perspective, thereby nurturing our own assumptions and prejudices. (Pike and Selby, 1988)

AN IDEOLOGY FOR FORMAL INTERNATIONAL EDUCATION

Four elements have now been identified as crucial in the creation of an ideology for formal education that will instil in learners 'a sense of values' without which '... they will never become citizens of the world nor give it their gifts as should those who have known a true international education' (Mattern, 1991). These elements are: the need for experiences that stress the global interdependent nature of our environment (global education); the creation of opportunities to explore different cultures starting from a personal perspective, to foster positive acknowledgement of diversity, and yet appreciate similarities (multicultural education); the development of social skills and modes of human interaction (journey outward); and, learning situations that 'extend the physical, mental and creative abilities' (Houston, 1982) of each individual (journey inward). I would now propose that a formal international education ideology is a dynamic equilibrium between these four elements.

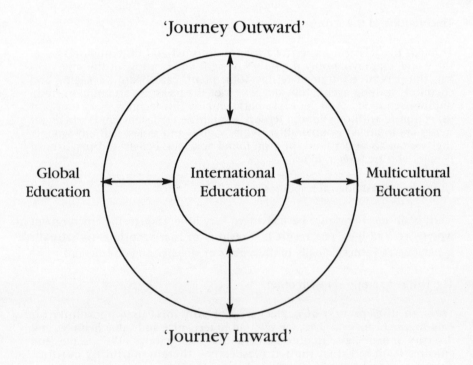

Figure 19.6 International education mode

Figure 19.6 is an attempt to put the principle into diagrammatic form. As can be seen, there is no fixed definition of formal international education. By nature it is both proactive and reactive.

The environment of the society, the climate of the school and the composition of the community will determine the nature of international education the students are experiencing. Clearly the dynamic balance of these four identified elements will differ from place to place. The ideal international education will be that which challenges the community towards greater international understanding, action and involvement.

Figures 19.7a, 19.7b and 19.7c are examples of different dynamic models of international education.

Figure 19.7a is an example of international education where the ideological emphasis is on aspects of global education and the development of personal potential. The challenges in a school with this model would be to foster a greater understanding of multiculturalism, social and cooperative learning.

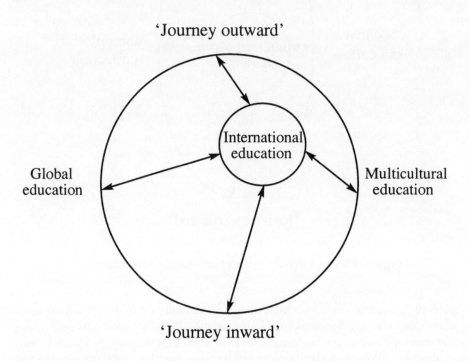

Figure 19.7a A dynamic model of international education

Figure 19.7b describes a school where there is little opportunity for multicultural education and limited global education. There is a good balance between the social and external knowledge aspects of learning and personal challenge and creativity. This establishment would challenge itself by trying to develop programmes and opportunities for multicultural learning and interaction. The other international element of global education also needs introduction into the school environment.

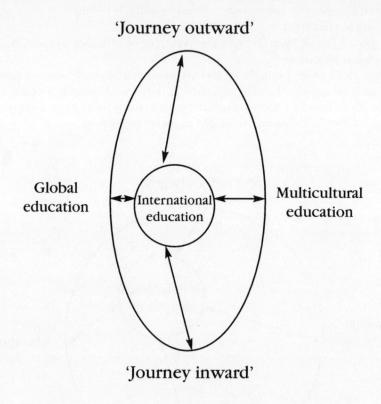

'Journey outward'

Global education

International education

Multicultural education

'Journey inward'

Figure 19.7b A dynamic model of international education

Figure 19.7c depicts a school which does not include any multicultural aspect or global education opportunities in its programme. There is little focus on the personal development of the students with areas such as, creativity; learning to learn and affective involvement being perceived as a low priority. Since three of the four elements cited as being essential in a formal international education are lacking, I would purport that this school, no matter what the external examination results or achievements in national standings may be, is failing to provide the 'essential elements in the preparation of young people for life in a pluralistic society and an increasingly inter-dependent world' (Foundation of the International School of Geneva, 1992).

It should be stressed once again that these are dynamic models. They are never static. For an education to be considered 'international' all four elements must be present. As the school grows and changes so does the form of international education.

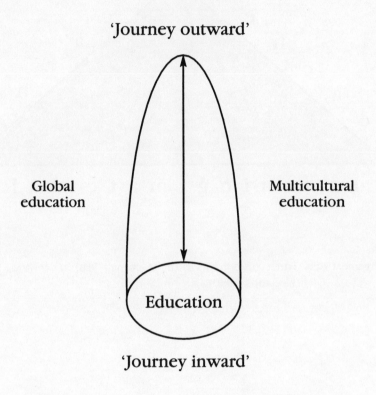

'Journey outward'

Global education

Multicultural education

Education

'Journey inward'

Figure 19.7c A dynamic model of international education

However, inherent within all these ideological components is the attitude of the teacher. The importance of the teacher–student relationship is critical in an educational environment laden with value-influencing experiences. It is at this pedagogical interface that the covert messages of international education are relayed. Neelands (1990) presents his perception of the change in the nature of teaching negotiation which he perceives is necessary in a values-learning environment.

Figure 19.8a represents the three components in the teaching–learning contract.

Figure 19.8b is how Neelands perceives the 'traditional transmission model' with the control of what is to be learnt always passing through the teacher.

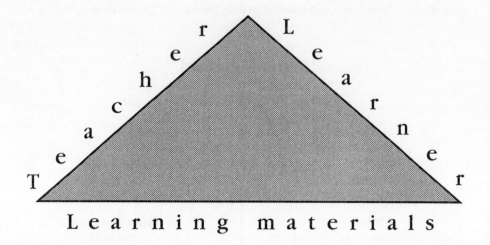

Figure 19.8a Three components in the teaching – learning contract (Neelands, 1990)

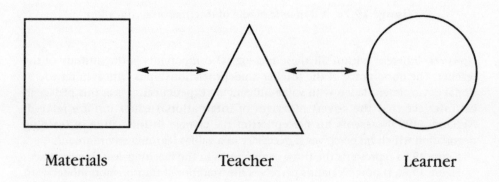

Figure 19.8b Traditional transmission model (Neelands, 1990)

The final model Neelands proposes, Figure 19.8c, suggests a different role for the teacher. Instead of acting as a 'transmitter' the teacher would now become the provider of a 'focusing lens' in the form of varied teaching strategies. To return to the words of Marshall McLuhan (1971): 'the medium is the message'. Only by examples of teaching methodologies that encourage trust and respect can the values, which subtend international education, be inculcated.

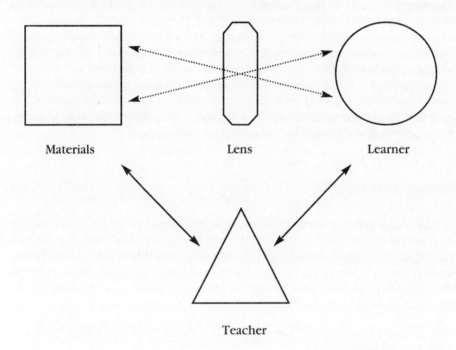

Figure 19.8c Teacher as 'focusing lens' (Neelands, 1990)

But the teacher is not alone in creating an environment for international education. From the classroom, to the corridor, to the playground, to the library, every aspect of school life must reinforce and support the values messages of international education. Figure 19.9 outlines some of the areas that must be considered. The entire school community (students, teachers, parents, administrators, etc) must contribute to and agree on a whole school perspective of international education. Every aspect of the school programme, including the curriculum, the extra-mural, the language policies and the balance of the four elements referred to earlier, must be discussed, clarified and accepted by the community.

Every teacher's classroom must reflect similar international value messages. The learning strategies and assessment policies must manifest equality of opportunity. The layout and organization of each classroom must suggest respect and tolerance, which must be supported by the general physical appearance of the entire establishment. The images on show in classrooms, corridors and libraries must display the international beliefs taken on by the school. These processes and role models of cooperative relationships will ensure that a whole school approach to international education is being pursued.

However, the essential base of an international philosophy lies in the dynamic equilibrium of the four elements. Many national systems have developed exciting programmes in each of the elements independently. In the United States and United Kingdom, Personal Study Skills and PSE (Personal and Social Education) programmes supported by Gestalt learning courses have encouraged 'Journey inward–Journey outward' experiences. In Switzerland, France and Finland education groups such as Zurich University, 'Educateurs sans Frontières' and 'Finnlda' have approached cultural diversity and development education in schools. But no national system has worked on a balance of the four elements. In essence this means that most national systems offer a limited international experience that cannot compete with the informal international education sector.

DREAMS AND REALITY

The challenging question in this chapter, 'Is international education a pipedream?' is a statement full of paradoxes. In many ways 'international education' is, or was, a pipedream. Dreams of globally interdependent world citizens have spurred idealistic educators into drawing up blueprints of international education systems. These 'mind's-eye pictures' are essential for future planning for, as the words of the song in the musical South Pacific assert:

> You gotta have a dream. If you don't have a dream, how's ya gonna have a dream come true?

However, these dreams must be linked to reality. No one person's dream is the same as that of anyone else. And so, in the transition from the abstract to the concrete, an evolution of the dream takes place to accommodate the different perspectives and experiences of those who will now begin to share the dream. But, even then, from group to group, the image of international education will undergo metamorphosis and adapt to the circumstances of the location. Only the fundamental elements, the recognition of interdependency; the affirmation of cultural pluralism; 'the desire (of the individual) to fulfil his wishes, and his acknowledgement of social responsibility' (Bronowski, 1976), will remain present. The realization of a 'pipedream' of international education has happened. Through the process of socialization selected aspects of internationalism have already instilled implicit values into a world community. The response of formal education to the outcomes of global interdependence and cultural migration has been slower and less concerted. As the smoke begins to clear from the pedagogical musings and the abstract images become processes then the different pipedreams of international education will become fleeting realities.

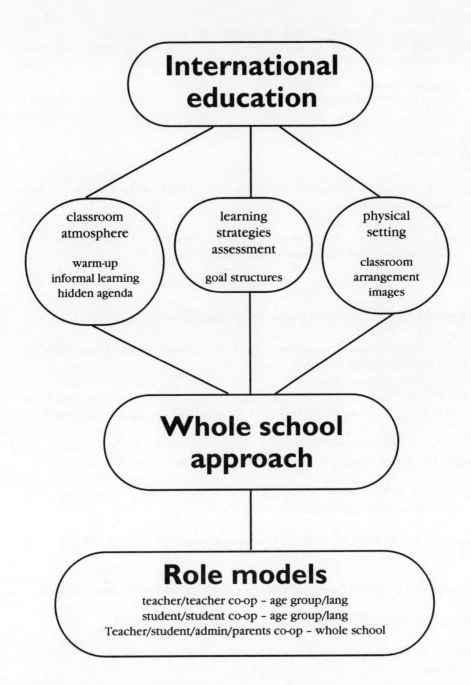

Figure 19.9 A whole school approach to international education

With regard to the electric light, much has been said for and against it, but I think I may say without contradiction that when the Paris Exhibition closes, electric light will close with it, and no more will be heard of it.

Erasmus Wilson
Oxford University professor, 1878

REFERENCES

Barlett, K (1993) Education in an International Context module, University of Bath Summer School, July

Beare, H, Caldwell, B J and Millikan, R M (1992) *Creating an Excellent School: Some New Management Techniques*, Routledge, London

Berry, W (1977) *The Unsettling of America*, Sierra Club Books, San Francisco

Bronowski, J (1976) *The Ascent of Man*, British Broadcasting Corporation, London

Cech, M (1990) *Globalchild: Multicultural Resources for Young Children*, Canadian Cataloguing in Publication Data, Ottawa

Deal, T E and Nolan, R R (1978) 'Alternative schools: a conceptual map', in V Lee and D Zeldin, *Planning the Curriculum: A Reader*, Hodder & Stoughton, London

Deutsch, M (1992) Review of Staub, E, *The Roots of Evil: The Origins of Genocide and Other Group Violence*, Cambridge University Press, Cambridge

Foundation of the International School of Geneva (1992) *Second Draft of the 'Curriculum Charter'*, published internally, October 1992

Hanvey, R G (1976) *An Attainable Global Perspective*, Global Perspective in Education, New York

Hodgkinson, C (1978) *Towards a Philosophy of Administration*, Blackwell, Oxford

Houston, J (1982) *The Possible Human*, J P Tarcher, Los Angeles, CA

Lawton, D (1978) *Theory and Practice of Curriculum Studies*, Routledge & Kegan Paul, London

McLuhan, M (1971) *From Cliché to Archetype*, Pocket Book edn, New York

Massey, I (1991) *More than Skin Deep*, Hodder & Stoughton, London

Mattern, G (1991) 'Random ruminations on the curriculum of the international school', in P L Jonietz and D Harris (eds), *World Yearbook of Education 1991: International Schools and International Education*, Kogan Page, London

Neelands, J (1990) *Making Sense of Drama*, Heinemann Educational Books, London

Pike, G and Selby, D (1988) *Global Teacher, Global Learner*, Hodder & Stoughton, London

Rogers, C (1983) *Freedom to Learn for the 80s*, Merrill Publishing Company, Ohio

Roszak, T (1978) *Person/Planet: The Creative Disentigration of Industrial Society*, Gollancz, London

Schaetti, B (1994) A profile of the 'global nomad' described in a workshop held at the International School of Geneva, 21 April

Staub,E (1992) *The Roots of Evil: The Origins of Genocide and Other Group Violence*, Cambridge University Press, Cambridge

Thompson, J J (1993) 'Education in an International Context module', University of Bath Summer School, July

Walkling, P (1990) 'Multicultural education', in Entwhistle, N (ed), *Handbook of Educational Ideas and Practices*, Routledge, London

20

TOWARDS A MODEL FOR INTERNATIONAL EDUCATION

Jeff Thompson

INTRODUCTION

There can be little doubt, based on the evidence provided by those contributing
their personal experiences and views to this book, that international education, as
practised in one or other of its many manifestations, is currently at a higher level of
activity than it has ever been. Along with the expansion in numbers of institutions
involved has come a corresponding increase in the diversity of practice existing
under the banner of international education. Such variety in provision is an understandable consequence of serious attempts to match the educational experience of
students to their needs in a wide range of educational and social contexts.
However, as indicated by several authors, especially in the latter part of this book,
such growth has not been accompanied by any fundamental achievement of an
overall rationale, against which those designing new courses or evaluating existing
practice can, with confidence, undertake such developments secure in the knowledge that they are doing so in a way which is conceptually defensible. At times it
has appeared as if the sheer diversity observed in practice has confounded attempts
to reach agreement in conceptual terms, yet there is a clear need, expressed most
often by those involved in the day-to-day practice of international education, for
such a consensus. Far from being a confounding factor, it is obvious from the contributions made to debate through this volume that diversity must be central in
any list of features that are likely to appear as essential elements in any such rationale. The purpose of this chapter is to attempt to reach such a goal; to identify
those aspects on which there is agreement concerning their presence in any conceptualization of international education and to explore the kinds of model that
could be of use in developing further our understanding of the nature of the practice
in which so many are engaged. If the ultimate objectives of international education
are related to the achievement of greater levels of mutual respect and harmonious
coexistence among nations, then the search for such an enabling framework within
which to strive for their achievement will be worth while.

We do know that some form of international education has existed for many years and, the more liberal minded may wish to argue, for many centuries. It is certainly true that the practice of young people moving around the world for educational purposes was well established in the nineteenth century, although not always with the support of those in national schools (including Birdsey Grant Northrop (1968) in Connecticut in 1873, who expressed, quite vehemently, a territorially defensive view about the dangers of sending youth overseas to gain an education). Such a stance seems at first glance unacceptably intolerant when seen against the views of the more globally aware individuals who are involved in promoting international education some century and a quarter later, but echoes of such territorial defensiveness still exist and can present barriers to progress in the implementation of international education, both within national systems of schools and within international schools situated in an educationally or politically antagonistic context. In spite of such resistance to the education of young people overseas, the practice was well established by the first quarter of the twentieth century, and many schools were set up in different parts of the world to cater for an increasingly mobile student population. However, as Mary Hayden observes (in Chapter 1), the existence of schools that were self-described as 'international' was no guarantee of the promotion of international education within them. Certainly little agreement existed about the 'aims and fundamental premises' of international education (Jonietz, 1991). Thus, due to a lack of such agreement, any attempt to infer the nature of international education by an examination of what went on in the so-called international schools was not seen to offer much of value in the early days, even when such a question was asked within the community.

More recent commentators have taken a different angle in defining international education, concentrating not so much on the nature of the providing institution but on what kinds of educational transactions and processes go on inside the institutions and inside the minds of the young people within them. As Belle-Isle asserted, 'The... mission of international education is to respond to the intellectual and emotional needs of the children of the world, bearing in mind the intellectual and cultural mobility not only of the individual but, most of all, of thought' (1986). This, in turn, focused attention on the nature of the curriculum within such schools, a dimension about which Gellar had already offered his own suggestion that:

the concept of international education demands a curriculum which is both concrete and specific, aimed at giving the student the skills that he needs to achieve the goal that he has chosen and broad enough to include those subjects that enable him to see the world from a much wider perspective than is generally required in national systems (Gellar, 1981).

Thus, a way forward for international education was seen to be through the curriculum offered in the schools.

AN INTERNATIONAL CURRICULUM

Attempts to define international education, and hence to find a way towards the design and implementation of an international curriculum, have sometimes revolved around the views of those involved in designing curricula across national boundaries on what constitutes internationalism *per se*. Thus, Stobart (1989) relates internationalism in the individual to the 'intensity of international living'. Translated into curricular terms, an international education is likely to be provided to the extent that the institution is able to make provision for the student to have access to international living through increasing levels of intensity. The employment of such a hierarchical approach to internationalism as a basis for the curriculum is paralleled by Hofstede's hierarchical portrayal of types of cultures and, given the relationship between internationalism and culture explored by the authors of contributions to this book, it may well be that it has something to offer the international curriculum planner. According to Hofstede (1991) culture can be described in increasing levels of manifestation: symbols, heroes, rituals and values.

The implications of such a scheme of 'cultural intensity' for the design of an international curriculum has never been explicitly acknowledged, although aspects of the different levels are reflected in the curricula produced for the international school circuit by a number of agencies and, indeed, by those responsible for curricular provision within the schools themselves. The notion of culture as a foundation for the curriculum is also explored by Lawton (1978), who starts from the premise that the curriculum is a selection from the culture of a society. Such an approach raises some very interesting questions about the basis on which the selection should be made when the nature of an 'international society' is itself unclear. It is interesting to note that from quite different ideological positions Phenix (1964) in the USA, and Hirst and Peters (1970) in the United Kingdom, offered ways in which a curriculum may be constructed based on an epistemological approach involving 'realms of meaning' and 'forms of knowledge' respectively, a perspective which was adopted, to a great extent, in the creation of the International Baccalaureate programme. These approaches raise at least as many problematic issues for curricular design, however, as do the alternatives briefly mentioned above.

Attempts to start from such cultural and ideological positions in order to find ways towards curricula which can be used internationally, as well as towards an international curriculum, have been well documented over a number of years, and such attempts seem to fall into well-recognized categories which could be identified as follows:

1. *Exportation*: the marketing abroad of existing national curricula and examinations has been a feature of education world-wide for a very long time, and there are numerous examples (including France, the UK and USA) of such a phenomenon. In these cases little attempt has been made to change the national curriculum or the national examination on the basis that what is offered is the same curriculum as, for example, an English student would receive in a school

in England. Those who are involved in promoting such a system would probably not wish, in general, to make many claims that an A-level syllabus from England, for example, contributes because of its nature to an international education. The value system is unapologetically that of the national country from which it is exported, but it does depend on an assumption of society identity between national country and receiver country. The literature is well supplied with examples of straight exportation of the curriculum from one country failing to find success in a second country because of the societal dissonance which takes place in, for example, Lawton's terms. In order for such curriculum exportation to succeed a society needs to be created within the 'foreign country' which will espouse the same value system as the original national context. Concession to any overt form of internationalism is slight, and is confined to the notion that the curriculum may be called 'international' only in the sense that it is used in a geographically dispersed market.

2. *Adaptation*: this can be said to take place when an acknowledgement is made in the selection of elements for the curriculum of the different contexts in which the curricula and examinations may be used. The International General Certificate of Secondary Education (IGCSE) and the Advanced International Certificate of Education (AICE), both from the University of Cambridge Local Examinations Syndicate in the UK, are examples of successful curricula (by market measures at least) in this category. Although content elements may constitute the major focus for the adaptation process, acknowledging context differences, the inherent value system may not change at all. Thus, the 'international value system' is automatically equated with the value system built into the national programme, so running the risk of a frequently unwitting, process of educational imperialism.

3. *Integration*: this occurs when 'best practices' from a range of 'successful' curricula are brought together to determine a curriculum that may be operated across a number of systems or countries. Such a process was at one time popular within Europe, when the Council of Europe often commissioned studies of the curricula of a number of member European countries in order to distil from the findings those curricular features that seemed to 'work' educationally and to bring them together in order to influence teaching and learning across different national systems in Europe (see, for example, Thompson, 1972). These kinds of study often served to provide a basis for improvement within national systems, so that claims to internationalism *per se* were necessarily limited. In the formulation of the European Baccalaureate in 1958 advantage was taken of such knowledge across the member states of the then European Economic Community to create a kind of internationalism, within a regionally restricted geographical context (Beardsmore, 1993). It can also be said that something of that kind of approach characterized the International Baccalaureate in its earliest days. Quite clearly, whatever the benefits of bringing together examples of good practice in pedagogy for a sharing of ideas across a number of systems, the dangers of confusing strategies from quite different, and often inconsistent, values or ideological positions are manifest. Under such circumstances this can often resemble a process

279

which results in – to use a chemical analogy – a mere mixture rather than a compound, little fundamental reaction having taken place! One is left with the question of whether a mixture of value systems is the way forward for international education.

4. *Creation*: this is the label I have given to the curriculum process which attempts to create a programme from first principles. Those principles will need clear exposition at the outset, a task that will be among the most challenging in the development of the entire programme. That is certainly true in the case of an international curriculum, for which value positions, agreement on the basis for selection of content, and a view of the nature of an international society are likely to be contentious. The International Baccalaureate, a 16–19 curriculum, is an example of a programme produced in this category. It clearly owes much to the epistemological approach of the 1950s and 1960s, during which period it was created, although elements of the other categories described above can be identified at different stages of its development. With the incorporation of the Middle Years Programme (IBMYP) and the Primary Years Programme (IBPYP) the International Baccalaureate Organization now has the challenge of creating a K- grade 12 coherence in international terms. It remains to be seen which category of curricular process described above, or mixture of such processes, it will adopt in rising to that challenge; it may well be that the opportunity will arise for a completely radical process to be developed. Perhaps the closest to date is that which has been employed by a group working under the auspices of the International Schools Association in Geneva (ISA), and which is described in part in Chapter 8 by Phil Thomas.

One of the most compelling influences on the evolution of an international curriculum in practice has been the external examination system, which represents a major goal for the end of the secondary phase of education, prior to student entry into higher education or employment. Attempts to achieve such a goal have often resulted in assessment systems being set up that not only relate directly to the final phase of education but also have a 'backwash effect' on earlier stages of institutional curricular planning. That effect can arise directly from attempts to meet external requirements associated with the testing process, such as those associated with IB, Advanced Placement (AP), AICE or even the national assessment demands of the host country national system, but it can also arise from a self-imposed testing regime within the school itself. Where the curricular objectives for teaching and learning are closely identified with those for assessment, the effect of the testing programme on the achievement of international curriculum goals may be extremely reinforcing, but where inconsistencies in that respect exist the potential for confusion, and subsequent damage to the efforts of both teachers and students, remains high. International examination systems hold particular responsibilities in such cases, where it is often extremely difficult to reward individual learning gains in some of the important curricular objectives relating to the international nature of the programme. In turn, that lack of visibility of such objectives in the testing arrangements leads easily to a lack of acknowledgement of their significance in the full education received by the students, with a corresponding decrease of the importance attached to them by parents, administrators, board members, sometimes by teachers in planning programmes and, most importantly, often by the students themselves, who may well devalue such aspects of their international education.

THE CONTRIBUTION OF TEACHERS

One of the most encouraging features of the movement to establish an international curriculum has been the contribution from those who are directly involved in the practice of international education in schools. That contribution has been as substantial in the extent of participation as it has been significant in terms of the quality of the output. There is, as has already been highlighted in earlier chapters of this book, a great diversity of provision and innovation, much of it arising from the creativity of those in schools and colleges. In some cases those contributions have come from individuals, working by themselves or in teams with other colleagues, to improve their own classrooms, subject areas, departments or whole school systems of organization and administration. In others, individuals have made direct contributions through membership of consortia of schools in a region (for example the work undertaken through the English Schools Foundation in Hong Kong), through international working parties organized for specific purposes of curriculum development (the International Baccalaureate, for instance), through in-service workshops and accreditation activities organized on an international basis (such as those organized through the European Council of International Schools) or through individual research work coordinated through a university department (such as the Centre for the study of Education in an International Context (CEIC) at the University of Bath, as one example). In all such activities the impact of the contribution such colleagues make to the process of international curriculum development is enhanced by the pragmatism which is added to subject knowledge and pedagogic expertise

While acknowledging the many pressures which arise for individuals, or teams of individuals, within institutions in planning for an international education, many schools have adopted a systematic approach to designing, delivering, monitoring and evaluating their specifically international curricular goals, often with spectacular success. One of the most well known examples, perhaps in part because it is the oldest international school, is that provided by the International School of Geneva, which has created a team approach to the generation of what they have termed 'Principles for an International Education' (1994). A list of eight such principles was produced from their joint discussions and is included in Malcolm McKenzie's chapter earlier in this book. The list has been used by that school as a framework for the development of a programme for international education within the institution, and one interesting feature of the list is the implication that so far as planning for international education is concerned the formal curriculum (in the sense of that element which directly affects classroom activities) is only one dimension, albeit an important one, of whole institutional strategy. The same school then went on to identify six features of an international education, which could be used not only in planning and designing an international education programme but also in helping to take decisions about resourcing and evaluating its success (ISG, 1995). Those features are:

1. use of communications technology to access information;
2. negotiating skills;
3. understanding of other nations' priorities;
4. awareness of different national 'mind-sets';
5. study which crosses national frontiers;
6. ability to perceive distinction between truth and falsehood.

That kind of evidence, generated through the efforts of teachers working in schools, often as members of subject, pastoral, extracurricular, whole institutional teams, or as individuals enquiring into their own practice as a part of a planned programme of research linked to a higher education institution, for example, is important and not only for the specific messages which arise from it that can be used by others in their approach to their own work. Because that example from Geneva could, no doubt, be replaced by a large number of other examples drawn from the international school circuit, it also relates directly to practical experience which is shared by a wide constituency and which therefore has more generalizability, and validity, than otherwise may have been the case.

FEATURES IMPORTANT TO INTERNATIONAL EDUCATION

Arising from such work in schools is an overall impression that, while there is a great deal which can be planned through the formal curriculum, there are a number of features of international education that are just as likely to arise from aspects of school that are outside the formal curricular arrangements. This understanding has also been supported through further research work carried out elsewhere. As has already been pointed out, empirical data generated from systematic study of international education in schools world-wide has been relatively uncommon. However, the outcomes of three related pieces of independent research work, undertaken through the CEIC, have added to our knowledge of the field in a number of important ways. In particular, and directly relevant to the discussion here, the work carried out has reinforced the importance attached to those features that are perceived to be a necessary part of the experience of international education, including those comprising aspects of the formal curriculum. Three groups of those most closely involved in the process of international education were surveyed for their views on the relative importance of a number of ingredients of international education that had already been identified through literature, through preliminary interviews with teachers, students and curriculum developers, and through published school-based work (in, for example, the *International Schools*

Journal) arising from the kind of teacher enquiry activity described above. The three groups surveyed were a sample of undergraduates in their first year at university who had gained experience of international education, two cohorts of students in school (16 and 18 year olds) who were engaged in international education programmes, and teachers in international schools claiming to be promoting international education.

Views from undergraduates

The research undertaken with undergraduates who had, self-judgementally, recently experienced an international education was part of a larger project set up to investigate the range of perceptions of international education by those most closely involved in it. The details of the undergraduate survey have been reported elsewhere (Hayden and Thompson, 1995), and here we shall be concerned only with the principal outcomes as they relate to provision of an international education within a school context. The survey, which was undertaken with a small opportunity sample of undergraduates in their first year at university, was concerned with establishing the retrospective views of students with respect to the factors that were most likely to have contributed to the development of an 'international attitude' during their time at school, this having already been established as an important goal of international education. What is of direct relevance to our current concerns is the relative importance attached by those responding to the interaction between students themselves, through both formal and informal contact, in the formation of an international attitude, and to the influence of parental attitudes, too. Of relatively less importance were the more formal curricular and organizational features of the institution and, interestingly, of the attitudes of individual teachers and administrators. In terms of statistical significance the factors were found to cluster into coherent groups which comprised: exposure to others of different cultures both within and outside school; informal aspects of school (including parents); formal curricular considerations (including teachers); and administrative and organizational aspects. These clusters were confirmed in their generality and examined from a range of different perspectives in the major part of the project, which involved an elucidation of the perceptions of students and teachers in relation to such issues.

Views from schools: students and teachers

A questionnaire survey instrument was developed and administered to a student population, selected from schools included in the *ECIS Directory,* which resulted in a return comprising subsamples of 18 year olds (total 1345), 17 year olds (total 451) and 16 year olds (total 1740). The same instrument was employed for all the student subsamples. Thus the views of a total population of over 3000 students, at or nearing the end of their secondary education in an international school, were available for study. The details of the range of outcomes from the analysis of the data have been reported elsewhere (Hayden and Thompson, 1995, 1996, 1997).

In terms of the issues relating to the relative importance of factors affecting the development of a programme of international education within a school context, the data were analysed using clusters of constructs similar to those which had emerged from the preliminary study with undergraduates, in order to find out how these perceptions sat, in terms of relative importance, alongside those indications gained from the undergraduate study. In addition, the views of a sample of teachers (total 226) drawn from secondary level international schools world-wide, were elicited from the data collected, and similar categories of factors to those arising from the student surveys were identified and evaluated in respect of their relative importance to the promotion of international education at secondary school level. The detailed analysis of the teacher survey has been reported elsewhere (Hayden and Thompson, 1998); here we report the outcomes only in a manner that will facilitate comparison between the various samples studied.

In order to effect such a comparison a common framework for reporting needed to be developed arising from the three subsamples. In fact, across the entire student and teacher responses a remarkable agreement was reached concerning the major clusters into which the responses to individual issues raised in the questionnaires could be grouped. Issues relating to senior management were not included in the teacher questionnaire, although perceptions of the importance of this aspect by teachers has been explored by other means. Common clusters of responses have been used, in Table 20.1, to aid comparison of views across the subsamples investigated. The relative rank orders for each of the groups is illustrated in Table 20.1.

One of the most striking features about Table 20.1 is the cross-group agreement about the prime importance of the feature of student exposure to other students of different cultures within the school. It is also interesting to note that exposure to others of different cultures outside school, maybe through community links, is not rated so highly except by the undergraduate group; perhaps those in the school system do not appreciate the relative importance of this further cross-cultural interaction until later. In a similar way the relative importance of the exemplary attitudes of teachers seems to decrease once the students leave school! It must be remembered that all of the clusters included in Table 20.1 are present because they share a high level of importance, and in comparing the relative importance within the cluster group we are almost in a position of considering *primus inter pares*.

CORE FEATURES OF INTERNATIONAL EDUCATION

On the basis of the perceived importance of all of those clusters, and bearing in mind the levels of agreement about their importance, it is possible to place the evidence from these survey enquiries alongside that obtained from other research work (follow-up interviews, literature surveys) and to identify a number of features that not only persist in the views expressed by others, but that also attract a high measure of support in their perceived level of importance. These features, it is here proposed, constitute a core list of those aspects that need to be considered closely by those designing a programme of international education, whether or not that be in an institution called an international school. They have already been highlighted by Bob Sylvester in Chapter 13. The list is derived from practice but, as will be shown later, it has validity in its relationship to work in cognate fields. The features identified to date are:

- exposure to others of different cultures within the school;
- teachers as exemplars of 'international-mindedness';
- exposure to others of different cultures outside the school;
- a balanced formal curriculum;
- a management regime which is value consistent with an institutional international philosophy.

The five core features above are obviously far from being discrete, both with respect to the manner in which they were generated from such a wide data set, and in the attempts to indicted how they may be manifested in practice. There is clearly a great deal of overlap and connection between them. The centrality of cultural diversity within the core features was expressed most vividly by one of the undergraduates from the University of Bath, when she was writing about her thoughts concerning where internationalism was located for her during her time at school:

Although my experience in class was not international, I did experience international education out of class, through clubs and societies at school. I was exposed to many different cultures and I began to appreciate them, especially as some of my closest friends were not of the same culture as me. I still have my own set of values and am still greatly influenced by my own culture, but I don't expect everyone to be like me, or to believe in everything I believe in. I can appreciate other cultures and at university I have made friends with people from cultures to which I have never before been exposed – yet I can still appreciate them and value them for what they are. (Hayden and Thompson 1995)

Table 20.1 Comparison of rank order of importance attached to categories of factors affecting international education for various samples of students and teachers

Cluster	Student sample 16+ yrs	Student sample 17+ yrs	Student sample 18+ yrs	U/grad sample	Teacher sample
Exposure to students of different cultures within school	1 =	1	1	1	1
Teachers as exemplars of international-mindedness	1 =	3	2	4	2
Exposure to others of different cultures outside school/links with local community	5	5	5	2	4
A balanced formal curriculum	3	2	3	5	3
Informal aspects of school	4	4	4	3	5

A MODEL FOR INTERNATIONAL EDUCATION

Consideration of the core features of an international education, identified above, leads to the conclusion that no single aspect of institutional arrangements is likely to act as a guarantee of delivery of an international education at the level of the individual student. It is certainly true that one can bring together a group of students from diverse cultural backgrounds, whether that be in a national or an international school, but that fact by itself will not result in any sense of internationalism by default. Lessons arising from work done in the field of intercultural learning indicate that in order to integrate such learning in the school, for example, it is likely that the process will be characterized by inter- and transdisciplinary approaches, extracurricular as well as formal curricular activities, long-term and ongoing learning rather than 'one-off' episodes, and a flexible position with regard to administrative and organizational matters such as timetabling, class structures and staffing deployment. It is also likely to be theme-oriented and person-centred, and will be closely linked with social learning (Fennes and Hapgood, 1997). This process will permeate every aspect of the school environment, from individual subjects and classrooms, through departmental structures, whole school issues and the relationship between the school and its various communities (local, regional, national and international). It is here suggested that 'internationalism' may be thought of in a similar way, using a 'brick wall' metaphor (Figure 20.1).

There will be opportunities in the formal classroom situation to incorporate international features such as a balanced approach to the teaching of a subject through the deployment of a range of teaching and learning strategies and the selection of materials drawn from a wide cultural base, for example. This is represented by the actual bricks in the wall, of different shapes and sizes because the collection of subjects and other planned activities that define the formal curriculum will be derived from different disciplines, methodologies and epistemologies and will therefore offer breadth in approach; the task of the teacher will be to ensure that they are organized so that they offer balance. Some of the opportunities that could be taken *within* a subject area will be teacher-led, and will be instructional in nature as a result. Many will seek to bring students together in team and group interactions that are more likely to encourage experiential learning.

To continue with the metaphor, there will also be opportunities for international learning that takes place *between* the subjects of the curriculum, and that arises from the various styles of inter- and transdisciplinary processes that are part of the planned and unplanned experience for the students and teachers. Such 'interstitial learning' is likely to involve not only those academic subjects that cross the boundaries between traditional interpretations of school subjects, but also to include learning associated with such structures as pastoral care, guidance, discipline codes, approaches to individual special needs, and what has become known as the hidden curriculum, all of which can make a contribution to the generation of an international attitude. Such learning is essentially experiential in nature and, in the terms of our metaphor, will constitute institutional 'cement' for internationalism.

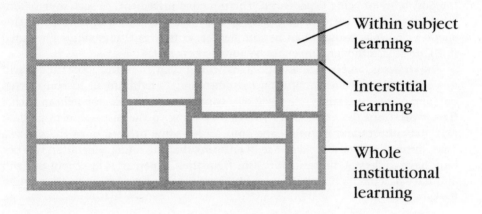

Within subject learning

Interstitial learning

Whole institutional learning

Figure 20.1 Metaphor for internationalism in an institutional setting

All those associated with school will also be learning at a whole institution level, and this will apply to all participants in the institutional process: students, teachers, administrators, board members, parents. This learning, which arises from the framework within which all participants will engage together, will relate to such organizational features as management style, decision-making processes, general organizational culture, and school mission statements; they will effectively constitute the ethos of the institution, a dimension that has already been acknowledged to contribute significantly to school effectiveness by a large number of authors in the literature. It will have a special place in a school that sets out to promote international education through a deliberate approach to all the learning that takes place there; it will be a total 'learning organization' (Senge, 1994).

Such a view of a school that is likely to be an enabling institution for international education is characterized more by experiential learning than by instructional learning, although both will have a part to play. This approach will require the establishment of a shared set of values so that all those involved with the school will be able to plan, deliver and evaluate the experiences of students together with confidence and with high expectations, aspects that are known to influence the levels of motivation and success of a school. So far as international education is concerned, the strong message coming from those most closely associated with its development in practice, not least from those who have contributed to this volume, is that it is most likely to be caught, not taught! The task of those directly responsible for the planning and organization of the school, involving most centrally board members, administrators, teachers and other staff, will be to arrange a *learning environment* that will provide opportunity, encouragement and support to those who are participating in it, and through which international education has the possibility of being experienced. The principal ingredients of such an environment as we know them to date have already been identified and noted in this chapter, and may perhaps best be summed up in the visual mnemonic illustrated in Figure 20.2, although it may not be quite so easy as ABC!

The students, and indeed all who work within such an institutional model, will not only experience learning from the educational environment so constructed but, and most importantly, they will also contribute to the development of such a framework from the experiences which they bring to the institution from their personal cultures and histories, and thus accept some ownership of the process. That, in turn, will go some distance in ensuring that the future generation will not only have understood internationalism from their experiences at school but will also have accepted a personal responsibility for making it a reality in their future lives.

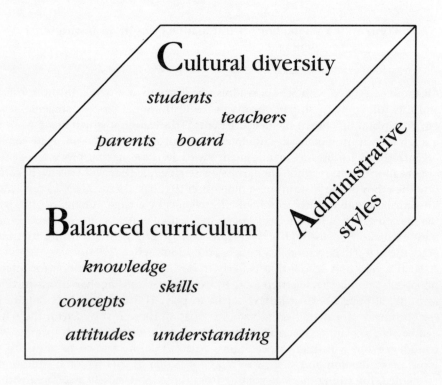

Figure 20.2 Model of a learning environment for international education

REFERENCES

Beardsmore, H B (1993) 'The European school model', in *European Models of Bilingual Education*, Multilingual Matters, Clevedon, Avon

Belle-Isle, R (1986) 'Learning for a new humanism', *International Schools Journal*, 11, pp 27–30

Fennes, H and Hapgood, K (1997) *Intercultural Learning in the Classroom: Crossing Borders*, Cassell, London

Gellar, C (1981) 'International education: some thoughts on what it is and what It might be', *International Schools Journal*, 1, pp 21–6

Hayden M C and Thompson, J J (1995) 'Perceptions of international education: a preliminary study', *International Review of Education*, **41**, 5, pp 389–404

Hayden, M C and Thompson, J J (1996) 'Potential difference: the driving force for international education', *International Schools Journal*, **XVI**, 1, pp 46–57

Hayden, M C and Thompson, J J (1997) 'Student perspectives on international education: A European dimension', *Oxford Review of Education*, **23**, 4, pp 459–78

Hayden, M C and Thompson, J J (1998) 'Teacher perceptions of international education', *International Review of Education*, 44, 5–6 in press

Hirst, P H and Peters, R S (1970) *The Logic of Education,* Routledge & Kegan Paul, London

Hofstede, G (1991) *Cultures and Organizations: Software of the Mind*, McGraw-Hill, Maidenhead

International School of Geneva (1994) 'Principles for an international education', internal school document

International School of Geneva (1995) 'Features of an international education', internal school document

Jonietz, P L (1991) 'International schools: developing a consensus of opinion', PhD thesis, Brunel University

Lawton, D (1978) *Theory and Practice of Curriculum Studies*, Routledge & Kegan Paul, London

Northrop, Birdsey Grant (1968), in Fraser, S E and Brickman, W W, *A History of International and Comparative Education: Nineteenth-century Documents*, Scott Foresman, Glenview, Ill

Phenix, P H (1964) *Realms of Meaning*, McGraw-Hill, New York

Senge, P M (1990) *The Fifth Discipline: The Art and Practice of the Learning Organisation*, Century, London

Stobart, M (1989) 'A new programme for a time of change', *Forum*, Council of Europe, Strasbourg

Thompson, J J (1972) *European Curriculum Studies Number 4: Chemistry*, Council of Europe, Strasbourg

Index